KEYSTONES OF DEMOCRACY

KEYSTONES OF DEMOCRACY

The Second Treatise of Government

John Locke

The Social Contract

Jean-Jacques Rousseau

Rights of Man

Thomas Paine

BARNES & NOBLE
NEW YORK

Originally published in 1690 (*The Second Treatise of Government*), 1762 (*The Social Contract*), and, as a pamphlet, 1792 (*Rights of Man*)

This edition published by Barnes & Noble Publishing, Inc.

Cover Design by Jeff Batzli

2005 Barnes & Noble Publishing, Inc.

ISBN 0-7607-7513-3

Printed and bound in the United States of America

1 3 5 7 9 10 8 6 4 2

CONTENTS

THE SOCIAL CONTRACT

JEAN-JACQUES ROUSSEAU

BOOK I

INTRODUCTION

For more than two thousand years, thinkers have speculated upon, analyzed, and debated the best forms of government, reasons for obeying the state, the rights of the individual, and the concepts of freedom, equality, and justice. At the dawn of the democratic Western political tradition in the eighteenth century, which grew out of the humanist intellectual sensibilities of the Scientific Revolution of the previous century, three great works of Enlightenment political philosophy, presented together in this volume, emerged as the keystones of democracy as we know it: John Locke's *The Second Treatise of Government,* Jean-Jacques Rousseau's *The Social Contract,* and Thomas Paine's *Rights of Man.*

John Locke's *Second Treatise of Government* (1690) is one of the most important works in the history of Western political thought. The central principles of what today is broadly known as political liberalism —individual liberty, the rule of law, government by consent of the people, and the right to private property—were made current in large part by Locke's *Second Treatise.*

At the foundation of Locke's theories are individual rights and natural law, as well as the argument that popular consent is necessary for legitimate government. Locke (1632–1704) asserts that individuals are naturally in a state of liberty and equality, but he also recognizes that there must be limitations on the individual—what he termed the law of nature—that stipulates that every individual must, despite inherent self-interest, seek to protect the life and liberty of everyone else. Locke suggests that an individual is more likely to limit his own freedom if he believes that his life and liberty are better served by doing so. For Locke, the desire for political association is natural law at work, uniting self-interest with public interest.

The Second Treatise makes clear that the protection of property interests is the fundamental purpose of government. Locke made the property right "natural," and therefore inalienable; he argued that unequal distribution of property also occurs naturally and that the primary function of government is to protect and preserve disparities in wealth, thereby increasing the stability and general welfare of the entire community. Locke did not ignore those without property, however. He supported individual liberty by stressing the ultimate sovereignty of the people, their right to establish the form of government and their right to revolution. Locke argues that government has an obligation to protect the interests not only of the propertied classes but also of those without. Moreover, Locke asserts that the rulers' *belief* in popular sovereignty provides greater restraint on political power than institutional structures or a system of checks and balances. *The Second Treatise* is, in this respect, a rhetorical tour de force. It succeeds in persuading the ruling class to advocate, and actually to put in place, a political system that constrains its own power out of self-interest, in order to take into account the interests of all.

The best-selling author of pre-Revolutionary France, Jean-Jacques Rousseau (1712–1778), remains today perhaps the greatest proponent of direct, participatory democracy. In his towering work of political philosophy, *The Social Contract,* Rousseau asks: Must people accept legalized domination and inequality in order to enjoy the benefits of social life? Is it our fate to choose between natural freedom and civilized servitude? The answer, Rousseau tells us, is *The Social Contract,* the result of his quest to find an alternative to the modern state as it was formulated by John Locke, who believed to varying degrees that the people must delegate power to government to avoid chaos and to protect property and individual rights.

At the beginning of the *Contract,* Rousseau proudly announces that he is a citizen of Geneva, Switzerland. Geneva was one of Europe's last free states or republics, governed by citizens collectively. European republics had largely disappeared, due to the nature of communal self-government and the need for free states to remain small. But republics would again emerge after the American and French Revolutions had transformed them into modern territorial states with systems of representation. In the *Contract,* however, Rousseau insists on *popular* sovereignty: the people, not rulers, together maintain sovereignty, or ultimate political authority. Furthermore, sovereignty cannot be relegated to representatives; "We the People" remain in charge.

More controversially, Rousseau develops a theory whereby the people unify their wills into a single common will: the General Will, the will of the community. Boldly, Rousseau claims that the General Will can never be directed at anything specific; it is in the general interest even when individual interests diverge. In the *Contract,* the meaning and significance of the General Will remains enigmatic, the goal being political consensus, a republic of collective consciousness.

The second half of the *Contract* abandons logic for the rhetoric of the classical political tradition. Rousseau revered the classical republics of Sparta and Rome, praising their forgotten practices and institutions, such as the assembly of the citizenry in public, essential in preventing tyranny, and civil religion, the civic rituals that united people and swayed them to serve the city-state. Rousseau was the first to romanticize the classical republics, infusing the *Contract* with nostalgia for a pure, vanished world of virtue and heroic devotion to the city-state.

In his masterpiece *Rights of Man* (1792), Thomas Paine presents an impassioned defense of the Enlightenment principles of freedom and equality. Though many more sophisticated thinkers of the day argued for the same principles, no one was better able to fire the hopes of the common man and stir him to political action. Paine (1737–1809) was one of the most influential proponents of American independence and is best remembered for his pamphlet *Common Sense* (1776), which was largely responsible for motivating the American colonists to declare independence from England. His *Rights of Man*—the only comprehensive account he gave of his understanding of Enlightenment humanism—is of enduring general interest to contemporary readers fascinated by the "age of revolutions" and to readers with a passion for economic justice and democracy movements today.

Rights of Man captures the revolutionary spirit of the most elevated Enlightenment authors, and brings their ideas to the level of the average reader. Loosely echoing Locke and Rousseau, Paine distinguishes between "society," the natural product of the association of peoples, and "government," the sole rational purpose of which is the protection of societies' members from threats to their pursuit of happiness and freedom. Paine argued that government unjustly redistributes through taxation the wealth of the majority to rich landowners and to royalty. In his detailed scheme for redistributing tax monies to the poor, Paine earned some fleeting friendships in revolutionary France, but, given the rise of capitalism, ultimately lost many allies in America and England.

The truth of the contemporary human condition, according to the *Rights of Man,* is as follows: Men are born by nature equal and good, content to live with a relatively equitable distribution of material goods, provided these are adequate to the maintenance of a comfortable life. But the majority of people are everywhere corrupted by a rapacious few who use force and deception to establish governments, the sole purpose of which is to satisfy their avarice. Such governments conduct wars simply to legitimate excessive taxation and to perpetuate the status quo; governments deprive their own people, driving them into desperate circumstances in order to pay for their rulers' excesses.

More than two hundred years later, these issues are still hotly debated. Paine's theories, as well as those of his predecessors Locke and Rousseau are as relevant today as when they were written. In our twenty-first-century world, where the polarized American democracy, the fledgling democracy of an evolving European Union, the emerging democratic movements in the former Soviet bloc, and especially the debate about the role of the industrialized West in promoting democratic change in the Middle East make up the pressing issues of our day, readers would be wise to contemplate the wellsprings of the Western political tradition, and to read closely the works in this collection that truly constitute the keystones of democratic thought.

THE SECOND TREATISE OF GOVERNMENT

John Locke

CHAPTER I

AN ESSAY CONCERNING THE TRUE ORIGINAL, EXTENT AND END OF CIVIL GOVERNMENT

1. It having been shown in the foregoing discourse:

Firstly. That Adam had not, either by natural right of fatherhood or by positive donation from God, any such authority over his children, nor dominion over the world, as is pretended.

Secondly. That if he had, his heirs yet had no right to it.

Thirdly. That if his heirs had, there being no law of Nature nor positive law of God that determines which is the right heir in all cases that may arise, the right of succession, and consequently of bearing rule, could not have been certainly determined.

Fourthly. That if even that had been determined, yet the knowledge of which is the eldest line of Adam's posterity being so long since utterly lost, that in the races of mankind and families of the world, there remains not to one above another the least pretence to be the eldest house, and to have the right of inheritance.

All these promises having, as I think, been clearly made out, it is impossible that the rulers now on earth should make any benefit, or derive any the least shadow of authority from that which is held to be the fountain of all power, "Adam's private dominion and paternal jurisdiction"; so that he that will not give just occasion to think that all government in the world is the product only of force and violence, and that men live together by no other rules but that of beasts, where the strongest carries it, and so lay a foundation for perpetual disorder and mischief, tumult, sedition, and rebellion (things that the followers of that hypothesis so loudly cry out against), must of necessity find out another rise of government, another original of political power, and another way of designing and knowing the persons that have it than what Sir Robert Filmer hath taught us.

2. To this purpose, I think it may not be amiss to set down what I take to be political power. That the power of a magistrate over a subject may be distinguished from that of a father over his children, a master over his servant, a husband over his wife, and a lord over his slave. All which distinct powers happening sometimes together in the same man, if he be considered under these different relations, it may help us to distinguish these powers one from another, and show the difference betwixt a ruler of a commonwealth, a father of a family, and a captain of a galley.

3. Political power, then, I take to be a right of making laws, with penalties of death, and consequently all less penalties for the regulating and preserving of property, and of employing the force of the community in the execution of such laws, and in the defence of the commonwealth from foreign injury, and all this only for the public good.

CHAPTER II

OF THE STATE OF NATURE

4. To understand political power aright, and derive it from its original, we must consider what estate all men are naturally in, and that is, a state of perfect freedom to order their actions, and dispose of their possessions and persons as they think fit, within the bounds of the law of Nature, without asking leave or depending upon the will of any other man.

A state also of equality, wherein all the power and jurisdiction is reciprocal, no one having more than another, there being nothing more evident than that creatures of the same species and rank, promiscuously born to all the same advantages of Nature, and the use of the same faculties, should also be equal one amongst another, without subordination or subjection, unless the lord and master of them all should, by any manifest declaration of his will, set one above another, and confer on him, by an evident and clear appointment, an undoubted right to dominion and sovereignty.

5. This equality of men by Nature, the judicious Hooker looks upon as so evident in itself, and beyond all question, that he makes it the foundation of that obligation to mutual love amongst men on which he builds the duties they owe one another, and from whence he derives the great maxims of justice and charity. His words are:

"The like natural inducement hath brought men to know that it is no less their duty to love others than themselves, for seeing those things which are equal, must needs all have one measure; if I cannot but wish to receive good, even as much at every man's hands, as any man can wish unto his own soul, how should I look to have any part of my desire herein satisfied, unless myself be careful to satisfy the like desire, which is undoubtedly in other men weak, being of one and the same nature: to have anything offered them repugnant to this desire must needs, in all respects, grieve them as much as me; so that if I do harm, I must look to suffer, there being no reason that others should show greater measure of love to me than they have by me showed unto them; my desire, therefore, to be loved of my equals in Nature, as much as possible may be, imposeth upon me a natural duty of bearing to themward fully the like affection. From which relation of equality between ourselves and them that are as ourselves, what several rules and canons natural reason hath drawn for direction of life no man is ignorant." (*Eccl. Pol.* i.)

6. But though this be a state of liberty, yet it is not a state of licence; though man in that state have an uncontrollable liberty to dispose of his person or possessions, yet he has not liberty to destroy himself, or so much as any creature in his possession, but where some nobler use than its bare preservation calls for it. The state of Nature has a law of Nature to govern it, which obliges every one, and reason, which is that law, teaches all mankind who will but consult it, that being all equal and independent, no one ought to harm another in his life, health, liberty or possessions; for men being all the workmanship of one omnipotent and infinitely wise Maker; all the servants of one sovereign Master, sent into the world by His order and about His business; they are His property, whose workmanship they are made to last during His, not one another's pleasure. And, being furnished with like faculties, sharing all in one community of Nature, there cannot be supposed any such subordination among us that may authorise us to destroy one another, as if we were made for one another's uses, as the inferior ranks of creatures are for ours. Every one as he is bound to preserve himself, and not to quit his station wilfully, so by the like reason, when his own preservation comes not in competition, ought he as much as he can to preserve the rest of mankind, and not unless it be to do justice on an offender, take away or impair the life, or what tends to the preservation of the life, the liberty, health, limb, or goods of another.

7. And that all men may be restrained from invading others' rights, and from doing hurt to one another, and the law of Nature be observed, which willeth the peace and preservation of all mankind, the execution of the law of Nature is in that state put into every man's hands, whereby every one has a right to punish the transgressors of that law to such a degree as may hinder its violation. For the law of Nature would, as all other laws that concern men in this world, be in vain if there were nobody that in the state of Nature had a power to execute that law, and thereby

preserve the innocent and restrain offenders; and if any one in the state of Nature may punish another for any evil he has done, every one may do so. For in that state of perfect equality, where naturally there is no superiority or jurisdiction of one over another, what any may do in prosecution of that law, every one must needs have a right to do.

8. And thus, in the state of Nature, one man comes by a power over another, but yet no absolute or arbitrary power to use a criminal, when he has got him in his hands, according to the passionate heats or boundless extravagancy of his own will, but only to retribute to him so far as calm reason and conscience dictate, what is proportionate to his transgression, which is so much as may serve for reparation and restraint. For these two are the only reasons why one man may lawfully do harm to another, which is that we call punishment. In transgressing the law of Nature, the offender declares himself to live by another rule than that of reason and common equity, which is that measure God has set to the actions of men for their mutual security, and so he becomes dangerous to mankind; the tie which is to secure them from injury and violence being slighted and broken by him, which being a trespass against the whole species, and the peace and safety of it, provided for by the law of Nature, every man upon this score, by the right he hath to preserve mankind in general, may restrain, or where it is necessary, destroy things noxious to them, and so may bring such evil on any one who hath transgressed that law, as may make him repent the doing of it, and thereby deter him, and, by his example, others from doing the like mischief. And in this case, and upon this ground, every man hath a right to punish the offender, and be executioner of the law of Nature.

9. I doubt not but this will seem a very strange doctrine to some men; but before they condemn it, I desire them to resolve me by what right any prince or state can put to death or punish an alien for any crime he commits in their country? It is certain their laws, by virtue of any sanction they receive from the promulgated will of the legislature, reach not a stranger. They speak not to him, nor, if they did, is he bound to hearken to them. The legislative authority by which they are in force over the subjects of that commonwealth hath no power over him. Those who have the supreme power of making laws in England, France, or Holland are, to an Indian, but like the rest of the world—men without authority. And therefore, if by the law of Nature every man hath not a power to punish offences against it, as he soberly judges the case to require, I see not how

the magistrates of any community can punish an alien of another country, since, in reference to him, they can have no more power than what every man naturally may have over another.

10. Besides the crime which consists in violating the laws, and varying from the right rule of reason, whereby a man so far becomes degenerate, and declares himself to quit the principles of human nature and to be a noxious creature, there is commonly injury done, and some person or other, some other man, receives damage by his transgression; in which case, he who hath received any damage has (besides the right of punishment common to him, with other men) a particular right to seek reparation from him that hath done it. And any other person who finds it just may also join with him that is injured, and assist him in recovering from the offender so much as may make satisfaction for the harm he hath suffered.

11. From these two distinct rights (the one of punishing the crime, for restraint and preventing the like offence, which right of punishing is in everybody, the other of taking reparation, which belongs only to the injured party) comes it to pass that the magistrate, who by being magistrate hath the common right of punishing put into his hands, can often, where the public good demands not the execution of the law, remit the punishment of criminal offences by his own authority, but yet cannot remit the satisfaction due to any private man for the damage he has received. That he who hath suffered the damage has a right to demand in his own name, and he alone can remit. The damnified person has this power of appropriating to himself the goods or service of the offender by right of self-preservation, as every man has a power to punish the crime to prevent its being committed again, by the right he has of preserving all mankind, and doing all reasonable things he can in order to that end. And thus it is that every man in the state of Nature has a power to kill a murderer, both to deter others from doing the like injury (which no reparation can compensate) by the example of the punishment that attends it from everybody, and also to secure men from the attempts of a criminal who, having renounced reason, the common rule and measure God hath given to mankind, hath, by the unjust violence and slaughter he hath committed upon one, declared war against all mankind, and therefore may be destroyed as a lion or a tiger, one of those wild savage beasts with whom men can have no society nor security. And upon this is grounded that great law of Nature, "Whoso sheddeth man's blood, by man shall his blood be shed." And Cain was so fully convinced that every

one had a right to destroy such a criminal, that, after the murder of his brother, he cries out, "Every one that findeth me shall slay me," so plain was it writ in the hearts of all mankind.

12. By the same reason may a man in the state of Nature punish the lesser breaches of that law, it will, perhaps, be demanded, with death? I answer: Each transgression may be punished to that degree, and with so much severity, as will suffice to make it an ill bargain to the offender, give him cause to repent, and terrify others from doing the like. Every offence that can be committed in the state of Nature may, in the state of Nature, be also punished equally, and as far forth, as it may, in a commonwealth. For though it would be beside my present purpose to enter here into the particulars of the law of Nature, or its measures of punishment, yet it is certain there is such a law, and that too as intelligible and plain to a rational creature and a studier of that law as the positive laws of commonwealths, nay, possibly plainer; as much as reason is easier to be understood than the fancies and intricate contrivances of men, following contrary and hidden interests put into words; for truly so are a great part of the municipal laws of countries, which are only so far right as they are founded on the law of Nature, by which they are to be regulated and interpreted.

13. To this strange doctrine—viz., That in the state of Nature every one has the executive power of the law of Nature—I doubt not but it will be objected that it is unreasonable for men to be judges in their own cases, that self-love will make men partial to themselves and their friends; and, on the other side, ill-nature, passion, and revenge will carry them too far in punishing others, and hence nothing but confusion and disorder will follow, and that therefore God hath certainly appointed government to restrain the partiality and violence of men. I easily grant that civil government is the proper remedy for the inconveniences of the state of Nature, which must certainly be great where men may be judges in their own case, since it is easy to be imagined that he who was so unjust as to do his brother an injury will scarce be so just as to condemn himself for it. But I shall desire those who make this objection to remember that absolute monarchs are but men; and if government is to be the remedy of those evils which necessarily follow from men being judges in their own cases, and the state of Nature is therefore not to be endured, I desire to know what kind of government that is, and how much better it is than the state of Nature, where one man commanding a multitude has the liberty to be judge in his own case, and may do to all his subjects whatever he

pleases without the least question or control of those who execute his pleasure? and in whatsoever he doth, whether led by reason, mistake, or passion, must be submitted to? which men in the state of Nature are not bound to do one to another. And if he that judges, judges amiss in his own or any other case, he is answerable for it to the rest of mankind.

14. It is often asked as a mighty objection, where are, or ever were, there any men in such a state of Nature? To which it may suffice as an answer at present, that since all princes and rulers of "independent" governments all through the world are in a state of Nature, it is plain the world never was, nor never will be, without numbers of men in that state. I have named all governors of "independent" communities, whether they are, or are not, in league with others; for it is not every compact that puts an end to the state of Nature between men, but only this one of agreeing together mutually to enter into one community, and make one body politic; other promises and compacts men may make one with another, and yet still be in the state of Nature. The promises and bargains for truck, etc., between the two men in Soldania, in or between a Swiss and an Indian, in the woods of America, are binding to them, though they are perfectly in a state of Nature in reference to one another for truth, and keeping of faith belongs to men as men, and not as members of society.

15. To those that say there were never any men in the state of Nature, I will not only oppose the authority of the judicious Hooker (*Eccl. Pol.* i. 10), where he says, "the laws which have been hitherto mentioned"—*i.e.*, the laws of Nature—"do bind men absolutely, even as they are men, although they have never any settled fellowship, never any solemn agreement amongst themselves what to do or not to do; but for as much as we are not by ourselves sufficient to furnish ourselves with competent store of things needful for such a life as our Nature doth desire, a life fit for the dignity of man, therefore to supply those defects and imperfections which are in us, as living single and solely by ourselves, we are naturally induced to seek communion and fellowship with others; this was the cause of men uniting themselves as first in politic societies." But I, moreover, affirm that all men are naturally in that state, and remain so till, by their own consents, they make themselves members of some politic society, and I doubt not, in the sequel of this discourse, to make it very clear.

CHAPTER III

OF THE STATE OF WAR

16. THE state of war is a state of enmity and destruction; and therefore declaring by word or action, not a passionate and hasty, but sedate, settled design upon another man's life puts him in a state of war with him against whom he has declared such an intention, and so has exposed his life to the other's power to be taken away by him, or any one that joins with him in his defence, and espouses his quarrel; it being reasonable and just I should have a right to destroy that which threatens me with destruction; for by the fundamental law of Nature, man being to be preserved as much as possible, when all cannot be preserved, the safety of the innocent is to be preferred, and one may destroy a man who makes war upon him, or has discovered an enmity to his being, for the same reason that he may kill a wolf or a lion, because they are not under the ties of the common law of reason, have no other rule but that of force and violence, and so may be treated as a beast of prey, those dangerous and noxious creatures that will be sure to destroy him whenever he falls into their power.

17. And hence it is that he who attempts to get another man into his absolute power does thereby put himself into a state of war with him; it being to be understood as a declaration of a design upon his life. For I have reason to conclude that he who would get me into his power without my consent would use me as he pleased when he had got me there, and destroy me too when he had a fancy to it; for nobody can desire to have me in his absolute power unless it be to compel me by force to that which is against the right of my freedom—*i.e.* make me a slave. To be free from such force is the only security of my preservation, and reason

bids me look on him as an enemy to my preservation who would take away that freedom which is the fence to it; so that he who makes an attempt to enslave me thereby puts himself into a state of war with me. He that in the state of Nature would take away the freedom that belongs to any one in that state must necessarily be supposed to have a design to take away everything else, that freedom being the foundation of all the rest; as he that in the state of society would take away the freedom belonging to those of that society or commonwealth must be supposed to design to take away from them everything else, and so be looked on as in a state of war.

18. This makes it lawful for a man to kill a thief who has not in the least hurt him, nor declared any design upon his life, any farther than by the use of force, so to get him in his power as to take away his money, or what he pleases, from him; because using force, where he has no right to get me into his power, let his pretence be what it will, I have no reason to suppose that he who would take away my liberty would not, when he had me in his power, take away everything else. And, therefore, it is lawful for me to treat him as one who has put himself into a state of war with me—*i.e.*, kill him if I can; for to that hazard does he justly expose himself whoever introduces a state of war, and is aggressor in it.

19. And here we have the plain difference between the state of Nature and the state of war, which however some men have confounded, are as far distant as a state of peace, goodwill, mutual assistance, and preservation; and a state of enmity, malice, violence and mutual destruction are one from another. Men living together according to reason without a common superior on earth, with authority to judge between them, is properly the state of Nature. But force, or a declared design of force upon the person of another, where there is no common superior on earth to appeal to for relief, is the state of war; and it is the want of such an appeal gives a man the right of war even against an aggressor, though he be in society and a fellow-subject. Thus, a thief whom I cannot harm, but by appeal to the law, for having stolen all that I am worth, I may kill when he sets on me to rob me but of my horse or coat, because the law, which was made for my preservation, where it cannot interpose to secure my life from present force, which if lost is capable of no reparation, permits me my own defence and the right of war, a liberty to kill the aggressor, because the aggressor allows not time to appeal to our common judge, nor the decision of the law, for remedy in a case where the mischief may

be irreparable. Want of a common judge with authority puts all men in a state of Nature; force without right upon a man's person makes a state of war both where there is, and is not, a common judge.

20. But when the actual force is over, the state of war ceases between those that are in society and are equally on both sides subject to the judge; and, therefore, in such controversies, where the question is put, "Who shall be judge?" it cannot be meant who shall decide the controversy; every one knows what Jephtha here tells us, that "the Lord the Judge" shall judge. Where there is no judge on earth the appeal lies to God in Heaven. That question then cannot mean who shall judge, whether another hath put himself in a state of war with me, and whether I may, as Jephtha did, appeal to Heaven in it? Of that I myself can only judge in my own conscience, as I will answer it at the great day to the Supreme Judge of all men.

CHAPTER IV

OF SLAVERY

21. THE natural liberty of man is to be free from any superior power on earth, and not to be under the will or legislative authority of man, but to have only the law of Nature for his rule. The liberty of man in society is to be under no other legislative power but that established by consent in the commonwealth, nor under the dominion of any will, or restraint of any law, but what that legislative shall enact according to the trust put in it. Freedom, then, is not what Sir Robert Filmer tells us: "A liberty for every one to do what he lists, to live as he pleases, and not to be tied by any laws"; but freedom of men under government is to have a standing rule to live by, common to every one of that society, and made by the legislative power erected in it. A liberty to follow my own will in all things where that rule prescribes not, not to be subject to the inconstant, uncertain, unknown, arbitrary will of another man, as freedom of nature is to be under no other restraint but the law of Nature.

22. This freedom from absolute, arbitrary power is so necessary to, and closely joined with, a man's preservation, that he cannot part with it but by what forfeits his preservation and life together. For a man, not having the power of his own life, cannot by compact or his own consent enslave himself to any one, nor put himself under the absolute, arbitrary power of another to take away his life when he pleases. Nobody can give more power than he has himself, and he that cannot take away his own life cannot give another power over it. Indeed, having by his fault forfeited his own life by some act that deserves death, he to whom he has forfeited it may, when he has him in his power, delay to take it, and make use of him to his own service; and he does him no injury by it.

For, whenever he finds the hardship of his slavery outweigh the value of his life, it is in his power, by resisting the will of his master, to draw on himself the death he desires.

23. This is the perfect condition of slavery, which is nothing else but the state of war continued between a lawful conqueror and a captive, for if once compact enter between them, and make an agreement for a limited power on the one side, and obedience on the other, the state of war and slavery ceases as long as the compact endures; for, as has been said, no man can by agreement pass over to another that which he hath not in himself—a power over his own life.

I confess, we find among the Jews, as well as other nations, that men did sell themselves; but it is plain this was only to drudgery, not to slavery; for it is evident the person sold was not under an absolute, arbitrary, despotical power, for the master could not have power to kill him at any time, whom at a certain time he was obliged to let go free out of his service; and the master of such a servant was so far from having an arbitrary power over his life that he could not at pleasure so much as maim him, but the loss of an eye or tooth set him free (Exod. xxi.).

CHAPTER V

OF PROPERTY

24. WHETHER we consider natural reason, which tells us that men, being once born, have a right to their preservation, and consequently to meat and drink and such other things as Nature affords for their subsistence, or "revelation," which gives us an account of those grants God made of the world to Adam, and to Noah and his sons, it is very clear that God, as King David says (Psalm cxv. 16), "has given the earth to the children of men," given it to mankind in common. But, this being supposed, it seems to some a very great difficulty how any one should ever come to have a property in anything, I will not content myself to answer, that, if it be difficult to make out "property" upon a supposition that God gave the world to Adam and his posterity in common, it is impossible that any man but one universal monarch should have any "property" upon a supposition that God gave the world to Adam and his heirs in succession, exclusive of all the rest of his posterity; but I shall endeavour to show how men might come to have a property in several parts of that which God gave to mankind in common, and that without any express compact of all the commoners.

25. God, who hath given the world to men in common, hath also given them reason to make use of it to the best advantage of life and convenience. The earth and all that is therein is given to men for the support and comfort of their being. And though all the fruits it naturally produces, and beasts it feeds, belong to mankind in common, as they are produced by the spontaneous hand of Nature, and nobody has originally a private dominion exclusive of the rest of mankind in any of them, as they are thus in their natural state, yet being given for the use of men,

there must of necessity be a means to appropriate them some way or other before they can be of any use, or at all beneficial, to any particular men. The fruit or venison which nourishes the wild Indian, who knows no enclosure, and is still a tenant in common, must be his, and so his—*i.e.*, a part of him, that another can no longer have any right to it before it can do him any good for the support of his life.

26. Though the earth and all inferior creatures be common to all men, yet every man has a "property" in his own "person." This nobody has any right to but himself. The "labour" of his body and the "work" of his hands, we may say, are properly his. Whatsoever, then, he removes out of the state that Nature hath provided and left it in, he hath mixed his labour with it, and joined to it something that is his own, and thereby makes it his property. It being by him removed from the common state Nature placed it in, it hath by this labour something annexed to it that excludes the common right of other men. For this "labour" being the unquestionable property of the labourer, no man but he can have a right to what that is once joined to, at least where there is enough, and as good left in common for others.

27. He that is nourished by the acorns he picked up under an oak, or the apples he gathered from the trees in the wood, has certainly appropriated them to himself. Nobody can deny but the nourishment is his. I ask, then, when did they begin to be his? when he digested? or when he ate? or when he boiled? or when he brought them home? or when he picked them up? And it is plain, if the first gathering made them not his, nothing else could. That labour put a distinction between them and common. That added something to them more than Nature, the common mother of all, had done, and so they became his private right. And will any one say he had no right to those acorns or apples he thus appropriated because he had not the consent of all mankind to make them his? Was it a robbery thus to assume to himself what belonged to all in common? If such a consent as that was necessary, man had starved, notwithstanding the plenty God had given him. We see in commons, which remain so by compact, that it is the taking any part of what is common, and removing it out of the state Nature leaves it in, which begins the property, without which the common is of no use. And the taking of this or that part does not depend on the express consent of all the commoners. Thus, the grass my horse has bit, the turfs my servant has cut, and the ore I have digged in any place, where I have a right to them in common

with others, become my property without the assignation or consent of anybody. The labour that was mine, removing them out of that common state they were in, hath fixed my property in them.

28. By making an explicit consent of every commoner necessary to any one's appropriating to himself any part of what is given in common. Children or servants could not cut the meat which their father or master had provided for them in common without assigning to every one his peculiar part. Though the water running in the fountain be every one's, yet who can doubt but that in the pitcher is his only who drew it out? His labour hath taken it out of the hands of Nature where it was common, and belonged equally to all her children, and hath thereby appropriated it to himself.

29. Thus this law of reason makes the deer that Indian's who hath killed it; it is allowed to be his goods who hath bestowed his labour upon it, though, before, it was the common right of every one. And amongst those who are counted the civilised part of mankind, who have made and multiplied positive laws to determine property, this original law of Nature for the beginning of property, in what was before common, still takes place, and by virtue thereof, what fish any one catches in the ocean, that great and still remaining common of mankind; or what ambergris any one takes up here is by the labour that removes it out of that common state Nature left it in, made his property who takes that pains about it. And even amongst us, the hare that any one is hunting is thought his who pursues her during the chase. For being a beast that is still looked upon as common, and no man's private possession, whoever has employed so much labour about any of that kind as to find and pursue her has thereby removed her from the state of Nature wherein she was common, and hath begun a property.

30. It will, perhaps, be objected to this, that if gathering the acorns or other fruits of the earth, etc., makes a right to them, then any one may engross as much as he will. To which I answer, Not so. The same law of Nature that does by this means give us property, does also bound that property too. "God has given us all things richly." Is the voice of reason confirmed by inspiration? But how far has He given it us—"to enjoy"? As much as any one can make use of to any advantage of life before it spoils, so much he may by his labour fix a property in. Whatever is beyond this is more than his share, and belongs to others. Nothing was made by God for man to spoil or destroy. And thus considering the

plenty of natural provisions there was a long time in the world, and the few spenders, and to how small a part of that provision the industry of one man could extend itself and engross it to the prejudice of others, especially keeping within the bounds set by reason of what might serve for his use, there could be then little room for quarrels or contentions about property so established.

31. But the chief matter of property being now not the fruits of the earth and the beasts that subsist on it, but the earth itself, as that which takes in and carries with it all the rest, I think it is plain that property in that too is acquired as the former. As much land as a man tills, plants, improves, cultivates, and can use the product of, so much is his property. He by his labour does, as it were, enclose it from the common. Nor will it invalidate his right to say everybody else has an equal title to it, and therefore he cannot appropriate, he cannot enclose, without the consent of all his fellow-commoners, all mankind. God, when He gave the world in common to all mankind, commanded man also to labour, and the penury of his condition required it of him. God and his reason commanded him to subdue the earth—*i.e.*, improve it for the benefit of life and therein lay out something upon it that was his own, his labour. He that, in obedience to this command of God, subdued, tilled, and sowed any part of it, thereby annexed to it something that was his property, which another had no title to, nor could without injury take from him.

32. Nor was this appropriation of any parcel of land, by improving it, any prejudice to any other man, since there was still enough and as good left, and more than the yet unprovided could use. So that, in effect, there was never the less left for others because of his enclosure for himself. For he that leaves as much as another can make use of does as good as take nothing at all. Nobody could think himself injured by the drinking of another man, though he took a good draught, who had a whole river of the same water left him to quench his thirst. And the case of land and water, where there is enough of both, is perfectly the same.

33. God gave the world to men in common, but since He gave it them for their benefit and the greatest conveniencies of life they were capable to draw from it, it cannot be supposed He meant it should always remain common and uncultivated. He gave it to the use of the industrious and rational (and labour was to be his title to it); not to the fancy or covetousness of the quarrelsome and contentious. He that had as good left for his improvement as was already taken up needed not complain, ought not to

meddle with what was already improved by another's labour; if he did it is plain he desired the benefit of another's pains, which he had no right to, and not the ground which God had given him, in common with others, to labour on, and whereof there was as good left as that already possessed, and more than he knew what to do with, or his industry could reach to.

34. It is true, in land that is common in England or any other country, where there are plenty of people under government who have money and commerce, no one can enclose or appropriate any part without the consent of all his fellow-commoners; because this is left common by compact—*i.e.,* by the law of the land, which is not to be violated. And, though it be common in respect of some men, it is not so to all mankind, but is the joint propriety of this country, or this parish. Besides, the remainder, after such enclosure, would not be as good to the rest of the commoners as the whole was, when they could all make use of the whole; whereas in the beginning and first peopling of the great common of the world it was quite otherwise. The law man was under was rather for appropriating. God commanded, and his wants forced him to labour. That was his property, which could not be taken from him wherever he had fixed it. And hence subduing or cultivating the earth and having dominion, we see, are joined together. The one gave title to the other. So that God, by commanding to subdue, gave authority so far to appropriate. And the condition of human life, which requires labour and materials to work on, necessarily introduce private possessions.

35. The measure of property Nature well set, by the extent of men's labour and the conveniency of life. No man's labour could subdue or appropriate all, nor could his enjoyment consume more than a small part; so that it was impossible for any man, this way, to entrench upon the right of another or acquire to himself a property to the prejudice of his neighbour, who would still have room for as good and as large a possession (after the other had taken out his) as before it was appropriated. Which measure did confine every man's possession to a very moderate proportion, and such as he might appropriate to himself without injury to anybody in the first ages of the world, when men were more in danger to be lost, by wandering from their company, in the then vast wilderness of the earth than to be straitened for want of room to plant in.

36. The same measure may be allowed still, without prejudice to anybody, full as the world seems. For, supposing a man or family, in the state they were at first, peopling of the world by the children of Adam or Noah, let him plant in some inland vacant places of America. We shall find that

the possessions he could make himself, upon the measures we have given, would not be very large, nor, even to this day, prejudice the rest of mankind or give them reason to complain or think themselves injured by this man's encroachment, though the race of men have now spread themselves to all the corners of the world, and do infinitely exceed the small number was at the beginning. Nay, the extent of ground is of so little value without labour that I have heard it affirmed that in Spain itself a man may be permitted to plough, sow, and reap, without being disturbed, upon land he has no other title to, but only his making use of it. But, on the contrary, the inhabitants think themselves beholden to him who, by his industry on neglected, and consequently waste land, has increased the stock of corn, which they wanted. But be this as it will, which I lay no stress on, this I dare boldly affirm, that the same rule of propriety— viz., that every man should have as much as he could make use of, would hold still in the world, without straitening anybody, since there is land enough in the world to suffice double the inhabitants, had not the invention of money, and the tacit agreement of men to put a value on it, introduced (by consent) larger possessions and a right to them; which, how it has done, I shall by and by show more at large.

37. This is certain, that in the beginning, before the desire of having more than men needed had altered the intrinsic value of things, which depends only on their usefulness to the life of man, or had agreed that a little piece of yellow metal, which would keep without wasting or decay, should be worth a great piece of flesh or a whole heap of corn, though men had a right to appropriate by their labour, each one to himself, as much of the things of Nature as he could use, yet this could not be much, nor to the prejudice of others, where the same plenty was still left, to those who would use the same industry.

Before the appropriation of land, he who gathered as much of the wild fruit, killed, caught, or tamed as many of the beasts as he could—he that so employed his pains about any of the spontaneous products of Nature as any way to alter them from the state Nature put them in, by placing any of his labour on them, did thereby acquire a propriety in them; but if they perished in his possession without their due use—if the fruits rotted or the venison putrefied before he could spend it, he offended against the common law of Nature, and was liable to be punished: he invaded his neighbour's share, for he had no right farther than his use called for any of them, and they might serve to afford him conveniencies of life.

38. The same measures governed the possession of land, too. Whatsoever he tilled and reaped, laid up and made use of before it spoiled, that was his peculiar right; whatsoever he enclosed, and could feed and make use of, the cattle and product was also his. But if either the grass of his enclosure rotted on the ground, or the fruit of his planting perished without gathering and laying up, this part of the earth, notwithstanding his enclosure, was still to be looked on as waste, and might be the possession of any other. Thus, at the beginning, Cain might take as much ground as he could till and make it his own land, and yet leave enough to Abel's sheep to feed on: a few acres would serve for both their possessions. But as families increased and industry enlarged their stocks, their possessions enlarged with the need of them; but yet it was commonly without any fixed property in the ground they made use of till they incorporated, settled themselves together, and built cities, and then, by consent, they came in time to set out the bounds of their distinct territories and agree on limits between them and their neighbours, and by laws within themselves settled the properties of those of the same society. For we see that in that part of the world which was first inhabited, and therefore like to be best peopled, even as low down as Abraham's time, they wandered with their flocks and their herds, which was their substance, freely up and down—and this Abraham did in a country where he was a stranger; whence it is plain that, at least, a great part of the land lay in common, that the inhabitants valued it not, nor claimed property in any more than they made use of; but when there was not room enough in the same place for their herds to feed together, they, by consent, as Abraham and Lot did (Gen. xiii. 5), separated and enlarged their pasture where it best liked them. And for the same reason, Esau went from his father and his brother, and planted in Mount Seir (Gen. xxxvi. 6).

39. And thus, without supposing any private dominion and property in Adam over all the world, exclusive of all other men, which can no way be proved, nor any one's property be made out from it, but supposing the world, given as it was to the children of men in common, we see how labour could make men distinct titles to several parcels of it for their private uses, wherein there could be no doubt of right, no room for quarrel.

40. Nor is it so strange as, perhaps, before consideration, it may appear, that the property of labour should be able to overbalance the community of land, for it is labour indeed that puts the difference of value on everything; and let any one consider what the difference is between an acre of

land planted with tobacco or sugar, sown with wheat or barley, and an acre of the same land lying in common without any husbandry upon it, and he will find that the improvement of labour makes the far greater part of the value. I think it will be but a very modest computation to say, that of the products of the earth useful to the life of man, nine-tenths are the effects of labour. Nay, if we will rightly estimate things as they come to our use, and cast up the several expenses about them—what in them is purely owing to Nature and what to labour—we shall find that in most of them ninety-nine hundredths are wholly to be put on the account of labour.

41. There cannot be a clearer demonstration of anything than several nations of the Americans are of this, who are rich in land and poor in all the comforts of life; whom Nature, having furnished as liberally as any other people with the materials of plenty—*i.e.*, a fruitful soil, apt to produce in abundance what might serve for food, raiment, and delight; yet, for want of improving it by labour, have not one hundredth part of the conveniencies we enjoy, and a king of a large and fruitful territory there feeds, lodges, and is clad worse than a day labourer in England.

42. To make this a little clearer, let us but trace some of the ordinary provisions of life, through their several progresses, before they come to our use, and see how much they receive of their value from human industry. Bread, wine, and cloth are things of daily use and great plenty; yet notwithstanding acorns, water, and leaves, or skins must be our bread, drink and clothing, did not labour furnish us with these more useful commodities. For whatever bread is more worth than acorns, wine than water, and cloth or silk than leaves, skins or moss, that is wholly owing to labour and industry. The one of these being the food and raiment which unassisted Nature furnishes us with; the other provisions which our industry and pains prepare for us, which how much they exceed the other in value, when any one hath computed, he will then see how much labour makes the far greatest part of the value of things we enjoy in this world; and the ground which produces the materials is scarce to be reckoned in as any, or at most, but a very small part of it; so little, that even amongst us, land that is left wholly to nature, that hath no improvement of pasturage, tillage, or planting, is called, as indeed it is, waste; and we shall find the benefit of it amount to little more than nothing.

43. An acre of land that bears here twenty bushels of wheat, and another in America, which, with the same husbandry, would do the like, are, without doubt, of the same natural, intrinsic value. But yet the

benefit mankind receives from one in a year is worth five pounds, and the other possibly not worth a penny; if all the profit an Indian received from it were to be valued and sold here, at least I may truly say, not one thousandth. It is labour, then, which puts the greatest part of value upon land, without which it would scarcely be worth anything; it is to that we owe the greatest part of all its useful products; for all that the straw, bran, bread, of that acre of wheat, is more worth than the product of an acre of as good land which lies waste is all the effect of labour. For it is not barely the ploughman's pains, the reaper's and thresher's toil, and the baker's sweat, is to be counted into the bread we eat; the labour of those who broke the oxen, who digged and wrought the iron and stones, who felled and framed the timber employed about the plough, mill, oven, or any other utensils, which are a vast number, requisite to this corn, from its sowing to its being made bread, must all be charged on the account of labour, and received as an effect of that; Nature and the earth furnished only the almost worthless materials as in themselves. It would be a strange catalogue of things that industry provided and made use of about every loaf of bread before it came to our use if we could trace them; iron, wood, leather, bark, timber, stone, bricks, coals, lime, cloth, dyeing-drugs, pitch, tar, masts, ropes, and all the materials made use of in the ship that brought any of the commodities made use of by any of the workmen, to any part of the work, all which it would be almost impossible, at least too long, to reckon up.

44. From all which it is evident, that though the things of Nature are given in common, man (by being master of himself, and proprietor of his own person, and the actions or labour of it) had still in himself the great foundation of property; and that which made up the great part of what he applied to the support or comfort of his being, when invention and arts had improved the conveniences of life, was perfectly his own, and did not belong in common to others.

45. Thus labour, in the beginning, gave a right of property, wherever any one was pleased to employ it, upon what was common, which remained a long while, the far greater part, and is yet more than mankind makes use of. Men at first, for the most part, contented themselves with what unassisted Nature offered to their necessities; and though afterwards, in some parts of the world, where the increase of people and stock, with the use of money, had made land scarce, and so of some value, the

several communities settled the bounds of their distinct territories, and, by laws, within themselves, regulated the properties of the private men of their society, and so, by compact and agreement, settled the property which labour and industry began. And the leagues that have been made between several states and kingdoms, either expressly or tacitly disowning all claim and right to the land in the other's possession, have, by common consent, given up their pretences to their natural common right, which originally they had to those countries; and so have, by positive agreement, settled a property amongst themselves, in distinct parts of the world; yet there are still great tracts of ground to be found, which the inhabitants thereof, not having joined with the rest of mankind in the consent of the use of their common money, lie waste, and are more than the people who dwell on it, do, or can make use of, and so still lie in common; though this can scarce happen amongst that part of mankind that have consented to the use of money.

46. The greatest part of things really useful to the life of man, and such as the necessity of subsisting made the first commoners of the world look after—as it doth the Americans now—are generally things of short duration, such as—if they are not consumed by use—will decay and perish of themselves. Gold, silver, and diamonds are things that fancy or agreement hath put the value on, more than real use and the necessary support of life. Now of those good things which Nature hath provided in common, every one hath a right (as hath been said) to as much as he could use, and had a property in all he could effect with his labour; all that his industry could extend to, to alter from the state Nature had put it in, was his. He that gathered a hundred bushels of acorns or apples had thereby a property in them; they were his goods as soon as gathered. He was only to look that he used them before they spoiled, else he took more than his share, and robbed others. And, indeed, it was a foolish thing, as well as dishonest, to hoard up more than he could make use of. If he gave away a part to anybody else, so that it perished not uselessly in his possession, these he also made use of. And if he also bartered away plums that would have rotted in a week, for nuts that would last good for his eating a whole year, he did no injury; he wasted not the common stock; destroyed no part of the portion of goods that belonged to others, so long as nothing perished uselessly in his hands. Again, if he would give his nuts for a piece of metal, pleased with its colour, or exchange his sheep for shells, or wool for a sparkling pebble or a diamond, and keep those by him all his life, he

invaded not the right of others; he might heap up as much of these durable things as he pleased; the exceeding of the bounds of his just property not lying in the largeness of his possession, but the perishing of anything uselessly in it.

47. And thus came in the use of money; some lasting thing that men might keep without spoiling, and that, by mutual consent, men would take in exchange for the truly useful but perishable supports of life.

48. And as different degrees of industry were apt to give men possessions in different proportions, so this invention of money gave them the opportunity to continue and enlarge them. For supposing an island, separate from all possible commerce with the rest of the world, wherein there were but a hundred families, but there were sheep, horses, and cows, with other useful animals, wholesome fruits, and land enough for corn for a hundred thousand times as many, but nothing in the island, either because of its commonness or perishableness, fit to supply the place of money. What reason could any one have there to enlarge his possessions beyond the use of his family, and a plentiful supply to its consumption, either in what their own industry produced, or they could barter for like perishable, useful commodities with others? Where there is not something both lasting and scarce, and so valuable to be hoarded up, there men will not be apt to enlarge their possessions of land, were it never so rich, never so free for them to take. For I ask, what would a man value ten thousand or an hundred thousand acres of excellent land, ready cultivated and well stocked, too, with cattle, in the middle of the inland parts of America, where he had no hopes of commerce with other parts of the world, to draw money to him by the sale of the product? It would not be worth the enclosing, and we should see him give up again to the wild common of Nature whatever was more than would supply the conveniences of life, to be had there for him and his family.

49. Thus, in the beginning, all the world was America, and more so than that is now; for no such thing as money was anywhere known. Find out something that hath the use and value of money amongst his neighbours, you shall see the same man will begin presently to enlarge his possessions.

50. But since gold and silver, being little useful to the life of man, in proportion to food, raiment, and carriage, has its value only from the consent of men—whereof labour yet makes in great part the measure—it is plain that the consent of men have agreed to a disproportionate and unequal possession of the earth—I mean out of the bounds of

society and compact; for in governments the laws regulate it; they having, by consent, found out and agreed in a way how a man may, rightfully and without injury, possess more than he himself can make use of by receiving gold and silver, which may continue long in a man's possession without decaying for the overplus, and agreeing those metals should have a value.

51. And thus, I think, it is very easy to conceive, without any difficulty, how labour could at first begin a title of property in the common things of Nature, and how the spending it upon our uses bounded it; so that there could then be no reason of quarrelling about title, nor any doubt about the largeness of possession it gave. Right and conveniency went together. For as a man had a right to all he could employ his labour upon, so he had no temptation to labour for more than he could make use of. This left no room for controversy about the title, nor for encroachment on the right of others. What portion a man carved to himself was easily seen; and it was useless, as well as dishonest, to carve himself too much, or take more than he needed.

CHAPTER VI

OF PATERNAL POWER

52. It may perhaps be censured an impertinent criticism in a discourse of this nature to find fault with words and names that have obtained in the world. And yet possibly it may not be amiss to offer new ones when the old are apt to lead men into mistakes, as this of paternal power probably has done, which seems so to place the power of parents over their children wholly in the father, as if the mother had no share in it; whereas if we consult reason or revelation, we shall find she has an equal title, which may give one reason to ask whether this might not be more properly called parental power? For whatever obligation Nature and the right of generation lays on children, it must certainly bind them equal to both the concurrent causes of it. And accordingly we see the positive law of God everywhere joins them together without distinction, when it commands the obedience of children: "Honour thy father and thy mother" (Exod. xx. 12); "Whosoever curseth his father or his mother" (Lev. xx. 9); "Ye shall fear every man his mother and his father" (Lev. xix. 3); "Children, obey your parents" (Eph. vi. 1), etc., is the style of the Old and New Testament.

53. Had but this one thing been well considered without looking any deeper into the matter, it might perhaps have kept men from running into those gross mistakes they have made about this power of parents, which however it might without any great harshness bear the name of absolute dominion and regal authority, when under the title of "paternal" power, it seemed appropriated to the father; would yet have sounded but oddly, and in the very name shown the absurdity, if this supposed absolute power over children had been called parental, and thereby discovered that it belonged to the mother too. For it will but very ill serve the turn of

those men who contend so much for the absolute power and authority of the fatherhood, as they call it, that the mother should have any share in it. And it would have but ill supported the monarchy they contend for, when by the very name it appeared that that fundamental authority from whence they would derive their government of a single person only was not placed in one, but two persons jointly. But to let this of names pass.

54. Though I have said above (2) "That all men by nature are equal," I cannot be supposed to understand all sorts of "equality." Age or virtue may give men a just precedency. Excellency of parts and merit may place others above the common level. Birth may subject some, and alliance or benefits others, to pay an observance to those to whom Nature, gratitude, or other respects, may have made it due; and yet all this consists with the equality which all men are in in respect of jurisdiction or dominion one over another, which was the equality I there spoke of as proper to the business in hand, being that equal right that every man hath to his natural freedom, without being subjected to the will or authority of any other man.

55. Children, I confess, are not born in this full state of equality, though they are born to it. Their parents have a sort of rule and jurisdiction over them when they come into the world, and for some time after, but it is but a temporary one. The bonds of this subjection are like the swaddling clothes they are wrapt up in and supported by in the weakness of their infancy. Age and reason as they grow up loosen them, till at length they drop quite off, and leave a man at his own free disposal.

56. Adam was created a perfect man, his body and mind in full possession of their strength and reason, and so was capable from the first instance of his being to provide for his own support and preservation, and govern his actions according to the dictates of the law of reason God had implanted in him. From him the world is peopled with his descendants, who are all born infants, weak and helpless, without knowledge or understanding. But to supply the defects of this imperfect state till the improvement of growth and age had removed them, Adam and Eve, and after them all parents were, by the law of Nature, under an obligation to preserve, nourish and educate the children they had begotten, not as their own workmanship, but the workmanship of their own Maker, the Almighty, to whom they were to be accountable for them.

57. The law that was to govern Adam was the same that was to govern all his posterity, the law of reason. But his offspring having another way of entrance into the world, different from him, by a natural birth, that

produced them ignorant, and without the use of reason, they were not presently under that law. For nobody can be under a law that is not promulgated to him; and this law being promulgated or made known by reason only, he that is not come to the use of his reason cannot be said to be under this law; and Adam's children being not presently as soon as born under this law of reason, were not presently free. For law, in its true notion, is not so much the limitation as the direction of a free and intelligent agent to his proper interest, and prescribes no farther than is for the general good of those under that law. Could they be happier without it, the law, as a useless thing, would of itself vanish; and that ill deserves the name of confinement which hedges us in only from bogs and precipices. So that however it may be mistaken, the end of law is not to abolish or restrain, but to preserve and enlarge freedom. For in all the states of created beings, capable of laws, where there is no law there is no freedom. For liberty is to be free from restraint and violence from others, which cannot be where there is no law; and is not, as we are told, "a liberty for every man to do what he lists." For who could be free, when every other man's humour might domineer over him? But a liberty to dispose and order freely as he lists his person, actions, possessions, and his whole property within the allowance of those laws under which he is, and therein not to be subject to the arbitrary will of another, but freely follow his own.

58. The power, then, that parents have over their children arises from that duty which is incumbent on them, to take care of their offspring during the imperfect state of childhood. To inform the mind, and govern the actions of their yet ignorant nonage, till reason shall take its place and ease them of that trouble, is what the children want, and the parents are bound to. For God having given man an understanding to direct his actions, has allowed him a freedom of will and liberty of acting, as properly belonging thereunto within the bounds of that law he is under. But whilst he is in an estate wherein he has no understanding of his own to direct his will, he is not to have any will of his own to follow. He that understands for him must will for him too; he must prescribe to his will, and regulate his actions, but when he comes to the estate that made his father a free man, the son is a free man too.

59. This holds in all the laws a man is under, whether natural or civil. Is a man under the law of Nature? What made him free of that law? what gave him a free disposing of his property, according to his own will, within the compass of that law? I answer, an estate wherein he might be

supposed capable to know that law, that so he might keep his actions within the bounds of it. When he has acquired that state, he is presumed to know how far that law is to be his guide, and how far he may make use of his freedom, and so comes to have it; till then, somebody else must guide him, who is presumed to know how far the law allows a liberty. If such a state of reason, such an age of discretion made him free, the same shall make his son free too. Is a man under the law of England? what made him free of that law—that is, to have the liberty to dispose of his actions and possessions, according to his own will, within the permission of that law ? a capacity of knowing that law. Which is supposed, by that law, at the age of twenty-one, and in some cases sooner. If this made the father free, it shall make the son free too. Till then, we see the law allows the son to have no will, but he is to be guided by the will of his father or guardian, who is to understand for him. And if the father die and fail to substitute a deputy in this trust, if he hath not provided a tutor to govern his son during his minority, during his want of understanding, the law takes care to do it: some other must govern him and be a will to him till he hath attained to a state of freedom, and his understanding be fit to take the government of his will. But after that the father and son are equally free, as much as tutor and pupil, after nonage, equally subjects of the same law together, without any dominion left in the father over the life, liberty, or estate of his son, whether they be only in the state and under the law of Nature, or under the positive laws of an established government.

60. But if through defects that may happen out of the ordinary course of Nature, any one comes not to such a degree of reason wherein he might be supposed capable of knowing the law, and so living within the rules of it, he is never capable of being a free man, he is never let loose to the disposure of his own will; because he knows no bounds to it, has not understanding, its proper guide, but is continued under the tuition and government of others all the time his own understanding is incapable of that charge. And so lunatics and idiots are never set free from the government of their parents: "Children who are not as yet come unto those years whereat they may have, and innocents, which are excluded by a natural defect from ever having." Thirdly, "Madmen, which, for the present, cannot possibly have the use of right reason to guide themselves, have, for their guide, the reason that guideth other men which are tutors over them, to seek and procure their good for them," says Hooker

(*Eccl. Pol.*, lib. i., s. 7). All which seems no more than that duty which God and Nature has laid on man, as well as other creatures, to preserve their offspring till they can be able to shift for themselves, and will scarce amount to an instance or proof of parents' regal authority.

61. Thus we are born free as we are born rational; not that we have actually the exercise of either: age that brings one, brings with it the other too. And thus we see how natural freedom and subjection to parents may consist together, and are both founded on the same principle. A child is free by his father's title, by his father's understanding, which is to govern him till he hath it of his own. The freedom of a man at years of discretion, and the subjection of a child to his parents, whilst yet short of it, are so consistent and so distinguishable that the most blinded contenders for monarchy, "by right of fatherhood," cannot miss of it; the most obstinate cannot but allow of it. For were their doctrine all true, were the right heir of Adam now known, and, by that title, settled a monarch in his throne, invested with all the absolute unlimited power Sir Robert Filmer talks of, if he should die as soon as his heir were born, must not the child, notwithstanding he were never so free, never so much sovereign, be in subjection to his mother and nurse, to tutors and governors, till age and education brought him reason and ability to govern himself and others? The necessities of his life, the health of his body, and the information of his mind would require him to be directed by the will of others and not his own; and yet will any one think that this restraint and subjection were inconsistent with, or spoiled him of, that liberty or sovereignty he had a right to, or gave away his empire to those who had the government of his nonage? This government over him only prepared him the better and sooner for it. If anybody should ask me when my son is of age to be free, I shall answer, just when his monarch is of age to govern. "But at what time," says the judicious Hooker (*Eccl. Pol.*, lib. i., s. 6), "a man may be said to have attained so far forth the use of reason as sufficeth to make him capable of those laws whereby he is then bound to guide his actions; this is a great deal more easy for sense to discern than for any one, by skill and learning, to determine."

62. Commonwealths themselves take notice of, and allow that there is a time when men are to begin to act like free men, and therefore, till that time, require not oaths of fealty or allegiance, or other public owning of, or submission to, the government of their countries.

63. The freedom then of man, and liberty of acting according to his own will, is grounded on his having reason, which is able to instruct him in that law he is to govern himself by, and make him know how far he is left to the freedom of his own will. To turn him loose to an unrestrained liberty, before he has reason to guide him, is not the allowing him the privilege of his nature to be free, but to thrust him out amongst brutes, and abandon him to a state as wretched and as much beneath that of a man as theirs. This is that which puts the authority into the parents' hands to govern the minority of their children. God hath made it their business to employ this care on their offspring, and hath placed in them suitable inclinations of tenderness and concern to temper this power, to apply it as His wisdom designed it, to the children's good as long as they should need to be under it.

64. But what reason can hence advance this care of the parents due to their offspring into an absolute, arbitrary dominion of the father, whose power reaches no farther than by such a discipline as he finds most effectual to give such strength and health to their bodies, such vigour and rectitude to their minds, as may best fit his children to be most useful to themselves and others, and; if it be necessary to his condition, to make them work when they are able for their own subsistence; but in this power the mother, too, has her share with the father.

65. Nay, this power so little belongs to the father by any peculiar right of Nature, but only as he is guardian of his children, that when he quits his care of them he loses his power over them, which goes along with their nourishment and education, to which it is inseparably annexed, and belongs as much to the foster-father of an exposed child as to the natural father of another. So little power does the bare act of begetting give a man over his issue, if all his care ends there, and this be all the title he hath to the name and authority of a father. And what will become of this paternal power in that part of the world where one woman hath more than one husband at a time? or in those parts of America where, when the husband and wife part, which happens frequently, the children are all left to the mother, follow her, and are wholly under her care and provision? And if the father die whilst the children are young, do they not naturally everywhere owe the same obedience to their mother, during their minority, as to their father, were he alive ? And will any one say that the mother hath a legislative power over her children that she can make standing rules which shall be of perpetual

obligation, by which they ought to regulate all the concerns of their property, and bound their liberty all the course of their lives, and enforce the observation of them with capital punishments? For this is the proper power of the magistrate, of which the father hath not so much as the shadow. His command over his children is but temporary, and reaches not their life or property. It is but a help to the weakness and imperfection of their nonage, a discipline necessary to their education. And though a father may dispose of his own possessions as he pleases when his children are out of danger of perishing for want, yet his power extends not to the lives or goods which either their own industry, or another's bounty, has made theirs, nor to their liberty neither, when they are once arrived to the enfranchisement of the years of discretion. The father's empire then ceases, and he can from thenceforward no more dispose of the liberty of his son than that of any other man. And it must be far from an absolute or perpetual jurisdiction from which a man may withdraw himself, having licence from Divine authority to "leave father and mother and cleave to his wife."

66. But though there be a time when a child comes to be as free from subjection to the will and command of his father as he himself is free from subjection to the will of anybody else, and they are both under no other restraint but that which is common to them both, whether it be the law of Nature or municipal law of their country, yet this freedom exempts not a son from that honour which he ought, by the law of God and Nature, to pay his parents, God having made the parents instruments in His great design of continuing the race of mankind and the occasions of life to their children. As He hath laid on them an obligation to nourish, preserve, and bring up their offspring, so He has laid on the children a perpetual obligation of honouring their parents, which, containing in it an inward esteem and reverence to be shown by all outward expressions, ties up the child from anything that may ever injure or affront, disturb or endanger the happiness or life of those from whom he received his, and engages him in all actions of defence, relief, assistance, and comfort of those by whose means he entered into being and has been made capable of any enjoyments of life. From this obligation no state, no freedom, can absolve children. But this is very far from giving parents a power of command over their children, or an authority to make laws and dispose as they please of their lives or liberties. It is one thing to owe honour, respect, gratitude, and assistance; another to

require an absolute obedience and submission. The honour due to parents a monarch on his throne owes his mother, and yet this lessens not his authority nor subjects him to her government.

67. The subjection of a minor places in the father a temporary government which terminates with the minority of the child; and the honour due from a child places in the parents a perpetual right to respect, reverence, support, and compliance, to more or less, as the father's care, cost, and kindness in his education has been more or less, and this ends not with minority, but holds in all parts and conditions of a man's life. The want of distinguishing these two powers which the father hath, in the right of tuition, during minority, and the right of honour all his life, may perhaps have caused a great part of the mistakes about this matter. For, to speak properly of them, the first of these is rather the privilege of children and duty of parents than any prerogative of paternal power. The nourishment and education of their children is a charge so incumbent on parents for their children's good, that nothing can absolve them from taking care of it. And though the power of commanding and chastising them go along with it, yet God hath woven into the principles of human nature such a tenderness for their offspring, that there is little fear that parents should use their power with too much rigour; the excess is seldom on the severe side, the strong bias of nature drawing the other way. And therefore God Almighty, when He would express His gentle dealing with the Israelites, He tells them that though He chastened them, "He chastened them as a man chastens his son" (Deut. viii. 5)—*i.e.*, with tenderness and affection, and kept them under no severer discipline than what was absolutely best for them, and had been less kindness to have slackened. This is that power to which children are commanded obedience, that the pains and care of their parents may not be increased or ill-rewarded.

68. On the other side, honour and support all that which gratitude requires to return; for the benefits received by and from them is the indispensable duty of the child and the proper privilege of the parents. This is intended for the parents' advantage, as the other is for the child's; though education, the parents' duty, seems to have most power, because the ignorance and infirmities of childhood stand in need of restraint and correction, which is a visible exercise of rule and a kind of dominion. And that duty which is comprehended in the word "honour" requires less obedience, though the obligation be stronger on grown than younger children.

For who can think the command, "Children, obey your parents," requires in a man that has children of his own the same submission to his father as it does in his yet young children to him, and that by this precept he were bound to obey all his father's commands, if, out of a conceit of authority, he should have the indiscretion to treat him still as a boy?

69. The first part, then, of paternal power, or rather duty, which is education, belongs so to the father that it terminates at a certain season. When the business of education is over it ceases of itself, and is also alienable before. For a man may put the tuition of his son in other hands; and he that has made his son an apprentice to another has discharged him, during that time, of a great part of his obedience, both to himself and to his mother. But all the duty of honour, the other part, remains nevertheless entire to them; nothing can cancel that. It is so inseparable from them both, that the father's authority cannot dispossess the mother of this right, nor can any man discharge his son from honouring her that bore him. But both these are very far from a power to make laws, and enforcing them with penalties that may reach estate, liberty, limbs, and life. The power of commanding ends with nonage, and though after that honour and respect, support and defence, and whatsoever gratitude can oblige a man to, for the highest benefits he is naturally capable of be always due from a son to his parents, yet all this puts no sceptre into the father's hand, no sovereign power of commanding. He has no dominion over his son's property or actions, nor any right that his will should prescribe to his son's in all things; however, it may become his son in many things, not very inconvenient to him and his family, to pay a deference to it.

70. A man may owe honour and respect to an ancient or wise man, defence to his child or friend, relief and support to the distressed, and gratitude to a benefactor, to such a degree that all he has, all he can do, cannot sufficiently pay it. But all these give no authority, no right of making laws to any one over him from whom they are owing. And it is plain all this is due, not to the bare title of father, not only because, as has been said, it is owing to the mother too, but because these obligations to parents, and the degrees of what is required of children, may be varied by the different care and kindness, trouble and expense, is often employed upon one child more than another.

71. This shows the reason how it comes to pass that parents in societies, where they themselves are subjects, retain a power over their children and have as much right to their subjection as those who are in the

state of Nature, which could not possibly be if all political power were only paternal, and that, in truth, they were one and the same thing; for then, all paternal power being in the prince, the subject could naturally have none of it. But these two powers, political and paternal, are so perfectly distinct and separate, and built upon so different foundations, and given to so different ends, that every subject that is a father has as much a paternal power over his children as the prince has over his. And every prince that has parents owes them as much filial duty and obedience as the meanest of his subjects do to theirs, and can therefore contain not any part or degree of that kind of dominion which a prince or magistrate has over his subject.

72. Though the obligation on the parents to bring up their children, and the obligation on children to honour their parents, contain all the power, on the one hand, and submission on the other, which are proper to this relation, yet there is another power ordinarily in the father, whereby he has a tie on the obedience of his children, which, though it be common to him with other men, yet the occasions of showing it, almost constantly happening to fathers in their private families and in instances of it elsewhere being rare, and less taken notice of, it passes in the world for a part of "paternal jurisdiction." And this is the power men generally have to bestow their estates on those who please them best. The possession of the father being the expectation and inheritance of the children ordinarily, in certain proportions, according to the law and custom of each country, yet it is commonly in the father's power to bestow it with a more sparing or liberal hand, according as the behaviour of this or that child hath comported with his will and humour.

73. This is no small tie to the obedience of children; and there being always annexed to the enjoyment of land a submission to the government of the country of which that land is a part, it has been commonly supposed that a father could oblige his posterity to that government of which he himself was a subject, that his compact held them; whereas, it being only a necessary condition annexed to the land which is under that government, reaches only those who will take it on that condition, and so is no natural tie or engagement, but a voluntary submission; for every man's children being, by Nature, as free as himself or any of his ancestors ever were, may, whilst they are in that freedom, choose what society they will join themselves to, what commonwealth they will put themselves under. But if they will enjoy the inheritance of their ancestors, they must take it

on the same terms their ancestors had it, and submit to all the conditions annexed to such a possession. By this power, indeed, fathers oblige their children to obedience to themselves even when they are past minority, and most commonly, too, subject them to this or that political power. But neither of these by any peculiar right of fatherhood, but by the reward they have in their hands to enforce and recompense such a compliance, and is no more power than what a Frenchman has over an Englishman, who, by the hopes of an estate he will leave him, will certainly have a strong tie on his obedience; and if when it is left him, he will enjoy it, he must certainly take it upon the conditions annexed to the possession of land in that country where it lies, whether it be France or England.

74. To conclude, then, though the father's power of commanding extends no farther than the minority of his children, and to a degree only fit for the discipline and government of that age; and though that honour and respect, and all that which the Latins called piety, which they indispensably owe to their parents all their lifetime, and in all estates, with all that support and defence, is due to them, gives the father no power of governing—*i.e.*, making laws and exacting penalties on his children; though by this he has no dominion over the property or actions of his son, yet it is obvious to conceive how easy it was, in the first ages of the world, and in places still where the thinness of people gives families leave to separate into unpossessed quarters, and they have room to remove and plant themselves in yet vacant habitations, for the father of the family to become the prince of it;[1] he had been a ruler from the beginning of the infancy of his children; and when they were grown up, since without some government it would be hard for them to live together, it was likeliest it should, by the express or tacit consent of the children, be in the father, where it seemed, without any change, barely to continue. And when, indeed, nothing more was required to it than the permitting the father to exercise alone in his family that executive power of the law of Nature which every free man naturally hath, and by that permission resigning up to him a monarchical power whilst they remained in it. But that this was not by any paternal right, but only by the consent of his children, is evident from hence, that nobody doubts but if a stranger, whom chance or business had brought to his family, had there killed any of his children, or committed any other act, he might condemn and put him to death, or otherwise have punished him as well as any of his children, which was impossible he should do by virtue of any paternal authority over one who

was not his child, but by virtue of that executive power of the law of Nature which, as a man, he had a right to; and he alone could punish him in his family where the respect of his children had laid by the exercise of such a power, to give way to the dignity and authority they were willing should remain in him above the rest of his family.

75. Thus it was easy and almost natural for children, by a tacit and almost natural consent, to make way for the father's authority and government. They had been accustomed in their childhood to follow his direction, and to refer their little differences to him; and when they were men, who was fitter to rule them? Their little properties and less covetousness seldom afforded greater controversies; and when any should arise, where could they have a fitter umpire than he, by whose care they had every one been sustained and brought up, and who had a tenderness for them all? It is no wonder that they made no distinction betwixt minority and full age, nor looked after one-and-twenty, or any other age, that might make them the free disposers of themselves and fortunes, when they could have no desire to be out of their pupilage. The government they had been under during it continued still to be more their protection than restraint; and they could nowhere find a greater security to their peace, liberties, and fortunes than in the rule of a father.

76. Thus the natural fathers of families, by an insensible change, became the politic monarchs of them too; and as they chanced to live long, and leave able and worthy heirs for several successions or otherwise, so they laid the foundations of hereditary or elective kingdoms under several constitutions and manors, according as chance, contrivance, or occasions happened to mould them. But if princes have their titles in the father's right, and it be a sufficient proof of the natural right of fathers to political authority, because they commonly were those in whose hands we find, *de facto,* the exercise of government, I say, if this argument be good, it will as strongly prove that all princes, nay, princes only, ought to be priests, since it is as certain that in the beginning "the father of the family was priest, as that he was ruler in his own household."

CHAPTER VII

OF POLITICAL OR CIVIL SOCIETY

77. God, having made man such a creature that, in His own judgment, it was not good for him to be alone, put him under strong obligations of necessity, convenience, and inclination, to drive him into society, as well as fitted him with understanding and language to continue and enjoy it. The first society was between man and wife, which gave beginning to that between parents and children, to which, in time, that between master and servant came to be added. And though all these might, and commonly did, meet together, and make up but one family, wherein the master or mistress of it had some sort of rule proper to a family, each of these, or all together, came short of "political society," as we shall see if we consider the different ends, ties, and bounds of each of these.

78. Conjugal society is made by a voluntary compact between man and woman, and though it consist chiefly in such a communion and right in one another's bodies as is necessary to its chief end, procreation, yet it draws with it mutual support and assistance, and a communion of interests too, as necessary not only to unite their care and affection, but also necessary to their common offspring, who have a right to be nourished and maintained by them till they are able to provide for themselves.

79. For the end of conjunction between male and female being not barely procreation, but the continuation of the species, this conjunction betwixt male and female ought to last, even after procreation, so long as is necessary to the nourishment and support of the young ones, who are to be sustained by those that got them till they are able to shift and provide for themselves. This rule, which the infinite wise Maker hath set to the works of His hands, we find the inferior creatures steadily obey. In

those vivaporous animals which feed on grass the conjunction between male and female lasts no longer than the very act of copulation, because the teat of the dam being sufficient to nourish the young till it be able to feed on grass, the male only begets, but concerns not himself for the female or young, to whose sustenance he can contribute nothing. But in beasts of prey the conjunction lasts longer, because the dam, not being able well to subsist herself and nourish her numerous offspring by her own prey alone (a more laborious as well as more dangerous way of living than by feeding on grass), the assistance of the male is necessary to the maintenance of their common family, which cannot subsist till they are able to prey for themselves, but by the joint care of male and female. The same is observed in all birds (except some domestic ones, where plenty of food excuses the cock from feeding and taking care of the young brood), whose young, needing food in the nest, the cock and hen continue mates till the young are able to use their wings and provide for themselves.

80. And herein, I think, lies the chief, if not the only reason, why the male and female in mankind are tied to a longer conjunction than other creatures—viz., because the female is capable of conceiving, and, *de facto,* is commonly with child again, and brings forth too a new birth, long before the former is out of a dependency for support on his parents' help and able to shift for himself, and has all the assistance due to him from his parents, whereby the father, who is bound to take care for those he hath begot, is under an obligation to continue in conjugal society with the same woman longer than other creatures, whose young, being able to subsist of themselves before the time of procreation returns again, the conjugal bond dissolves of itself, and they are at liberty till Hymen, at his usual anniversary season, summons them again to choose new mates. Wherein one cannot but admire the wisdom of the great Creator, who, having given to man an ability to lay up for the future as well as supply the present necessity, hath made it necessary that society of man and wife should be more lasting than of male and female amongst other creatures, that so their industry might be encouraged, and their interest better united, to make provision and lay up goods for their common issue, which uncertain mixture, or easy and frequent solutions of conjugal society, would mightily disturb.

81. But though these are ties upon mankind which make the conjugal bonds more firm and lasting in a man than the other species of animals, yet it would give one reason to inquire why this compact, where procreation

and education are secured and inheritance taken care for, may not be made determinable, either by consent, or at a certain time, or upon certain conditions, as well as any other voluntary compacts, there being no necessity, in the nature of the thing, nor to the ends of it, that it should always be for life—I mean, to such as are under no restraint of any positive law which ordains all such contracts to be perpetual.

82. But the husband and wife, though they have but one common concern, yet having different understandings, will unavoidably sometimes have different wills too. It therefore being necessary that the last determination *(i.e.,* the rule) should be placed somewhere, it naturally falls to the man's share as the abler and the stronger. But this, reaching but to the things of their common interest and property, leaves the wife in the full and true possession of what by contract is her peculiar right, and at least gives the husband no more power over her than she has over his life; the power of the husband being so far from that of an absolute monarch that the wife has, in many cases, a liberty to separate from him where natural right or their contract allows it, whether that contract be made by themselves in the state of Nature or by the customs or laws of the country they live in, and the children, upon such separation, fall to the father or mother's lot as such contract does determine.

83. For all the ends of marriage being to be obtained under politic government, as well as in the state of Nature, the civil magistrate doth not abridge the right or power of either, naturally necessary to those ends—viz., procreation and mutual support and assistance whilst they are together, but only decides any controversy that may arise between man and wife about them. If it were otherwise, and that absolute sovereignty and power of life and death naturally belonged to the husband, and were necessary to the society between man and wife, there could be no matrimony in any of these countries where the husband is allowed no such absolute authority. But the ends of matrimony requiring no such power in the husband, it was not at all necessary to it. The condition of conjugal society put it not in him; but whatsoever might consist with procreation and support of the children till they could shift for themselves—mutual assistance, comfort, and maintenance—might be varied and regulated by that contract which first united them in that society, nothing being necessary to any society that is not necessary to the ends for which it is made.

84. The society betwixt parents and children, and the distinct rights and powers belonging respectively to them, I have treated of so largely in the foregoing chapter that I shall not here need to say anything of it; and I think it is plain that it is far different from a politic society.

85. Master and servant are names as old as history, but given to those of far different condition; for a free man makes himself a servant to another by selling him for a certain time the service he undertakes to do in exchange for wages he is to receive; and though this commonly puts him into the family of his master, and under the ordinary discipline thereof, yet it gives the master but a temporary power over him, and no greater than what is contained in the contract between them. But there is another sort of servant which by a peculiar name we call slaves, who being captives taken in a just war are, by the right of Nature, subjected to the absolute dominion and arbitrary power of their masters. These men having, as I say, forfeited their lives and, with it, their liberties, and lost their estates, and being in the state of slavery, not capable of any property, cannot in that state be considered as any part of civil society, the chief end whereof is the preservation of property.

86. Let us therefore consider a master of a family with all these subordinate relations of wife, children, servants and slaves, united under the domestic rule of a family, with what resemblance soever it may have in its order, offices, and number too, with a little commonwealth, yet is very far from it both in its constitution, power, and end; or if it must be thought a monarchy, and the paterfamilias the absolute monarch in it, absolute monarchy will have but a very shattered and short power, when it is plain by what has been said before, that the master of the family has a very distinct and differently limited power both as to time and extent over those several persons that are in it; for excepting the slave (and the family is as much a family, and his power as paterfamilias as great, whether there be any slaves in his family or no) he has no legislative power of life and death over any of them, and none too but what a mistress of a family may have as well as he. And he certainly can have no absolute power over the whole family who has but a very limited one over every individual in it. But how a family, or any other society of men, differ from that which is properly political society, we shall best see by considering wherein political society itself consists.

87. Man being born, as has been proved, with a title to perfect freedom and an uncontrolled enjoyment of all the rights and privileges of the law of Nature, equally with any other man, or number of men in the

world, hath by nature a power not only to preserve his property—that is, his life, liberty, and estate, against the injuries and attempts of other men, but to judge of and punish the breaches of that law in others, as he is persuaded the offence deserves, even with death itself, in crimes where the heinousness of the fact, in his opinion, requires it. But because no political society can be, nor subsist, without having in itself the power to preserve the property, and in order thereunto punish the offences of all those of that society, there, and there only, is political society where every one of the members hath quitted this natural power, resigned it up into the hands of the community in all cases that exclude him not from appealing for protection to the law established by it. And thus all private judgment of every particular member being excluded, the community comes to be umpire, and by understanding indifferent rules and men authorised by the community for their execution, decides all the differences that may happen between any members of that society concerning any matter of right, and punishes those offences which any member hath committed against the society with such penalties as the law has established; whereby it is easy to discern who are, and are not, in political society together. Those who are united into one body, and have a common established law and judicature to appeal to, with authority to decide controversies between them and punish offenders, are in civil society one with another; but those who have no such common appeal, I mean on earth, are still in the state of Nature, each being where there is no other, judge for himself and executioner; which is, as I have before showed it, the perfect state of Nature.

88. And thus the commonwealth comes by a power to set down what punishment shall belong to the several transgressions they think worthy of it, committed amongst the members of that society (which is the power of making laws), as well as it has the power to punish any injury done unto any of its members by any one that is not of it (which is the power of war and peace); and all this for the preservation of the property of all the members of that society, as far as is possible. But though every man entered into society has quitted his power to punish offences against the law of Nature in prosecution of his own private judgment, yet with the judgment of offences which he has given up to the legislative, in all cases where he can appeal to the magistrate, he has given up a right to the commonwealth to employ his force for the execution of the judgments of the commonwealth whenever he shall be called to it,

which, indeed, are his own judgments, they being made by himself or his representative. And herein we have the original of the legislative and executive power of civil society, which is to judge by standing laws how far offences are to be punished when committed within the commonwealth; and also by occasional judgments founded on the present circumstances of the fact, how far injuries from without are to be vindicated, and in both these to employ all the force of all the members when there shall be need.

89. Wherever, therefore, any number of men so unite into one society as to quit every one his executive power of the law of Nature, and to resign it to the public, there and there only is a political or civil society. And this is done wherever any number of men, in the state of Nature, enter into society to make one people one body politic under one supreme government: or else when any one joins himself to, and incorporates with any government already made. For hereby he authorises the society, or which is all one, the legislative thereof, to make laws for him as the public good of the society shall require, to the execution whereof his own assistance (as to his own decrees) is due. And this puts men out of a state of Nature into that of a commonwealth, by setting up a judge on earth with authority to determine all the controversies and redress the injuries that may happen to any member of the commonwealth, which judge is the legislative or magistrates appointed by it. And wherever there are any number of men, however associated, that have no such decisive power to appeal to, there they are still in the state of Nature.

90. And hence it is evident that absolute monarchy, which by some men is counted for the only government in the world, is indeed inconsistent with civil society, and so can be no form of civil government at all. For the end of civil society being to avoid and remedy those inconveniencies of the state of Nature which necessarily follow from every man's being judge in his own case, by setting up a known authority to which every one of that society may appeal upon any injury received, or controversy that may arise, and which every one of the society ought to obey.[1] Wherever any persons are who have not such an authority to appeal to, and decide any difference between them there, those persons are still in the state of Nature. And so is every absolute prince in respect of those who are under his dominion.

91. For he being supposed to have all, both legislative and executive, power in himself alone, there is no judge to be found, no appeal lies open to any one, who may fairly and indifferently, and with authority decide,

and from whence relief and redress may be expected of any injury or inconveniency that may be suffered from him, or by his order. So that such a man, however entitled, Czar, or Grand Signior, or how you please, is as much in the state of Nature, with all under his dominion, as he is with the rest of mankind. For wherever any two men are, who have no standing rule and common judge to appeal to on earth, for the determination of controversies of right betwixt them, there they are still in the state of Nature, and under all the inconveniencies of it, with only this woeful difference to the subject, or rather slave of an absolute prince.[2] That whereas, in the ordinary state of Nature, he has a liberty to judge of his right, according to the best of his power to maintain it; but whenever his property is invaded by the will and order of his monarch, he has not only no appeal, as those in society ought to have, but, as if he were degraded from the common state of rational creatures, is denied a liberty to judge of, or defend his right, and so is exposed to all the misery and inconveniencies that a man can fear from one, who being in the unrestrained state of Nature, is yet corrupted with flattery and armed with power.

92. For he that thinks absolute power purifies men's blood, and corrects the baseness of human nature, need read but the history of this, or any other age, to be convinced to the contrary. He that would have been insolent and injurious in the woods of America would not probably be much better on a throne, where perhaps learning and religion shall be found out to justify all that he shall do to his subjects, and the sword presently silence all those that dare question it. For what the protection of absolute monarchy is, what kind of fathers of their countries it makes princes to be, and to what a degree of happiness and security it carries civil society, where this sort of government is grown to perfection, he that will look into the late relation of Ceylon may easily see.

93. In absolute monarchies, indeed, as well as other governments of the world, the subjects have an appeal to the law, and judges to decide any controversies, and restrain any violence that may happen betwixt the subjects themselves, one amongst another. This every one thinks necessary, and believes; he deserves to be thought a declared enemy to society and mankind who should go about to take it away. But whether this be from a true love of mankind and society, and such a charity as we owe all one to another, there is reason to doubt. For this is no more than what every man, who loves his own power, profit, or greatness, may, and naturally must do, keep those animals from hurting or destroying one another who

labour and drudge only for his pleasure and advantage; and so are taken care of, not out of any love the master has for them, but love of himself, and the profit they bring him. For if it be asked what security, what fence is there in such a state against the violence and oppression of this absolute ruler, the very question can scarce be borne. They are ready to tell you that it deserves death only to ask after safety. Betwixt subject and subject, they will grant, there must be measures, laws, and judges for their mutual peace and security. But as for the ruler, he ought to be absolute, and is above all such circumstances; because he has a power to do more hurt and wrong, it is right when he does it. To ask how you may be guarded from harm or injury on that side, where the strongest hand is to do it, is presently the voice of faction and rebellion. As if when men, quitting the state of Nature, entered into society, they agreed that all of them but one should be under the restraint of laws; but that he should still retain all the liberty of the state of Nature, increased with power, and made licentious by impunity. This is to think that men are so foolish that they take care to avoid what mischiefs may be done them by polecats or foxes, but are content, nay, think it safety, to be devoured by lions.

94. But, whatever flatterers may talk to amuse people's understandings, it never hinders men from feeling; and when they perceive that any man, in what station soever, is out of the bounds of the civil society they are of, and that they have no appeal, on earth, against any harm they may receive from him, they are apt to think themselves in the state of Nature, in respect of him whom they find to be so; and to take care, as soon as they can, to have that safety and security, in civil society, for which it was first instituted, and for which only they entered into it. And therefore, though perhaps at first, as shall be showed more at large hereafter, in the following part of this discourse, some one good and excellent man having got a pre-eminency amongst the rest, had this deference paid to his goodness and virtue, as to a kind of natural authority, that the chief rule, with arbitration of their differences, by a tacit consent devolved into his hands, without any other caution but the assurance they had of his uprightness and wisdom; yet when time giving authority, and, as some men would persuade us, sacredness to customs, which the negligent and unforeseeing innocence of the first ages began, had brought in successors of another stamp, the people finding their properties not secure under the government as then it was[3] (whereas government has no other end but the preservation of

property), could never be safe, nor at rest, nor think themselves in civil society, till the legislative was so placed in collective bodies of men, call them senate, parliament, or what you please, by which means every single person became subject equally, with other the meanest men, to those laws, which he himself, as part of the legislative, had established; nor could any one, by his own authority, avoid the force of the law, when once made, nor by any pretence of superiority plead exemption, thereby to license his own, or the miscarriages of any of his dependants. No man in civil society can be exempted from the laws of it. For if any man may do what he thinks fit and there be no appeal on earth for redress or security against any harm he shall do, I ask whether he be not perfectly still in the state of Nature, and so can be no part or member of that civil society, unless any one will say the state of Nature and civil society are one and the same thing, which I have never yet found any one so great a patron of anarchy as to affirm.[4]

CHAPTER VIII

OF THE BEGINNING OF POLITICAL SOCIETIES

95. MEN being, as has been said, by nature all free, equal, and independent, no one can be put out of this estate and subjected to the political power of another without his own consent, which is done by agreeing with other men, to join and unite into a community for their comfortable, safe, and peaceable living, one amongst another, in a secure enjoyment of their properties, and a greater security against any that are not of it. This any number of men may do, because it injures not the freedom of the rest; they are left, as they were, in the liberty of the state of Nature. When any number of men have so consented to make one community or government, they are thereby presently incorporated, and make one body politic, wherein the majority have a right to act and conclude the rest.

96. For, when any number of men have, by the consent of every individual, made a community, they have thereby made that community one body, with a power to act as one body, which is only by the will and determination of the majority. For that which acts any community, being only the consent of the individuals of it, and it being one body, must move one way, it is necessary the body should move that way whither the greater force carries it, which is the consent of the majority, or else it is impossible it should act or continue one body, one community, which the consent of every individual that united into it agreed that it should; and so every one is bound by that consent to be concluded by the majority. And therefore we see that in assemblies empowered to act by positive laws where no number is set by that positive law which empowers

them, the act of the majority passes for the act of the whole, and of course determines as having, by the law of Nature and reason, the power of the whole.

97. And thus every man, by consenting with others to make one body politic under one government, puts himself under an obligation to every one of that society to submit to the determination of the majority, and to be concluded by it; or else this original compact, whereby he with others incorporates into one society, would signify nothing, and be no compact if he be left free and under no other ties than he was in before in the state of Nature. For what appearance would there be of any compact? What new engagement if he were no farther tied by any decrees of the society than he himself thought fit and did actually consent to? This would be still as great a liberty as he himself had before his compact, or any one else in the state of Nature, who may submit himself and consent to any acts of it if he thinks fit.

98. For if the consent of the majority shall not in reason be received as the act of the whole, and conclude every individual, nothing but the consent of every individual can make anything to be the act of the whole, which, considering the infirmities of health and avocations of business, which in a number though much less than that of a commonwealth, will necessarily keep many away from the public assembly; and the variety of opinions and contrariety of interests which unavoidably happen in all collections of men, it is next impossible ever to be had. And, therefore, if coming into society be upon such terms, it will be only like Cato's coming into the theatre, *tantum ut exiret.* Such a constitution as this would make the mighty leviathan of a shorter duration than the feeblest creatures, and not let it outlast the day it was born in, which cannot be supposed till we can think that rational creatures should desire and constitute societies only to be dissolved. For where the majority cannot conclude the rest, there they cannot act as one body, and consequently will be immediately dissolved again.

99. Whosoever, therefore, out of a state of Nature unite into a community, must be understood to give up all the power necessary to the ends for which they unite into society to the majority of the community, unless they expressly agreed in any number greater than the majority. And this is done by barely agreeing to unite into one political society, which is all the compact that is, or needs be, between the individuals that enter into or make up a commonwealth. And thus, that which begins and actually

constitutes any political society is nothing but the consent of any number of freemen capable of majority, to unite and incorporate into such a society. And this is that, and that only, which did or could give beginning to any lawful government in the world.

100. To this I find two objections made: 1. That there are no instances to be found in story of a company of men, independent and equal one amongst another, that met together, and in this way began and set up a government. 2. It is impossible of right that men should do so, because all men, being born under government, they are to submit to that, and are not at liberty to begin a new one.

101. To the first there is this to answer: That it is not at all to be wondered that history gives us but a very little account of men that lived together in the state of Nature. The inconveniencies of that condition, and the love and want of society, no sooner brought any number of them together, but they presently united and incorporated if they designed to continue together. And if we may not suppose men ever to have been in the state of Nature, because we hear not much of them in such a state, we may as well suppose the armies of Salmanasser or Xerxes were never children, because we hear little of them till they were men and embodied in armies. Government is everywhere antecedent to records, and letters seldom come in amongst a people till a long continuation of civil society has, by other more necessary arts, provided for their safety, ease, and plenty. And then they begin to look after the history of their founders, and search into their original when they have outlived the memory of it. For it is with commonwealths as with particular persons, they are commonly ignorant of their own births and infancies; and if they know anything of it, they are beholding for it to the accidental records that others have kept of it. And those that we have of the beginning of any polities in the world, excepting that of the Jews, where God Himself immediately interposed, and which favours not at all paternal dominion, are all either plain instances of such a beginning as I have mentioned, or at least have manifest footsteps of it.

102. He must show a strange inclination to deny evident matter of fact, when it agrees not with his hypothesis, who will not allow that the beginning of Rome and Venice were by the uniting together of several men, free and independent one of another, amongst whom there was no natural superiority or subjection. And if Josephus Acosta's word may be taken, he tells us that in many parts of America there was no government

at all. "There are great and apparent conjectures," says he, "that these men (speaking of those of Peru) for a long time had neither kings nor commonwealths, but lived in troops, as they do this day in Florida—the Cheriquanas, those of Brazil, and many other nations, which have no certain kings, but, as occasion is offered in peace or war, they choose their captains as they please" (lib. i. cap. 25). If it be said, that every man there was born subject to his father, or the head of his family, that the subjection due from a child to a father took not away his freedom of uniting into what political society he thought fit, has been already proved; but be that as it will, these men, it is evident, were actually free; and whatever superiority some politicians now would place in any of them, they themselves claimed it not; but, by consent, were all equal, till, by the same consent, they set rulers over themselves. So that their politic societies all began from a voluntary union, and the mutual agreement of men freely acting in the choice of their governors and forms of government.

103. And I hope those who went away from Sparta, with Palantus, mentioned by Justin, will be allowed to have been freemen independent one of another, and to have set up a government over themselves by their own consent. Thus I have given several examples out of history of people, free and in the state of Nature, that, being met together, incorporated and began a commonwealth. And if the want of such instances be an argument to prove that government were not nor could not be so begun, I suppose the contenders for paternal empire were better let it alone than urge it against natural liberty; for if they can give so many instances out of history of governments began upon paternal right, I think (though at least an argument from what has been to what should of right be of no great force) one might, without any great danger, yield them the cause. But if I might advise them in the case, they would do well not to search too much into the original of governments as they have begun *de facto*, lest they should find at the foundation of most of them something very little favourable to the design they promote, and such a power as they contend for.

104. But, to conclude: reason being plain on our side that men are naturally free; and the examples of history showing that the governments of the world, that were begun in peace, had their beginning laid on that foundation, and were made by the consent of the people; there can be little room for doubt, either where the right is, or what has been the opinion or practice of mankind about the first erecting of governments.

105. I will not deny that if we look back, as far as history will direct us, towards the original of commonwealths, we shall generally find them under the government and administration of one man. And I am also apt to believe that where a family was numerous enough to subsist by itself, and continued entire together, without mixing with others, as it often happens, where there is much land and few people, the government commonly began in the father. For the father having, by the law of Nature, the same power, with every man else, to punish, as he thought fit, any offences against that law, might thereby punish his transgressing children, even when they were men, and out of their pupilage; and they were very likely to submit to his punishment, and all join with him against the offender in their turns, giving him thereby power to execute his sentence against any transgression, and so, in effect, make him the law-maker and governor over all that remained in conjunction with his family. He was fittest to be trusted; paternal affection secured their property and interest under his care, and the custom of obeying him in their childhood made it easier to submit to him rather than any other. If, therefore, they must have one to rule them, as government is hardly to be avoided amongst men that live together, who so likely to be the man as he that was their common father, unless negligence, cruelty, or any other defect of mind or body, made him unfit for it? But when either the father died, and left his next heir—for want of age, wisdom, courage, or any other qualities—less fit for rule, or where several families met and consented to continue together, there, it is not to be doubted, but they used their natural freedom to set up him whom they judged the ablest and most likely to rule well over them. Conformable hereunto we find the people of America, who—living out of the reach of the conquering swords and spreading domination of the two great empires of Peru and Mexico—enjoyed their own natural freedom, though, *cæteris paribus,* they commonly prefer the heir of their deceased king; yet, if they find him any way weak or incapable, they pass him by, and set up the stoutest and bravest man for their ruler.

106. Thus, though looking back as far as records give us any account of peopling the world, and the history of nations, we commonly find the government to be in one hand, yet it destroys not that which I affirm—viz., that the beginning of politic society depends upon the consent of the individuals to join into and make one society, who, when they are thus incorporated, might set up what form of government they thought fit. But this having given occasion to men to mistake and think that, by

Nature, government was monarchical, and belonged to the father, it may not be amiss here to consider why people, in the beginning, generally pitched upon this form, which, though perhaps the father's preeminency might, in the first institution of some commonwealths, give a rise to and place in the beginning the power in one hand, yet it is plain that the reason that continued the form of government in a single person was not any regard or respect to paternal authority, since all petty monarchies—that is, almost all monarchies, near their original, have been commonly, at least upon occasion, elective.

107. First, then, in the beginning of things, the father's government of the childhood of those sprung from him having accustomed them to the rule of one man, and taught them that where it was exercised with care and skill, with affection and love to those under it, it was sufficient to procure and preserve men (all the political happiness they sought for in society), it was no wonder that they should pitch upon and naturally run into that form of government which, from their infancy, they had been all accustomed to, and which, by experience, they had found both easy and safe. To which if we add, that monarchy being simple and most obvious to men, whom neither experience had instructed in forms of government, nor the ambition or insolence of empire had taught to beware of the encroachments of prerogative or the inconveniencies of absolute power, which monarchy, in succession, was apt to lay claim to and bring upon them; it was not at all strange that they should not much trouble themselves to think of methods of restraining any exorbitances of those to whom they had given the authority over them, and of balancing the power of government by placing several parts of it in different hands. They had neither felt the oppression of tyrannical dominion, nor did the fashion of the age, nor their possessions or way of living, which afforded little matter for covetousness or ambition, give them any reason to apprehend or provide against it; and, therefore, it is no wonder they put themselves into such a frame of government as was not only, as I said, most obvious and simple, but also best suited to their present state and condition, which stood more in need of defence against foreign invasions and injuries than of multiplicity of laws where there was but very little property, and wanted not variety of rulers and abundance of officers to direct and look after their execution where there were but few trespassers and few offenders. Since, then, those who liked one another so well as to join into society cannot but be supposed to have some acquaintance and

friendship together, and some trust one in another, they could not but have greater apprehensions of others than of one another; and, therefore, their first care and thought cannot but be supposed to be, how to secure themselves against foreign force. It was natural for them to put themselves under a frame of government which might best serve to that end, and choose the wisest and bravest man to conduct them in their wars and lead them out against their enemies, and in this chiefly be their ruler.

108. Thus we see that the kings of the Indians, in America, which is still a pattern of the first ages in Asia and Europe, whilst the inhabitants were too few for the country, and want of people and money gave men no temptation to enlarge their possessions of land or contest for wider extent of ground, are little more than generals of their armies; and though they command absolutely in war, yet at home, and in time of peace, they exercise very little dominion, and have but a very moderate sovereignty, the resolutions of peace and war being ordinarily either in the people or in a council, though the war itself, which admits not of pluralities of governors, naturally evolves the command into the king's sole authority.

109. And thus, in Israel itself, the chief business of their judges and first kings seems to have been to be captains in war and leaders of their armies, which (besides what is signified by "going out and in before the people," which was, to march forth to war and home again at the heads of their forces) appears plainly in the story of Jephtha. The Ammonites making war upon Israel, the Gileadites, in fear, send to Jephtha, a bastard of their family, whom they had cast off, and article with him, if he will assist them against the Ammonites, to make him their ruler, which they do in these words: "And the people made him head and captain over them" (Judges xi. 11), which was, as it seems, all one as to be judge. "And he judged Israel" (Judges xii. 7)—that is, was their captain-general—"six years." So when Jotham upbraids the Shechemites with the obligation they had to Gideon, who had been their judge and ruler, he tells them: "He fought for you, and adventured his life for, and delivered you out of the hands of Midian" (Judges ix. 17). Nothing mentioned of him but what he did as a general, and, indeed, that is all is found in his history, or in any of the rest of the judges. And Abimelech particularly is called king, though at most he was but their general. And when, being weary of the ill-conduct of Samuel's sons, the children of Israel desired a king, "like all the nations, to judge them, and to go out before them, and to fight their battles" (I Sam. viii. 20), God, granting their desire, says to Samuel, "I will

send thee a man, and thou shalt anoint him to be captain over my people Israel, that he may save my people out of the hands of the Philistines" (ch. ix. 16). As if the only business of a king had been to lead out their armies and fight in their defence; and, accordingly, at his inauguration, pouring a vial of oil upon him, declares to Saul that "the Lord had anointed him to be captain over his inheritance" (ch. x. 1). And therefore those who, after Saul being solemnly chosen and saluted king by the tribes at Mispah, were unwilling to have him their king, make no other objection but this, "How shall this man save us?" (ch. x. 27), as if they should have said: "This man is unfit to be our king, not having skill and conduct enough in war to be able to defend us." And when God resolved to transfer the government to David, it is in these words: "But now thy kingdom shall not continue: the Lord hath sought Him a man after His own heart, and the Lord hath commanded him to be captain over His people" (ch. xiii. 14). As if the whole kingly authority were nothing else but to be their general; and therefore the tribes who had stuck to Saul's family, and opposed David's reign, when they came to Hebron with terms of submission to him, they tell him, amongst other arguments, they had to submit to him as to their king, that he was, in effect, their king in Saul's time, and therefore they had no reason but to receive him as their king now. "Also," say they, "in time past, when Saul was king over us, thou wast he that leddest out and broughtest in Israel, and the Lord said unto thee, Thou shalt feed my people Israel, and thou shalt be a captain over Israel."

110. Thus, whether a family, by degrees, grew up into a commonwealth, and the fatherly authority being continued on to the elder son, every one in his turn growing up under it tacitly submitted to it, and the easiness and equality of it not offending any one, every one acquiesced till time seemed to have confirmed it and settled a right of succession by prescription; or whether several families, or the descendants of several families, whom chance, neighbourhood, or business brought together, united into society; the need of a general whose conduct might defend them against their enemies in war, and the great confidence the innocence and sincerity of that poor but virtuous age, such as are almost all those which begin governments that ever come to last in the world, gave men one of another, made the first beginners of commonwealths generally put the rule into one man's hand, without any other express limitation or restraint but what the nature of the thing and the end of government

required. It was given them for the public good and safety, and to those ends, in the infancies of commonwealths, they commonly used it; and unless they had done so, young societies could not have subsisted. Without such nursing fathers, without this care of the governors, all governments would have sunk under the weakness and infirmities of their infancy, the prince and the people had soon perished together.

111. But the golden age (though before vain ambition, and *amor sceleratus habendi,* evil concupiscence had corrupted men's minds into a mistake of true power and honour) had more virtue, and consequently better governors, as well as less vicious subjects; and there was then no stretching prerogative on the one side to oppress the people, nor, consequently, on the other, any dispute about privilege, to lessen or restrain the power of the magistrate; and so no contest betwixt rulers and people about governors or government.[1] Yet, when ambition and luxury, in future ages, would retain and increase the power, without doing the business for which it was given, and aided by flattery, taught princes to have distinct and separate interests from their people, men found it necessary to examine more carefully the original and rights of government, and to find out ways to restrain the exorbitances and prevent the abuses of that power, which they having entrusted in another's hands, only for their own good, they found was made use of to hurt them.

112. Thus we may see how probable it is that people that were naturally free, and, by their own consent, either submitted to the government of their father, or united together, out of different families, to make a government, should generally put the rule into one man's hands, and choose to be under the conduct of a single person, without so much, as by express conditions, limiting or regulating his power, which they thought safe enough in his honesty and prudence; though they never dreamed of monarchy being *jure Divino,* which we never heard of among mankind till it was revealed to us by the divinity of this last age, nor ever allowed paternal power to have a right to dominion or to be the foundation of all government. And thus much may suffice to show that, as far as we have any light from history, we have reason to conclude that all peaceful beginnings of government have been laid in the consent of the people. I say "peaceful," because I shall have occasion, in another place, to speak of conquest, which some esteem a way of beginning of governments.

The other objection, I find, urged against the beginning of polities, in the way I have mentioned, is this, viz.:

113. "That all men being born under government, some or other, it is impossible any of them should ever be free and at liberty to unite together and begin a new one, or ever be able to erect a lawful government." If this argument be good, I ask, How came so many lawful monarchies into the world ? For if anybody, upon this supposition, can show me any one man, in any age of the world, free to begin a lawful monarchy, I will be bound to show him ten other free men at liberty, at the same time, to unite and begin a new government under a regal or any other form. It being demonstration that if any one born under the dominion of another may be so free as to have a right to command others in a new and distinct empire, every one that is born under the dominion of another may be so free too, and may become a ruler or subject of a distinct separate government. And so, by this their own principle, either all men, however born, are free, or else there is but one lawful prince, one lawful government in the world; and then they have nothing to do but barely to show us which that is, which, when they have done, I doubt not but all mankind will easily agree to pay obedience to him.

114. Though it be a sufficient answer to their objection to show that it involves them in the same difficulties that it doth those they use it against, yet I shall endeavour to discover the weakness of this argument a little farther.

"All men," say they, "are born under government, and therefore they cannot be at liberty to begin a new one. Every one is born a subject to his father or his prince, and is therefore under the perpetual tie of subjection and allegiance." It is plain mankind never owned nor considered any such natural subjection that they were born in, to one or to the other, that tied them, without their own consents, to a subjection to them and their heirs.

115. For there are no examples so frequent in history, both sacred and profane, as those of men withdrawing themselves and their obedience from the jurisdiction they were born under, and the family or community they were bred up in, and setting up new governments in other places, from whence sprang all that number of petty commonwealths in the beginning of ages, and which always multiplied as long as there was room enough, till the stronger or more fortunate swallowed the weaker; and those great ones, again breaking to pieces, dissolved into lesser dominions; all which are so many testimonies against paternal sovereignty, and plainly prove that it was not the natural right of the father descending to his heirs that made governments in the beginning; since it

was impossible, upon that ground, there should have been so many little kingdoms but only one universal monarchy if men had not been at liberty to separate themselves from their families and their government, be it what it will that was set up in it, and go and make distinct commonwealths and other governments as they thought fit.

116. This has been the practice of the world from its first beginning to this day; nor is it now any more hindrance to the freedom of mankind, that they are born under constituted and ancient polities that have established laws and set forms of government, than if they were born in the woods amongst the unconfined inhabitants that run loose in them. For those who would persuade us that by being born under any government we are naturally subjects to it, and have no more any title or pretence to the freedom of the state of Nature, have no other reason (bating that of paternal power, which we have already answered) to produce for it, but only because our fathers or progenitors passed away their natural liberty, and thereby bound up themselves and their posterity to a perpetual subjection to the government which they themselves submitted to. It is true that whatever engagements or promises any one made for himself, he is under the obligation of them, but cannot by any compact whatsoever bind his children or posterity. For his son, when a man, being altogether as free as the father, any act of the father can no more give away the liberty of the son than it can of anybody else. He may, indeed, annex such conditions to the land he enjoyed, as a subject of any commonwealth, as may oblige his son to be of that community, if he will enjoy those possessions which were his father's, because that estate being his father's property, he may dispose or settle it as he pleases.

117. And this has generally given the occasion to the mistake in this matter; because commonwealths not permitting any part of their dominions to be dismembered, nor to be enjoyed by any but those of their community, the son cannot ordinarily enjoy the possessions of his father but under the same terms his father did, by becoming a member of the society, whereby he puts himself presently under the government he finds there established, as much as any other subject of that commonweal. And thus the consent of free men, born under government, which only makes them members of it, being given separately in their turns, as each comes to be of age, and not in a multitude together, people take no notice of it, and thinking it not done at all, or not necessary, conclude they are naturally subjects as they are men.

118. But it is plain governments themselves understand it otherwise; they claim no power over the son because of that they had over the father; nor look on children as being their subjects, by their fathers being so. If a subject of England have a child by an Englishwoman in France, whose subject is he? Not the King of England's; for he must have leave to be admitted to the privileges of it. Nor the King of France's, for how then has his father a liberty to bring him away, and breed him as he pleases; and whoever was judged as a traitor or deserter, if he left, or warred against a country, for being barely born in it of parents that were aliens there? It is plain, then, by the practice of governments themselves, as well as by the law of right reason, that a child is born a subject of no country nor government. He is under his father's tuition and authority till he come to age of discretion, and then he is a free man, at liberty what government he will put himself under, what body politic he will unite himself to. For if an Englishman's son born in France be at liberty, and may do so, it is evident there is no tie upon him by his father being a subject of that kingdom, nor is he bound up by any compact of his ancestors; and why then hath not his son, by the same reason, the same liberty, though he be born anywhere else? Since the power that a father hath naturally over his children is the same wherever they be born, and the ties of natural obligations are not bounded by the positive limits of kingdoms and commonwealths.

119. Every man being, as has been showed, naturally free, and nothing being able to put him into subjection to any earthly power, but only his own consent, it is to be considered what shall be understood to be a sufficient declaration of a man's consent to make him subject to the laws of any government. There is a common distinction of an express and a tacit consent, which will concern our present case. Nobody doubts but an express consent of any man, entering into any society, makes him a perfect member of that society, a subject of that government. The difficulty is, what ought to be looked upon as a tacit consent, and how far it binds—*i.e.*, how far any one shall be looked on to have consented, and thereby submitted to any government, where he has made no expressions of it at all. And to this I say, that every man that hath any possession or enjoyment of any part of the dominions of any government doth hereby give his tacit consent, and is as far forth obliged to obedience to the laws of that government, during such enjoyment, as any one under it, whether this his possession be of land to him and his heirs for ever, or a lodging only for a

week; or whether it be barely travelling freely on the highway; and, in effect, it reaches as far as the very being of any one within the territories of that government.

120. To understand this the better, it is fit to consider that every man when he at first incorporates himself into any commonwealth, he, by his uniting himself thereunto, annexes also, and submits to the community those possessions which he has, or shall acquire, that do not already belong to any other government. For it would be a direct contradiction for any one to enter into society with others for the securing and regulating of property, and yet to suppose his land, whose property is to be regulated by the laws of the society, should be exempt from the jurisdiction of that government to which he himself, and the property of the land, is a subject. By the same act, therefore, whereby any one unites his person, which was before free, to any commonwealth, by the same he unites his possessions, which were before free, to it also; and they become, both of them, person and possession, subject to the government and dominion of that commonwealth as long as it hath a being. Whoever therefore, from thenceforth, by inheritance, purchases permission, or otherwise enjoys any part of the land so annexed to, and under the government of that commonweal, must take it with the condition it is under—that is, of submitting to the government of the commonwealth, under whose jurisdiction it is, as far forth as any subject of it.

121. But since the government has a direct jurisdiction only over the land and reaches the possessor of it (before he has actually incorporated himself in the society) only as he dwells upon and enjoys that, the obligation any one is under by virtue of such enjoyment to submit to the government begins and ends with the enjoyment; so that whenever the owner, who has given nothing but such a tacit consent to the government will, by donation, sale or otherwise, quit the said possession, he is at liberty to go and incorporate himself into any other commonwealth, or agree with others to begin a new one *in vacuis locis,* in any part of the world they can find free and unpossessed; whereas he that has once, by actual agreement and any express declaration, given his consent to be of any commonweal, is perpetually and indispensably obliged to be, and remain unalterably a subject to it, and can never be again in the liberty of the state of Nature, unless by any calamity the government he was under comes to be dissolved.

122. But submitting to the laws of any country, living quietly and enjoying privileges and protection under them, makes not a man a member of that society; it is only a local protection and homage due to and from all those who, not being in a state of war, come within the territories belonging to any government, to all parts whereof the force of its law extends. But this no more makes a man a member of that society, a perpetual subject of that commonwealth, than it would make a man a subject to another in whose family he found it convenient to abide for some time, though, whilst he continued in it, he were obliged to comply with the laws and submit to the government he found there. And thus we see that foreigners, by living all their lives under another government, and enjoying the privileges and protection of it, though they are bound, even in conscience, to submit to its administration as far forth as any denizen, yet do not thereby come to be subjects or members of that commonwealth. Nothing can make any man so but his actually entering into it by positive engagement and express promise and compact. This is that which, I think, concerning the beginning of political societies, and that consent which makes any one a member of any commonwealth.

CHAPTER IX

OF THE ENDS OF POLITICAL SOCIETY AND GOVERNMENT

123. If man in the state of Nature be so free as has been said, if he be absolute lord of his own person and possessions, equal to the greatest and subject to nobody, why will he part with his freedom, this empire, and subject himself to the dominion and control of any other power? To which it is obvious to answer, that though in the state of Nature he hath such a right, yet the enjoyment of it is very uncertain and constantly exposed to the invasion of others; for all being kings as much as he, every man his equal, and the greater part no strict observers of equity and justice, the enjoyment of the property he has in this state is very unsafe, very insecure. This makes him willing to quit this condition which, however free, is full of fears and continual dangers; and it is not without reason that he seeks out and is willing to join in society with others who are already united, or have a mind to unite for the mutual preservation of their lives, liberties and estates, which I call by the general name—property.

124. The great and chief end, therefore, of men uniting into commonwealths, and putting themselves under government, is the preservation of their property; to which in the state of Nature there are many things wanting.

Firstly, there wants an established, settled, known law, received and allowed by common consent to be the standard of right and wrong, and the common measure to decide all controversies between them. For though the law of Nature be plain and intelligible to all rational creatures, yet men, being biased by their interest, as well as ignorant for want of study of it, are not apt to allow of it as a law binding to them in the application of it to their particular cases.

125. Secondly, in the state of Nature there wants a known and indifferent judge, with authority to determine all differences according to the established law. For every one in that state being both judge and executioner of the law of Nature, men being partial to themselves, passion and revenge is very apt to carry them too far, and with too much heat in their own cases, as well as negligence and unconcernedness, make them too remiss in other men's.

126. Thirdly, in the state of Nature there often wants power to back and support the sentence when right, and to give it due execution. They who by any injustice offended will seldom fail where they are able by force to make good their injustice. Such resistance many times makes the punishment dangerous, and frequently destructive to those who attempt it.

127. Thus mankind, notwithstanding all the privileges of the state of Nature, being but in an ill condition while they remain in it are quickly driven into society. Hence it comes to pass, that we seldom find any number of men live any time together in this state. The inconveniencies that they are therein exposed to by the irregular and uncertain exercise of the power every man has of punishing the transgressions of others, make them take sanctuary under the established laws of government, and therein seek the preservation of their property. It is this makes them so willingly give up every one his single power of punishing to be exercised by such alone as shall be appointed to it amongst them, and by such rules as the community, or those authorised by them to that purpose, shall agree on. And in this we have the original right and rise of both the legislative and executive power as well as of the governments and societies themselves.

128. For in the state of Nature to omit the liberty he has of innocent delights, a man has two powers. The first is to do whatsoever he thinks fit for the preservation of himself and others within the permission of the law of Nature; by which law, common to them all, he and all the rest of mankind are one community, make up one society distinct from all other creatures, and were it not for the corruption and viciousness of degenerate men, there would be no need of any other, no necessity that men should separate from this great and natural community, and associate into lesser combinations. The other power a man has in the state of

Nature is the power to punish the crimes committed against that law. Both these he gives up when he joins in a private, if I may so call it, or particular political society, and incorporates into any commonwealth separate from the rest of mankind.

129. The first power—viz., of doing whatsover he thought fit for the preservation of himself and the rest of mankind, he gives up to be regulated by laws made by the society, so far forth as the preservation of himself and the rest of that society shall require; which laws of the society in many things confine the liberty he had by the law of Nature.

130. Secondly, the power of punishing he wholly gives up, and engages his natural force, which he might before employ in the execution of the law of Nature, by his own single authority, as he thought fit, to assist the executive power of the society as the law thereof shall require. For being now in a new state, wherein he is to enjoy many conveniencies from the labour, assistance, and society of others in the same community, as well as protection from its whole strength, he is to part also with as much of his natural liberty, in providing for himself, as the good, prosperity, and safety of the society shall require, which is not only necessary but just, since the other members of the society do the like.

131. But though men when they enter into society give up the equality, liberty, and executive power they had in the state of Nature in the hands of the society, to be so far disposed of by the legislative as the good of the society shall require, yet it being only with an intention in every one the better to preserve himself, his liberty and property (for no rational creature can be supposed to change his condition with an intention to be worse), the power of the society or legislative constituted by them can never be supposed to extend farther than the common good, but is obliged to secure every one's property by providing against those three defects above mentioned that made the state of Nature so unsafe and uneasy. And so, whoever has the legislative or supreme power of any commonwealth, is bound to govern by established standing laws, promulgated and known to the people, and not by extemporary decrees, by indifferent and upright judges, who are to decide controversies by those laws; and to employ the force of the community at home only in the execution of such laws, or abroad to prevent or redress foreign injuries and secure the community from inroads and invasion. And all this to be directed to no other end but the peace, safety, and public good of the people.

CHAPTER X

OF THE FORMS OF A COMMONWEALTH

132. THE majority having, as has been showed, upon men's first uniting into society, the whole power of the community naturally in them, may employ all that power in making laws for the community from time to time, and executing those laws by officers of their own appointing, and then the form of the government is a perfect democracy; or else may put the power of making laws into the hands of a few select men, and their heirs or successors, and then it is an oligarchy; or else into the hands of one man, and then it is a monarchy; if to him and his heirs, it is a hereditary monarchy; if to him only for life, but upon his death the power only of nominating a successor, to return to them, an elective monarchy. And so accordingly of these make compounded and mixed forms of government, as they think good. And if the legislative power be at first given by the majority to one or more persons only for their lives, or any limited time, and then the supreme power to revert to them again, when it is so reverted the community may dispose of it again anew into what hands they please, and so constitute a new form of government; for the form of government depending upon the placing the supreme power, which is the legislative, it being impossible to conceive that an inferior power should prescribe to a superior, or any but the supreme make laws, according as the power of making laws is placed, such is the form of the commonwealth.

133. By "commonwealth" I must be understood all along to mean not a democracy, or any form of government, but any independent community which the Latins signified by the word *civitas,* to which the word which best answers in our language is "commonwealth," and most

properly expresses such a society of men which "community" does not (for there may be subordinate communities in a government), and "city" much less. And therefore, to avoid ambiguity, I crave leave to use the word "commonwealth" in that sense, in which sense I find the word used by King James himself, which I think to be its genuine signification, which, if anybody dislike, I consent with him to change it for a better.

CHAPTER XI

OF THE EXTENT OF THE LEGISLATIVE POWER

134. THE great end of men's entering into society being the enjoyment of their properties in peace and safety, and the great instrument and means of that being the laws established in that society, the first and fundamental positive law of all commonwealths is the establishing of the legislative power, as the first and fundamental natural law which is to govern even the legislative. Itself is the preservation of the society and (as far as will consist with the public good) of every person in it. this legislative is not only the supreme power of the commonwealth, but sacred and unalterable in the hands where the community have once placed it. Nor can any edict of anybody else, in what form soever conceived, or by what power soever backed, have the force and obligation of a law which has not its sanction from that legislative which the public has chosen and appointed; for without this the law could not have that which is absolutely necessary to its being a law, the consent of the society, over whom nobody can have a power to make laws[1] but by their own consent and by authority received from them; and therefore all the obedience, which by the most solemn ties any one can be obliged to pay, ultimately terminates in this supreme power, and is directed by those laws which it enacts. Nor can any oaths to any foreign power whatsoever, or any domestic subordinate power, discharge any member of the society from his obedience to the legislative, acting pursuant to their trust, nor oblige him to any obedience contrary to the laws so enacted or farther than they do allow, it being ridiculous to imagine one can be tied ultimately to obey any power in the society which is not the supreme.

135. Though the legislative, whether placed in one or more, whether it be always in being or only by intervals, though it be the supreme power in every commonwealth, yet, first, it is not, nor can possibly be, absolutely arbitrary over the lives and fortunes of the people. For it being but the joint power of every member of the society given up to that person or assembly which is legislator, it can be no more than those persons had in a state of Nature before they entered into society, and gave it up to the community. For nobody can transfer to another more power than he has in himself, and nobody has an absolute arbitrary power over himself, or over any other, to destroy his own life, or take away the life or property of another. A man, as has been proved, cannot subject himself to the arbitrary power of another; and having, in the state of Nature, no arbitrary power over the life, liberty, or possession of another, but only so much as the law of Nature gave him for the preservation of himself and the rest of mankind, this is all he doth, or can give up to the commonwealth, and by it to the legislative power, so that the legislative can have no more than this. Their power in the utmost bounds of it is limited to the public good of the society.[2] It is a power that hath no other end but preservation, and therefore can never have a right to destroy, enslave, or designedly to impoverish the subjects; the obligations of the law of Nature cease not in society, but only in many cases are drawn closer, and have, by human laws, known penalties annexed to them to enforce their observation. Thus the law of Nature stands as an eternal rule to all men, legislators as well as others. The rules that they make for other men's actions must, as well as their own and other men's actions, be comformable to the law of Nature—*i.e.*, to the will of God, of which that is a declaration, and the fundamental law of Nature being the preservation of mankind, no human sanction can be good or valid against it.

136. Secondly, the legislative or supreme authority cannot assume to itself a power to rule by extemporary arbitrary decrees, but is bound to dispense justice and decide the rights of the subject by promulgated standing laws,[3] and known authorised judges. For the law of Nature being unwritten, and so nowhere to be found but in the minds of men, they who, through passion or interest, shall miscite or misapply it, cannot so easily be convinced of their mistake where there is no established judge; and so it serves not as it aught, to determine the rights and fence the properties of those that live under it, especially where every one is judge, interpreter, and executioner of it too, and that in

his own case; and he that has right on his side, having ordinarily but his own single strength, hath not force enough to defend himself from injuries or punish delinquents. To avoid these inconveniencies which disorder men's properties in the state of Nature, men unite into societies that they may have the united strength of the whole society to secure and defend their properties, and may have standing rules to bound it by which every one may know what is his. To this end it is that men give up all their natural power to the society they enter into, and the community put the legislative power into such hands as they think fit, with this trust, that they shall be governed by declared laws, or else their peace, quiet, and property will still be at the same uncertainty as it was in the state of Nature.

137. Absolute arbitrary power, or governing without settled standing laws, can neither of them consist with the ends of society and government, which men would not quit the freedom of the state of Nature for, and tie themselves up under, were it not to preserve their lives, liberties, and fortunes, and by stated rules of right and property to secure their peace and quiet. It cannot be supposed that they should intend, had they a power so to do, to give any one or more an absolute arbitrary power over their persons and estates, and put a force into the magistrate's hand to execute his unlimited will arbitrarily upon them; this were to put themselves into a worse condition than the state of Nature, wherein they had a liberty to defend their right against the injuries of others, and were upon equal terms of force to maintain it, whether invaded by a single man or many in combination. Whereas by supposing they have given up themselves to the absolute arbitrary power and will of a legislator, they have disarmed themselves, and armed him to make a prey of them when he pleases; he being in a much worse condition that is exposed to the arbitrary power of one man who has the command of a hundred thousand than he that is exposed to the arbitrary power of a hundred thousand single men, nobody being secure, that his will who has such a command is better than that of other men, though his force be a hundred thousand times stronger. And, therefore, whatever form the commonwealth is under, the ruling power ought to govern by declared and received laws, and not by extemporary dictates and undetermined resolutions, for then mankind will be in a far worse condition than in the state of Nature if they shall have armed one or a few men with the joint power of a multitude, to force them to obey at pleasure the exorbitant

and unlimited decrees of their sudden thoughts, or unrestrained, and till that moment, unknown wills, without having any measures set down which may guide and justify their actions. For all the power the government has, being only for the good of the society, as it ought not to be arbitrary and at pleasure, so it ought to be exercised by established and promulgated laws, that both the people may know their duty, and be safe and secure within the limits of the law, and the rulers, too, kept within their due bounds, and not be tempted by the power they have in their hands to employ it to purposes, and by such measures as they would not have known, and own not willingly.

138. Thirdly, the supreme power cannot take from any man any part of his property without his own consent. For the preservation of property being the end of government, and that for which men enter into society, it necessarily supposes and requires that the people should have property, without which they must be supposed to lose that by entering into society which was the end for which they entered into it; too gross an absurdity for any man to own. Men, therefore, in society having property, they have such a right to the goods, which by the law of the community are theirs, that nobody hath a right to take them, or any part of them, from them without their own consent; without this they have no property at all. For I have truly no property in that which another can by right take from me when he pleases against my consent. Hence it is a mistake to think that the supreme or legislative power of any commonwealth can do what it will, and dispose of the estates of the subject arbitrarily, or take any part of them at pleasure. This is not much to be feared in governments where the legislative consists wholly or in part in assemblies which are variable, whose members upon the dissolution of the assembly are subjects under the common laws of their country, equally with the rest. But in governments where the legislative is in one lasting assembly, always in being, or in one man as in absolute monarchies, there is danger still, that they will think themselves to have a distinct interest from the rest of the community, and so will be apt to increase their own riches and power by taking what they think fit from the people. For a man's property is not at all secure, though there be good and equitable laws to set the bounds of it between him and his fellow-subjects, if he who commands those subjects have power to take from any private man what part he pleases of his property, and use and dispose of it as he thinks good.

139. But government, into whosesoever hands it is put, being as I have before showed, entrusted with this condition, and for this end, that men might have and secure their properties, the prince or senate, however it may have power to make laws for the regulating of property between the subjects one amongst another, yet can never have a power to take to themselves the whole, or any part of the subjects' property, without their own consent; for this would be in effect to leave them no property at all. And to let us see that even absolute power, where it is necessary, is not arbitrary by being absolute, but is still limited by that reason, and confined to those ends which required it in some cases to be absolute, we need look no farther than the common practice of martial discipline. For the preservation of the army, and in it of the whole commonwealth, requires an absolute obedience to the command of every superior officer, and it is justly death to disobey or dispute the most dangerous or unreasonable of them; but yet we see that neither the sergeant that could command a soldier to march up to the mouth of a cannon, or stand in a breach where he is almost sure to perish, can command that soldier to give him one penny of his money; nor the general that can condemn him to death for deserting his post, or not obeying the most desperate orders, cannot yet with all his absolute power of life and death dispose of one farthing of that soldier's estate, or seize one jot of his goods; whom yet he can command anything, and hang for the least disobedience. Because such a blind obedience is necessary to that end for which the commander has his power—viz., the preservation of the rest, but the disposing of his goods has nothing to do with it.

140. It is true governments cannot be supported without great charge, and it is fit every one who enjoys his share of the protection should pay out of his estate his proportion for the maintenance of it. But still it must be with his own consent—*i.e.*, the consent of the majority, giving it either by themselves or their representatives chosen by them; for if any one shall claim a power to lay and levy taxes on the people by his own authority, and without such consent of the people, he thereby invades the fundamental law of property, and subverts the end of government. For what property have I in that which another may by right take when he pleases to himself?

141. Fourthly. The legislative cannot transfer the power of making laws to any other hands, for it being but a delegated power from the people, they who have it cannot pass it over to others. The people alone can appoint the form of the commonwealth, which is by constituting

the legislative, and appointing in whose hands that shall be. And when the people have said, "We will submit, and be governed by laws made by such men, and in such forms," nobody else can say other men shall make laws for them; nor can they be bound by any laws but such as are enacted by those whom they have chosen and authorised to make laws for them.

142. These are the bounds which the trust that is put in them by the society and the law of God and Nature have set to the legislative power of every commonwealth, in all forms of government. First: They are to govern by promulgated established laws, not to be varied in particular cases, but to have one rule for rich and poor, for the favourite at Court, and the countryman at plough. Secondly: These laws also ought to be designed for no other end ultimately but the good of the people. Thirdly: They must not raise taxes on the property of the people without the consent of the people given by themselves or their deputies. And this properly concerns only such governments where the legislative is always in being, or at least where the people have not reserved any part of the legislative to deputies, to be from time to time chosen by themselves. Fourthly: Legislative neither must nor can transfer the power of making laws to anybody else, or place it anywhere but where the people have.

CHAPTER XII

THE LEGISLATIVE, EXECUTIVE, AND FEDERATIVE POWER OF THE COMMONWEALTH

143. THE legislative power is that which has a right to direct how the force of the commonwealth shall be employed for preserving the community and the members of it. Because those laws which are constantly to be executed, and whose force is always to continue, may be made in a little time, therefore there is no need that the legislative should be always in being, not having always business to do. And because it may be too great temptation to human frailty, apt to grasp at power, for the same persons who have the power of making laws to have also in their hands the power to execute them, whereby they may exempt themselves from obedience to the laws they make, and suit the law, both in its making and execution, to their own private advantage, and thereby come to have a distinct interest from the rest of the community, contrary to the end of society and government. Therefore in well-ordered commonwealths, where the good of the whole is so considered as it ought, the legislative power is put into the hands of divers persons who, duly assembled, have by themselves, or jointly with others, a power to make laws, which when they have done, being separated again, they are themselves subject to the laws they have made; which is a new and near tie upon them to take care that they make them for the public good.

144. But because the laws that are at once, and in a short time made, have a constant and lasting force, and need a perpetual execution, or an attendance thereunto, therefore it is necessary there should be a

power always in being which should see to the execution of the laws that are made, and remain in force. And thus the legislative and executive power come often to be separated.

145. There is another power in every commonwealth which one may call natural, because it is that which answers to the power every man naturally had before he entered into society. For though in a commonwealth the members of it are distinct persons, still, in reference to one another, and, as such, are governed by the laws of the society, yet, in reference to the rest of mankind, they make one body, which is, as every member of it before was, still in the state of Nature with the rest of mankind, so that the controversies that happen between any man of the society with those that are out of it are managed by the public, and an injury done to a member of their body engages the whole in the reparation of it. So that under this consideration the whole community is one body in the state of Nature in respect of all other states or persons out of its community.

146. This, therefore, contains the power of war and peace, leagues and alliances, and all the transactions with all persons and communities without the commonwealth, and may be called federative if any one pleases. So the thing be understood, I am indifferent as to the name.

147. These two powers, executive and federative, though they be really distinct in themselves, yet one comprehending the execution of the municipal laws of the society within itself upon all that are parts of it, the other the management of the security and interest of the public without with all those that it may receive benefit or damage from, yet they are always almost united. And though this federative power in the well or ill management of it be of great moment to the commonwealth, yet it is much less capable to be directed by antecedent, standing, positive laws than the executive, and so must necessarily be left to the prudence and wisdom of those whose hands it is in, to be managed for the public good. For the laws that concern subjects one amongst another, being to direct their actions, may well enough precede them. But what is to be done in reference to foreigners depending much upon their actions, and the variation of designs and interests, must be left in great part to the prudence of those who have this power committed to them, to be managed by the best of their skill for the advantage of the commonwealth.

148. Though, as I said, the executive and federative power of every community be really distinct in themselves, yet they are hardly to be separated and placed at the same time in the hands of distinct persons. For

both of them requiring the force of the society for their exercise, it is almost impracticable to place the force of the commonwealth in distinct and not subordinate hands, or that the executive and federative power should be placed in persons that might act separately, whereby the force of the public would be under different commands, which would be apt some time or other to cause disorder and ruin.

CHAPTER XIII

OF THE SUBORDINATION OF THE POWERS OF THE COMMONWEALTH

149. THOUGH in a constituted commonwealth standing upon its own basis and acting according to its own nature—that is, acting for the preservation of the community, there can be but one supreme power, which is the legislative, to which all the rest are and must be subordinate, yet the legislative being only a fiduciary power to act for certain ends, there remains still in the people a supreme power to remove or alter the legislative, when they find the legislative act contrary to the trust reposed in them. For all power given with trust for the attaining an end being limited by that end, whenever that end is manifestly neglected or opposed, the trust must necessarily be forfeited, and the power devolve into the hands of those that gave it, who may place it anew where they shall think best for their safety and security. And thus the community perpetually retains a supreme power of saving themselves from the attempts and designs of anybody, even of their legislators, whenever they shall be so foolish or so wicked as to lay and carry on designs against the liberties and properties of the subject. For no man or society of men having a power to deliver up their preservation, or consequently the means of it, to the absolute will and arbitrary dominion of another, whenever any one shall go about to bring them into such a slavish condition, they will always have a right to preserve what they have not a power to part with, and to rid themselves of those who invade this fundamental, sacred, and unalterable law of self-preservation for which they entered into society. And thus the community may be

said in this respect to be always the supreme power, but not as considered under any form of government, because this power of the people can never take place till the government be dissolved.

150. In all cases whilst the government subsists, the legislative is the supreme power. For what can give laws to another must needs be superior to him, and since the legislative is no otherwise legislative of the society but by the right it has to make laws for all the parts, and every member of the society prescribing rules to their actions, and giving power of execution where they are transgressed, the legislative must needs be the supreme, and all other powers in any members or parts of the society derived from and subordinate to it.

151. In some commonwealths where the legislative is not always in being, and the executive is vested in a single person who has also a share in the legislative, there that single person, in a very tolerable sense, may also be called supreme; not that he has in himself all the supreme power, which is that of law-making, but because he has in him the supreme execution from whom all inferior magistrates derive all their several subordinate powers, or, at least, the greatest part of them; having also no legislative superior to him, there being no law to be made without his consent, which cannot be expected should ever subject him to the other part of the legislative, he is properly enough in this sense supreme. But yet it is to be observed that though oaths of allegiance and fealty are taken to him, it is not to him as supreme legislator, but as supreme executor of the law made by a joint power of him with others, allegiance being nothing but an obedience according to law, which, when he violates, he has no right to obedience, nor can claim it otherwise than as the public person vested with the power of the law, and so is to be considered as the image, phantom, or representative of the commonwealth, acted by the will of the society declared in its laws, and thus he has no will, no power, but that of the law. But when he quits this representation, this public will, and acts by his own private will, he degrades himself, and is but a single private person without power and without will; the members owing no obedience but to the public will of the society.

152. The executive power placed anywhere but in a person that has also a share in the legislative is visibly subordinate and accountable to it, and may be at pleasure changed and displaced; so that it is not the supreme executive power that is exempt from subordination, but the supreme executive power vested in one, who having a share in the legislative, has no

distinct superior legislative to be subordinate and accountable to, farther than he himself shall join and consent, so that he is no more subordinate than he himself shall think fit, which one may certainly conclude will be but very little. Of other ministerial and subordinate powers in a commonwealth we need not speak, they being so multiplied with infinite variety in the different customs and constitutions of distinct commonwealths, that it is impossible to give a particular account of them all. Only thus much which is necessary to our present purpose we may take notice of concerning them, that they have no manner of authority, any of them, beyond what is by positive grant and commission delegated to them, and are all of them accountable to some other power in the commonwealth.

153. It is not necessary—no, nor so much as convenient—that the legislative should be always in being; but absolutely necessary that the executive power should, because there is not always need of new laws to be made, but always need of execution of the laws that are made. When the legislative hath put the execution of the laws they make into other hands, they have a power still to resume it out of those hands when they find cause, and to punish for any maladministration against the laws. The same holds also in regard of the federative power, that and the executive being both ministerial and subordinate to the legislative, which, as has been shown, in a constituted commonwealth is the supreme, the legislative also in this case being supposed to consist of several persons; for if it be a single person it cannot but be always in being, and so will, as supreme, naturally have the supreme executive power, together with the legislative, may assemble and exercise their legislative at the times that either their original constitution or their own adjournment appoints, or when they please, if neither of these hath appointed any time, or there be no other way prescribed to convoke them. For the supreme power being placed in them by the people, it is always in them, and they may exercise it when they please, unless by their original constitution they are limited to certain seasons, or by an act of their supreme power they have adjourned to a certain time, and when that time comes they have a right to assemble and act again.

154. If the legislative, or any part of it, be of representatives, chosen for that time by the people, which afterwards return into the ordinary state of subjects, and have no share in the legislative but upon a new choice, this power of choosing must also be exercised by the people, either at certain appointed seasons, or else when they are summoned to

it; and, in this latter case, the power of convoking the legislative is ordinarily placed in the executive, and has one of these two limitations in respect of time:—that either the original constitution requires their assembling and acting at certain intervals; and then the executive power does nothing but ministerially issue directions for their electing and assembling according to due forms; or else it is left to his prudence to call them by new elections when the occasions or exigencies of the public require the amendment of old or making of new laws, or the redress or prevention of any inconveniencies that lie on or threaten the people.

155. It may be demanded here, what if the executive power, being possessed of the force of the commonwealth, shall make use of that force to hinder the meeting and acting of the legislative, when the original constitution or the public exigencies require it? I say, using force upon the people, without authority, and contrary to the trust put in him that does so, is a state of war with the people, who have a right to reinstate their legislative in the exercise of their power. For having erected a legislative with an intent they should exercise the power of making laws, either at certain set times, or when there is need of it, when they are hindered by any force from what is so necessary to the society, and wherein the safety and preservation of the people consists, the people have a right to remove it by force. In all states and conditions the true remedy of force without authority is to oppose force to it. The use of force without authority always puts him that uses it into a state of war as the aggressor, and renders him liable to be treated accordingly.

156. The power of assembling and dismissing the legislative, placed in the executive, gives not the executive a superiority over it, but is a fiduciary trust placed in him for the safety of the people in a case where the uncertainty and variableness of human affairs could not bear a steady fixed rule. For it not being possible that the first framers of the government should by any foresight be so much masters of future events as to be able to prefix so just periods of return and duration to the assemblies of the legislative, in all times to come, that might exactly answer all the exigencies of the commonwealth, the best remedy could be found for this defect was to trust this to the prudence of one who was always to be present, and whose business it was to watch over the public good. Constant, frequent meetings of the legislative, and long continuations of their assemblies, without necessary occasion, could not but be burdensome to the people, and must necessarily in time produce more dangerous inconveniencies, and yet the

quick turn of affairs might be sometimes such as to need their present help; any delay of their convening might endanger the public; and sometimes, too, their business might be so great that the limited time of their sitting might be too short for their work, and rob the public of that benefit which could be had only from their mature deliberation. What, then, could be done in this case to prevent the community from being exposed some time or other to imminent hazard on one side or the other, by fixed intervals and periods set to the meeting and acting of the legislative, but to entrust it to the prudence of some who, being present and acquainted with the state of public affairs, might make use of this prerogative for the public good? And where else could this be so well placed as in his hands who was entrusted with the execution of the laws for the same end? Thus, supposing the regulation of times for the assembling and sitting of the legislative not settled by the original constitution, it naturally fell into the hands of the executive; not as an arbitrary power depending on his good pleasure, but with this trust always to have it exercised only for the public weal, as the occurrences of times and change of affairs might require. Whether settled periods of their convening, or a liberty left to the prince for convoking the legislative, or perhaps a mixture of both, hath the least inconvenience attending it, it is not my business here to inquire, but only to show that, though the executive power may have the prerogative of convoking and dissolving such conventions of the legislative, yet it is not thereby superior to it.

157. Things of this world are in so constant a flux that nothing remains long in the same state. Thus people, riches, trade, power, change their stations; flourishing mighty cities come to ruin, and prove in time neglected desolate corners, whilst other unfrequented places grow into populous countries filled with wealth and inhabitants. But things not always changing equally, and private interest often keeping up customs and privileges when the reasons of them are ceased, it often comes to pass that in governments where part of the legislative consists of representatives chosen by the people, that in tract of time this representation becomes very unequal and disproportionate to the reasons it was at first established upon. To what gross absurdities the following of custom when reason has left it may lead, we may be satisfied when we see the bare name of a town, of which there remains not so much as the ruins, where scarce so much housing as a sheepcote, or more inhabitants than a shepherd is to be found, send as many representatives to the

grand assembly of law-makers as a whole county numerous in people and powerful in riches. This strangers stand amazed at, and every one must confess needs a remedy; though most think it hard to find one, because the constitution of the legislative being the original and supreme act of the society, antecedent to all positive laws in it, and depending wholly on the people, no inferior power can alter it. And, therefore, the people when the legislative is once constituted, having in such a government as we have been speaking of no power to act as long as the government stands, this inconvenience is thought incapable of a remedy.

158. *Salus populi suprema lex* is certainly so just and fundamental a rule, that he who sincerely follows it cannot dangerously err. If, therefore, the executive who has the power of convoking the legislative, observing rather the true proportion than fashion of representation, regulates not by old custom, but true reason, the number of members in all places, that have a right to be distinctly represented, which no part of the people, however incorporated, can pretend to, but in proportion to the assistance which it affords to the public, it cannot be judged to have set up a new legislative, but to have restored the old and true one, and to have rectified the disorders which succession of time had insensibly as well as inevitably introduced; for it being the interest as well as intention of the people to have a fair and equal representative, whoever brings it nearest to that is an undoubted friend to and establisher of the government, and cannot miss the consent and approbation of the community; prerogative being nothing but a power in the hands of the prince to provide for the public good in such cases which, depending upon unforeseen and uncertain occurrences, certain and unalterable laws could not safely direct. Whatsoever shall be done manifestly for the good of the people, and establishing the government upon its true foundations is, and always will be, just prerogative. The power of erecting new corporations, and therewith new representatives, carries with it a supposition that in time the measures of representation might vary, and those have a just right to be represented which before had none; and by the same reason, those cease to have a right, and be too inconsiderable for such a privilege, which before had it. It is not a change from the present state which, perhaps, corruption or decay has introduced, that makes an inroad upon the government, but the tendency of it to injure or oppress the people, and to set up one part or party with a distinction from and an unequal subjection of the rest. Whatsoever cannot but be acknowledged

to be of advantage to the society and people in general, upon just and lasting measures, will always, when done, justify itself; and whenever the people shall choose their representatives upon just and undeniably equal measures, suitable to the original frame of the government, it cannot be doubted to be the will and act of the society, whoever permitted or proposed to them so to do.

CHAPTER XIV

OF PREROGATIVE

159. WHERE the legislative and executive power are in distinct hands, as they are in all moderated monarchies and well-framed governments, there the good of the society requires that several things should be left to the discretion of him that has the executive power. For the legislators not being able to foresee and provide by laws for all that may be useful to the community, the executor of the laws, having the power in his hands, has by the common law of Nature a right to make use of it for the good of the society, in many cases where the municipal law has given no direction, till the legislative can conveniently be assembled to provide for it; nay, many things there are which the law can by no means provide for, and those must necessarily be left to the discretion of him that has the executive power in his hands, to be ordered by him as the public good and advantage shall require; nay, it is fit that the laws themselves should in some cases give way to the executive power, or rather to this fundamental law of Nature and government—viz., that as much as may be all the members of the society are to be preserved. For since many accidents may happen wherein a strict and rigid observation of the laws may do harm, as not to pull down an innocent man's house to stop the fire when the next to it is burning; and a man may come sometimes within the reach of the law, which makes no distinction of persons, by an action that may deserve reward and pardon; it is fit the ruler should have a power in many cases to mitigate the severity of the law, and pardon some offenders, since the end of government being the preservation of all as much as may be, even the guilty are to be spared where it can prove no prejudice to the innocent.

160. This power to act according to discretion for the public good, without the prescription of the law and sometimes even against it, is that which is called prerogative; for since in some governments the law-making power is not always in being and is usually too numerous, and so too slow for the dispatch requisite to execution, and because, also, it is impossible to foresee and so by laws to provide for all accidents and necessities that may concern the public, or make such laws as will do no harm, if they are executed with an inflexible rigour on all occasions and upon all persons that may come in their way, therefore there is a latitude left to the executive power to do many things of choice which the laws do not prescribe.

161. This power, whilst employed for the benefit of the community and suitably to the trust and ends of the government, is undoubted prerogative, and never is questioned. For the people are very seldom or never scrupulous or nice in the point or questioning of prerogative whilst it is in any tolerable degree employed for the use it was meant—that is, the good of the people, and not manifestly against it. But if there comes to be a question between the executive power and the people about a thing claimed as a prerogative, the tendency of the exercise of such prerogative, to the good or hurt of the people, will easily decide that question.

162. It is easy to conceive that in the infancy of governments, when commonwealths differed little from families in number of people, they differed from them too but little in number of laws; and the governors being as the fathers of them, watching over them for their good, the government was almost all prerogative. A few established laws served the turn, and the discretion and care of the ruler supplied the rest. But when mistake or flattery prevailed with weak princes, to make use of this power for private ends of their own and not for the public good, the people were fain, by express laws, to get prerogative determined in those points wherein they found disadvantage from it, and declared limitations of prerogative in those cases which they and their ancestors had left in the utmost latitude to the wisdom of those princes who made no other but a right use of it—that is, for the good of their people.

163. And therefore they have a very wrong notion of government who say that the people have encroached upon the prerogative when they have got any part of it to be defined by positive laws. For in so doing they have not pulled from the prince anything that of right belonged to him, but only declared that that power which they indefinitely left in his or his

ancestors' hands, to be exercised for their good, was not a thing they intended him, when he used it otherwise. For the end of government being the good of the community, whatsoever alterations are made in it tending to that end cannot be an encroachment upon anybody; since nobody in government can have a right tending to any other end; and those only are encroachments which prejudice or hinder the public good. Those who say otherwise speak as if the prince had a distinct and separate interest from the good of the community, and was not made for it; the root and source from which spring almost all those evils and disorders which happen in kingly governments. And, indeed, if that be so, the people under his government are not a society of rational creatures, entered into a community for their mutual good, such as have set rulers over themselves, to guard and promote that good; but are to be looked on as a herd of inferior creatures under the dominion of a master, who keeps them and works them for his own pleasure or profit. If men were so void of reason and brutish as to enter into society upon such terms, prerogative might indeed be, what some men would have it, an arbitrary power to do things hurtful to the people.

164. But since a rational creature cannot be supposed, when free, to put himself into subjection to another for his own harm (though where he finds a good and a wise ruler he may not, perhaps, think it either necessary or useful to set precise bounds to his power in all things), prerogative can be nothing but the people's permitting their rulers to do several things of their own free choice where the law was silent, and sometimes too against the direct letter of the law, for the public good and their acquiescing in it when so done. For as a good prince, who is mindful of the trust put into his hands and careful of the good of his people, cannot have too much prerogative—that is, power to do good, so a weak and ill prince, who would claim that power his predecessors exercised, without the direction of the law, as a prerogative belonging to him by right of his office, which he may exercise at his pleasure to make or promote an interest distinct from that of the public, gives the people an occasion to claim their right and limit that power, which, whilst it was exercised for their good, they were content should be tacitly allowed.

165. And therefore he that will look into the history of England will find that prerogative was always largest in the hands of our wisest and best princes, because the people observing the whole tendency of their actions to be the public good, or if any human frailty or mistake (for

princes are but men, made as others) appeared in some small declinations from that end, yet it was visible the main of their conduct tended to nothing but the care of the public. The people, therefore, finding reason to be satisfied with these princes, whenever they acted without, or contrary to the letter of the law, acquiesced in what they did, and without the least complaint, let them enlarge their prerogative as they pleased, judging rightly that they did nothing herein to the prejudice of their laws, since they acted conformably to the foundation and end of all laws—the public good.

166. Such God-like princes, indeed, had some title to arbitrary power by that argument that would prove absolute monarchy the best government, as that which God Himself governs the universe by, because such kings partake of His wisdom and goodness. Upon this is founded that saying, "That the reigns of good princes have been always most dangerous to the liberties of their people." For when their successors, managing the government with different thoughts, would draw the actions of those good rulers into precedent and make them the standard of their prerogative—as if what had been done only for the good of the people was a right in them to do for the harm of the people, if they so pleased—it has often occasioned contest, and sometimes public disorders, before the people could recover their original right and get that to be declared not to be prerogative which truly was never so; since it is impossible anybody in the society should ever have a right to do the people harm, though it be very possible and reasonable that the people should not go about to set any bounds to the prerogative of those kings or rulers who themselves transgressed not the bounds of the public good. For "prerogative is nothing but the power of doing public good without a rule."

167. The power of calling parliaments in England, as to precise time, place, and duration, is certainly a prerogative of the king, but still with this trust, that it shall be made use of for the good of the nation as the exigencies of the times and variety of occasion shall require. For it being impossible to foresee which should always be the fittest place for them to assemble in, and what the best season, the choice of these was left with the executive power, as might be best subservient to the public good and best suit the ends of parliament.

168. The old question will be asked in this matter of prerogative, "But who shall be judge when this power is made a right use of?" I answer: Between an executive power in being, with such a prerogative,

and a legislative that depends upon his will for their convening, there can be no judge on earth. As there can be none between the legislative and the people, should either the executive or the legislative, when they have got the power in their hands, design, or go about to enslave or destroy them, the people have no other remedy in this, as in all other cases where they have no judge on earth, but to appeal to Heaven; for the rulers in such attempts, exercising a power the people never put into their hands, who can never be supposed to consent that anybody should rule over them for their harm, do that which they have not a right to do. And where the body of the people, or any single man, are deprived of their right, or are under the exercise of a power without right, having no appeal on earth they have a liberty to appeal to Heaven whenever they judge the cause of sufficient moment. And therefore, though the people cannot be judge, so as to have, by the constitution of that society, any superior power to determine and give effective sentence in the case, yet they have reserved that ultimate determination to themselves which belongs to all mankind, where there lies no appeal on earth, by a law antecedent and paramount to all positive laws of men, whether they have just cause to make their appeal to Heaven. And this judgment they cannot part with, it being out of a man's power so to submit himself to another as to give him a liberty to destroy him; God and Nature never allowing a man so to abandon himself as to neglect his own preservation. And since he cannot take away his own life, neither can he give another power to take it. Nor let any one think this lays a perpetual foundation for disorder; for this operates not till the inconvenience is so great that the majority feel it, and are weary of it, and find a necessity to have it amended. And this the executive power, or wise princes, never need come in the danger of; and it is the thing of all others they have most need to avoid, as, of all others, the most perilous.

CHAPTER XV

OF PATERNAL, POLITICAL AND DESPOTICAL POWER, CONSIDERED TOGETHER

169. THOUGH I have had occasion to speak of these separately before, yet the great mistakes of late about government having, as I suppose, arisen from confounding these distinct powers one with another, it may not perhaps be amiss to consider them here together.

170. First, then, paternal or parental power is nothing but that which parents have over their children to govern them, for the children's good, till they come to the use of reason, or a state of knowledge, wherein they may be supposed capable to understand that rule, whether it be the law of Nature or the municipal law of their country, they are to govern themselves by—capable, I say, to know it, as well as several others, who live as free men under that law. The affection and tenderness God hath planted in the breasts of parents towards their children makes it evident that this is not intended to be a severe arbitrary government, but only for the help, instruction, and preservation of their offspring. But happen as it will, there is, as I have proved, no reason why it should be thought to extend to life and death, at any time, over their children, more than over anybody else, or keep the child in subjection to the will of his parents when grown to a man and the perfect use of reason, any farther than as having received life and education from his parents obliges him to respect, honour, gratitude, assistance, and support, all his life, to both father and mother. And thus, it is true, the paternal is a natural government, but not at all extending itself to the ends and jurisdictions of that which is political. The power of the father doth not reach at all to the property of the child, which is only in his own disposing.

171. Secondly, political power is that power which every man having in the state of Nature has given up into the hands of the society, and therein to the governors whom the society hath set over itself, with this express or tacit trust, that it shall be employed for their good and the preservation of their property. Now this power, which every man has in the state of Nature, and which he parts with to the society in all such cases where the society can secure him, is to use such means for the preserving of his own property as he thinks good and Nature allows him; and to punish the breach of the law of Nature in others so as (according to the best of his reason) may most conduce to the preservation of himself and the rest of mankind; so that the end and measure of this power, when in every man's hands, in the state of Nature, being the preservation of all of his society—that is, all mankind in general—it can have no other end or measure, when in the hands of the magistrate, but to preserve the members of that society in their lives, liberties, and possessions, and so cannot be an absolute, arbitrary power over their lives and fortunes, which are as much as possible to be preserved; but a power to make laws, and annex such penalties to them as may tend to the preservation of the whole, by cutting off those parts, and those only, which are so corrupt that they threaten the sound and healthy, without which no severity is lawful. And this power has its original only from compact and agreement and the mutual consent of those who make up the community.

172. Thirdly, despotical power is an absolute, arbitrary power one man has over another, to take away his life whenever he pleases; and this is a power which neither Nature gives, for it has made no such distinction between one man and another, nor compact can convey. For man, not having such an arbitrary power over his own life, cannot give another man such a power over it, but it is the effect only of forfeiture which the aggressor makes of his own life when he puts himself into the state of war with another. For having quitted reason, which God hath given to be the rule betwixt man and man, and the peaceable ways which that teaches, and made use of force to compass his unjust ends upon another where he has no right, he renders himself liable to be destroyed by his adversary whenever he can, as any other noxious and brutish creature that is destructive to his being. And thus captives, taken in a just and lawful war, and such only, are subject to a despotical power, which, as it arises not from compact, so neither is it capable of any, but is the state of war continued. For what compact can be made with a man that is not master of

his own life? What condition can he perform? And if he be once allowed to be master of his own life, the despotical, arbitrary power of his master ceases. He that is master of himself and his own life has a right, too, to the means of preserving it; so that as soon as compact enters, slavery ceases, and he so far quits his absolute power and puts an end to the state of war who enters into conditions with his captive.

173. Nature gives the first of these—viz., paternal power to parents for the benefit of their children during their minority, to supply their want of ability and understanding how to manage their property. (By property I must be understood here, as in other places, to mean that property which men have in their persons as well as goods.) Voluntary agreement gives the second—viz., political power to governors, for the benefit of their subjects, to secure them in the possession and use of their properties. And forfeiture gives the third—despotical power to lords for their own benefit over those who are stripped of all property.

174. He that shall consider the distinct rise and extent, and the different ends of these several powers, will plainly see that paternal power comes as far short of that of the magistrate as despotical exceeds it; and that absolute dominion, however placed, is so far from being one kind of civil society that it is as inconsistent with it as slavery is with property. Paternal power is only where minority makes the child incapable to manage his property; political where men have property in their own disposal; and despotical over such as have no property at all.

CHAPTER XVI

OF CONQUEST

175. THOUGH governments can originally have no other rise than that before mentioned, nor polities be founded on anything but the consent of the people, yet such have been the disorders ambition has filled the world with, that in the noise of war, which makes so great a part of the history of mankind, this consent is little taken notice of; and, therefore, many have mistaken the force of arms for the consent of the people, and reckon conquest as one of the originals of government. But conquest is as far from setting up any government as demolishing a house is from building a new one in the place. Indeed, it often makes way for a new frame of a commonwealth by destroying the former; but, without the consent of the people, can never erect a new one.

176. That the aggressor, who puts himself into the state of war with another, and unjustly invades another man's right, can, by such an unjust war, never come to have a right over the conquered, will be easily agreed by all men, who will not think that robbers and pirates have a right of empire over whomsoever they have force enough to master, or that men are bound by promises which unlawful force extorts from them. Should a robber break into my house, and, with a dagger at my throat, make me seal deeds to convey my estate to him, would this give him any title? Just such a title by his sword has an unjust conqueror who forces me into submission. The injury and the crime is equal, whether committed by the wearer of a crown or some petty villain. The title of the offender and the number of his followers make no difference in the offence, unless it be to aggravate it. The only difference is, great robbers punish little ones to keep them in their obedience; but the great ones

are rewarded with laurels and triumphs, because they are too big for the weak hands of justice in this world, and have the power in their own possession which should punish offenders. What is my remedy against a robber that so broke into my house? Appeal to the law for justice. But perhaps justice is denied, or I am crippled and cannot stir; robbed, and have not the means to do it. If God has taken away all means of seeking remedy, there is nothing left but patience. But my son, when able, may seek the relief of the law, which I am denied; he or his son may renew his appeal till he recover his right. But the conquered, or their children, have no court—no arbitrator on earth to appeal to. Then they may appeal, as Jephtha did, to Heaven, and repeat their appeal till they have recovered the native right of their ancestors, which was to have such a legislative over them as the majority should approve and freely acquiesce in. If it be objected this would cause endless trouble, I answer, no more than justice does, where she lies open to all that appeal to her. He that troubles his neighbour without a cause is punished for it by the justice of the court he appeals to. And he that appeals to Heaven must be sure he has right on his side, and a right, too, that is worth the trouble and cost of the appeal, as he will answer at a tribunal that cannot be deceived, and will be sure to retribute to every one according to the mischiefs he hath created to his fellow-subjects—that is, any part of mankind. From whence it is plain that he that conquers in an unjust war can thereby have no title to the subjection and obedience of the conquered.

177. But supposing victory favours the right side, let us consider a conqueror in a lawful war, and see what power he gets, and over whom.

First, it is plain he gets no power by his conquest over those that conquered with him. They that fought on his side cannot suffer by the conquest, but must, at least, be as much free men as they were before. And most commonly they serve upon terms, and on condition to share with their leader, and enjoy a part of the spoil and other advantages that attend the conquering sword, or, at least, have a part of the subdued country bestowed upon them. And the conquering people are not, I hope, to be slaves by conquest, and wear their laurels only to show they are sacrifices to their leader's triumph. They that found absolute monarchy upon the title of the sword make their heroes, who are the founders of such monarchies, arrant "draw-can-sirs," and forget they had any officers and soldiers that fought on their side in the battles they won, or assisted them in the subduing, or shared in possessing the countries they mastered. We are told by some that the English monarchy is founded in the Norman Conquest, and that our princes have thereby a title to absolute dominion, which, if it were true (as by the history it appears otherwise), and that William had a right to make war on this island, yet his dominion by conquest could reach no farther than to the Saxons and Britons that were then inhabitants of this country. The Normans that came with him and helped to conquer, and all descended from them, are free men and no subjects by conquest, let that give what dominion it will. And if I or anybody else shall claim freedom as derived from them, it will be very hard to prove the contrary; and it is plain, the law that has made no distinction between the one and the other intends not there should be any difference in their freedom or privileges.

178. But supposing, which seldom happens, that the conquerors and conquered never incorporate into one people under the same laws and freedom; let us see next what power a lawful conqueror has over the subdued, and that I say is purely despotical. He has an absolute power over the lives of those who, by an unjust war, have forfeited them, but not over the lives or fortunes of those who engaged not in the war, nor over the possessions even of those who were actually engaged in it.

179. Secondly, I say, then, the conqueror gets no power but only over those who have actually assisted, concurred, or consented to that unjust force that is used against him. For the people having given to their governors no power to do an unjust thing, such as is to make an unjust war (for they never had such a power in themselves), they ought not to be charged as guilty of the violence and injustice that is committed in an unjust war any farther than they actually abet it, no more than they are to be thought guilty of any violence or oppression their governors should use upon the people themselves or any part of their fellow-subjects, they having empowered them no more to the one than to the other. Conquerors, it is true, seldom trouble themselves to make the distinction, but they willingly permit the confusion of war to sweep all together; but yet this alters not the right; for the conqueror's power over the lives of the conquered being only because they have used force to do or maintain an injustice, he can have that power only over those who have concurred in that force; all the rest are innocent, and he has no more title over the people of that country who have done him no injury, and so have made no forfeiture of their lives, than he has over any other who, without any injuries or provocations, have lived upon fair terms with him.

180. Thirdly, the power a conqueror gets over those he overcomes in a just war is perfectly despotical; he has an absolute power over the lives of those who, by putting themselves in a state of war, have forfeited them, but he has not thereby a right and title to their possessions. This I doubt not but at first sight will seem a strange doctrine, it being so quite contrary to the practice of the world; there being nothing more familiar in speaking of the dominion of countries than to say such an one conquered it, as if conquest, without any more ado, conveyed a right of possession. But when we consider that the practice of the strong and powerful, how universal soever it may be, is seldom the rule of right, however it be one part of the subjection of the conquered not to argue against the conditions cut out to them by the conquering swords.

181. Though in all war there be usually a complication of force and damage, and the aggressor seldom fails to harm the estate when he uses force against the persons of those he makes war upon, yet it is the use of force only that puts a man into the state of war. For whether by force he begins the injury, or else having quietly and by fraud done the injury, he refuses to make reparation, and by force maintains it, which is the same thing as at first to have done it by force; it is the unjust use of force that makes the war. For he that breaks open my house and violently turns me out of doors, or having peaceably got in, by force keeps me out, does, in effect, the same thing; supposing we are in such a state that we have no common judge on earth whom I may appeal to, and to whom we are both obliged to submit, for of such I am now speaking. It is the unjust use of force, then, that puts a man into the state of war with another, and thereby he that is guilty of it makes a forfeiture of his life. For quitting reason, which is the rule given between man and man, and using force, the way of beasts, he becomes liable to be destroyed by him he uses force against, as any savage ravenous beast that is dangerous to his being.

182. But because the miscarriages of the father are no faults of the children, who may be rational and peaceable, notwithstanding the brutishness and injustice of the father, the father, by his miscarriages and violence, can forfeit but his own life, and involves not his children in his guilt or destruction. His goods which Nature, that willeth the preservation of all mankind as much as is possible, hath made to belong to the children to keep them from perishing, do still continue to belong to his children. For supposing them not to have joined in the war either through infancy or choice, they have done nothing to forfeit them, nor

has the conqueror any right to take them away by the bare right of having subdued him that by force attempted his destruction, though, perhaps, he may have some right to them to repair the damages he has sustained by the war, and the defence of his own right, which how far it reaches to the possessions of the conquered we shall see by-and-by; so that he that by conquest has a right over a man's person, to destroy him if he pleases, has not thereby a right over his estate to possess and enjoy it. For it is the brutal force the aggressor has used that gives his adversary a right to take away his life and destroy him, if he pleases, as a noxious creature; but it is damage sustained that alone gives him title to another man's goods; for though I may kill a thief that sets on me in the highway, yet I may not (which seems less) take away his money and let him go; this would be robbery on my side. His force, and the state of war he put himself in, made him forfeit his life, but gave me no title to his goods. The right, then, of conquest extends only to the lives of those who joined in the war, but not to their estates, but only in order to make reparation for the damages received and the charges of the war, and that, too, with reservation of the right of the innocent wife and children.

183. Let the conqueror have as much justice on his side as could be supposed, he has no right to seize more than the vanquished could forfeit; his life is at the victor's mercy, and his service and goods he may appropriate to make himself reparation; but he cannot take the goods of his wife and children, they too had a title to the goods he enjoyed, and their shares in the estate he possessed. For example, I in the state of Nature (and all commonwealths are in the state of Nature one with another) have injured another man, and refusing to give satisfaction, it is come to a state of war wherein my defending by force what I had gotten unjustly makes me the aggressor. I am conquered; my life, it is true, as forfeit, is at mercy, but not my wife's and children's. They made not the war, nor assisted in it. I could not forfeit their lives, they were not mine to forfeit. My wife had a share in my estate, that neither could I forfeit. And my children also, being born of me, had a right to be maintained out of my labour or substance. Here then is the case: The conqueror has a title to reparation for damages received, and the children have a title to their father's estate for their subsistence. For as to the wife's share, whether her own labour or compact gave her a title to it, it is plain her husband could not forfeit what was hers. What must be done in the case? I answer: The fundamental law of Nature being that

all, as much as may be, should be preserved, it follows that if there be not enough fully to satisfy both—viz., for the conqueror's losses and children's maintenance, he that hath and to spare must remit something of his full satisfaction, and give way to the pressing and preferable title of those who are in danger to perish without it.

184. But supposing the charge and damages of the war are to be made up to the conqueror to the utmost farthing, and that the children of the vanquished, spoiled of all their father's goods, are to be left to starve and perish, yet the satisfying of what shall, on this score, be due to the conqueror will scarce give him a title to any country he shall conquer. For the damages of war can scarce amount to the value of any considerable tract of land in any part of the world, where all the land is possessed, and none lies waste. And if I have not taken away the conqueror's land which, being vanquished, it is impossible I should, scarce any other spoil I have done him can amount to the value of mine, supposing it of an extent any way coming near what I had overrun of his, and equally cultivated too. The destruction of a year's product or two (for it seldom reaches four or five) is the utmost spoil that usually can be done. For as to money, and such riches and treasure taken away, these are none of Nature's goods, they have but a phantastical imaginary value; Nature has put no such upon them. They are of no more account by her standard than the Wampompeke of the Americans to an European prince, or the silver money of Europe would have been formerly to an American. And five years' product is not worth the perpetual inheritance of land, where all is possessed and none remains waste, to be taken up by him that is disseised, which will be easily granted, if one do but take away the imaginary value of money, the disproportion being more than between five and five thousand; though, at the same time, half a year's product is more worth than the inheritance where, there being more land than the inhabitants possess and make use of, any one has liberty to make use of the waste. But their conquerors take little care to possess themselves of the lands of the vanquished. No damage therefore that men in the state of Nature (as all princes and governments are in reference to one another) suffer from one another can give a conqueror power to dispossess the posterity of the vanquished, and turn them out of that inheritance which ought to be the possession of them and their descendants to all generations. The conqueror indeed will be apt to think himself master; and it is the very condition of

the subdued not to be able to dispute their right. But, if that be all, it gives no other title than what bare force gives to the stronger over the weaker; and, by this reason, he that is strongest will have a right to whatever he pleases to seize on.

185. Over those, then, that joined with him in the war, and over those of the subdued country that opposed him not, and the posterity even of those that did, the conqueror, even in a just war, hath, by his conquest, no right of dominion. They are free from any subjection to him, and if their former government be dissolved, they are at liberty to begin and erect another to themselves.

186. The conqueror, it is true, usually by the force he has over them, compels them, with a sword at their breasts, to stoop to his conditions, and submit to such a government as he pleases to afford them; but the inquiry is, what right he has to do so? If it be said they submit by their own consent, then this allows their own consent to be necessary to give the conqueror a title to rule over them. It remains only to be considered whether promises, extorted by force, without right, can be thought consent, and how far they bind. To which I shall say, they bind not at all; because whatsoever another gets from me by force, I still retain the right of, and he is obliged presently to restore. He that forces my horse from me ought presently to restore him, and I have still a right to retake him. By the same reason, he that forced a promise from me ought presently to restore it—*i.e.*, quit me of the obligation of it; or I may resume it myself—*i.e.*, choose whether I will perform it. For the law of Nature laying an obligation on me, only by the rules she prescribes, cannot oblige me by the violation of her rules; such is the extorting anything from me by force. Nor does it at all alter the case, to say I gave my promise, no more than it excuses the force, and passes the right, when I put my hand in my pocket and deliver my purse myself to a thief who demands it with a pistol at my breast.

187. From all which it follows that the government of a conqueror, imposed by force on the subdued, against whom he had no right of war, or who joined not in the war against him, where he had right, has no obligation upon them.

188. But let us suppose that all the men of that community being all members of the same body politic, may be taken to have joined in that unjust war, wherein they are subdued, and so their lives are at the mercy of the conqueror.

189. I say this concerns not their children who are in their minority. For since a father hath not, in himself, a power over the life or liberty of his child, no act of his can possibly forfeit it; so that the children, whatever may have happened to the fathers, are free men, and the absolute power of the conqueror reaches no farther than the persons of the men that were subdued by him, and dies with them; and should he govern them as slaves, subjected to his absolute, arbitrary power, he has no such right of dominion over their children. He can have no power over them but by their own consent, whatever he may drive them to say or do, and he has no lawful authority, whilst force, and not choice, compels them to submission.

190. Every man is born with a double right. First, a right of freedom to his person, which no other man has a power over, but the free disposal of it lies in himself. Secondly, a right before any other man, to inherit, with his brethren, his father's goods.

191. By the first of these, a man is naturally free from subjection to any government, though he be born in a place under its jurisdiction. But if he disclaim the lawful government of the country he was born in, he must also quit the right that belonged to him, by the laws of it, and the possessions there descending to him from his ancestors, if it were a government made by their consent.

192. By the second, the inhabitants of any country, who are descended and derive a title to their estates from those who are subdued, and had a government forced upon them, against their free consents, retain a right to the possession of their ancestors, though they consent not freely to the government, whose hard conditions were, by force, imposed on the possessors of that country. For the first conqueror never having had a title to the land of that country, the people, who are the descendants of, or claim under those who were forced to submit to the yoke of a government by constraint, have always a right to shake it off, and free themselves from the usurpation or tyranny the sword hath brought in upon them, till their rulers put them under such a frame of government as they willingly and of choice consent to (which they can never be supposed to do, till either they are put in a full state of liberty to choose their government and governors, or at least till they have such standing laws to which they have, by themselves or their representatives, given their free consent, and also till they are allowed their due property, which is so to be proprietors of what they have that nobody can take away any part of it without their own consent, without which, men under any government are not in the state of

free men, but are direct slaves under the force of war). And who doubts but the Grecian Christians, descendants of the ancient possessors of that country, may justly cast off the Turkish yoke they have so long groaned under, whenever they have a power to do it?

193. But granting that the conqueror, in a just war, has a right to the estates, as well as power over the persons of the conquered, which, it is plain, he hath not, nothing of absolute power will follow from hence in the continuance of the government. Because the descendants of these being all free men, if he grants them estates and possessions to inhabit his country, without which it would be worth nothing, whatsoever he grants them they have so far as it is granted property in; the nature whereof is, that, without a man's own consent, it cannot be taken from him.

194. Their persons are free by a native right, and their properties, be they more or less, are their own, and at their own dispose, and not at his; or else it is no property. Supposing the conqueror gives to one man a thousand acres, to him and his heirs for ever; to another he lets a thousand acres, for his life, under the rent of £50 or £500 per annum. Has not the one of these a right to his thousand acres for ever, and the other during his life, paying the said rent? And hath not the tenant for life a property in all that he gets over and above his rent, by his labour and industry, during the said term, supposing it be double the rent? Can any one say, the king, or conqueror, after his grant, may, by his power of conqueror, take away all, or part of the land, from the heirs of one, or from the other during his life, he paying the rent? Or, can he take away from either the goods or money they have got upon the said land at his pleasure? If he can, then all free and voluntary contracts cease, and are void in the world; there needs nothing but power enough to dissolve them at any time, and all the grants and promises of men in power are but mockery and collusion. For can there be anything more ridiculous than to say, I give you and yours this for ever, and that in the surest and most solemn way of conveyance can be devised, and yet it is to be understood that I have right, if I please, to take it away from you again to-morrow?

195. I will not dispute now whether princes are exempt from the laws of their country, but this I am sure, they owe subjection to the laws of God and Nature. Nobody, no power can exempt them from the obligations of that eternal law. Those are so great and so strong in the case of promises, that Omnipotency itself can be tied by them. Grants, promises, and oaths are bonds that hold the Almighty, whatever some flatterers say to princes

of the world, who, all together, with all their people joined to them, are, in comparison of the great God, but as a drop of the bucket, or a dust on the balance—inconsiderable, nothing!

196. The short of the case in conquest, is this: The conqueror, if he have a just cause, has a despotical right over the persons of all that actually aided and concurred in the war against him, and a right to make up his damage and cost out of their labour and estates, so he injure not the right of any other. Over the rest of the people, if there were any that consented not to the war, and over the children of the captives themselves or the possessions of either he has no power, and so can have, by virtue of conquest, no lawful title himself to dominion over them, or derive it to his posterity; but is an aggressor, and puts himself in a state of war against them, and has no better a right of principality, he, nor any of his successors, than Hingar, or Hubba, the Danes, had here in England, or Spartacus, had he conquered Italy, which is to have their yoke cast off as soon as God shall give those under their subjection courage and opportunity to do it. Thus, notwithstanding whatever title the kings of Assyria had over Judah, by the sword, God assisted Hezekiah to throw off the dominion of that conquering empire. "And the Lord was with Hezekiah, and he prospered; wherefore he went forth, and he rebelled against the king of Assyria, and served him not" (2 Kings xviii. 7). Whence it is plain that shaking off a power which force, and not right, hath set over any one, though it hath the name of rebellion, yet is no offence before God, but that which He allows and countenances, though even promises and covenants, when obtained by force, have intervened. For it is very probable, to any one that reads the story of Ahaz and Hezekiah attentively, that the Assyrians subdued Ahaz, and deposed him, and made Hezekiah king in his father's lifetime, and that Hezekiah, by agreement, had done him homage, and paid him tribute till this time.

CHAPTER XVII

OF USURPATION

197. As conquest may be called a foreign usurpation, so usurpation is a kind of domestic conquest, with this difference—that an usurper can never have right on his side, it being no usurpation but where one is got into the possession of what another has right to. This, so far as it is usurpation, is a change only of persons, but not of the forms and rules of the government; for if the usurper extend his power beyond what, of right, belonged to the lawful princes or governors of the commonwealth, it is tyranny added to usurpation.

198. In all lawful governments the designation of the persons who are to bear rule being as natural and necessary a part as the form of the government itself, and that which had its establishment originally from the people—the anarchy being much alike, to have no form of government at all, or to agree that it shall be monarchical, yet appoint no way to design the person that shall have the power and be the monarch—all commonwealths, therefore, with the form of government established, have rules also of appointing and conveying the right to those who are to have any share in the public authority; and whoever gets into the exercise of any part of the power by other ways than what the laws of the community have prescribed hath no right to be obeyed, though the form of the commonwealth be still preserved, since he is not the person the laws have appointed, and, consequently, not the person the people have consented to. Nor can such an usurper, or any deriving from him, ever have a title till the people are both at liberty to consent, and have actually consented, to allow and confirm in him the power he hath till then usurped.

CHAPTER XVIII

OF TYRANNY

199. As usurpation is the exercise of power which another hath a right to, so tyranny is the exercise of power beyond right, which nobody can have a right to; and this is making use of the power any one has in his hands, not for the good of those who are under it, but for his own private, separate advantage. When the governor, however entitled, makes not the law, but his will, the rule, and his commands and actions are not directed to the preservation of the properties of his people, but the satisfaction of his own ambition, revenge, covetousness, or any other irregular passion.

200. If one can doubt this to be truth or reason because it comes from the obscure hand of a subject, I hope the authority of a king will make it pass with him. King James, in his speech to the Parliament, 1603, tells them thus: "I will ever prefer the weal of the public and of the whole commonwealth, in making of good laws and constitutions, to any particular and private ends of mine, thinking ever the wealth and weal of the commonwealth to be my greatest weal and worldly felicity—a point wherein a lawful king doth directly differ from a tyrant; for I do acknowledge that the special and greatest point of difference that is between a rightful king and an usurping tyrant is this— that whereas the proud and ambitious tyrant doth think his kingdom and people are only ordained for satisfaction of his desires and unreasonable appetites, the righteous and just king doth, by the contrary, acknowledge himself to be ordained for the procuring of the wealth and property of his people." And again, in his speech to the Parliament, 1609, he hath these words: "The king binds himself, by a double oath, to the observation of the fundamental laws of his kingdom—tacitly, as by being a king, and so

bound to protect, as well the people as the laws of his kingdom; and expressly by his oath at his coronation; so as every just king, in a settled kingdom, is bound to observe that paction made to his people, by his laws, in framing his government agreeable thereunto, according to that paction which God made with Noah after the deluge: 'Hereafter, seed-time, and harvest, and cold, and heat, and summer, and winter, and day, and night, shall not cease while the earth remaineth.' And therefore a king, governing in a settled kingdom, leaves to be a king, and degenerates into a tyrant, as soon as he leaves off to rule according to his laws." And a little after: "Therefore, all kings that are not tyrants, or perjured, will be glad to bound themselves within the limits of their laws, and they that persuade them the contrary are vipers, pests, both against them and the commonwealth." Thus, that learned king, who well understood the notions of things, makes the difference betwixt a king and a tyrant to consist only in this: that one makes the laws the bounds of his power and the good of the public the end of his government; the other makes all give way to his own will and appetite.

201. It is a mistake to think this fault is proper only to monarchies. Other forms of government are liable to it as well as that; for wherever the power that is put in any hands for the government of the people and the preservation of their properties is applied to other ends, and made use of to impoverish, harass, or subdue them to the arbitrary and irregular commands of those that have it, there it presently becomes tyranny, whether those that thus use it are one or many. Thus we read of the thirty tyrants at Athens, as well as one at Syracuse; and the intolerable dominion of the Decemviri at Rome was nothing better.

202. Wherever law ends, tyranny begins, if the law be transgressed to another's harm; and whosoever in authority exceeds the power given him by the law, and makes use of the force he has under his command to compass that upon the subject which the law allows not, ceases in that to be a magistrate, and acting without authority may be opposed, as any other man who by force invades the right of another. This is acknowledged in subordinate magistrates. He that hath authority to seize my person in the street may be opposed as a thief and a robber if he endeavours to break into my house to execute a writ, notwithstanding that I know he has such a warrant and such a legal authority as will empower him to arrest me abroad. And why this should not hold in the highest, as well as in the most inferior magistrate, I would gladly be

informed. Is it reasonable that the eldest brother, because he has the greatest part of his father's estate, should thereby have a right to take away any of his younger brothers' portions ? Or that a rich man, who possessed a whole country, should from thence have a right to seize, when he pleased, the cottage and garden of his poor neighbour? The being rightfully possessed of great power and riches, exceedingly beyond the greatest part of the sons of Adam, is so far from being an excuse, much less a reason for rapine and oppression, which the endamaging another without authority is, that it is a great aggravation of it. For exceeding the bounds of authority is no more a right in a great than a petty officer, no more justifiable in a king than a constable. But so much the worse in him as that he has more trust put in him, is supposed, from the advantage of education and counsellors, to have better knowledge and less reason to do it, having already a greater share than the rest of his brethren.

203. May the commands, then, of a prince be opposed? May he be resisted, as often as any one shall find himself aggrieved, and but imagine he has not right done him? This will unhinge and overturn all polities, and instead of government and order, leave nothing but anarchy and confusion.

204. To this I answer: That force is to be opposed to nothing but to unjust and unlawful force. Whoever makes any opposition in any other case draws on himself a just condemnation, both from God and man; and so no such danger or confusion will follow, as is often suggested. For—

205. First. As in some countries the person of the prince by the law is sacred, and so whatever he commands or does, his person is still free from all question or violence, not liable to force, or any judicial censure or condemnation. But yet opposition may be made to the illegal acts of any inferior officer or other commissioned by him, unless he will, by actually putting himself into a state of war with his people, dissolve the government, and leave them to that defence, which belongs to every one in the state of Nature. For of such things, who can tell what the end will be? And a neighbour kingdom has showed the world an odd example. In all other cases the sacredness of the person exempts him from all inconveniencies, whereby he is secure, whilst the government stands, from all violence and harm whatsoever, than which there cannot be a wiser constitution. For the harm he can do in his own person not being likely to happen often, nor to extend itself far, nor being able by his single

strength to subvert the laws nor oppress the body of the people, should any prince have so much weakness and ill-nature as to be willing to do it. The inconveniency of some particular mischiefs that may happen sometimes when a heady prince comes to the throne are well recompensed by the peace of the public and security of the government in the person of the chief magistrate, thus set out of the reach of danger; it being safer for the body that some few private men should be sometimes in danger to suffer than that the head of the republic should be easily and upon slight occasions exposed.

206. Secondly. But this privilege, belonging only to the king's person, hinders not but they may be questioned, opposed, and resisted, who use unjust force, though they pretend a commission from him which the law authorises not; as is plain in the case of him that has the king's writ to arrest a man which is a full commission from the king, and yet he that has it cannot break open a man's house to do it, nor execute this command of the king upon certain days nor in certain places, though this commission have no such exception in it; but they are the limitations of the law, which, if any one transgress, the king's commission excuses him not. For the king's authority being given him only by the law, he cannot empower any one to act against the law, or justify him by his commission in so doing. The commission or command of any magistrate where he has no authority, being as void and insignificant as that of any private man, the difference between the one and the other being that the magistrate has some authority so far and to such ends, and the private man has none at all; for it is not the commission but the authority that gives the right of acting, and against the laws there can be no authority. But notwithstanding such resistance, the king's person and authority are still both secured, and so no danger to governor or government.

207. Thirdly. Supposing a government wherein the person of the chief magistrate is not thus sacred, yet this doctrine of the lawfulness of resisting all unlawful exercises of his power will not, upon every slight occasion, endanger him or embroil the government; for where the injured party may be relieved and his damages repaired by appeal to the law, there can be no pretence for force, which is only to be used where a man is intercepted from appealing to the law. For nothing is to be accounted hostile force but where it leaves not the remedy of such an appeal, and it is such force alone that puts him that uses it into a state of war, and makes it lawful to resist him. A man with a sword in his hand demands my purse on

the highway, when perhaps I have not 12d. in my pocket. This man I may lawfully kill. To another I deliver £100 to hold only whilst I alight, which he refuses to restore me when I am got up again, but draws his sword to defend the possession of it by force. I endeavour to retake it. The mischief this man does me is a hundred, or possibly a thousand times more than the other perhaps intended me (whom I killed before he really did me any); and yet I might lawfully kill the one and cannot so much as hurt the other lawfully. The reason whereof is plain; because the one using force which threatened my life, I could not have time to appeal to the law to secure it, and when it was gone it was too late to appeal. The law could not restore life to my dead carcass. The loss was irreparable; which to prevent the law of Nature gave me a right to destroy him who had put himself into a state of war with me and threatened my destruction. But in the other case, my life not being in danger, I might have the benefit of appealing to the law, and have reparation for my £100 that way.

208. Fourthly. But if the unlawful acts done by the magistrate be maintained (by the power he has got), and the remedy, which is due by law, be by the same power obstructed, yet the right of resisting, even in such manifest acts of tyranny, will not suddenly, or on slight occasions, disturb the government. For if it reach no farther than some private men's cases, though they have a right to defend themselves, and to recover by force what by unlawful force is taken from them, yet the right to do so will not easily engage them in a contest wherein they are sure to perish; it being as impossible for one or a few oppressed men to disturb the government where the body of the people do not think themselves concerned in it, as for a raving madman or heady malcontent to overturn a well-settled state, the people being as little apt to follow the one as the other.

209. But if either these illegal acts have extended to the majority of the people, or if the mischief and oppression has light only on some few, but in such cases as the precedent and consequences seem to threaten all, and they are persuaded in their consciences that their laws, and with them, their estates, liberties, and lives are in danger, and perhaps their religion too, how they will be hindered from resisting illegal force used against them I cannot tell. This is an inconvenience, I confess, that attends all governments whatsoever, when the governors have brought it to this pass, to be generally suspected of their people, the most dangerous state they can possibly put themselves in; wherein they are the less to be pitied, because it is so easy to be avoided. It being as impossible for a

governor, if he really means the good of his people, and the preservation of them and their laws together, not to make them see and feel it, as it is for the father of a family not to let his children see he loves and takes care of them.

210. But if all the world shall observe pretences of one kind, and actions of another, arts used to elude the law, and the trust of prerogative (which is an arbitrary power in some things left in the prince's hand to do good, not harm, to the people) employed contrary to the end for which it was given; if the people shall find the ministers and subordinate magistrates chosen, suitable to such ends, and favoured or laid by proportionably as they promote or oppose them; if they see several experiments made of arbitrary power, and that religion underhand favoured, though publicly proclaimed against, which is readiest to introduce it, and the operators in it supported as much as may be; and when that cannot be done, yet approved still, and liked the better, and a long train of acting show the counsels all tending that way, how can a man any more hinder himself from being persuaded in his own mind which way things are going; or, from casting about how to save himself, than he could from believing the captain of a ship he was in was carrying him and the rest of the company to Algiers, when he found him always steering that course, though cross winds, leaks in his ship, and want of men and provisions did often force him to turn his course another way for some time, which he steadily returned to again as soon as the wind, weather, and other circumstances would let him?

CHAPTER XIX

OF THE DISSOLUTION OF GOVERNMENT

211. He that will, with any clearness, speak of the dissolution of government, ought in the first place to distinguish between the dissolution of the society and the dissolution of the government. That which makes the community, and brings men out of the loose state of Nature into one politic society, is the agreement which every one has with the rest to incorporate and act as one body, and so be one distinct commonwealth. The usual, and almost only way whereby this union is dissolved, is the inroad of foreign force making a conquest upon them. For in that case (not being able to maintain and support themselves as one entire and independent body) the union belonging to that body, which consisted therein, must necessarily cease, and so every one return to the state he was in before, with a liberty to shift for himself and provide for his own safety, as he thinks fit, in some other society. Whenever the society is dissolved, it is certain the government of that society cannot remain. Thus conquerors' swords often cut up governments by the roots, and mangle societies to pieces, separating the subdued or scattered multitude from the protection of and dependence on that society which ought to have preserved them from violence. The world is too well instructed in, and too forward to allow of this way of dissolving of governments, to need any more to be said of it; and there wants not much argument to prove that where the society is dissolved, the government cannot remain; that being as impossible as for the frame of a house to subsist when the materials of it are scattered and displaced by a whirlwind, or jumbled into a confused heap by an earthquake.

212. Besides this overturning from without, governments are dissolved from within:

First. When the legislative is altered, civil society being a state of peace amongst those who are of it, from whom the state of war is excluded by the umpirage which they have provided in their legislative for the ending all differences that may arise amongst any of them; it is in their legislative that the members of a commonwealth are united and combined together into one coherent living body. This is the soul that gives form, life, and unity to the commonwealth; from hence the several members have their mutual influence, sympathy, and connection; and therefore when the legislative is broken, or dissolved, dissolution and death follows. For the essence and union of the society consisting in having one will, the legislative, when once established by the majority, has the declaring and, as it were, keeping of that will. The constitution of the legislative is the first and fundamental act of society, whereby provision is made for the continuation of their union under the direction of persons and bonds of laws, made by persons authorised thereunto, by the consent and appointment of the people, without which no one man, or number of men, amongst them can have authority of making laws that shall be binding to the rest. When any one, or more, shall take upon them to make laws whom the people have not appointed so to do, they make laws without authority, which the people are not therefore bound to obey; by which means they come again to be out of subjection, and may constitute to themselves a new legislative, as they think best, being in full liberty to resist the force of those who, without authority, would impose anything upon them. Every one is at the disposure of his own will, when those who had, by the delegation of the society, the declaring of the public will, are excluded from it, and others usurp the place who have no such authority or delegation.

213. This being usually brought about by such in the commonwealth, who misuse the power they have, it is hard to consider it aright, and know at whose door to lay it, without knowing the form of government in which it happens. Let us suppose, then, the legislative placed in the concurrence of three distinct persons:—First, a single hereditary person having the constant, supreme, executive power, and with it the power of convoking and dissolving the other two within certain periods of time. Secondly, an assembly of hereditary nobility. Thirdly, an assembly of representatives chosen, *pro tempore,* by the people. Such a form of government supposed, it is evident:

214. First, that when such a single person or prince sets up his own arbitrary will in place of the laws which are the will of the society declared by the legislative, then the legislative is changed. For that being, in effect, the legislative whose rules and laws are put in execution, and required to be obeyed, when other laws are set up, and other rules pretended and enforced than what the legislative, constituted by the society, have enacted, it is plain that the legislative is changed. Whoever introduces new laws, not being thereunto authorised, by the fundamental appointment of the society, or subverts the old, disowns and overturns the power by which they were made, and so sets up a new legislative.

215. Secondly, when the prince hinders the legislative from assembling in its due time, or from acting freely, pursuant to those ends for which it was constituted, the legislative is altered. For it is not a certain number of men—no, nor their meeting, unless they have also freedom of debating and leisure of perfecting what is for the good of the society, wherein the legislative consists; when these are taken away, or altered, so as to deprive the society of the due exercise of their power, the legislative is truly altered. For it is not names that constitute governments, but the use and exercise of those powers that were intended to accompany them; so that he who takes away the freedom, or hinders the acting of the legislative in its due seasons, in effect takes away the legislative, and puts an end to the government.

216. Thirdly, when, by the arbitrary power of the prince, the electors or ways of election are altered without the consent and contrary to the common interest of the people, there also the legislative is altered. For if others than those whom the society hath authorised thereunto do choose, or in another way than what the society hath prescribed, those chosen are not the legislative appointed by the people.

217. Fourthly, the delivery also of the people into the subjection of a foreign power, either by the prince or by the legislative, is certainly a change of the legislative, and so a dissolution of the government. For the end why people entered into society being to be preserved one entire, free, independent society, to be governed by its own laws, this is lost whenever they are given up into the power of another.

218. Why, in such a constitution as this, the dissolution of the government in these cases is to be imputed to the prince is evident, because he, having the force, treasure, and offices of the State to employ, and often persuading himself or being flattered by others, that, as supreme magistrate,

he is incapable of control; he alone is in a condition to make great advances towards such changes under pretence of lawful authority, and has it in his hands to terrify or suppress opposers as factious, seditious, and enemies to the government; whereas no other part of the legislative, or people, is capable by themselves to attempt any alteration of the legislative without open and visible rebellion, apt enough to be taken notice of, which, when it prevails, produces effects very little different from foreign conquest. Besides, the prince, in such a form of government, having the power of dissolving the other parts of the legislative, and thereby rendering them private persons, they can never, in opposition to him, or without his concurrence, alter the legislative by a law, his consent being necessary to give any of their decrees that sanction. But yet so far as the other parts of the legislative any way contribute to any attempt upon the government, and do either promote, or not, what lies in them, hinder such designs, they are guilty, and partake in this, which is certainly the greatest crime men can be guilty of one towards another.

219. There is one way more whereby such a government may be dissolved, and that is: When he who has the supreme executive power neglects and abandons that charge, so that the laws already made can no longer be put in execution ; this is demonstratively to reduce all to anarchy, and so effectively to dissolve the government. For laws not being made for themselves, but to be, by their execution, the bonds of the society to keep every part of the body politic in its due place and function. When that totally ceases, the government visibly ceases, and the people become a confused multitude without order or connection. Where there is no longer the administration of justice for the securing of men's rights, nor any remaining power within the community to direct the force, or provide for the necessities of the public, there certainly is no government left. Where the laws cannot be executed it is all one as if there were no laws, and a government without laws is, I suppose, a mystery in politics inconceivable to human capacity, and inconsistent with human society.

220. In these, and the like cases, when the government is dissolved, the people are at liberty to provide for themselves by erecting a new legislative differing from the other by the change of persons, or form, or both, as they shall find it most for their safety and good. For the society can never, by the fault of another, lose the native and original right it has to preserve itself, which can only be done by a settled legislative and a

fair and impartial execution of the laws made by it. But the state of mankind is not so miserable that they are not capable of using this remedy till it be too late to look for any. To tell people they may provide for themselves by erecting a new legislative, when, by oppression, artifice, or being delivered over to a foreign power, their old one is gone, is only to tell them they may expect relief when it is too late, and the evil is past cure. This is, in effect, no more than to bid them first be slaves, and then to take care of their liberty, and, when their chains are on, tell them they may act like free men. This, if barely so, is rather mockery than relief, and men can never be secure from tyranny if there be no means to escape it till they are perfectly under it; and, therefore, it is that they have not only a right to get out of it, but to prevent it.

221. There is, therefore, secondly, another way whereby governments are dissolved, and that is, when the legislative, or the prince, either of them act contrary to their trust.

For the legislative acts against the trust reposed in them when they endeavour to invade the property of the subject, and to make themselves, or any part of the community, masters or arbitrary disposers of the lives, liberties, or fortunes of the people.

222. The reason why men enter into society is the preservation of their property; and the end while they choose and authorise a legislative is that there may be laws made, and rules set, as guards and fences to the properties of all the society, to limit the power and moderate the dominion of every part and member of the society. For since it can never be supposed to be the will of the society that the legislative should have a power to destroy that which every one designs to secure by entering into society, and for which the people submitted themselves to legislators of their own making: whenever the legislators endeavour to take away and destroy the property of the people, or to reduce them to slavery under arbitrary power, they put themselves into a state of war with the people, who are thereupon absolved from any farther obedience, and are left to the common refuge which God hath provided for all men against force and violence. Whensoever, therefore, the legislative shall transgress this fundamental rule of society, and either by ambition, fear, folly, or corruption, endeavour to grasp themselves, or put into the hands of any other, an absolute power over the lives, liberties, and estates of the people, by this breach of trust they forfeit the power the people had put into their hands for quite contrary ends, and it devolves to the people, who

have a right to resume their original liberty, and by the establishment of a new legislative (such as they shall think fit), provide for their own safety and security, which is the end for which they are in society. What I have said here concerning the legislative in general holds true also concerning the supreme executor, who having a double trust put in him, both to have a part in the legislative and the supreme execution of the law, acts against both, when he goes about to set up his own arbitrary will as the law of the society. He acts also contrary to his trust when he employs the force, treasure, and offices of the society to corrupt the representatives and gain them to his purposes, when he openly pre-engages the electors, and prescribes, to their choice, such whom he has, by solicitation, threats, promises, or otherwise, won to his designs, and employs them to bring in such who have promised beforehand what to vote and what to enact. Thus to regulate candidates and electors, and new model the ways of election, what is it but to cut up the government by the roots, and poison the very fountain of public security? For the people having reserved to themselves the choice of their representatives as the fence to their properties, could do it for no other end but that they might always be freely chosen, and so chosen, freely act and advise as the necessity of the commonwealth and the public good should, upon examination and mature debate, be judged to require. This, those who give their votes before they hear the debate, and have weighed the reasons on all sides, are not capable of doing. To prepare such an assembly as this, and endeavour to set up the declared abettors of his own will, for the true representatives of the people, and the law-makers of the society, is certainly as great a breach of trust, and as perfect a declaration of a design to subvert the government, as is possible to be met with. To which, if one shall add rewards and punishments visibly employed to the same end, and all the arts of perverted law made use of to take off and destroy all that stand in the way of such a design, and will not comply and consent to betray the liberties of their country, it will be past doubt what is doing. What power they ought to have in the society who thus employ it contrary to the trust went along with it in its first institution, is easy to determine; and one cannot but see that he who has once attempted any such thing as this cannot any longer be trusted.

223. To this, perhaps, it will be said that the people being ignorant and always discontented, to lay the foundation of government in the unsteady opinion and uncertain humour of the people, is to expose it to

certain ruin; and no government will be able long to subsist if the people may set up a new legislative whenever they take offence at the old one. To this I answer, quite the contrary. People are not so easily got out of their old forms as some are apt to suggest. They are hardly to be prevailed with to amend the acknowledged faults in the frame they have been accustomed to. And if there be any original defects, or adventitious ones introduced by time or corruption, it is not an easy thing to get them changed, even when all the world sees there is an opportunity for it. This slowness and aversion in the people to quit their old constitutions has in the many revolutions have been seen in this kingdom, in this and former ages, still kept us to, or after some interval of fruitless attempts, still brought us back again to our old legislative of king, lords and commons; and whatever provocations have made the crown be taken from some of our princes' heads, they never carried the people so far as to place it in another line.

224. But it will be said this hypothesis lays a ferment for frequent rebellion. To which I answer:

First: no more than any other hypothesis. For when the people are made miserable, and find themselves exposed to the ill usage of arbitrary power, cry up their governors as much as you will for sons of Jupiter, let them be sacred and divine, descended or authorised from Heaven; give them out for whom or what you please, the same will happen. The people generally ill treated, and contrary to right, will be ready upon any occasion to ease themselves of a burden that sits heavy upon them. They will wish and seek for the opportunity, which in the change, weakness, and accidents of human affairs, seldom delays long to offer itself. He must have lived but a little while in the world, who has not seen examples of this in his time; and he must have read very little who cannot produce examples of it in all sorts of governments in the world.

225. Secondly: I answer, such revolutions happen not upon every little mismanagement in public affairs. Great mistakes in the ruling part, many wrong and inconvenient laws, and all the slips of human frailty will be borne by the people without mutiny or murmur. But if a long train of abuses, prevarications, and artifices, all tending the same way, make the design visible to the people, and they cannot but feel what they lie under, and see whither they are going, it is not to be wondered that they should then rouse themselves, and endeavour to put the rule into such hands

which may secure to them the ends for which government was at first erected, and without which, ancient names and specious forms are so far from being better, that they are much worse than the state of Nature or pure anarchy; the inconveniencies being all as great and as near, but the remedy farther off and more difficult.

226. Thirdly: I answer, that this power in the people of providing for their safety anew by a new legislative when their legislators have acted contrary to their trust by invading their property, is the best fence against rebellion, and the probablest means to hinder it. For rebellion being an opposition, not to persons, but authority, which is founded only in the constitutions and laws of the government: those, whoever they be, who, by force, break through, and, by force, justify their violation of them, are truly and properly rebels. For when men, by entering into society and civil government, have excluded force, and introduced laws for the preservation of property, peace, and unity amongst themselves, those who set up force again in opposition to the laws, do *rebellare*— that is, bring back again the state of war, and are properly rebels, which they who are in power, by the pretence they have to authority, the temptation of force they have in their hands, and the flattery of those about them being likeliest to do, the properest way to prevent the evil is to show them the danger and injustice of it who are under the greatest temptation to run into it.

227. In both the forementioned cases, when either the legislative is changed, or the legislators act contrary to the end for which they were constituted, those who are guilty are guilty of rebellion. For if any one by force takes away the established legislative of any society, and the laws by them made, pursuant to their trust, he thereby takes away the umpirage which every one had consented to for a peaceable decision of all their controversies, and a bar to the state of war amongst them. They who remove or change the legislative take away this decisive power, which nobody can have but by the appointment and consent of the people, and so destroying the authority which the people did, and nobody else can set up, and introducing a power which the people hath not authorised, actually introduce a state of war, which is that of force without authority; and thus by removing the legislative established by the society, in whose decisions the people acquiesced and united as to that of their own will, they untie the knot, and expose the people anew to the state of war. And if those, who by force take away

the legislative, are rebels, the legislators themselves, as has been shown, can be no less esteemed so, when they who were set up for the protection and preservation of the people, their liberties and properties shall by force invade and endeavour to take them away; and so they putting themselves into a state of war with those who made them the protectors and guardians of their peace, are properly, and with the greatest aggravation, *rebellantes,* rebels.

228. But if they who say it lays a foundation for rebellion mean that it may occasion civil wars or intestine broils to tell the people they are absolved from obedience when illegal attempts are made upon their liberties or properties, and may oppose the unlawful violence of those who were their magistrates when they invade their properties, contrary to the trust put in them, and that, therefore, this doctrine is not to be allowed, being so destructive to the peace of the world; they may as well say, upon the same ground, that honest men may not oppose robbers or pirates, because this may occasion disorder or bloodshed. If any mischief come in such cases, it is not to be charged upon him who defends his own right, but on him that invades his neighbour's. If the innocent honest man must quietly quit all he has for peace sake to him who will lay violent hands upon it, I desire it may be considered what a kind of peace there will be in the world which consists only in violence and rapine, and which is to be maintained only for the benefit of robbers and oppressors. Who would not think it an admirable peace betwixt the mighty and the mean, when the lamb, without resistance, yielded his throat to be torn by the imperious wolf? Polyphemus's den gives us a perfect pattern of such a peace. Such a government wherein Ulysses and his companions had nothing to do but quietly to suffer themselves to be devoured. And no doubt Ulysses, who was a prudent man, preached up passive obedience, and exhorted them to a quiet submission by representing to them of what concernment peace was to mankind, and by showing the inconveniencies might happen if they should offer to resist Polyphemus, who had now the power over them.

229. The end of government is the good of mankind; and which is best for mankind, that the people should be always exposed to the boundless will of tyranny, or that the rulers should be sometimes liable to be opposed when they grow exorbitant in the use of their power, and employ it for the destruction, and not the preservation, of the properties of their people?

230. Nor let any one say that mischief can arise from hence as often as it shall please a busy head or turbulent spirit to desire the alteration of the government. It is true such men may stir whenever they please, but it will be only to their own just ruin and perdition. For till the mischief be grown general, and the ill designs of the rulers become visible, or their attempts sensible to the greater part, the people, who are more disposed to suffer than right themselves by resistance, are not apt to stir. The examples of particular injustice or oppression of here and there an unfortunate man moves them not. But if they universally have a persuasion grounded upon manifest evidence that designs are carrying on against their liberties, and the general course and tendency of things cannot but give them strong suspicions of the evil intention of their governors, who is to be blamed for it? Who can help it if they, who might avoid it, bring themselves into this suspicion? Are the people to be blamed if they have the sense of rational creatures, and can think of things no otherwise than as they find and feel them? And is it not rather their fault who put things in such a posture that they would not have them thought as they are? I grant that the pride, ambition, and turbulency of private men have sometimes caused great disorders in commonwealths, and factions have been fatal to states and kingdoms. But whether the mischief hath oftener begun in the people's wantonness, and a desire to cast off the lawful authority of their rulers, or in the rulers' insolence and endeavours to get and exercise an arbitrary power over their people, whether oppression or disobedience gave the first rise to the disorder, I leave it to impartial history to determine. This I am sure, whoever, either ruler or subject, by force goes about to invade the rights of either prince or people, and lays the foundation for overturning the constitution and frame of any just government, he is guilty of the greatest crime I think a man is capable of, being to answer for all those mischiefs of blood, rapine, and desolation, which the breaking to pieces of governments bring on a country; and he who does it is justly to be esteemed the common enemy and pest of mankind, and is to be treated accordingly.

231. That subjects or foreigners attempting by force on the properties of any people may be resisted with force is agreed on all hands; but that magistrates doing the same thing may be resisted, hath of late been denied; as if those who had the greatest privileges and advantages by the law had thereby a power to break those laws by which alone they were

set in a better place than their brethren; whereas their offence is thereby the greater, both as being ungrateful for the greater share they have by the law, and breaking also that trust which is put into their hands by their brethren.

232. Whosoever uses force without right—as every one does in society who does it without law—puts himself into a state of war with those against whom he so uses it, and in that state all former ties are cancelled, all other rights cease, and every one has a right to defend himself, and to resist the aggressor. This is so evident that Barclay himself—that great assertor of the power and sacredness of kings—is forced to confess that it is lawful for the people, in some cases, to resist their king, and that, too, in a chapter wherein he pretends to show that the Divine law shuts up the people from all manner of rebellion. Whereby it is evident, even by his own doctrine, that since they may, in some cases, resist, all resisting of princes is not rebellion. His words are these: "Quod siquis dicat, Ergone populus tyrannicæ crudelitati et furori jugulum semper præbebit? Ergone multitudo civitates suas fame, ferro, et flammâ vastari, seque, conjuges, et liberos fortunæ ludibrio et tyranni libidini exponi, inque omnia vitæ pericula omnesque miserias et molestias à rege deduci patientur? Num illis quod omni animantium generi est à naturâ tributum, denegari debet, ut sc. vim vi repellant, seseque ab injuriâ tueantur? Huic breviter responsum sit, populo universo negari defensionem, quæ juris naturalis est, neque ultionem quæ præter naturam est adversus regem concedi debere. Quapropter si rex non in singulares tantum personas aliquot privatum odium exerceat, sed corpus etiam reipublicæ, cujus ipse caput est—*i.e.*, totum populum, vel insignem aliquam ejus partem immani et intolerandâ sævitiâ seu tyrannide divexet; populo, quidem hoc casu resistendi ac tuendi se ab injuriâ potestas competit, sed tuendi se tantum, non enim in principem invadendi: et restituendæ injuriæ illatæ, non recedendi à debitâ reverentiâ propter acceptum injuriam. Præsentem denique impetum propulsandi non vim præteritam ulciscendi jus habet. Horum enim alterum à naturâ est, ut vitam scilicet corpusque tueamur. Alterum vero contra naturam, ut inferior de superiori supplicium sumat. Quod itaque populus malum, antequam factum sit, impedire potest, ne fiat, id postquam factum est, in regem authorem sceleris vindicare non potest, populus igitur hoc ampliùs quam privatus quispiam habet: Quod huic, vel ipsis adversariis

judicibus, excepto Buchanano, nullum nisi in patientia remedium superest. Cum ille si intolerabilis tyrannis est (modicum enim ferre omnino debet) resistere cum reverentiâ possit."—Barclay, *Contra Monarchomachos,* 1. iii., c. 8.

In English thus:—

233. "But if any one should ask: Must the people, then, always lay themselves open to the cruelty and rage of tyranny—must they see their cities pillaged and laid in ashes, their wives and children exposed to the tyrant's lust and fury, and themselves and families reduced by their king to ruin and all the miseries of want and oppression, and yet sit still—must men alone be debarred the common privilege of opposing force with force, which Nature allows so freely to all other creatures for their preservation from injury? I answer: Self-defence is a part of the law of Nature; nor can it be denied the community, even against the king himself; but to revenge themselves upon him must, by no means, be allowed them, it being not agreeable to that law. Wherefore, if the king shall show an hatred, not only to some particular persons, but sets himself against the body of the commonwealth, whereof he is the head, and shall, with intolerable ill-usage, cruelly tyrannise over the whole, or a considerable part of the people; in this case the people have a right to resist and defend themselves from injury; but it must be with this caution, that they only defend themselves, but do not attack their prince. They may repair the damages received, but must not, for any provocation, exceed the bounds of due reverence and respect. They may repulse the present attempt, but must not revenge past violences. For it is natural for us to defend life and limb, but that an inferior should punish a superior is against nature. The mischief which is designed them the people may prevent before it be done, but, when it is done, they must not revenge it on the king, though author of the villany. This, therefore, is the privilege of the people in general above what any private person hath: That particular men are allowed, by our adversaries themselves (Buchanan only excepted), to have no other remedy but patience; but the body of the people may, with respect, resist intolerable tyranny, for when it is but moderate they ought to endure it."

234. Thus far that great advocate of monarchical power allows of resistance.

235. It is true, he has annexed two limitations to it, to no purpose:

First. He says it must be with reverence.

Secondly. It must be without retribution or punishment; and the reason he gives is, "because an inferior cannot punish a superior."

First. How to resist force without striking again, or how to strike with reverence, will need some skill to make intelligible. He that shall oppose an assault only with a shield to receive the blows, or in any more respectful posture, without a sword in his hand to abate the confidence and force of the assailant, will quickly be at an end of his resistance, and will find such a defence serve only to draw on himself the worse usage. This is as ridiculous a way of resisting as Juvenal thought it of fighting: *Ubi tu pulsas, ego vapulo tantum.* And the success of the combat will be unavoidably the same he there describes it:

> Libertas pauperis hæc est;
> Pulsatus rogat, et pugnis concisus, adorat,
> Ut liceat paucis cum dentibus inde reverti.

This will always be the event of such an imaginary resistance, where men may not strike again. He, therefore, who may resist must be allowed to strike. And then let our author, or anybody else, join a knock on the head or a cut on the face with as much reverence and respect as he thinks fit. He that can reconcile blows and reverence may, for aught I know, deserve for his pains a civil, respectful cudgelling wherever he can meet with it.

Secondly. As to his second—"An inferior cannot punish a superior"—that is true, generally speaking, whilst he is his superior. But to resist force with force, being the state of war that levels the parties, cancels all former relation of reverence, respect, and superiority; and then the odds that remains is—that he who opposes the unjust aggressor has this superiority over him, that he has a right, when he prevails, to punish the offender, both for the breach of the peace and all the evils that followed upon it. Barclay, therefore, in another place, more coherently to himself, denies it to be lawful to resist a king in any case. But he there assigns two cases whereby a king may unking himself. His words are:

"Quid ergo, nulline casus incidere possunt quibus populo sese erigere atque in regem impotentius dominantem arma capere et invadere jure suo suâque authoritate liceat? Nulli certe quamdiu rex manet. Semper enim ex divinis id obstat, Regem honorificato, et qui potestati resistit, Dei ordinationi resistit; non aliàs igitur in eum populo potestas est quam si id committat propter quod ipso jure rex esse desinat. Tunc enim se ipse principatu exuit atque in privatis constituit liber; hoc modo populus et superior efficitur, reverso ad eum scilicet jure illo quod ante regem inauguratum in interregno habuit. At sunt paucorum generum commissa ejusmodi quæ hunc effectum pariunt. At ego cum plurima animo perlustrem, duo tantum invenio, duos, inquam, casus quibus rex ipso facto ex rege non regem se facit et omni honore et dignitate regali atque in subditos potestate destituit; quorum etiam meminit Winzerus. Horum unus est, si regnum disperdat, quemadmodum de Nerone fertur, quod is nempe senatum populumque Romanum atque adeo urbem ipsam ferro flammaque vastare, ac novas sibi sedes quærere decrevisset. Et de Caligula, quod palam denunciarit se neque civem neque principem senatui amplius fore, inque animo habuerit, interempto utriusque ordinis electissimo, quoque Alexandriam commigrare, ac ut populum uno ictu interimeret, unam ei cervicem optavit. Talia cum rex aliquis meditatur et molitur serio, omnem regnandi curam et animum ilico abjicit, ac proinde imperium in subditos amittit, ut dominus servi pro derelicto habiti, dominium.

236. "Alter casus est, si rex in alicujus clientelam se contulit, ac regnum quod liberum à majoribus et populo traditum accepit, alienæ ditioni mancipavit. Nam tunc quamvis forte non eâ mente id agit populo plane ut incommodet; tamen quia quod præcipuum est regiæ dignitatis amisit, ut summus scilicet in regno secundum Deum sit, et solo Deo inferior, atque populum etiam totum ignorantem vel invitum, cujus libertatem sartam et tectam conservare debuit, in alterius gentis ditionem et potestatem dedidit; hâc velut quadam rengi abalienatione effecit, ut nec quod ipse in regno imperium habuit retineat, nec in eum cui collatum voluit, juris quicquam transferat, atque ita eo facto liberum jam et suæ potestatis populum relinquit, cujus rei exemplum unum annales Scotici suppeditant."—Barclay, *Contra Monarchomachos,* l. iii., c. 16.

Which may be thus Englished:—

237. "What, then, can there no case happen wherein the people may of right, and by their own authority, help themselves, take arms, and set upon their king, imperiously domineering over them ? None at all whilst he remains a king. 'Honour the king,' and 'he that resists the power, resists the ordinance of God,' are Divine oracles that will never permit it. The people, therefore, can never come by a power over him

unless he does something that makes him cease to be a king; for then he divests himself of his crown and dignity, and returns to the state of a private man, and the people become free and superior; the power which they had in the interregnum, before they crowned him king, devolving to them again. But there are but few miscarriages which bring the matter to this state. After considering it well on all sides, I can find but two. Two cases there are, I say, whereby a king, *ipso facto,* becomes no king, and loses all power and regal authority over his people, which are also taken notice of by Winzerus. The first is, if he endeavour to overturn the government—that is, if he have a purpose and design to ruin the kingdom and commonwealth, as it is recorded of Nero that he resolved to cut off the senate and people of Rome, lay the city waste with fire and sword, and then remove to some other place; and of Caligula, that he openly declared that he would be no longer a head to the people or senate, and that he had it in his thoughts to cut off the worthiest men of both ranks, and then retire to Alexandria; and he wished that the people had but one neck that he might dispatch them all at a blow. Such designs as these, when any king harbours in his thoughts, and seriously promotes, he immediately gives up all care and thought of the commonwealth, and, consequently, forfeits the power of governing his subjects, as a master does the dominion over his slaves whom he hath abandoned.

238. "The other case is, when a king makes himself the dependent of another, and subjects his kingdom, which his ancestors left him, and the people put free into his hands, to the dominion of another. For however, perhaps, it may not be his intention to prejudice the people, yet because he has hereby lost the principal part of regal dignity—viz., to be next and immediately under God, supreme in his kingdom; and also because he betrayed or forced his people, whose liberty he ought to have carefully preserved, into the power and dominion of a foreign nation. By this, as it were, alienation of his kingdom, he himself loses the power he had in it before, without transferring any the least right to those on whom he would have bestowed it; and so by this act sets the people free, and leaves them at their own disposal. One example of this is to be found in the Scotch annals."

239. In these cases Barclay, the great champion of absolute monarchy, is forced to allow that a king may be resisted, and ceases to be a king. That is in short—not to multiply cases—in whatsoever he has no

authority, there he is no king, and may be resisted: for wheresoever the authority ceases, the king ceases too, and becomes like other men who have no authority. And these two cases that he instances differ little from those above mentioned, to be destructive to governments, only that he has omitted the principle from which his doctrine flows, and that is the breach of trust in not preserving the form of government agreed on, and in not intending the end of government itself, which is the public good and preservation of property. When a king has dethroned himself, and put himself in a state of war with his people, what shall hinder them from prosecuting him who is no king, as they would any other man, who has put himself into a state of war with them, Barclay, and those of his opinion, would do well to tell us. Bilson, a bishop of our Church, and a great stickler for the power and prerogative of princes, does, if I mistake not, in his treatise of "Christian Subjection," acknowledge that princes may forfeit their power and their title to the obedience of their subjects; and if there needed authority in a case where reason is so plain, I could send my reader to Bracton, Fortescue, and the author of the "Mirror," and others, writers that cannot be suspected to be ignorant of our government, or enemies to it. But I thought Hooker alone might be enough to satisfy those men who, relying on him for their ecclesiastical polity, are by a strange fate carried to deny those principles upon which he builds it. Whether they are herein made the tools of cunninger workmen, to pull down their own fabric, they were best look. This I am sure, their civil policy is so new, so dangerous, and so destructive to both rulers and people, that as former ages never could bear the broaching of it, so it may be hoped those to come, redeemed from the impositions of these Egyptian under-taskmasters, will abhor the memory of such servile flatterers, who, whilst it seemed to serve their turn, resolved all government into absolute tyranny, and would have all men born to what their mean souls fitted them—slavery.

240. Here it is like the common question will be made: Who shall be judge whether the prince or legislative act contrary to their trust? This, perhaps, ill-affected and factious men may spread amongst the people, when the prince only makes use of his due prerogative. To this I reply, The people shall be judge; for who shall be judge whether his trustee or deputy acts well and according to the trust reposed in him, but he who deputes him and must, by having deputed him, have still a power

to discard him when he fails in his trust? If this be reasonable in particular cases of private men, why should if be otherwise in that of the greatest moment, where the welfare of millions is concerned and also where the evil, if not prevented, is greater, and the redress very difficult, dear, and dangerous?

241. But, farther, this question, Who shall be judge? cannot mean that there is no judge at all. For where there is no judicature on earth to decide controversies amongst men, God in heaven is judge. He alone, it is true, is judge of the right. But every man is judge for himself, as in all other cases so in this, whether another hath put himself into a state of war with him, and whether he should appeal to the supreme Judge, as Jephtha did.

242. If a controversy arise betwixt a prince and some of the people in a matter where the law is silent or doubtful, and the thing be of great consequence, I should think the proper umpire in such a case should be the body of the people. For in such cases where the prince hath a trust reposed in him, and is dispensed from the common, ordinary rules of the law, there, if any men find themselves aggrieved, and think the prince acts contrary to, or beyond that trust, who so proper to judge as the body of the people (who at first lodged that trust in him) how far they meant it should extend? But if the prince, or whoever they be in the administration, decline that way of determination, the appeal then lies nowhere but to Heaven. Force between either persons who have no known superior on earth, or which permits no appeal to a judge on earth, being properly a state of war, wherein the appeal lies only to Heaven; and in that state the injured party must judge for himself when he will think fit to make use of that appeal and put himself upon it.

243. To conclude. The power that every individual gave the society when he entered into it can never revert to the individuals again, as long as the society lasts, but will always remain in the community; because without this there can be no community—no commonwealth, which is contrary to the original agreement; so also when the society hath placed the legislative in any assembly of men, to continue in them and their successors, with direction and authority for providing such successors, the legislative can never revert to the people whilst that government lasts; because, having provided a legislative with power to continue for ever, they have given up their political power to the legislative, and cannot resume it. But if they have set limits to the duration of their legislative,

and made this supreme power in any person or assembly only temporary; or else when, by the miscarriages of those in authority, it is forfeited; upon the forfeiture of their rulers, or at the determination of the time set, it reverts to the society, and the people have a right to act as supreme, and continue the legislative in themselves or place it in a new form, or new hands, as they think good.

ENDNOTES

CHAPTER VI

[1] "It is no improbable opinion, therefore, which the arch-philosopher was of, That the chief person in every household was always, as it were, a king; so when numbers of households joined themselves in civil societies together, kings were the first kind of governors among them, which is also, as it seemeth, the reason why the name of fathers continued still in them, who of fathers were made rulers; as also the ancient custom of governors to do as Melchizedec; and being kings, to exercise the office of priests, which fathers did, at the first, grew, perhaps, by the same occasion. Howbeit, this is not the only kind of regimen that has been received in the world. The inconveniencies of one kind have caused sundry others to be devised, so that, in a word, all public regimen, of what kind soever, seemeth evidently to have risen from the deliberate advice, consultation and composition between men, judging it convenient and behoveful, there being no impossibility in Nature, considered by itself, but that man might have lived without any public regimen." —Hooker (*Eccl. Pol.,* lib. i., s. 10).

CHAPTER VII

[1] "The public power of all society is above every soul contained in the same society, and the principal use of that power is to give laws unto all that are under it, which laws in such cases we must obey, unless there be reason showed which may necessarily enforce that the law of reason or of God doth enjoin the contrary."— Hooker (*Eccl. Pol.,* lib. i., s. 16).

[2] "To take away all such mutual grievances, injuries, and wrongs— *i.e.,* such as attend men in the state of Nature, there was no way but only by growing into composition and agreement amongst themselves by ordaining some kind of government public, and by yielding themselves subject thereunto, that unto whom they granted authority to rule and govern, by them the peace, tranquillity, and happy estate of the rest might be procured. Men always knew that where force and injury was offered, they might be defenders of themselves. They knew that, however men may seek their own commodity, yet if this were done with injury unto others, it was not to be suffered, but by all men and all good means to be withstood. Finally, they knew that no man might, in reason, take upon him to determine his own right, and according to his own determination proceed in maintenance thereof, in as much as every man is towards himself, and them whom he greatly

affects, partial; and therefore, that strifes and troubles would be endless, except they gave their common consent, all to be ordered by some whom they should agree upon, without which consent there would be no reason that one man should take upon him to be lord or judge over another."—Hooker (*ibid.,* s. 10).

3 "At the first, when some certain kind of regimen was once approved, it may be that nothing was then further thought upon for the manner of governing, but all permitted unto their wisdom and discretion which were to rule till, by experience, they found this for all parts very inconvenient, so as the thing which they had devised for a remedy did indeed but increase the sore which it should have cured. They saw that to live by one man's will became the cause of all men's misery. This constrained them to come unto laws wherein all men might see their duty beforehand, and know the penalties of transgressing them."—Hooker (*Eccl. Pol.,* lib. i., s. 10).

4 "Civil law, being the act of the whole body politic, doth therefore overrule each several part of the same body."—Hooker (*ibid.*).

CHAPTER VIII

1 "At the first, when some certain kind of regimen was once approved, it may be that nothing was then further thought upon for the manner of governing, but all permitted unto their wisdom and discretion, which were to rule till, by experience, they found this for all parts very inconvenient, so as the thing which they had devised for a remedy did indeed but increase the sore which it should have cured. They saw that to live by one man's will became the cause of all men's misery. This constrained them to come unto laws wherein all men might see their duty beforehand, and know the penalties of transgressing them." —Hooker (*Eccl. Pol.,* lib. i., s. 10).

CHAPTER XI

1 "The lawful power of making laws to command whole politic societies of men, belonging so properly unto the same entire societies, that for any prince or potentate, of what kind soever upon earth, to exercise the same of himself, and not by express commission immediately and personally received from God, or else by authority derived at the first from their consent, upon whose persons they impose laws, it is no better than mere tyranny. Laws they are not, therefore, which public approbation hath not made so."—Hooker (*Eccl. Pol.,* lib. i., s. 10). "Of this point, therefore, we are to note that such men naturally have no full and perfect power to command whole politic multitudes of men, therefore utterly without our consent we could in such sort be at no man's commandment living. And to be commanded, we do consent when that society, whereof we be a part, hath at any time before consented, without revoking the same after by the like universal agreement.

"Laws therefore human, of what kind soever, are available by consent."—Hooker (*Eccl. Pol.*).

2 "Two foundations there are which bear up public societies; the one a natural inclination whereby all men desire sociable life and fellowship; the other an order, expressly or secretly agreed upon, touching the manner of their union in living together. The latter

is that which we call the law of a commonweal, the very soul of a politic body, the parts whereof are by law animated, held together, and set on work in such actions as the common good requireth. Laws politic, ordained for external order and regimen amongst men, are never framed as they should be, unless presuming the will of man to be inwardly obstinate, rebellious, and averse from all obedience to the sacred laws of his nature; in a word, unless presuming man to be in regard of his depraved mind little better than a wild beast, they do accordingly provide notwithstanding, so to frame his outward actions, that they be no hindrance unto the common good, for which societies are instituted. Unless they do this they are not perfect."—Hooker (*Eccl. Pol.,* lib. i., s. 10.).

3 "Human laws are measures in respect of men whose actions they must direct, howbeit such measures they are as have also their higher rules to be measured by, which rules are two—the law of God and the law of Nature; so that laws human must be made according to the general laws of Nature, and without contradiction to any positive law of Scripture, otherwise they are ill made."—Hooker (*Eccl. Pol.,* lib. iii., s. 9).

"To constrain men to anything inconvenient doth seem unreasonable."—*Ibid.,* i., 10.)

THE SOCIAL CONTRACT

Jean-Jacques Rousseau

FOREWORD

THIS little treatise is part of a longer work, which I began years ago without realizing my limitations, and long since abandoned. Of the various fragments that might have been extracted from what I wrote, this is the most considerable, and, I think, the least unworthy of being offered to the public. The rest no longer exists.

BOOK I

I mean to inquire if, in the civil order, there can be any sure and legitimate rule of administration, men being taken as they are and laws as they might be. In this inquiry I shall endeavor always to unite what right sanctions with what is prescribed by interest, in order that justice and utility may in no case be divided.

I enter upon my task without proving the importance of the subject. I shall be asked if I am a prince or a legislator, to write on politics. I answer that I am neither, and that is why I do so. If I were a prince or a legislator, I should not waste time in saying what wants doing; I should do it, or hold my peace.

As I was born a citizen of a free State, and a member of the Sovereign, I feel that, however feeble the influence my voice can have on public affairs, the right of voting on them makes it my duty to study them: and I am happy, when I reflect upon governments, to find my inquiries always furnish me with new reasons for loving that of my own country.

I

SUBJECT OF THE FIRST BOOK

MAN is born free; and everywhere he is in chains. One thinks himself the master of others, and still remains a greater slave than they. How did this change come about? I do not know. What can make it legitimate? That question I think I can answer.

If I took into account only force, and the effects derived from it, I should say: "As long as a people is compelled to obey, and obeys, it does well; as soon as it can shake off the yoke, and shakes it off, it does still better; for, regaining its liberty by the same right as took it away, either it is justified in resuming it, or there was no justification for those who took it away." But the social order is a sacred right which is the basis of all other rights. Nevertheless, this right does not come from nature, and must therefore be founded on conventions. Before coming to that, I have to prove what I have just asserted.

II

THE FIRST SOCIETIES

THE most ancient of all societies, and the only one that is natural, is the family: and even so the children remain attached to the father only so long as they need him for their preservation. As soon as this need ceases, the natural bond is dissolved. The children, released from the obedience they owed to the father, and the father, released from the care he owed his children, return equally to independence. If they remain united, they continue so no longer naturally, but voluntarily; and the family itself is then maintained only by convention.

This common liberty results from the nature of man. His first law is to provide for his own preservation, his first cares are those which he owes to himself; and, as soon as he reaches years of discretion, he is the sole judge of the proper means of preserving himself, and consequently becomes his own master.

The family then may be called the first model of political societies: the ruler corresponds to the father, and the people to the children; and all, being born free and equal, alienate their liberty only for their own advantage. The whole difference is that, in the family, the love of the father for his children repays him for the care he takes of them, while, in the State, the pleasure of commanding takes the place of the love which the chief cannot have for the peoples under him.

Grotius denies that all human power is established in favor of the governed, and quotes slavery as an example. His usual method of reasoning is constantly to establish right by fact.[1] It would be possible to employ a more logical method, but none could be more favorable to tyrants.

It is then, according to Grotius, doubtful whether the human race belongs to a hundred men, or that hundred men to the human race: and, throughout his book, he seems to incline to the former alternative, which is also the view of Hobbes. On this showing, the human species is divided into so many herds of cattle, each with its ruler, who keeps guard over them for the purpose of devouring them.

As a shepherd is of a nature superior to that of his flock, the shepherds of men, i.e. their rulers, are of a nature superior to that of the peoples under them. Thus, Philo tells us, the Emperor Caligula reasoned, concluding equally well either that kings were gods, or that men were beasts.

The reasoning of Caligula agrees with that of Hobbes and Grotius. Aristotle, before any of them, had said that men are by no means equal naturally, but that some are born for slavery, and others for dominion.

Aristotle was right; but he took the effect for the cause. Nothing can be more certain than that every man born in slavery is born for slavery. Slaves lose everything in their chains, even the desire of escaping from them: they love their servitude, as the comrades of Ulysses loved their brutish condition.[2] If then there are slaves by nature, it is because there have been slaves against nature. Force made the first slaves, and their cowardice perpetuated the condition.

I have said nothing of King Adam, or Emperor Noah, father of the three great monarchs who shared out the universe, like the children of Saturn, whom some scholars have recognized in them. I trust to getting due thanks for my moderation; for, being a direct descendant of one of these princes, perhaps of the eldest branch, how do I know that a verification of titles might not leave me the legitimate king of the human race? In any case, there can be no doubt that Adam was sovereign of the world, as Robinson Crusoe was of his island, as long as he was its only inhabitant; and this empire had the advantage that the monarch, safe on his throne, had no rebellions, wars, or conspirators to fear.

III

THE RIGHT OF THE STRONGEST

THE strongest is never strong enough to be always the master, unless he transforms strength into right, and obedience into duty. Hence the right of the strongest, which, though to all seeming meant ironically, is really laid down as a fundamental principle. But are we never to have an explanation of this phrase? Force is a physical power, and I fail to see what moral effect it can have. To yield to force is an act of necessity, not of will —at most, an act of prudence. In what sense can it be a duty?

Suppose for a moment that this so-called "right" exists. I maintain that the sole result is a mass of inexplicable nonsense. For, if force creates right, the effect changes with the cause: every force that is greater than the first succeeds to its right. As soon as it is possible to disobey with impunity, disobedience is legitimate; and, the strongest being always in the right, the only thing that matters is to act so as to become the strongest. But what kind of right is that which perishes when force fails? If we must obey perforce, there is no need to obey because we ought; and if we are not forced to obey, we are under no obligation to do so. Clearly, the word 'right' adds nothing to force: in this connection, it means absolutely nothing.

Obey the powers that be. If this means yield to force, it is a good precept, but superfluous: I can answer for its never being violated. All power comes from God, I admit; but so does all sickness: does that mean that we are forbidden to call in the doctor? A brigand surprises me at the edge of a wood: must I not merely surrender my purse on compulsion; but, even if I could withhold it, am I in conscience bound to give it up? For certainly the pistol he holds is also a power.

Let us then admit that force does not create right, and that we are obliged to obey only legitimate powers. In that case, my original question recurs.

IV

SLAVERY

SINCE no man has a natural authority over his fellow, and force creates no right, we must conclude that conventions form the basis of all legitimate authority among men.

If an individual, says Grotius, can alienate his liberty and make himself the slave of a master, why could not a whole people do the same and make itself subject to a king? There are in this passage plenty of ambiguous words which would need explaining; but let us confine ourselves to the word *alienate.* To alienate is to give or to sell. Now, a man who becomes the slave of another does not give himself; he sells himself, at least for his subsistence: but for what does a people sell itself? A king is so far from furnishing his subjects with their subsistence that he gets his own only from them; and, according to Rabelais, kings do not live on nothing. Do subjects then give their persons on condition that the king takes their goods also? I fail to see what they have left to preserve.

It will be said that the despot assures his subjects civil tranquillity. Granted; but what do they gain, if the wars his ambition brings down upon them, his insatiable avidity, and the vexatious conduct of his ministers press harder on them than their own dissensions would have done? What do they gain, if the very tranquillity they enjoy is one of their miseries? Tranquillity is found also in dungeons; but is that enough to make them desirable places to live in? The Greeks imprisoned in the cave of the Cyclops lived there very tranquilly, while they were awaiting their turn to be devoured.

To say that a man gives himself gratuitiously, is to say what is absurd and inconceivable; such an act is null and illegitimate, from the mere fact that he who does it is out of his mind. To say the same of a whole people is to suppose a people of madmen; and madness creates no right.

Even if each man could alienate himself, he could not alienate his children: they are born men and free; their liberty belongs to them, and no one but they has the right to dispose of it. Before they come to years of discretion, the father can, in their name, lay down conditions for their preservation and well-being, but he cannot give them irrevocably and without conditions: such a gift is contrary to the ends of nature, and exceeds the rights of paternity. It would therefore be necessary, in order to legitimize an arbitrary government, that in every generation the people should be in a position to accept or reject it; but, were this so, the government would be no longer arbitrary.

To renounce liberty is to renounce being a man, to surrender the rights of humanity and even its duties. For him who renounces everything no indemnity is possible. Such a renunciation is incomparable with man's nature; to remove all liberty from his will is to remove all morality from his acts. Finally, it is an empty and contradictory convention that sets up, on the one side, absolute authority, and, on the other, unlimited obedience. Is it not clear that we can be under no obligation to a person from whom we have the right to exact everything? Does not this condition alone, in the absence of equivalence or exchange, in itself involve the nullity of the act? For what right can my slave have against me, when all that he has belongs to me, and, his right being mine, this right of mine against myself is a phrase devoid of meaning?

Grotius and the rest find in war another origin for the so-called right of slavery. The victor having, as they hold, the right of killing the vanquished, the latter can buy back his life at the price of his liberty; and this convention is the more legitimate because it is to the advantage of both parties.

But it is clear that this supposed right to kill the conquered is by no means deducible from the state of war. Men, from the mere fact that, while they are living in their primitive independence, they have no mutual relations stable enough to constitute either the state of peace or the state of war, cannot be naturally enemies. War is constituted by a relation between things, and not between persons; and, as the state of war cannot arise out of simple personal relations, but only out of real relations, private war, or war of man with man, can exist neither in the state of nature, where there is no constant property, nor in the social state, where everything is under the authority of the laws.

Individual combats, duels, and encounters, are acts which cannot constitute a state; while the private wars, authorized by the Establishments of Louis IX, King of France, and suspended by the Peace of God, are abuses of feudalism, in itself an absurd system if ever there was one, and contrary to the principles of natural right and to all good polity.

War then is a relation, not between man and man, but between State and State, and individuals are enemies only accidentally, not as men, nor even as citizens,[1] but as soldiers; not as members of their country, but as its defenders. Finally, each State can have for enemies only other States, and not men; for between things disparate in nature there can be no real relation.

Furthermore, this principle is in conformity with the established rules of all times and the constant practice of all civilized peoples. Declarations of war are intimations less to powers then to their subjects. The foreigner, whether king, individual, or people, who robs, kills, or detains the subjects, without declaring war on the prince, is not an enemy, but a brigand. Even in real war, a just prince, while laying hands, in the enemy's country, on all that belongs to the public, respects the lives and goods of individuals: he respects rights on which his own are founded. The object of the war being the destruction of the hostile State, the other side has a right to kill its defenders, while they are bearing arms; but as soon as they lay them down and surrender, they cease to be enemies or instruments of the enemy, and become once more merely men, whose life no one has any right to take. Sometimes it is possible to kill the State without killing a single one of its members; and war gives no right which is not necessary to the gaining of its object. These principles are not those of Grotius: they are not based on the authority of poets, but derived from the nature of reality and based on reason.

The right of conquest has no foundation other than the right of the strongest. If war does not give the conqueror the right to massacre the conquered peoples, the right to enslave them cannot be based upon a right which does not exist. No one has a right to kill an enemy except when he cannot make him a slave, and the right to enslave him cannot therefore be derived from the right to kill him. It is accordingly an unfair exchange to make him buy at the price of his liberty his life, over which the victor holds no right. Is it not clear that there is a vicious circle in founding the right of life and death on the right of slavery, and the right of slavery on the right of life and death?

Even if we assume this terrible right to kill everybody, I maintain that a slave made in war, or a conquered people, is under no obligation to a master, except to obey him as far as he is compelled to do so. By taking an equivalent for his life, the victor has not done him a favor; instead of killing him without profit, he has killed him usefully. So far then is he from acquiring over him any authority in addition to that of force, that the state of war continues to subsist between them: their mutual relation is the effect of it, and the usage of the right of war does not imply a treaty of peace. A convention has indeed been made; but this convention, so far from destroying the state of war, presupposes its continuance.

So, from whatever aspect we regard the question, the right of slavery is null and void, not only as being illegitimate, but also because it is absurd and meaningless. The words *slave* and *right* contradict each other, and are mutually exclusive. It will always be equally foolish for a man to say to a man or to a people: "I make with you a convention wholly at your expense and wholly to my advantrage; I shall keep it as long as I like, and you will keep it as long as I like."

V

THAT WE MUST ALWAYS GO BACK TO A FIRST CONVENTION

EVEN if I granted all that I have been refuting, the friends of despotism would be no better off. There will always be a great difference between subduing a multitude and ruling a society. Even if scattered individuals were successively enslaved by one man, however numerous they might be, I still see no more than a master and his slaves, and certainly not a people and its ruler; I see what may be termed an aggregation, but not an association; there is as yet neither public good nor body politic. The man in question, even if he has enslaved half the world, is still only an individual; his interest, apart from that of others, is still purely private interest. If this same man comes to die, his empire, after him, remains scattered and without unity, as an oak falls and dissolves into a heap of ashes when the fire has consumed it.

A people, says Grotius, can give itself to a king. Then, according to Grotius, a people is a people before it gives itself. The gift is itself a civil act, and implies public deliberation. It would be better, before examining the act by which a people gives itself to a king, to examine that by which it has become a people; for this act, being necessarily prior to the other, is the true foundation of society.

Indeed, if there were no prior convention, where, unless the election were unanimous, would be the obligation on the minority to submit to the choice of the majority? How have a hundred men who wish for a master the right to vote on behalf of ten who do not? The law of majority voting is itself something established by convention, and presupposes unanimity, on one occasion at least.

VI

THE SOCIAL COMPACT

I suppose men to have reached the point at which the obstacles in the way of their preservation in the state of nature show their power of resistance to be greater than the resources at the disposal of each individual for his maintenance in that state. That primitive condition can then subsist no longer; and the human race would perish unless it changed its manner of existence.

But, as men cannot engender new forces, but only unite and direct existing ones, they have no other means of preserving themselves than the formation, by aggregation, of a sum of forces great enough to overcome the resistance. These they have to bring into play by means of a single motive power, and cause to act in concert.

This sum of forces can arise only where several persons come together: but, as the force and liberty of each man are the chief instruments of his self-preservation, how can he pledge them without harming his own interests, and neglecting the care he owes to himself? This difficulty, in its bearing on my present subject, may be stated in the following terms:

"The problem is to find a form of association which will defend and protect with the whole common force the person and goods of each associate, and in which each, while uniting himself with all, may still obey himself alone, and remain as free as before." This is the fundamental problem of which the *Social Contract* provides the solution.

The clauses of this contract are so determined by the nature of the act that the slightest modification would make them vain and ineffective; so that, although they have perhaps never been formally set forth, they are everywhere the same and everywhere tacitly admitted and recognized, until, on the violation of the social compact, each regains his original rights and resumes his natural liberty, while losing the conventional liberty in favor of which he renounced it.

These clauses, properly understood, may be reduced to one—the total alienation of each associate, together with all his rights, to the whole community; for, in the first place, as each gives himself absolutely, the conditions are the same for all; and, this being so, no one has any interest in making them burdensome to others.

Moreover, the alienation being without reserve, the union is as perfect as it can be, and no associate has anything more to demand: for, if the individuals retained certain rights, as there would be no common superior to decide between them and the public, each, being on one point his own judge, would ask to be so on all; the state of nature would thus continue, and the association would necessarily become inoperative or tyrannical.

Finally, each man, in giving himself to all, gives himself to nobody; and as there is no associate over which he does not acquire the same right as he yields others over himself, he gains an equivalent for everything he loses, and an increase of force for the preservation of what he has.

If then we discard from the social compact what is not of its essence, we shall find that it reduces itself to the following terms:

"Each of us puts his person and all his power in common under the supreme direction of the general will, and, in our corporate capacity, we receive each member as an indivisible part of the whole."

At once, in place of the individual personality of each contracting party, this act of association creates a moral and collective body composed of as many members as the assembly contains voters, and receiving from this act its unity, its common identity, its life, and its will. The public person, so formed by the union of all other persons, formerly took the name of *city,*[1] and now takes that of *Republic* or *body politic;* it is called by its members *State* when passive, *Sovereign* when active, and *Power* when compared with others like itself. Those who are associated in it take collectively the name of *people,* and severally are called *citizens,* as sharing in the sovereign power, and *subjects,* as being under the laws of the State. But these terms are often confused and taken one for another: it is enough to know how to distinguish them when they are being used with precision.

VII

THE SOVEREIGN

THIS formula shows us that the act of association comprises a mutual undertaking between the public and the individuals, and that each individual, in making a contract, as we may say, with himself, is bound in a double capacity; as a member of the Sovereign he is bound to the individuals, and as a member of the State to the Sovereign. But the maxim of civil right, that no one is bound by undertakings made to himself does not apply in this case; for there is a great difference between incurring an obligation to yourself and incurring one to a whole of which you form a part.

Attention must further be called to the fact that public deliberation, while competent to bind all the subjects to the Sovereign, because of the two different capacities in which each of them may be regarded, cannot, for the opposite reason, bind the Sovereign to itself; and that it is consequently against the nature of the body politic for the Sovereign to impose on itself a law which it cannot infringe. Being able to regard itself in only one capacity, it is in the position of an individual who makes a contract with himself; and this makes it clear that there neither is nor can be any kind of fundamental law binding on the body of the people—not even the social contract itself. This does not mean that the body politic cannot enter into undertakings with others, provided the contract is not infringed by them; for in relation to what is external to it, it becomes a simple being, an individual.

But the body politic or the Sovereign, drawing its being wholly from the sanctity of the contract, can never bind itself, even to an outsider, to do anything derogatory to the original act, for instance, to alienate any part of itself, or to submit to another Sovereign. Violation of the act by which it exists would be self-annihilation; and that which is itself nothing can create nothing.

As soon as this multitude is so united in one body, it is impossible to offend against one of the members without attacking the body, and still more to offend against the body without the members resenting it. Duty and interest therefore equally oblige the two contracting parties to give each other help; and the same men should seek to combine, in their double capacity, all the advantages dependent upon that capacity.

Again, the Sovereign, being formed wholly of the individuals who compose it, neither has nor can have any interest contrary to theirs; and consequently the sovereign power need give no guarantee to its subjects, because it is impossible for the body to wish to hurt all its members. We shall also see later on that it cannot hurt any in particular. The Sovereign, merely by virtue of what it is, is always what it should be.

This, however, is not the case with the relation of the subjects to the Sovereign, which, despite the common interest, would have no security that they would fulfil their undertakings, unless it found means to assure itself of their fidelity.

In fact, each individual, as a man, may have a particular will contrary or dissimilar to the general will which he has as a citizen. His particuilar interest may speak to him quite differently from the common interest: his absolute and naturally independent existence may make him look upon what he owes to the common cause as a gratuitous contribution, the loss of which will do no less harm to others than the payment of it is burdensome to himself; and, regarding the moral person which constitutes the State as a *persona ficta,* because not a man, he may wish to enjoy the rights of citizenship without being ready to fulfil the duties of a subject. The continuance of such an injustice could not but prove the undoing of the body politic.

In order then that the social compact may not be an empty formula, it tacitly includes the undertaking, which alone can give force to the rest, that whoever refuses to obey the general will shall be compelled to do so by the whole body. This means nothing less than that he will be forced to be free; for this is the condition which, by giving each citizen to his country, secures him against all personal dependence. In this lies the key to the working of the political machine; this alone legitimizes civil undertakings, which, without it, would be absurd, tyrannical, and liable to the most frightful abuses.

VIII

THE CIVIL STATE

THE passage from the state of nature to the civil state produces a very remarkable change in man, by substituting justice for instinct in his conduct, and giving his actions the morality they had formerly lacked. Then only, when the voice of duty takes the place of physical impulses and right of appetite, does man, who so far had considered only himself, find that he is forced to act on different principles, and to consult his reason before listening to his inclinations. Although, in this state, he deprives himself of some advantages which he got from nature, he gains in return others so great, his faculties are so stimulated and developed, his ideas so extended, his feelings so ennobled, and his whole soul so uplifted, that, did not the abuses of this new condition often degrade him below that which he left, he would be bound to bless continually the happy moment which took him from it for ever, and, instead of a stupid and unimaginative animal, made him an intelligent being and a man.

Let us draw up the whole account in terms easily commensurable. What man loses by the social contract is his natural liberty and an unlimited right to everything he tries to get and succeeds in getting; what he gains is civil liberty and the proprietorship of all he possesses. If we are to avoid mistake in weighing one against the other, we must clearly distinguish natural liberty, which is bounded only by the strength of the individual from civil liberty, which is limited by the general will and possession, which is merely the effect of force or the right of the first occupier, from property, which can be founded only on a positive title.

We might, over and above all this, add, to what man acquires in the civil state, moral liberty, which alone makes him truly master of himself; for the mere impulse of appetite is slavery, while obedience to a law which we prescribe to ourselves is liberty. But I have already said too much on this head, and the philosophical meaning of the word liberty does not now concern us.

IX

REAL PROPERTY

EACH member of the community gives himself to it, at the moment of its foundation, just as he is, with all the resources at his command, including the goods he possesses. This act does not make possession, in changing hands, change its nature, and become property in the hands of the Sovereign; but, as the forces of the city are incomparably greater than those of an individual, public possession is also, in fact, stronger and more irrevocable, without being any more legitimate, at any rate from the point of view of foreigners. For the State, in relation to its members, is master of all their goods by the social contract, which, within the State, is the basis of all rights; but, in relation to other powers, it is so only by the right of the first occupier, which it holds from its members.

The right of the first occupier, though more real than the right of the strongest, becomes a real right only when the right of property has already been established. Every man has naturally a right to everything he needs; but the positive act which makes him proprietor of one thing excludes him from everything else. Having his share, he ought to keep to it, and can have no further right against the community. This is why the right of the first occupier, which in the state of nature is so weak, claims the respect of every man in civil society. In this right we are respecting not so much what belongs to another as what does not belong to ourselves.

In general, to establish the right of the first occupier over a plot of ground, the following conditions are necessary: first, the land must not yet be inhabited; secondly, a man must occupy only the amount he needs for his subsistence; and, in the third place, possession must be taken, not by an empty ceremony, but by labor and cultivation, the only sign of proprietorship that should be respected by others, in default of a legal title.

In granting the right of first occupancy to necessity and labor, are we not really stretching it as far as it can go? Is it possible to leave such a right unlimited? Is it to be enough to set foot on a plot of common ground, in order to be able to call yourself at once the master of it? Is it to be enough that a man has the strength to expel others for a moment, in order to establish his right to prevent them from ever returning? How can a man or a people seize an immense territory and keep it from the rest of the world except by a punishable usurpation, since all others are being robbed, by such an act, of the place of habitation and the means of subsistence which nature gave them in common? When Nuñez Balbao, standing on the seashore, took possession of the South Seas and the whole of South America in the name of the crown of Castille, was that enough to dispossess all their actual inhabitants, and to shut out from them all the princes of the world? On such a showing, these ceremonies are idly multiplied, and the Catholic King need only take possession all at once, from his apartment, of the whole universe, merely making a subsequent reservation about what was already in the possession of other princes.

We can imagine how the lands of individuals, where they were contiguous and came to be united, became the public territory, and how the right of Sovereignty, extending from the subjects over the lands they held, became at once real and personal. The possessors were thus made more dependent, and the forces at their command used to guarantee their fidelity. The advantage of this does not seem to have been felt by ancient monarchs, who called themselves King of the Persians, Scythians, or Macedonians, and seemed to regard themselves more as rulers of men than as masters of a country. Those of the present day more cleverly call themselves Kings of France, Spain, England, etc.: thus holding the land, they are quite confident of holding the inhabitants.

The peculiar fact about this alienation is that, in taking over the goods of individuals, the community, so far from despoiling them, only assures them legitimate possession, and changes usurpation into a true right and enjoyment into proprietorship. Thus the possessors, being regarded as depositaries of the public good, and having their rights respected by all the members of the State and maintained against foreign aggression by all its forces, have, by a cession which benefits both the public and still more themselves, acquired, so to speak, all that they gave up. This paradox may easily be explained by the distinction between the rights which the Sovereign and the proprietor have over the same estate, as we shall see later on.

It may also happen that men begin to unite one with another before they possess anything, and that, subsequently occupying a tract of country which is enough for all, they enjoy it in common, or share it out among themselves, either equally or according to a scale fixed by the Sovereign. However the acquisition be made, the right which each individual has to his own estate is always subordinate to the right which the community has over all: without this, there would be neither stability in the social tie, nor real force in the exercise of Sovereignty.

I shall end this chapter and this book by remarking on a fact on which the whole social system should rest: i.e. that, instead of destroying natural inequality, the fundamental compact substitutes, for such physical inequality as nature may have set up between men, an equality that is moral and legitimate, and that men, who may be unequal in strength or intelligence, become every one equal by convention and legal right.[1]

BOOK II

I

THAT SOVEREIGNTY IS INALIENABLE

THE first and most important deduction from the principles we have so far laid down is the general will alone can direct the State according to the object for which it was instituted, i.e. the common good: for if the clashing of particular interests made the establishment of societies necessary, the agreement of these very interests made it possible. The common element in these different interests is what forms the social tie; and, were there no point of agreement between them all, no society could exist. It is solely on the basis of this common interest that every society should be governed.

I hold then that Sovereignty, being nothing less then the exercise of the general will, can never be alienated, and that the Sovereign, who is no less than a collective being, cannot be represented except by himself: the power indeed may be transmitted, but not the will.

In reality, if it is not impossible for a particular will to agree on some point with the general will, it is at least impossible for the agreement to be lasting and constant; for the particular will tends, by its very nature, to partiality, while the general will tends to equality. It is even more impossible to have any guarantee of this agreement; for even if it should always exist, it would be the effect not of art, but of chance. The Sovereign may indeed say: "I now will actually what this man wills, or at least what he says he wills"; but it cannot say: "What he wills to-morrow, I too shall will" because it is absurd for the will to bind itself for the future, nor is it incumbent on any will to consent to anything that is not for the good of the being who wills. If then the people promises simply to obey, by that very act it dissolves itself and loses what makes it a people; the moment a master exists, there is no longer a Sovereign, and from that moment the body politic has ceased to exist.

This does not mean that the commands of the rulers cannot pass for general wills, so long as the Sovereign, being free to oppose them, offers no opposition. In such a case, universal silence is taken to imply the consent of the people. This will be explained later on.

II

THAT SOVEREIGNTY IS INDIVISIBLE

SOVEREIGNTY, for the same reason as makes it inalienable, is indivisible; for will either is, or is not general;[1] it is the will either of the body of the people, or only of a part of it. In the first case, the will, when declared, is an act of Sovereignty and constitutes law: in the second, it is merely a particular will, or act of magistracy—at the most a decree.

But our political theorists, unable to divide Sovereignty in principle, divide it according to its object: into force and will; into legislative power and executive power; into rights of taxation, justice, and war; into internal administration and power of foreign treaty. Sometimes they confuse all these sections, and sometimes they distinguish them; they turn the Sovereign into a fantastic being composed of several connected pieces: it is as if they were making man of several bodies, one with eyes, one with arms, another with feet, and each with nothing besides. We are told that the jugglers of Japan dismember a child before the eyes of the spectators; then they throw all the members into the air one after another, and the child falls down alive and whole. The conjuring tricks of our political theorists are very like that; they first dismember the body politic by an illusion worthy of a fair, and then join it together again we know not how.

This error is due to a lack of exact notions concerning the Sovereign authority, and to taking for parts of it what are only emanations from it. Thus, for example, the acts of declaring war and making peace have been regarded as acts of Sovereignty; but this is not the case, as these acts do not consititute law, but merely the application of a law, a particular act which decides how the law applies, as we shall see clearly when the idea attached to the word "law" has been defined.

If we examined the other divisions in the same manner, we should find that, whenever Sovereignty seems to be divided, there is an illusion: the rights which are taken as being part of Sovereignty are really all subordinate, and always imply supreme wills of which they only sanction the execution.

It would be impossible to estimate the obscurity this lack of exactness has thrown over the decisions of writers who have dealt with political right, when they have used the principles laid down by them to pass judgment on the respective rights of kings and peoples. Every one can see, in Chapters III and IV of the first book of Grotius, how the learned man and his translator, Barbeyrac, entangle and tie themselves up in their own sophistries, for fear of saying too little or too much of what they think, and so offending the interests they have to conciliate. Grotius, a refugee in France, ill content with his own country, and desirous of paying his court to Louis XIII, to whom his book is dedicated, spares no pains to rob the peoples of all their rights and invest kings with them by every conceivable artifice. This would also have been much to the taste of Barbeyrac, who dedicated his translation to George I of England. But unfortunately the expulsion of James II, which he called his "abdication," compelled him to use all reserve, to shuffle and to tergiversate, in order to avoid making William out a usurper. If these two writers had adopted the true principles, all difficulties would have been removed, and they would have been always consistent; but it would have been a sad truth for them to tell, and would have paid court for them to no one save the people. Moreover, truth is no road to fortune, and the people dispenses neither ambassadorships, nor professorships, nor pensions.

III

WHETHER THE GENERAL WILL IS FALLIBLE

It follows from what has gone before that the general will is always right and tends to the public advantage; but it does not follow that the deliberations of the people are always equally correct. Our will is always for our own good, but we do not always see what that is; the people is never corrupted, but it is often deceived, and on such occasions only does it seem to will what is bad.

There is often a great deal of difference between the will of all and the general will; the latter considers only the common interest, while the former takes private interest into account, and is no more than a sum of particular wills: but take away from these same wills the pluses and minuses that cancel one another,[1] and the general will remains as the sum of the differences.

If, when the people, being furnished with adequate information, held its deliberations, the citizens had no communication one with another, the grand total of the small differences would always give the general will, and the decision would always be good. But when factions arise, and partial associations are formed at the expense of the great association, the will of each of these associations becomes general in relation to its members, while it remains particular in relation to the State: it may then be said that there are no longer as many votes as there are men, but only as many as there are associations. The differences become less numerous and give a less general result. Lastly, when one of these associations is so great as to prevail over all the rest, the result is no longer a sum of small differences, but a single difference; in this case there is no longer a general will, and the opinion which prevails is purely particular.

It is therefore essential, if the general will is to be able to express itself, that there should be no partial society within the State, and that each citizen should think only his own thoughts:[2] which was indeed the sublime and unique system established by the great Lycurgus. But if there are partial societies, it is best to have as many as possible and to prevent them from being unequal, as was done by Solon, Numa and Servius. These precautions are the only ones that can guarantee that the general will shall be always enlightened, and that the people shall in no way deceive itself.

IV

THE LIMITS OF THE SOVEREIGN POWER

If the State is a moral person whose life is in the union of its members, and if the most important of its cares is the care for its own preservation, it must have a universal and compelling force, in order to move and dispose each part as may be most advantageous to the whole. As nature gives each man absolute power over all his members, the social compact gives the body politic absolute power over all its members also; and it is this power which, under the direction of the general will, bears, as I have said, the name of Sovereignty.

But, besides the public person, we have to consider the private persons composing it, whose life and liberty are naturally independent of it. We are bound then to distinguish clearly between the respective rights of the citizens and the Sovereign,[1] and between the duties the former have to fulfil as subjects, and the natural rights they should enjoy as men.

Each man alienates, I admit, by the social compact, only such part of his powers, goods, and liberty as it is important for the community to control; but it must also be granted that the Sovereign is sole judge of what is important.

Every service a citizen can render the State he ought to render as soon as the Sovereign demands it; but the Sovereign, for its part, cannot impose upon its subjects any fetters that are useless to the community, nor can it even wish to do so; for no more by the law of reason than by the law of nature can anything occur without a cause.

The undertakings which bind us to the social body are obligatory only because they are mutual; and their nature is such that in fulfilling them we cannot work for others without working for ourselves. Why is it that the general will is always in the right, and that all continually will the happiness of each one, unless it is because there is not a man who does not think of 'each' as meaning him, and consider himself in voting for all? This proves that equality of rights and the idea of justice which such equality creates originate in the preference each man gives to himself, and accordingly in the very nature of man. It proves that the general will, to be really such, must be general in its object as well as its essence; that it must both come from all and apply to all; and that it loses its natural rectitude when it is directed to some particular and determinate object, because in such a case we are judging of something foreign to us, and have no true principle of equity to guide us.

Indeed, as soon as a question of particular fact or right arises on a point not previously regulated by a general convention, the matter becomes contentious. It is a case in which the individuals concerned are one party, and the public the other, but in which I can see neither the law that ought to be followed nor the judge who ought to give the decision. In such a case, it would be absurd to propose to refer the question to an express decision of the general will, which can be only the conclusion reached by one of the parties and in consequence will be, for the other party, merely an external and particular will, inclined on this occasion to injustice and subject to error. Thus, just as a particular will cannot stand for the general will, the general will, in turn, changes its nature, when its object is particular, and, as general, cannot pronounce on a man or a fact. When, for instance, the people of Athens nominated or displaced its rulers, decreed honors to one, and imposed penalties on another, and, by a multitude of particular decrees, exercised all the functions of government indiscriminately, it had in such cases no longer a general will in the strict sense; it was acting no longer as Sovereign, but as magistrate. This will seem contrary to current views; but I must be given time to expound my own.

It should be seen from the foregoing that what makes the will general is less the number of voters than the common interest uniting them; for, under this system, each necessarily submits to the conditions he imposes on other: and this admirable agreement between interest and justice gives to the common deliberations an equitable character which at once vanishes when any particular question is discussed, in the absence of a common interest to unite and identify the ruling of the judge with that of the party.

From whatever side we approach our principle, we reach the same conclusion, that the social compact sets up among the citizens an equality of such a kind, that they all bind themselves to observe the same conditions and should therefore all enjoy the same rights. Thus, from the very nature of the compact, every act of Sovereignty, i.e. every authentic act of the general will, binds or favors all the citizens equally; so that the Sovereign recognizes only the body of the nation, and draws no distinctions between those of whom it is made up. What, then, strictly speaking, is an act of Sovereignty? It is not a convention between a superior and an inferior, but a convention between the body and each of its members. It is legitimate, because based on the social contract, and equitable, because common to all; useful, because it can have no other object than the general good, and stable because guaranteed by the public force and the supreme power. So long as the subjects have to submit only to conventions of this sort, they obey no one but their own will; and to ask how far the respective rights of the Sovereign and the citizens extend, is to ask up to what point the latter can enter into undertakings with themselves, each with all, and all with each.

We can see from this that the sovereign power, absolute, sacred, and inviolable as it is, does not and cannot exceed the limits of general conventions, and that every man may dispose at will of such goods and liberty as these conventions leave him; so that the Sovereign never has a right to lay more charges on one subject than on another, because, in that case, the question becomes particular, and ceases to be within its competency.

When these distinctions have once been admitted, it is seen to be so untrue that there is, in the social contract, any real renunciation on the part of the individuals, that the position in which they find themselves as a result of the contract is really preferable to that in which they were before. Instead of a renunciation, they have made an advantageous exchange: instead of an uncertain and precarious way of living they have got one that is better and more secure; instead of natural independence they have got liberty, instead of the power to harm others security for themselves, and instead of their strength, which others might overcome, a right which social union makes invincible. Their very life, which they have devoted to the State, is by it constantly protected; and when they risk it in the State's defense, what more are they doing than giving back what they have received from it? What are they doing that they would not do more often and with greater danger in the state of nature, in which they would inevitably have to fight battles at the peril of their lives in defense of that which is the means of their preservation? All have indeed to fight when their country needs them; but then no one has ever to fight for himself. Do we not gain something by running, on behalf of what gives us our security, only some of the risks we should have to run for ourselves, as soon as we lost it?

V

THE RIGHT OF LIFE AND DEATH

THE question is often asked how individuals, having no right to dispose of their own lives, can transfer to the Sovereign a right which they do not possess. The difficulty of answering this question seems to me to lie in its being wrongly stated. Every man has a right to risk his own life in order to preserve it. Has it ever been said that a man who throws himself out of the window to escape from a fire is guilty of suicide? Has such a crime ever been laid to the charge of him who perishes in a storm because, when he went on board, he knew of the danger?

The social treaty has for its end the preservation of the contracting parties. He who wills the end wills the means also, and the means must involve some risks, and even some losses. He who wishes to preserve his life at others' expense should also, when it is necessary, be ready to give it up for their sake. Furthermore, the citizen is no longer the judge of the dangers to which the law desires him to expose himself; and when the prince says to him: "It is expedient for the State that you should die," he ought to die, because it is only on that condition that he has been living in security up to the present, and because his life is no longer a mere bounty of nature, but a gift made conditionally by the State.

The death-penalty inflicted upon criminals may be looked on in much the same light: it is in order that we may not fall victims to an assassin that we consent to die if we ourselves turn assassins. In this treaty, so far from disposing of our own lives, we think only of securing them, and it is not to be assumed that any of the parties then expects to get hanged.

Again, every malefactor, by attacking social rights, becomes on forfeit a rebel and a traitor to his country; by violating its laws he ceases to be a member of it; he even makes war upon it. In such a case the preservation of the State is inconsistent with his own, and one or the other must perish; in putting the guilty to death, we slay not so much the citizen as an enemy. The trial and the judgment are the proofs that he has broken the social treaty, and is in consequence no longer a member of the State. Since, then, he has recognized himself to be such by living there, he must be removed by exile as a violator of the compact, or by death as a public enemy; for such an enemy is not a moral person but merely a man; and in such a case the right of war is to kill the vanquished.

But, it will be said, the condemnation of a criminal is a particular act. I admit it: but such condemnation is not a function of the Sovereign; it is a right the Sovereign can confer without being able itself to exert it. All my ideas are consistent, but I cannot expound them all at once.

We may add that frequent punishments are always a sign of weakness or remissness on the part of the government. There is not a single ill-doer who could not be turned to some good. The State has no right to put to death, even for the sake of making an example, any one whom it can leave alive without danger.

The right of pardoning or exempting the guilty from a penalty imposed by the law and pronounced by the judge belongs only to the authority which is superior to both judge and law, i.e. the Sovereign; even its right in this matter is far from clear, and the cases for exercising it are extremely rare. In a well-governed State, there are few punishments, not because there are many pardons, but because criminals are rare; it is when a State is in decay that the multitude of crimes is a guarantee of impunity. Under the Roman Republic, neither the senate nor the consuls ever attempted to pardon; even the people never did so, though it sometimes revoked its own decision. Frequent pardons mean that crime will soon need them no longer, and no one can help seeing whither that leads. But I feel my heart protesting and restraining my pen; let us leave these questions to the just man who has never offended, and would himself stand in no need of pardon.

VI

LAW

By the social compact we have given the body politic existence and life; we have now by legislation to give it movement and will. For the original act by which the body is formed and united still in no respect determines what it ought to do for its preservation.

What is well and in conformity with order is so by the nature of things and independently of human conventions. All justice comes from God, who is its sole source; but if we knew how to receive so high an inspiration, we should need neither government nor laws. Doubtless, there is a universal justice emanating from reason alone; but this justice, to be admitted among us, must be mutual. Humanly speaking, in default of natural sanctions, the laws of justice are ineffective among men: they merely make for the good of the wicked and the undoing of the just, when the just man observes them towards everybody and nobody observes them towards him. Conventions and laws are therefore needed to join rights to duties and refer justice to its object. In the state of nature, where everything is common, I owe nothing to him whom I have promised nothing; I recognize as belonging to others only what is of no use to me. In the state of society all rights are fixed by law, and the case becomes different.

But what, after all, is a law? As long as we remain satisfied with attaching purely metaphysical ideas to the word, we shall go on arguing without arriving at an understanding; and when we have defined a law of nature, we shall be no nearer the definition of a law of the State.

I have already said that there can be no general will directed to a particular object. Such an object must be either within or outside the State. If outside, a will which is alien to it cannot be, in relation to it, general; if within, it is part of the State, and in that case there arises a relation between whole and part which makes them two separate beings, of which the part is one, and the whole minus the part the other. But the whole minus a part cannot be the whole; and while this relation persists, there can be no whole, but only two unequal parts; and it follows that the will of one is no longer in any respect general in relation to the other.

But when the whole people decrees for the whole people, it is considering only itself; and if a relation is then formed, it is between two aspects of the entire object, without there being any division of the whole. In that case the matter about which the decree is made is, like the decreeing will, general. This act is what I call a law.

When I say that the object of laws is always general, I mean that law considers subjects *en masse* and actions in the abstract, and never a particular person or action. Thus the law may indeed decree that there shall be privileges, but cannot confer them on anybody by name. It may set up several classes of citizens, and even lay down the qualifications for membership of these classes, but it cannot nominate such and such persons as belonging to them; it may establish a monarchical government and hereditary succession, but it cannot choose a king, or nominate a royal family. In a word, no function which has a particular object belongs to the legislative power.

On this view, we at once see that it can no longer be asked whose business it is to make laws, since they are acts of the general will; nor whether the prince is above the law, since he is a member of the State; nor whether the law can be unjust, since no one is unjust to himself; nor how we can be both free and subject to the laws, since they are but registers of our wills.

We see further that, as the law unites universality of will with universality of object, what a man, whoever he be, commands of his own motion cannot be a law; and even with the Sovereign commands with regard to a particular matter is no nearer being a law, but is a decree, an act, not of sovereignty, but of magistracy.

I therefore give the name "Republic" to every State that is governed by laws, no matter what the form of its administration may be: for only in such a case does the public interest govern and the *res publica* rank as a *reality*. Every legitimate government is republican,[1] what government is I will explain later on.

Laws are, properly speaking, only the conditions of civil association. The people, being subject to the laws, ought to be their author: the conditions of the society ought to be regulated solely by those who come together to form it. But how are they to regulate them? Is it to be by common agreement, by a sudden inspiration? Has the body politic an organ to declare its will? Who can give it the foresight to formulate and announce its acts in advance? Or how is it to announce them in the hour of need? How can a blind multitude, which often does not know what it wills, because it rarely knows what is good for it, carry out for itself so great and difficult an enterprise as a system of legislation? Of itself the people will always the good, but of itself it by no means always sees it. The general will is always in the right, but the judgment which guides it is not always enlightened. It must be got to see objects as they are, and sometimes as they ought to appear to it; it must be shown the good road it is in search of, secured from the seductive influences of individual wills, taught to see times and spaces as a series, and made to weight the attractions of present and sensible advantages against the danger of distant and hidden evils. The individuals see the good they reject; the public wills the good it does not see. All stand equally in need of guidance. The former must be compelled to bring their wills into conformity with their reason; the latter must be taught to know what it wills. If that is done, public enlightenment leads to the union of understanding and will in the social body: the parts are made to work exactly together, and the whole is raised to its highest power. This makes a legislator necessary.

VII

THE LEGISLATOR

IN order to discover the rules of society best suited to nations, a superior intelligence beholding all the passions of men without experiencing any of them would be needed. This intelligence would have to be wholly unrelated to our nature, while knowing it through and through; its happiness would have to be independent of us, and yet ready to occupy itself with ours; and lastly, it would have, in the march of time, to look forward to a distant glory, and, working in one century, to be able to enjoy in the next.[1] It would take gods to give men laws.

What Caligula argued from the facts, Plato, in the dialogue called the *Politicus,* argued in defining the civil or kingly man, on the basis of right. But if great princes are rare, how much more so are great legislators! The former have only to follow the pattern which the latter have to lay down. The legislator is the engineer who invents the machine, the prince merely the mechanic who sets it up and makes it go. "At the birth of societies," says Montesquieu, "the rulers of Republics establish institutions, and afterwards the institutions mold the rulers."[2]

He who dares to undertake the making of a people's institutions ought to feel himself capable, so to speak, of changing human nature, of transforming each individual, who is by himself a complete and solitary whole, into part of a greater whole from which he in a manner receives his life and being; of altering man's constitution for the purpose of strengthening it; and of substituting a partial and moral existence for the physical and independent existence nature has conferred on us all. He must, in a word, take away from man his own resources and give him instead new ones alien to him, and incapable of being made use of without the help of other men. The more completely these natural resources are annihilated, the greater and the more lasting are those which he acquires, and the more stable and perfect the new institutions; so that if each citizen is nothing and can do nothing without the rest, and the resources acquired by the whole are equal or superior to the aggregate of the resources of all the individuals, it may be said that legislation is at the highest possible point of perfection.

The legislator occupies in every respect an extraordinary position in the State. If he should do so by reason of his genius, he does so no less by reason of his office, which is neither magistracy, nor Sovereignty. This office, which sets up the Republic, nowhere enters into its constitution; it is an individual and superior function, which has nothing in common with human empire; for if he who holds command over men ought not to have command over the laws, he who has command over the laws ought not any more to have it over men; or else his laws would be the ministers of his passions and would often merely serve to perpetuate his injustices: his private aims would inevitably mar the sanctity of his work.

When Lycurgus gave laws to his country, he began by resigning the throne. It was the custom of most Greek towns to entrust the establishment of their laws to foreigners. The Republics of modern Italy in many cases followed this example; Geneva did the same and profited by it.[3] Rome, when it was most prosperous, suffered a revival of all the crimes of tyranny, and was brought to the verge of destruction, because it put the legislative authority and the sovereign power into the same hands.

Nevertheless, the decemvirs themselves never claimed the right to pass any law merely on their own authority. "Nothing we propose to you," they said to the people, "can pass into law without your consent. Romans, be yourselves the authors of the laws which are to make you happy."

He, therefore, who draws up the laws has, or should have, no right of legislation, and the people cannot, even if it wishes, deprive itself of this incommunicable right, because, according to the fundamental compact, only the general will can bind the individuals, and there can be no assurance that a particular will is in conformity with the general will, until it has been put to the free vote of the people. This I have said already; but it is worth while to repeat it.

Thus in the task of legislation we find together two things which appear to be incompatible: an enterprise too difficult for human powers, and, for its execution, an authority that is no authority.

There is a farther difficulty that deserves attention. Wise men, if they try to speak their language to the common herd instead of its own, cannot possibly make themselves understood. There are a thousand kinds of ideas which it is impossible to translate into popular language. Conceptions that are too general and objects that are too remote are equally out of its range: each individual, having no taste for any other plan of government than that which suits his particular interest, finds it difficult to realize the advantages he might hope to draw from the continual privations good laws impose. For a young people to be able to relish sound principles of political theory and follow the fundamental rules of statecraft, the effect would have to become the cause; the social spirit which should be created by these institutions, would have to preside over their very foundation; and men would have to be before law what they should become by means of law. The legislator therefore, being unable to appeal to either force or reason, must have recourse to an authority of a different order, capable of constraining without violence and persuading without convincing.

This is what has, in all ages, compelled the fathers of nations to have recourse to devine intervention and credit the gods with their own wisdom, in order that the peoples, submitting to the laws of the State as to those of nature, and recognizing the same power in the formation of the city as in that of man, might obey freely, and bear with docility the yoke of the public happiness.

This sublime reason, far above the range of the common herd, is that whose decisions the legislator puts into the mouth of the immortals, in order to constrain by divine authority those whom human prudence could not move.[4] But it is not anybody who can make the gods speak, or get himself believed when he proclaims himself their intepreter. The great soul of the legislator is the only miracle that can prove his mission. Any man may grave tablets of stone, or buy an oracle, or feign secret intercourse with some divinity, or train a bird to whisper in his ear, or find other vulgar ways of imposing on the people. He whose knowledge goes no further may perhaps gather round him a band of fools; but he will never found an empire, and his extravagances will quickly perish with him. Idle tricks form a passing tie; only wisdom can make it lasting. The Judaic law, which still subsists, and that of the child of Ishmael, which, for ten centuries, has ruled half the world, still proclaim the great men who laid them down; and, while the pride of philosophy or the blind spirit of faction sees in them no more than lucky impostures, the true political theorist admires, in the institutions they set up, the great and powerful genius which presides over things made to endure.

We should not, with Warburton, conclude from this that politics and religion have among us a common object, but that, in the first periods of nations, the one is used as an instrument for the other.

VIII

THE PEOPLE

As, before putting up a large building, the architect surveys and sounds the site to see if it will bear the weight, the wise legislator does not begin by laying down laws good in themselves, but by investigating the fitness of the people for which they are destined, to receive them. Plato refused to legislate for the Arcadians and the Cyrenaeans, because he knew that both peoples were rich and could not put up with equality; and good laws and bad men were found together in Crete, because Minos had inflicted discipline on a people already burdened with vice.

A thousand nations have achieved earthly greatness, that could never have endured good laws; even such as could have endured them could have done so only for a very brief period of their long history. Most peoples, like most men, are docile only in youth; as they grow old they become incorrigible. When once customs have become established and prejudices inveterate, it is dangerous and useless to attempt their reformation; the people, like the foolish and cowardly patients who rave at sight of the doctor, can no longer bear that any one should lay hands on its faults to remedy them.

There are indeed times in the history of States when, just as some kinds of illness turn men's heads and make them forget the past, periods of violence and revolutions do to peoples what these crises do to individuals: horror of the past takes the place of forgetfulness, and the State, set on fire by civil wars, is born again, so to speak, from its ashes, and takes on anew, fresh from the jaws of death, the vigor of youth. Such were Sparta at the time of Lycurgus, Rome after the Tarquins, and, in modern times, Holland and Switzerland after the expulsion of the tyrants.

But such events are rare; they are exceptions, the cause of which is always to be found in the particular constitution of the State concerned. They cannot even happen twice to the same people, for it can make itself free as long as it remains barbarous, but not when the civic impulse has lost its vigor. Then disturbances may destroy it, but revolutions cannot mend it: it needs a master, and not a liberator. Free peoples, be mindful of this maxim: "Liberty may be gained, but can never be recovered."

Youth is not infancy. There is for nations, as for men, a period of youth, or, shall we say, maturity, before which they should not be made subject to laws; but the maturity of a people is not always easily recognizable, and, if it is anticipated, the work is spoilt. One people is amenable to discipline from the beginning; another, not after ten centuries. Russia will never be really civilized, because it was civilized too soon. Peter had a genius for imitation; but he lacked true genius, which is creative and makes all from nothing. He did some good things, but most of what he did was out of place. He saw that his people was barbarous, but did not see that it was not ripe for civilization: he wanted to civilize it when it needed only hardening. His first wish was to make Germans or Englishmen, when he ought to have been making Russians; and he prevented his subjects from ever becoming what they might have been by persuading them that they were what they are not. In this fashion too a French teacher turns out his pupil to be an infant prodigy, and for the rest of his life to be nothing whatsoever. The empire of Russia will aspire to conquer Europe, and will itself be conquered. The Tartars, its subjects or neighbors, will become its masters and ours, by a revolution which I regard as inevitable. Indeed, all the kings of Europe are working in concert to hasten its coming.

IX

THE PEOPLE (CONTINUED)

As nature has set bounds to the stature of a well-made man, and, outside those limits, makes nothing but giants or dwarfs, similarly, for the constitution of a State to be at its best, it is possible to fix limits that will make it neither too large for good government, nor too small for self-maintenance. In every body politic there is a maximum strength which it cannot exceed and which it only loses by increasing in size. Every extension of the social tie means it relaxation; and, generally speaking, a small State is stronger in proportion than a great one.

A thousand arguments could be advanced in favor of this principle. First, long distances make administration more difficult, just as a weight becomes heavier at the end of a longer lever. Administration therefore becomes more and more burdensome as the distance grows greater; for, in the first place, each city has its own, which is paid for by the people: each district its own, still paid for by the people: then comes each province, and then the great governments, satrapies, and viceroyalties, always costing more the higher you go, and always at the expense of the unfortunate people. Last of all comes the supreme administration, which eclipes all the rest. All these overcharges are a continual drain upon the subjects; so far from being better governed by all these different orders, they are worse governed than if there were only a single authority over them. In the meantime, there scarce remain resources enough to meet emergencies; and, when recourse must be had to these, the State is always on the eve of destruction.

This is not all; not only has the government less vigor and promptitude for securing the observance of the laws, preventing nuisances, correcting abuses, and guarding against seditious undertakings begun in distant places; the people has less affection for its rulers, whom it never sees, for its country, which, to its eyes, seems like the world, and for its fellow citizens, most of whom are unknown to it. The same laws cannot suit so many diverse provinces with different customs, situated in the most various climates, and incapable of enduring a uniform government. Different laws lead only to trouble and confusion among peoples which, living under the same rulers and in constant communication one with another, intermingle and intermarry, and, coming under the sway of new customs, never know if they can call their very patrimony their own. Talent is buried, virtue unknown, and vice unpunished, among such a multitude of men who do not know one another, gathered together in one place at the seat of the central administration. The leaders, overwhelmed with business, see nothing for themselves; the State is governed by clerks. Finally, the measures which have to be taken to maintain the general authority, which all these distant officials wish to escape or to impose upon, absorb all the energy of the public, so that there is none left for the happiness of the people. There is hardly enough to defend it when need arises, and thus a body which is too big for its constitution gives way and falls crushed under its own weight.

Again, the State must assure itself a safe foundation, if it is to have stability, and to be able to resist the shocks it cannot help experiencing, as well as the efforts it will be forced to make for its maintenance; for all peoples have a kind of centrifugal force that makes them continually act one against another, and tend to aggrandize themselves at their neighbors' expense, like the vortices of Descartes. Thus the weak run the risk of being soon swallowed up; and it is almost impossible for any one to preserve itself except by putting itself in a state of equilibrium with all, so that the pressure is on all sides practically equal.

It may therefore be seen that there are reasons for expansion and reasons for contraction; and it is no small part of the statesman's skill to hit between them the mean that is most favorable to the preservation of the State. It may be said that the reason for expansion, being merely external and relative, ought to be subordinate to the reasons for contraction, which are internal and absolute. A strong and healthy constitution is the first thing to look for; and it is better to count on the vigor which comes of good government than on the resources a great territory furnishes.

It may be added that there have been known States so constituted that the necessity of making conquests entered into their very constitution, and that, in order to maintain themselves, they were forced to expand carelessly. It may be that they congratulated themselves greatly on this fortunate necessity, which none the less indicated to them, along with the limits of their greatness, the inevitable moment of their fall.

X

THE PEOPLE (CONTINUED)

A body politic may be measured in two ways—either by the extent of its territory, or by the number of its people; and there is, between these two measurements, a right relation which makes the State really great. The men make the State, and the territory sustains the men; the right relation therefore is that the land should suffice for the maintenance of the inhabitants, and that there should be as many inhabitants as the land can maintain. In this proportion lies the maximum strength of a given number of people; for, if there is too much land, it is troublesome to guard and inadequately cultivated, produces more than is needed, and soon gives rise to wars of defense; if there is not enough, the State depends on its neighbors for what it needs over and above, and this soon gives rise to wars of offense. Every people, to which its situation gives no choice save that between commerce and war, is weak in itself: it depends on its neighbors, and on circumstances; its existence can never be more than short and uncertain. It either conquers others, and changes its situation, or it is conquered and becomes nothing. Only insignificance or greatness can keep it free.

No fixed relation can be stated between the extent of territory and the population that are adequate one to the other, both because of the differences in the quality of land, in its fertility, in the nature of its products, and in the influence of climate, and because of the different tempers of those who inhabit it; for some in a fertile country consume little, and others on an ungrateful soil much. The greater or less fecundity of women, the conditions that are more or less favorable in each country to the growth of population, and the influence the legislator can hope to exercise by his institutions, must also be taken into account. The legislator therefore should not go by what he sees, but by what he foresees; he should stop not so much at the state in which he actually finds the population, as at that to which it ought naturally to attain. Lastly, there are countless cases in which the particular local circumstances demand or allow the acquisition of a greater territory than seems necessary. Thus, expansion will be great in a mountainous country, where the natural products, i.e. woods and pastures, need less labor, where we know from experience that women are more fertile than in the plains, and where a great expanse of slope affords only a small level tract that can be counted on for vegetation. On the other hand, contraction is possible on the coast, even in lands of rocks and nearly barren sands, because there fishing makes up to a great extent for the lack of land produce, because the inhabitants have to congregate together more in order to repel pirates, and further because it is easier to unburden the country of its superfluous inhabitants by means of colonies.

To these conditions of law-giving must be added one other which, though it cannot take the place of the rest, renders them all useless when it is absent. This is the enjoyment of peace and plenty; for the moment at which a State sets its house in order is, like the moment when a battalion is forming up, that when its body is least capable of offering resistance and easiest to destroy. A better resistance could be made at a time of absolute disorganization than at a moment of fermentation, when each is occupied with his own position and not with the danger. If war, famine, or sedition arises at this time of crisis, the State will inevitably be overthrown.

Not that many governments have not been set up during such storms; but in such cases these governments are themselves the State's destroyers. Usurpers always bring about or select troublous times to get passed, under the cover of the public terror, destructive laws, which the people would never adopt in cold blood. The moment chosen is one of the surest means of distinguishing the work of the legislator from that of the tyrant.

What people, then, is a fit subject for legislation? One which, already bound by some unity of origin, interest, or convention, has never yet felt the real yoke of law; one that has neither customs nor superstitions deeply ingrained, one which stands in no fear of being overwhelmed by sudden invasion; one which, without entering into its neighbors' quarrels, can resist each of them single-handed, or get the help of one to repel another; one in which every member may be known by every other, and there is no need to lay on any man burdens too heavy for a man to bear;

one which can do without other peoples, and without which all others can do;[1] one which is neither rich nor poor, but self-sufficient; and, lastly, one which unites the consistency of an ancient people with the docility of a new one. Legislation is made difficult less by what is necessary to build up than by what has to be destroyed; and what makes success so rare is the impossiblity of finding natural simplicity together with social requirements. All these conditions are indeed rarely found united, and therefore few States have good constitutions.

There is still in Europe one country capable of being given laws—Corsica. The valor and persistency with which that brave people has regained and defended its liberty well deserves that some wise man should teach it how to preserve what it has won. I have a feeling that some day that little island will astonish Europe.

XI

THE VARIOUS SYSTEMS OF LEGISLATION

If we ask in what precisely consists the greatness good of all, which should be the end of every system of legislation, we shall find it reduce itself to two main objects, liberty and equality—liberty, because all particular dependence means so much force taken from the body of the State, and equality, because liberty cannot exist without it.

I have already defined civil liberty; by equality, we should understand, not that the degrees of power and riches are to be absolutely identical for everybody; but that power shall never be great enough for violence, and shall always be exercised by virtue of rank and law; and that, in respect of riches, no citizen shall ever be wealthy enough to buy another, and none poor enough to be forced to sell himself;[1] which implies, on the part of the great, moderation in goods and position, and, on the side of the common sort, moderation in avarice and covetousness.

Such equality, we are told, is an unpractical ideal that cannot actually exist. But if its abuse is inevitable, does it follow that we should not at least make regulations concerning it? It is precisely because the force of circumstances tends continually to destroy equality that the force of legislation should always tend to its maintenance.

But these general objects of every good legislative system need modifying in every country; in accordance with the local situation and the temper of the inhabitants; and these circumstances should determine, in each case, the particular system of institutions which is best, not perhaps in itself, but for the State for which it is destined. If, for instance, the soil is barren and unproductive, or the land too crowded for its inhabitants, the people should turn to industry and the crafts, and exchange what they produce for the commodities they lack. If, on the other hand, a people dwells in rich plains and fertile slopes, or, in a good land, lacks inhabitants, it should give all its attention to agriculture, which causes men to multiply, and should drive out the crafts, which would only result in depopulation, by grouping in a few localities the few inhabitants there are.[2] If a nation dwells on an extensive and convenient coastline, let it cover the sea with ships and foster commerce and navigation. It will have a life that will be short and glorious. If, on its coasts, the sea washes nothing but almost inaccessible rocks, let it remain barbarous and ichthyophagous: it will have a quieter, perhaps a better, and certainly a happier life. In a word, besides the principles that are common to all, every nation has in itself something that gives them a particular application, and makes its legislation peculiarly its own. Thus, among the Jews long ago and more recently among the Arabs, the chief object was religion, among the Athenians letters, at Carthage and Tyre commerce, at Rhodes shipping, at Sparta war, at Rome virtue. The author of *The Spirit of the Laws* has shown with many examples by what art the legislator directs the constitution towards each of these objects.

What makes the constitution of a State really solid and lasting is the due observance of what is proper, so that the natural relations are always in agreement with the laws on every point, and law only serves, so to speak, to assure, accompany and rectify them. But if the legislator mistakes his object and adopts a principle other than circumstances naturally direct; if his principle makes for servitude, while they make for liberty, or if it makes for riches, while they make for populousness, or if it makes for peace, while they make for conquest—the laws will insensibly lose their influence, the constitution will alter, and the State will have no rest from trouble till it is either destroyed or changed, and nature has resumed her invincible sway.

XII

THE DIVISION OF THE LAWS

IF the whole is to be set in order, and the commonwealth put into the best possible shape, there are various relations to be considered. First, there is the action of the complete body upon itself, the relation of the whole to the whole, of the Sovereign to the State; and this relation, as we shall see, is made up of the relations of the intermediate terms.

The laws which regulate this relation bear the name of political laws, and are also called fundamental laws, not without reason if they are wise. For, if there is, in each State, only one good system, the people that is in possession of it should hold fast to this; but if the established order is bad, why should laws that prevent men from being good be regarded as fundamental? Besides in any case, a people is always in a position to change its laws, however good; for, if it choose to do itself harm, who can have a right to stop it?

The second relation is that of the members one to another, or to the body as a whole; and this relation should be in the first respect as unimportant, and in the second as important, as possible. Each citizen would then be perfectly independent of all the rest, and at the same time very dependent on the city which is brought about always by the same means, as the strength of the State can alone secure the liberty of its members. From this second relation arise civil laws.

We may consider also a third kind of relation between the individual and the law, a relation of disobedience to its penalty. This gives rise to the setting up of criminal laws, which, at bottom, are less a particular class of law than the sanction behind all the rest.

Along with these three kinds of law goes a fourth, most important of all, which is not graven on tablets of marble or brass, but on the hearts of the citizens. This forms the real constitution of the States, takes on every day new powers, whether other laws decay or die out, restores them or takes their place, keeps a people in the ways in which it was meant to go, and insensibly replaces authority by the force of habit. I am speaking of morality, of custom, above all of public opinion; a power unknown to political thinkers, on which none the less success in everything else depends. With this the great legislator concerns himself in secret, though he seems to confine himself to particular regulations; for these are only the arc of the arch, while manners and morals, slower to arise, form in the end its immovable keystone.

Among the different classes of laws, the political, which determine the form of the government, are alone relevant to my subject.

BOOK III

BEFORE speaking of the different forms of government, let us try to fix the exact sense of the word, which has not yet been very clearly explained.

I

GOVERNMENT IN GENERAL

I warn the reader that this chapter requires careful reading, and that I am unable to make myself clear to those who refuse to be attentive.

Every free action is produced by the concurrence of two causes; one moral, i.e. the will which determines the act; the other physical, i.e. the power which executes it. When I walk towards an object, it is necessary first that I should will to go there, and, in the second place, that my feet should carry me. If a paralytic wills to run and an active man wills not to, they will both stay where they are. The body politic has the same motive powers; here too force and will are distinguished, will under the name of legislative power and force under that of executive power. Without their concurrence, nothing is, or should be, done.

We have seen that the legislative power belongs to the people, and can belong to it alone. It may, on the other hand, readily be seen, from the principles laid down above, that the executive power cannot belong to the generality as legislature or Sovereign, because it consists wholly of particular acts which fall outside the competency of the law, and consequently of the Sovereign, whose acts must always be laws.

The public force therefore needs an agent of its own to bind it together and set it to work under the direction of the general will, to serve as a means of communication between the State and the Sovereign, and to do for the collective person more or less what the union of soul and body does for man. Here we have what is, in the State, the basis of government, often wrongly confused with the Sovereign, whose minister it is.

What then is government? An intermediate body set up between the subjects and the Sovereign, to secure their mutual correspondence, charged with the execution of the laws and the maintenance of liberty, both civil and political.

The members of this body are called magistrates or *kings,* that is to say *governors,* and the whole body bears the name *prince.*[1] Thus those who hold that the act, by which a people puts itself under a prince, is not a contract, are certainly right. It is simply and solely a commission, an employment, in which the rulers, mere officials of the Sovereign, exercise in their own name the power of which it makes them depositaries. This power it can limit, modify, or recover at pleasure; for the alienation of such a right is incompatible with the nature of the social body, and contrary to the end of association.

I call then *government,* or supreme administration, the legitimate exercise of the executive power, and prince or magistrate the man or the body entrusted with that administration.

In government reside the intermediate forces whose relations make up that of the whole to the whole, or of the Sovereign to the State. This last relation may be represented as that between the extreme terms of a continuous proportion, which has government as its mean proportional. The government gets from the Sovereign the orders it gives the people, and, for the State to be properly balanced, there must, when everything is reckoned in, be equality between the product or power of the government taken in itself, and the product or power of the citizens, who are on the one hand sovereign and on the other subject.

Furthermore, none of these three terms can be altered without the equality being instantly destroyed. If the Sovereign desires to govern, or the magistrate to give laws, or if the subjects refuse to obey, disorder takes the place of regularity, force and will no longer act together, and the State is dissolved and falls into despotism or anarchy. Lastly, as there is only one mean proportional between each relation, there is also only one good government possible for a State. But, as countless events may change the relations of a people, not only may different governments be good for different peoples, but also for the same people at different times.

In attempting to give some idea of the various relations that may hold between these two extreme terms, I shall take as an example the number of a people, which is the most easily expressible.

Suppose the State is composed of ten thousand citizens. The Sovereign can only be considered collectively and as a body; but each member, as being a subject, is regarded as an individual: thus the Sovereign is to the subject as ten thousand to one, i.e. each member of the State has as his share only a ten-thousandth part of the sovereign authority, although he is wholly under its control. If the people numbers a hundred thousand, the condition of the subject undergoes no change, and each equally is under the whole authority of the laws, while his vote, being reduced to one hundred thousandth part, has ten times less induence in drawing them up. The subject therefore remaining always a unit, the relation between him and the Sovereign increases with the number of the citizens. From this it follows that, the larger the State, the less the liberty.

When I say the relation increases, I mean that it grows more unequal. Thus the greater it is in the geometrical sense, the less relation there is in the ordinary sense of the word. In the former sense, the relation, considered according to quantity, is expressed by the quotient; in the latter, considered according to identity, it is reckoned by similarity.

Now, the less relation the particular wills have to the general will, that is, morals and manners to laws, the more should the repressive force be increased. The government, then, to be good, should be proportionately stronger as the people is more numerous.

On the other hand, as the growth of the State gives the depositaries of the public authority more temptations and chances of abusing their power, the greater the force with which the government ought to be endowed for keeping the people in hand, the greater too should be the force at the disposal of the Sovereign for keeping the government in hand. I am speaking, not of absolute force, but of the relative force of the different parts of the State.

It follows from this double relation that the continuous proportion between the Sovereign, the prince, and the people, is by no means an arbitrary idea, but a necessary consequence of the nature of the body politic. It follows further that, one of the extreme terms, viz. the people, are subject, being fixed and represented by unity, whenever the duplicate ratio increases or diminishes, the simple ratio does the same, and is changed accordingly. From this we see that there is not a single unique and absolute form of government, but as many governments differing in nature as there are States differing in size.

If, ridiculing this system, any one were to say that, in order to find the mean proportional and give form to the body of the government, it is only necessary, according to me, to find the square root of the number of the people, I should answer that I am here taking this number only as an instance; that the relations of which I am speaking are not measured by the number of men alone, but generally by the amount of action, which is a combination of a multitude of causes; and that, further, if, to save words, I borrow for a moment the terms of geometry, I am none the less well aware that moral quantities do not allow of geometrical accuracy.

The government is on a small scale what the body politic which includes it is on a great one. It is a moral person endowed with certain faculties, active like the Sovereign and passive like the State, and capable of being resolved into other similar relations. This accordingly gives rise to a new proportion, within which there is yet another, according to the arrangement of the magistracies, till an indivisible middle term is reached, i.e. a single ruler or supreme magistrate, who may be represented, in the midst of this progression, as the unity between the fractional and the ordinal series.

Without encumbering ourselves with this multiplication of terms, let us rest content with regarding government as a new body within the State, distinct from the people and the Sovereign, and intermediate between them.

There is between these two bodies this essential difference, that the State exists by itself, and the government only through the Sovereign. Thus the dominant will of the prince is, or should be, nothing but the general will or the law; his force is only the public force concentrated in his hands, and, as soon as he tries to base any absolute and independent act on his own authority, the tie that binds the whole together begins to be loosened. If finally the prince should come to have a particular will more active than the will of the Sovereign, and should employ the public force in his hands in obedience to this particular will, there would be, so to speak, two Sovereigns, one rightful and the other actual, the social union would evaporate instantly, and the body politic would be dissolved.

However, in order that the government may have a true existence and a real life distinguishing it from the body of the State, and in order that all its members may be able to act in concert and fulfill the end for which it was set up, it must have a particular personality, a sensibility common to its members, and a force and will of its own making for its preservation.

This particular existence implies assemblies, councils, power of deliberation and decision, rights, titles, and privileges belonging exclusively to the prince and making the office of magistrate more honorable in proportion as it is more troublesome. The difficulties lie in the manner of so ordering this subordinate whole within the whole, that it in no way alters the general constitution by affirmation of its own, and always distinguishes the particular force it possesses, which is destined to aid in its preservation, from the public force, which is destined to the preservation of the State; and, in a word, is always ready to sacrifice the government to the people, and never to sacrifice the people to the government.

Furthermore, although the artificial body of the government is the work of another artificial body, and has, we may say, only a borrowed and subordinate life, this does not prevent it from being able to act with more or less vigor or promptitude, or from being, so to speak, in more or less robust health. Finally, without departing directly from the end for which it was instituted, it may deviate more or less from it, according to the manner of its constitution.

From all these differences arise the various relations which the government ought to bear to the body of the State, according to the accidental and particular relations by which the State itself is modified, for often the government that is best in itself will become the most pernicious, if the relations in which it stands have altered according to the defects of the body politic to which it belongs.

II

THE CONSTITUENT PRINCIPLE IN THE VARIOUS FORMS OF GOVERNMENT

To set forth the general cause of the above differences, we must here distinguish between government and its principle, as we did before between the State and the Sovereign.

The body of the magistrates may be composed of a greater or a less number of members. We said that the relation of the Sovereign to the subjects was greater in proportion as the people was more numerous, and, by a clear analogy, we may say the same of the relation of the government to the magistrates.

But the total force of the government, being always that of the State, is invariable; so that, the more of this force it expends on its own members, the less it has left to employ on the whole people.

The more numerous the magistrates, therefore, the weaker the government. This principle being fundamental, we must do our best to make it clear.

In the person of the magistrate we can distinguish three essentially different wills: first, the private will of the individual, tending only to his personal advantage; secondly, the common will of the magistrates, which is relative solely to the advantage of the prince, and may be called corporate will, being general in relation to the government, and particular in relation to the State, of which the government forms part; and, in the third place, the will of the people or the sovereign will, which is general both in relation to the State regarded as the whole, and to the government regarded as a part of the whole.

In a perfect act of legislation, the individual or particular will should be at zero; the corporate will belonging to the government should occupy a very subordinate position; and consequently, the general or sovereign will should always predominate and should be the sole guide of all the rest.

According to the natural order, on the other hand, these different wills become more active in proportion as they are concentrated. Thus, the general will is always the weakest, the corporate will second, and the individual will strongest of all: so that, in the government, each member is first of all himself, then a magistrate, and then a citizen—in an order exactly the reverse of what the social system requires.

This granted, if the whole government is in the hands of one man, the particular and the corporate will are wholly united, and consequently the latter is at its highest possible degree of intensity. But, as the use to which the force is put depends on the degree reached by the will, and as the absolute force of the government is invariable, it follows that the most active government is that of one man.

Suppose, on the other hand, we unite the government with the legislative authority, and make the Sovereign prince also, and all the citizens so many magistrates: then the corporate will, being confounded with the general will, can possess no greater activity than that will, and must leave the particular will as strong as it can possibly be. Thus, the government, having always the same absolute force, will be at the lowest point of its relative force or activity.

These relations are incontestable, and there are other considerations which still further confirm them. We can see, for instance, that each magistrate is more active in the body to which he belongs than each citizen in that to which he belongs, and that consequently the particular will has much more influence on the acts of the government than on those of the Sovereign; for each magistrate is almost always charged with some governmental function, while each citizen, taken singly, exercises no function of Sovereignty. Furthermore, the bigger the State grows, the more its real force increases, though not in direct proportion to its growth; but, the State remaining the same, the number of magistrates may increase to any extent, without the government gaining any greater real force; for its force is that of the State, the dimension of which remains equal. Thus the relative force or activity of the government decreases, while its absolute or real force cannot increase.

Moreover, it is a certainty that promptitude in execution diminishes as more people are put in charge of it: where prudence is made too much of, not enough is made of fortune; opportunity is let slip, and deliberation results in the loss of its object.

I have just proved that the government grows remiss in proportion as the number of the magistrates increases; and I previously proved that, the more numerous the people, the greater should be the repressive force. From this it follows that the relation of the magistrates to the government should vary inversely to the relation of the subjects to the Sovereign; that is to say, the larger the State, the more should the government be tightened, so that the number of the rulers diminish in proportion to the increase of that of the people.

It should be added that I am here speaking of the relative strength of the government, and not of its rectitude: for, on the other hand, the more numerous the magistracy, the nearer the corporate will comes to the general will; while, under a single magistrate, the corporate will is, as I said, merely a particular will. Thus, what may be gained on one side is lost on the other, and the art of the legislator is to know how to fix the point at which the force and the will of the government, which are always in inverse proportion, meet in the relation that is most to the advantage of the State.

III

THE DIVISION OF GOVERNMENTS

WE saw in the last chapter what causes the various kinds of forms of government to be distinguished according to the number of the members composing them: it remains in this to discover how the division is made.

In the first place, the Sovereign may commit the charge of the government to the whole people or to the majority of the people, so that more citizens are magistrates than are mere private individuals. This form of government is called *democracy.*

Or it may restrict the government to a small number, so that there are more private citizens than magistrates; and this is named *aristocracy.*

Lastly, it may concentrate the whole government in the hands of a single magistrate from whom all others hold their power. This third form is the most usual, and is called *monarchy,* or royal government.

It should be remarked that all these forms, or at least the first two, admit of degree, and even of very wide differences; for democracy may include the whole people, or may be restricted to half. Aristocracy, in its turn, may be restricted indefinitely from half the people down to the smallest possible number. Even royalty is susceptible of a measure of distribution. Sparta always had two kings, as its constitution provided; and the Roman Empire saw as many as eight emperors at once, without its being possible to say that the Empire was split up. Thus there is a point at which each form of government passes into the next, and it becomes clear that, under three comprehensive denominations, government is really susceptible of as many diverse forms as the State has citizens.

There are even more: for, as the government may also, in certain aspects, be subdivided into other parts, one administered in one fashion and one in another, the combination of the three forms may result in a multitude of mixed forms, each of which admits of multiplication by all the simple forms.

There has been at all times much dispute concerning the best form of government, without consideration of the fact that each is in some cases the best, and in others the worst.

If, in the different States, the number of supreme magistrates should be in inverse ratio to the number of citizens, it follows that, generally, democratic government suits small States, aristocratic government those of middle size, and monarchy great ones. This rule is immediately deducible from the principle laid down. But it is impossible to count the innumerable circumstances which may furnish exceptions.

IV

DEMOCRACY

He who makes the law knows better than any one else how it should be executed and interpreted. It seems then impossible to have a better constitution than that in which the executive and legislative powers are united; but this very fact renders the government in certain respects inadequate, because things which should be distinguished are confounded, and the prince and the Sovereign, being the same person, form, so to speak, no more than a government without government.

It is not good for him who makes the laws to execute them, or for the body of the people to turn its attention away from a general standpoint and devote it to particular objects. Nothing is more dangerous than the influence of private interests in public affairs, and the abuse of the laws by the government is a less evil than the corruption of the legislator, which is the inevitable sequel to a particular standpoint. In such a case, the State being altered in substance, all reformation becomes impossible. A people that would never misuse governmental powers would never misuse independence; a people that would always govern well would not need to be governed.

If we take the term in the strict sense, there never has been a real democracy, and there never will be. It is against the natural order for the many to govern and the few to be governed. It is unimaginable that the people should remain continually assembled to devote their time to public affairs, and it is clear that they cannot set up commissions for that purpose without the form of administration being changed.

In fact, I can confidently lay down as a principle that, when the functions of government are shared by several tribunals, the less numerous sooner or later acquire the greatest authority, of only because they are in position to expedite affairs, and power thus naturally comes into their hands.

Besides, how many conditions that are difficult to unite does such a government presuppose! First, a very small State, where the people can readily be got together and where each citizen can with ease know all the rest; secondly, great simplicity of manners, to prevent business from multiplying and raising thorny problems; next, a large measure of equality in rank and fortune, without which equality of rights and authority cannot long subsist; lastly, little or no luxury—for luxury either comes of riches or makes them necessary; it corrupts at once rich and poor, the rich by possession and the poor by covetousness; it sells the country to softness and vanity, and takes away from the State all its citizens, to make them slaves one to another, and one and all to public opinion.

This is why a famous writer has made virtue the fundamental principle of Republics; for all these conditions could not exist without virtue. But, for want of the necessary distinctions, that great thinker was often inexact, and sometimes obscure, and did not see that, the sovereign authority being everywhere the same, the same principle should be found in every well-constituted State, in a greater or less degree, it is true, according to the form of the government.

It may be added that there is no government so subject to civil wars and intestine agitations as democratic or popular government, because there is none which has so strong and continual a tendency to change to another form, or which demands more vigilance and courage for its maintenance as it is. Under such a constitution above all, the citizen should arm himself with strength and constancy, and say, every day of his life, what a virtuous Count Palatine[1] said in the Diet of Poland: "Malo periculosam libertatem quam quietum servitium."

Were there a people of gods, their government would be democratic. So perfect a government is not for men.

V

ARISTOCRACY

We have here two quite distinct moral persons, the government and the Sovereign, and in consequence two general wills, one general in relation to all the citizens, the other only for the members of the administration. Thus, although the government may regulate its internal policy as it pleases, it can never speak to the people save in the name of the Sovereign, that is, of the people itself, a fact which must not be forgotten.

The first societies governed themselves aristocratically. The heads of families took counsel together on public affairs. The young bowed without question to the authority of experience. Hence such names as *priests, elders, senate,* and *gerontes.* The savages of North America govern themselves in this way even now, and their government is admirable.

But, in proportion as artificial inequality produced by institutions became predominant over natural inequality, riches or power[1] were put before age, and aristocracy became elective. Finally, the transmission of the father's power along with his goods to his children, by creating patrician families, made government hereditary, and there came to be senators of twenty.

There are then three sorts of aristocracy—natural, elective, and hereditary. The first is only for simple peoples; the third is the worst of all governments; the second is the best, and is aristocracy properly so called.

Besides the advantage that lies in the distinction between the two powers, it presents that of its members being chosen; for, in popular government, all the citizens are born magistrates; but here magistracy is confined to a few, who become such only by election.[2] By this means uprightness, understanding, experience, and all other claims to pre-eminence and public esteem become so many further guarantees of wise government.

Morever, assemblies are more easily held, affairs better discussed and carried out with more order and diligence, and the credit of the State is better sustained abroad by venerable senators than by a multitude that is unknown or despised.

In a word, it is the best and most natural arrangement that the wisest should govern the many, when it is assured that they will govern for its profit, and not for their own. There is no need to multiply instruments, or get twenty thousand men to do what a hundred picked men can do even better. But it must not be forgotten that corporate interest here begins to direct the public power less under the regulation of the general will, and that a further inevitable propensity takes away from the laws part of the executive power.

If we are to speak of what is individually desirable, neither should the State be so small, nor a people so simple and upright, that the execution of the laws follows immediately from the public will, as it does in a good democracy. Nor should the nation be so great that the rulers have to scatter in order to govern it and are able to play the Sovereign each in his own department, and, beginning by making themselves independent, end by becoming masters.

But if aristocracy does not demand all the virtues needed by popular government, it demands others which are peculiar to itself; for instance, moderation on the side of the rich and contentment on that of the poor; for it seems that thoroughgoing equality would be out of place, as it was not found even at Sparta.

Furthermore, if this form of government carries with it a certain inequality of fortune, this is justifiable in order that as a rule the administration of public affairs may be entrusted to those who are most able to give them their whole time, but not, as Aristotle maintains, in order that the rich may always be put first. On the contrary, it is of importance that an opposite choice should occasionally teach the people that the deserts of men offer claims to pre-eminence more important than those of riches.

VI

MONARCHY

So far, we have considered the prince as a moral and collective person, unified by the force of the laws, and the depositary in the State of the executive power. We have now to consider this power when it is gathered together into the hands of a natural person, a real man, who alone has the right to dispose of it in accordance with the laws. Such a person is called a monarch or king.

In contrast with other forms of administration, in which a collective being stands for an individual, in this form an individual stands for a collective being; so that the moral unity that constitutes the prince is at the same time a physical unity, and all the qualities, which in the other case are only with difficulty brought together by the law, are found naturally united.

Thus the will of the people, the will of the prince, the public force of the State, and the particular force of the government, all answer to a single motive power; all of the springs of the machine are in the same hands, the whole moves towards the same end; there are no conflicting movements to cancel one another, and no kind of constitution can be imagined in which a less amount of effort produces a more considerable amount of action. Archimedes, seated quietly on the bank and easily drawing a great vessel afloat, stands to my mind for a skillful monarch, governing vast states from his study, and moving everything while he seems himself unmoved.

But if no government is more vigorous than this, there is also none in which the particular will holds more sway and rules the rest more easily. Everything moves towards the same end indeed, but this end is by no means that of the public happiness, and even the force of the administration constantly shows itself prejudicial to the State.

Kings desire to be absolute, and men are always crying out to them from afar that the best means of being so is to get themselves loved by their people. This precept is all very well, and even in some respects very true. Unfortunately, it will always be derided at court. The power which comes of a people's love is no doubt the greatest; but it is precarious and conditional, and princes will never rest content with it. The best kings desire to be in a position to be wicked, if they please, without forfeiting their mastery: political sermonizers may tell them to their hearts' content that, the people's strength being their own, their first interest is that the people should be prosperous, numerous, and formidable; they are well aware that this is untrue. Their first personal interest is that the people should be weak, wretched, and unable to resist them. I admit that, provided the subjects remained always in submission, the prince's interest would indeed be that it should be powerful, in order that its power, being his own, might make him formidable to his neighbors; but, this interest being merely secondary and subordinate, and strength being incompatible with submission, princes naturally give the preference always to the principle that is more to their immediate advantage. This is what Samuel put strongly before the Hebrews, and what Machiavelli has clearly shown. He professed to teach kings; but it was the people he really taught. His *Prince* is the book of Republicans.[1]

We found, on general grounds, that monarchy is suitable only for great States, and this is confirmed when we examine it in itself. The more numerous the public administration, the smaller becomes the relation between the prince and the subjects, and the nearer it comes to equality, so that in democracy the ratio is unity, or absolute equality. Again, as the government is restricted in numbers the ratio increases and reaches its maximum when the government is in the hands of a single person. There is then too great a distance between prince and people, and the State lacks a bond of union. To form such a bond, there must be intermediate orders, and princes, personages, and nobility to compose them. But no such things suit a small State, to which all class differences mean ruin.

If, however, it is hard for a great State to be well governed, it is much harder for it to be so by a single man; and every one knows what happens when kings substitute others for themselves.

An essential and inevitable defect, which will always rank monarchical below republican government, is that in a republic the public voice hardly ever raises to the highest positions men who are not enlightened and capable, and such as to fill them with honor; while in monarchies those who rise to the top are most often merely petty blunderers, petty swindlers, and petty intriguers, whose petty talents cause them to get into the highest positions at court, but, as soon as they have got there, serve only to make their ineptitude clear to the public. The people is far less often mistaken in its choice than the prince; and a man of real worth among the king's ministers is almost as rare as a fool at the head of a republican government. Thus, when, by some fortunate chance, one of these born governors takes the helm of State in some monarchy that has been nearly overwhelmed by swarms of "gentlemanly" administrators, there is nothing but amazement at the resources he discovers, and his coming marks an era in his country's history.

For a monarchical State to have a chance of being well governed, its population and extent must be proportionate to the abilities of its governor. It is easier to conquer than to rule. With a long enough lever, the world could be moved with a single finger; to sustain it needs the shoulders of Hercules. However small a State may be, the prince is hardly ever big enough for it. When, on the other hand, it happens that the State is too small for its ruler, in these rare cases too it is ill governed, because the ruler, constantly pursuing his great designs, forgets the interests of the people and makes it no less wretched by misusing the talents he has, than a ruler of less capacity would make it for want of those he had not. A kingdom should, so to speak, expand or contract with each reign, according to the prince's capabilities; but, the abilities of a senate being more constant in quantity, the State can then have permanent frontiers without the administration suffering.

The disadvantage that is most felt in monarchical government is the want of the continuous succession which, in both the other forms, provides an unbroken bond of union. When one king dies, another is needed; elections leave dangerous intervals and are full of storms; and unless the citizens are disinterested and upright to a degree which very seldom goes with this kind of government, intrigue and corruption abound. He to whom the State has sold itself can hardly help selling it in his turn and repaying himself, at the expense of the weak, the money the powerful have wrung from him. Under such an administration, venality sooner or later spreads through every part, and peace so enjoyed under a king is worse than the disorders of an interregnum.

What has been done to prevent these evils? Crowns have been made hereditary in certain families, and an order of succession has been set up, to prevent disputes from arising on the death of kings. That is to say, the disadvantages of regency have been put in place of those of election, apparent tranquillity has been preferred to wise administration, and men have chosen rather to risk having children, monstrosities, or embeciles as rulers to having disputes over the choice of good kings. It has not been taken into account that, in so exposing ourselves to the risks this possibility entails, we are setting almost all the chances against us. There was sound sense in what the younger Dionysius said to his father, who reproached him for doing some shameful deed by asking: "Did I set you the example?" "No," answered his son, "but your father was not king."

Everything conspires to take away from a man who is set in authority over others the sense of justice and reason. Much trouble, we are told, is taken to teach young princes the art of reigning; but their education seems to do them no good. It would be better to begin by teaching them the art of obeying. The greatest kings whose praises history tells were not brought up to reign: reigning is a science we are never so far from possessing as when we have learnt too much of it, and one we acquire better by obeying than by commanding. "Nam utilissimus idem ac brevissimus bonarum malarumque rerum delectus cogitare quid aut nolueris sub alio principe, aut volueris."[2]

One result of this lack of coherence is the inconstancy of royal government, which, regulated now on one scheme and now on another, according to the character of the reigning prince or those who reign for him, cannot for long have a fixed object or a consistent policy—and this variability, not found in the other forms of government, where the prince is always the same, causes the State to be always shifting from principle to principle and from project to project. Thus we may say that generally, if a court is more subtle in intrigue, there is more wisdom in a senate, and Republics advance towards their ends by more consistent and better considered policies; while every revolution in a royal ministry creates a revolution in the State; for the principle common to all ministers and nearly all kings is to do in every respect the reverse of what was done by their predecessors.

This incoherence further clears up a sophism that is very familiar to royalist political writers; not only is civil government likened to domestic government, and the prince to the father of a family—this error has already been refuted—but the prince is also freely credited with all the virtues he ought to possess, and is supposed to be always what he should be. This supposition once made, royal government is clearly preferable to all others, because it is incontestably the strongest, and, to be the best also, wants only a corporate will more in conformity with the general will.

But if, according to Plato,[3] the "king by nature" is such a rarity, how often will nature and fortune conspire to give him a crown? And, if royal education necessarily corrupts those who receive it, what is to be hoped from a series of men brought up to reign? It is, then, wanton self-deception to confuse royal government with government by a good king. To see such government as it is in itself, we must consider it as it is under princes who are incompetent or wicked: for either they will come to the throne wicked or incompetent, or the throne will make them so.

These difficulties have not escaped our writers, who, all the same, are not troubled by them. The remedy, they say, is to obey without a murmur: God sends bad kings in His wrath, and they must be borne as the scourges of Heaven. Such talk is doubtless edifying; but it would be more in place in a pulpit than in a political book. What are we to think of a doctor who promises miracles, and whose whole art is to exhort the sufferer to patience? We know for ourselves that we must put up with a bad government when it is there; the question is how to find a good one.

VII

MIXED GOVERNMENTS

STRICTLY speaking, there is no such thing as a simple government. An isolated ruler must have subordinate magistrates; a popular government must have a head. There is therefore, in the distribution of the executive power, always a gradation from the greater to the lesser number, with the difference that sometimes the greater number is dependent on the smaller, and sometimes the smaller on the greater.

Sometimes the distribution is equal, when either the constituent parts are in mutual dependence, as in the government of England, or the authority of each section is independent, but imperfect, as in Poland. This last form is bad; for it secures no unity in the government, and the State is left without a bond of union.

Is a simple or a mixed government the better? Political writers are always debating the question, which must be answered as we have already answered a question about all forms of government.

Simple government is better in itself, just because it is simple. But when the executive power is not sufficiently dependent upon the legislative power, i.e. when the prince is more closely related to the Sovereign than the people to the prince, this lack of proportion must be curved by the division of the government; for all the parts have then no less authority over the subjects, while their division makes them all together less strong against the Sovereign.

The same disadvantage is also prevented by the appointment of intermediate magistrates, who leave the government entire, and have the effect only of balancing the two powers and maintaining their respective rights. Government is then not mixed, but moderated.

The opposite disadvantages may be similarly cured, and, when the government is too lax, tribunals may be set up to concentrate it. This is done in all democracies. In the first case, the government is divided to make it weak; in the second, to make it strong: for the maxima of both strength and weakness are found in simple governments, while the mixed forms result in a mean strength.

VIII

THAT ALL FORMS OF GOVERNMENT DO NOT SUIT ALL COUNTRIES

LIBERTY, not being a fruit of all climates, is not within the reach of all peoples. The more this principle, laid down by Montesquieu, is considered, the more its truth is felt; the more it is combated, the more chance is given to confirm it by new proofs.

In all the governments that there are, the public person consumes without producing. Whence then does it get what it consumes? From the labor of its members. The necessities of the public are supplied out of the superfluities of individuals. It follows that the civil State can subsist only so long as men's labor brings them a return greater than their needs.

The amount of this excess is not the same in all countries. In some it is considerable, in others middling, in yet others nil, in some even negative. The relation of product to subsistence depends on the fertility of the climate, on the sort of labor the land demands, on the nature of its products, on the strength of its inhabitants, on the greater or less consumption they find necessary, and on several further considerations of which the whole relation is made up.

On the other side, all governments are not of the same nature: some are less voracious than others, and the differences between them are based on this second principle, that the further from their source the public contributions are removed, the more burdensome they become. The charge should be measured not by the amount of the impositions, but by the path they have to travel in order to get back to those from whom they came. When the circulation is prompt and well established, it does not matter whether much or little is paid; the people is always rich and, financially speaking, all is well. On the contrary, however little the people gives, if that little does not return to it, it is soon exhausted by living continually: the State is then never rich, and the people is always a people of beggars.

It follows that, the more the distance between people and government increases, the more burdensome tribute becomes: thus, in a democracy, the people bears the least charge; in an aristocracy, a greater charge; and, in monarchy, the weight becomes heaviest. Monarchy therefore suits only wealthy nations; aristocracy, States of middling size and wealth; and democracy, States that are small and poor.

In fact, the more we reflect, the more we find the difference between free and monarchical States to be this: in the former, everything is used for the public advantage; in the latter, the public forces and those of individuals are affected by each other, and either increases as the other grows weak; finally, instead of governing subjects to make them happy, despotism makes them wretched in order to govern them.

We find then, in every climate, natural causes according to which the form of government which it requires can be assigned, and we can even say what sort of inhabitants it should have.

Unfriendly and barren lands, where the product does not repay the labor, should remain desert and uncultivated, or peopled only by savages; lands where men's labor brings in no more than the exact minimum necessary to subsistence should be inhabited by barbarous peoples: in such places all polity is impossible. Lands where the surplus of product over labor is only middling are suitable for free peoples; those in which the soil is abundant and fertile and gives a great product for a little labor call for monarchical government, in order that the surplus of superfluities among the subjects may be consumed by the luxury of the prince: for it is better for this excess to be absorbed by the government than dissipated among the individuals. I am aware that there are exceptions; but these exceptions themselves confirm the rule, in that sooner or later they produce revolutions which restore things to the natural order.

General laws should always be distinguished from individual causes that may modify their effects. If all the South were covered with Republics and all the North were despotic States, it would be none the less true that, in point of climate, despotism is suitable to hot countries, barbarism to cold countries, and good polity to temperate regions. I see also that, the principle being granted, there may be disputes on its application; it may be said that there are cold countries that are very fertile, and tropical countries that are very unproductive. But this difficulty exists only for those who do not consider the question in all its aspects. We must, as I have already said, take labor, strength, consumption, etc., into account.

Take two tracts of equal extent, one of which brings in five and the other ten. If the inhabitants of the first consume four and those of the second nine, the surplus of the first product will be a fifth and that of the second a tenth. The ratio of these two surpluses will then be inverse to that of the products, and the tract which produces only five will give a surplus double that of the tract which produces ten.

But there is no question of a double product, and I think no one would put the fertility of cold countries, as a general rule, on an equality with that of hot ones. Let us, however, suppose this equality to exist: let us, if you will, regard England as on the same level as Sicily, and Poland as Egypt—further south, we shall have Africa and the Indies; further north, nothing at all. To get this equality of product, what a difference there must be in tillage; in Sicily, there is only need to scratch the ground; in England, how men must toil! But, where more hands are needed to get the same product, the superfluity must necessarily be less.

Consider, besides, that the same number of men consume much less in hot countries. The climate requires sobriety for the sake of health; and Europeans who try to live there as they would at home all perish of dysentery and indigestion. "We are," says Chardin, "carnivorous animals, wolves, in comparison with the Asiatics. Some attribute the sobriety of the Persians to the fact that their country is less cultivated; but it is my belief that their country abounds less in commodities because the inhabitants need less. If their frugality," he goes on, "were the effect of the nakedness of the land, only the poor would eat little; but everybody does so. Again, less or more would be eaten in various provinces, according to the land's fertility; but the same sobriety is found throughout the kingdom. They are very proud of their manner of life, saying that you have only to look at their hue to recognize how far it excels that of the Christians. In fact, the Persians are of an even hue; their skins are fair, fine and smooth; while the hue of their subjects, the Armenians, who live after the European fashion, is rough and blotchy, and their bodies are gross and unwieldy."

The nearer you get to the equator, the less people live on. Meat they hardly touch: rice, maize, couscous, millet, and cassava are their ordinary food. There are in the Indies millions of men whose subsistence does not cost a halfpenny a day. Even in Europe we find considerable differences of appetite between Northern and Southern peoples. A Spaniard will live for a week on a German's dinner. In the countries in which men are more voracious, luxury therefore turns in the direction of consumption. In England, luxury appears in a well-filled table; in Italy, you feast on sugar and flowers.

Luxury in clothes shows similar differences. In climates in which the changes of season are prompt and violent, men have better and simpler clothes; where they clothe themselves only for adornment, what is striking is more thought of than what is useful; clothes themselves are then a luxury. At Naples, you may see daily walking in the Pausilippeum men in gold-embroidered upper garments and nothing else. It is the same with buildings; magnificence is the sole consideration where there is nothing to fear from the air. In Paris and London, you desire to be lodged warmly and comfortably; in Madrid, you have superb salons, but not a window that closes, and you go to bed in a mere hole.

In hot countries foods are much more substantial and succulent; and the third difference cannot but have an influence on the second. Why are so many vegetables eaten in Italy? Because there they are good, nutritious, and excellent in taste. In France, where they are nourished only on water, they are far from nutritious and are thought nothing of at table. They take up all the same no less ground, and cost at least as much pains to cultivate. It is a proved fact that the wheat of Barbary, in other respects inferior to that of France, yields much more flour, and that the wheat of France in turn yields more than that of northern countries; from which it may be inferred that a like gradation in the same direction, from equator to pole, is found generally. But is it not an obvious disadvantage for an equal product to contain less nourishment?

To all these points may be added another, which at once depends on and strengthens them. Hot countries need inhabitants less than cold countries, and can support more of them. There is thus a double surplus, which is all to the advantage of despotism. The greater the territory occupied by a fixed number of inhabitants, the more difficult revolt becomes, because rapid or secret concerted action is impossible, and the government can easily unmask projects and cut communications; but the more a numerous people is gathered together, the less can the government usurp the Sovereign's place: the people's leaders can deliberate as safely in their houses as the prince in council, and the crowd gathers as rapidly in the squares as the prince's troops in their quarters. The advantage of tyrannical government therefore lies in acting at great distances. With the help of the rallying-points it establishes, its strength, like that of the lever,[1] grows with distance. The strength of the people, on the other hand, acts only when concentrated: when spread abroad, it evaporates and is lost, like powder scattered on the ground, which catches fire only grain by grain. The east populous countries are thus the fittest for tyranny: fierce animals reign only in deserts.

IX

THE MARKS OF A GOOD GOVERNMENT

THE question "What absolutely is the best government?" is unanswerable as well as indeterminate; or rather, there are as many good answers as there are possible combinations in the absolute and relative situations of all nations.

But if it is asked by what sign we may know that a given people is well or ill governed, that is another matter, and the question, being one of fact, admits of an answer.

It is not, however, answered, because everyone wants to answer it in his own way. Subjects extol public tranquillity, citizens individual liberty; the one class prefers security of possessions, the other that of person; the one regards as the best government that which is most severe, the other maintains that the mildest is the best; the one wants crimes punished, the other wants them prevented; the one wants the State to be feared by its neighbors, the other prefers that it should be ignored; the one is content if money circulates, the other demands that the people shall have bread. Even if an agreement were come to on these and similar points, should we have got any further? As moral qualities do not admit of exact measurement, agreement about the mark does not mean agreement about the valuation.

For my part, I am continually astonished that a mark so simple is not recognized, or that men are of so bad faith as not to admit it. What is the end of political association? The preservation and prosperity of its members. And what is the surest mark of their preservation and prosperity? Their numbers and population. Seek then nowhere else this mark that is in dispute. The rest being equal, the government under which, without external aids, without naturalization or colonies, the citizens increase and multiply most is beyond question the best. The government under which a people wanes and diminishes is the worst. Calculations, it is left for you to count, to measure, to compare.[1]

X

THE ABUSES OF GOVERNMENT AND ITS TENDENCY TO DEGENERATE

As the particular will acts constantly in opposition to the general will, the government continually exerts itself against the Sovereignty. The greater this exertion becomes, the more the constitution changes; and, as there is in this case no other corporate will to create an equilibrium by resisting the will of the prince, sooner or later the prince must inevitably suppress the Sovereign and break the social treaty. This is the unavoidable and inherent defect which, from the very birth of the body politic, tends ceaselessly to destroy it, as age and death end by destroying the human body.

There are two general courses by which government degenerates: i.e. when it undergoes contraction, or when the State is dissolved.

Government undergoes contraction when it passes from the many to the few, that is, from democracy to aristocracy, and from aristocracy to royalty. To do so is its natural propensity.[1] If it took the backward course from the few to the many, it could be said that it was relaxed; but this inverse sequence is impossible.

Indeed, governments never change their form except when their energy is exhausted and leaves them too weak to keep what they have. If a government at once extended its sphere and relaxed its stringency, its force would become absolutely nil, and it would persist still less. It is therefore necessary to wind up the spring and tighten the hold as it gives way: or else the State it sustains will come to grief.

The dissolution of the State may come about in either of two ways.

First, when the prince ceases to administer the State in accordance with the laws, and usurps the Sovereign power. A remarkable change then occurs: not the government, but the State, undergoes contraction; I mean that the great State is dissolved, and another is formed within it, composed solely of the members of the government, which becomes for the rest of the people merely master and tyrant. So that the moment of the government usurps the Sovereignty, the social compact is broken, and all private citizens recover by right their natural liberty, and are forced, but not bound, to obey.

The same thing happens when the members of the government severally usurp the power they should exercise only as a body; this is as great an infraction of the laws, and results in even greater disorders. There are then, so to speak, as many princes as there are magistrates, and the State, no less divided than the government, either perishes or changes its form.

When the State is dissolved, the abuse of government, whatever it is, bears the common name of *anarchy.* To distinguish, democracy degenerates into *ochlocracy,* and aristocracy into *oligarchy;* and I would add that royalty degenerates into *tyranny;* but this last word is ambiguous and needs explanation.

In vulgar usage, a tyrant is a king who governs violently and without regard for justice and law. In the exact sense, a tyrant is an individual who arrogates to himself the royal authority without having a right to it. This is how the Greeks understood the word "tyrant": they applied it indifferently to good and bad princes whose authority was not legitimate.[2] *Tyrant* and *usurper* are thus perfectly synonymous terms.

In order that I may give different things different names, I call him who usurps the royal authority a *tyrant,* and him who usurps the sovereign power a *despot.* The tyrant is he who thrusts himself in contrary to the laws to govern in accordance with the laws; the despot is he who sets himself above the laws themselves. Thus the tyrant cannot be a despot, but the despot is always a tyrant.

XI

THE DEATH OF THE BODY POLITIC

SUCH is the natural and inevitable tendency of the best constituted governments. If Sparta and Rome perished, what State can hope to endure for ever? If we would set up a long-lived form of government, let us not even dream of making it eternal. If we are to succeed, we must not attempt the impossible, or flatter ourselves that we are endowing the work of man with a stability of which human conditions do not permit.

The body politic, as well as the human body, begins to die as soon as it is born, and carries in itself the causes of its destruction. But both may have a constitution that is more or less robust and suited to preserve them a longer or a shorter time. The constitution of man is the work of nature; that of the State the work of art. It is not in men's power to prolong their own lives; but it is for them to prolong as much as possible the life of the State, by giving it the best possible constitution. The best constituted State will have an end; but it will end later than any other, unless some unforeseen accident brings about its untimely destruction.

The life-principle of the body politic lies in the sovereign authority. The legislative power is the heart of the State; the executive power is its brain, which causes the movement of all the parts. The brain may become paralyzed and the individual still live. A man may remain an imbecile and live; but as soon as the heart ceases to perform its functions, the animal is dead.

The State subsists by means not of the laws, but of the legislative power. Yesterday's law is not binding to-day; but silence is taken for tacit consent, and the Sovereign is held to confirm incessantly the laws it does not abrogate as it might. All that it has once declared itself to will it wills always, unless it revokes its declaration.

Why then is so much respect paid to old laws? For this very reason. We must believe that nothing but the excellence of old acts of will can have preserved them so long: if the Sovereign had not recognized them as throughout salutary, it would have revoked them a thousand times. This is why, so far from growing weak, the laws continually gain new strength in any well constituted State; the precedent of antiquity makes them daily more venerable: while wherever the laws grow weak as they become old, this proves that there is no longer a legislative power, and that the State is dead.

XII

HOW THE SOVEREIGN AUTHORITY MAINTAINS ITSELF

THE Sovereign, having no force other than the legislative power, acts only by means of the laws; and the laws being solely the authentic acts of the general will, the Sovereign cannot act save when the people is assembled. The people in assembly, I shall be told, is a mere chimera. It is so today, but two thousand years ago it was not so. Has man's nature changed?

The bounds of possibility, in moral matters, are less narrow than we imagine: it is our weaknesses, our vices, and our prejudices that confine them. Base souls have no belief in great men; vile slaves smile in mockery at the name of liberty.

Let us judge of what can be done by what has been done. I shall say nothing of the Republics of ancient Greece; but the Roman Republic was, to my mind, a great State, and the town of Rome a great town. The last census showed that there were in Rome four hundred thousand citizens capable of bearing arms, and the last computation of the population of the Empire showed over four million citizens, excluding subjects, foreigners, women, children, and slaves.

What difficulties might not be supposed to stand in the way of the frequent assemblage of the vast population of this capital and its neighborhood. Yet few weeks passed without the Roman people being in assembly, and even being so several times. It exercised not only the rights of Sovereignty, but also a part of those of government. It dealt with certain matters, and judged certain cases, and this whole people was found in the public meeting-place hardly less often as magistrates than as citizens.

If we went back to the earliest history of nations, we should find that most ancient governments, even those of monarchical form, such as the Macedonian and the Frankish, had similar councils. In any case, the one incontestable fact I have given is an answer to all difficulties; it is good logic to reason from the actual to the possible.

XIII

HOW THE SOVEREIGN AUTHORITY MAINTAINS ITSELF (CONTINUED)

IT is not enough for the assembled people to have once fixed the constitution of the State by giving its sanction to a body of law; it is not enough for it to have set up a perpetual government, or provided once for all for the election of magistrates. Besides the extraordinary assemblies unforeseen circumstances may demand, there must be fixed periodical assemblies which cannot be abrogated or prorogued, so that on the proper day the people is legitimately called together by law, without need of any formal summoning.

But, apart from these assemblies authorized by their date alone, every assembly of the people not summoned by the magistrates appointed for that purpose, and in accordance with the prescribed forms, should be regarded as unlawful, and all its acts as null and void, because the command to assemble should itself proceed from the law.

The greater or less frequency with which lawful assemblies should occur depends on so many considerations that no exact rules about them can be given. It can only be said generally that the stronger the government the more often should the Sovereign show itself.

This, I shall be told, may do for a single town; but what is to be done when the State includes several? Is the sovereign authority to be divided? Or is it to be concentrated in a single town to which all the rest are made subject?

Neither the one nor the other, I reply. First, the sovereign authority is one and simple, and cannot be divided without being destroyed. In the second place, one town cannot, any more than one nation, legitimately be made subject to another, because the essence of the body politic lies in the reconciliation of obedience and liberty, and the words subject and Sovereign are identical correlatives the idea of which meets in the single word "citizen."

I answer further that the union of several towns in a single city is always bad, and that, if we wish to make such a union, we should not expect to avoid its natural disadvantages. It is useless to bring up abuses that belong to great States against one who desires to see only small ones; but how can small States be given the strength to resist great ones, as formerly the Greek towns resisted the Great King, and more recently Holland and Switzerland have resisted the House of Austria?

Nevertheless, if the State cannot be reduced to the right limits, there remains still one resource; this is, to allow no capital, to make the seat of government move from town to town, and to assemble by turn in each the Provincial Estates of the country.

People the territory evenly, extend everywhere the same rights, bear to every place in it abundance and life: by these means will the State become at once as strong and as well governed as possible. Remember that the walls of towns are built of the ruins of the houses of the countryside. For every palace I see raised in the capital, my mind's eye sees a whole country made desolate.

XIV

HOW THE SOVEREIGN AUTHORITY MAINTAINS ITSELF (CONTINUED)

THE moment the people is legitimately assembled as a sovereign body, the jurisdiction of the government wholly lapses, the executive power is suspended, and the person of the meanest citizen is as sacred and inviolable as that of the first magistrate; for in the presence of the person represented, representatives no longer exist. Most of the tumults that arose in the comitia at Rome were due to ignorance or neglect of this rule. The consuls were in them merely the presidents of the people; the tribunes were mere speakers;[1] the senate was nothing at all.

These intervals of suspension, during which the prince recognizes or ought to recognize an actual superior, have always been viewed by him with alarm; and these assemblies of the people, which are the aegis of the body politic and the curb on the government, have at all times been the horror of rulers: who therefore never spare pains, objections, difficulties, and promises, to stop the citizens from having them. When the citizens are greedy, cowardly, and pusillanimous, and love ease more than liberty, they do not long hold out against the redoubled efforts of the government; and thus, as the resisting force incessantly grows, the sovereign authority ends by disappearing, and most cities fall and perish before their time.

But between the sovereign authority and arbitrary government there sometimes intervenes a mean power of which something must be said.

XV

DEPUTIES OR REPRESENTATIVES

As soon as public service ceases to be the chief business of the citizens, and they would rather serve with their money than with their persons, the State is not far from its fall. When it is necessary to march out to war, they pay troops and stay at home: when it is necessary to meet in council, they name deputies and stay at home. By reason of idleness and money, they end by having soldiers to enslave their country and representatives to sell it.

It is through the hustle of commerce and the arts, through the greedy self-interest of profit, and through softness and love of amenities that personal services are replaced by money payments. Men surrender a part of their profits in order to have time to increase them at leisure. Make gifts of money, and you will not be long without chains. The word "finance" is a slavish word, unknown in the city-state. In a country that is truly free, the citizens do everything with their own arms and nothing by means of money; so far from paying to be exempted from their duties, they would even pay for the privilege of fulfilling them themselves. I am far from taking the common view: hold enforced labor to be less opposed to liberty than taxes.

The better the constitution of a State is, the more do public affairs encroach on private in the minds of the citizens. Private affairs are even of much less importance, because the aggregate of the common happiness furnishes a greater proportion to that of each individual, so that there is less for him to seek in particular cares. In a well-ordered city every man flies to the assemblies: under a bad government no one cares to stir a step to get to them, because no one is interested in what happens there, because it is foreseen that the general will will not prevail, and lastly because domestic cares are all-absorbing. Good laws lead to the making of better ones; bad ones bring about worse. As soon as any man says of the affairs of the state *What does it matter to me?* the State may be given up for lost.

The lukewarmness of patriotism, the activity of private interest, the vastness of States, conquest, and the abuse of government suggested the method of having deputies or representatives of the people in the national assemblies. These are what, in some countries, men have presumed to call the Third Estate. Thus the individual interest of two orders is put first and second; the public interest occupies only the third place.

Sovereignty, for the same reason as makes it inalienable, cannot be represented; it lies essentially in the general will, and will does not admit of representation: it is either the same, or other; there is no intermediate possibility. The deputies of the people, therefore, are not and cannot be its representatives: they are merely its stewards, and can carry through no definitive acts. Every law the people has not ratified in person is null and void—is, in fact, not a law. The people of England regards itself as free; but it is grossly mistaken; it is free only during the election of members of parliament. As soon as they are elected, slavery overtakes it, and it is nothing. The use it makes of the short moments of liberty it enjoys shows indeed that it deserves to lose them.

The idea of representation is modern; it comes to us from feudal government, from that iniquitous and absurd system which degrades humanity and dishonors the name of man. In ancient republics and even in monarchies, the people never had representatives; the word itself was unknown. It is very singular that in Rome, where the tribunes were so sacrosanct, it was never even imagined that they could usurp the functions of the people, and that in the midst of so great a multitude they never attempted to pass on their own authority a single *plebiscitum.* We can, however, form an idea of the difficulties caused sometimes by the people being so numerous, from what happened in the time of the Gracchi, when some of the citizens had to cast their votes from the roofs of buildings.

Where right and liberty are everything, disadvantages count for nothing. Among this wise people everything was given its just value, its lictors were allowed to do what its tribunes would never have dared to attempt; for it had no fear that its lictors would try to represent it.

To explain, however, in what way the tribunes did sometimes represent it, it is enough to conceive how the government represents the Sovereign. Law being purely the declaration of the general will, it is clear that, in the exercise of the legislative power, the people cannot be represented; but in that of the executive power, which is only the force that is applied to give the law effect, it both can and should be represented. We thus see that if we looked closely into the matter we should find that very few nations have any laws. However that may be, it is certain that the tribunes, possessing no executive power, could never represent the Roman people by right of the powers entrusted to them, but only by usurping those of the senate.

In Greece, all that the people had to do, it did for itself; it was constantly assembled in the public square. The Greeks lived in a mild climate; they had no natural greed; slaves did their work for them; their great concern was with liberty. Lacking the same advantages, how can you preserve the same rights? Your severer climates add to your needs;[1] for half the year your public squares are uninhabitable; the flatness of your languages unfits them for being heard in the open air; you sacrifice more for profit than for liberty, and fear slavery less than poverty.

What then? Is liberty maintained only by the help of slavery? It may be so. Extremes meet. Everything that is not in the course of nature has its disadvantages, civil society most of all. There are some unhappy circumstances in which we can only keep our liberty at others' expense, and where the citizen can be perfectly free only when the slave is most a slave. Such was the case with Sparta. As for you, modern peoples, you have no slaves, but you are slaves yourselves; you pay for their liberty with your own. It is in vain that you boast of this preference; I find in it more cowardice than humanity.

I do not mean by all this that it is necessary to have slaves, or that the right of slavery is legitimate: I am merely giving the reasons why modern peoples, believing themselves to be free, have representatives, while ancient peoples had none. In any case, the moment a people allows itself to be represented, it is no longer free: it no longer exists.

All things considered, I do not see that it is possible henceforth for the Sovereign to preserve among us the exercise of its rights, unless the city is very small. But if it is very small, will it be conquered? No. I will show later on how the external strength of a great people[2] may be combined with the convenient polity and good order of a small State.

XVI

THAT THE INSTITUTION OF GOVERNMENT IS NOT A CONTRACT

THE legislative power once well established, the next thing is to establish similarly the executive power; for this latter, which operates only by particular acts, not being of the essence of the former, is naturally separate from it. Were it possible for the Sovereign, as such, to possess the executive power, right and fact would be so confounded that no one could tell what was law and what was not; and the body politic, thus figured, would soon fall a prey to the violence it was instituted to prevent.

As the citizens, by the social contract, are all equal, all can prescribe what all should do, but no one has a right to demand that another shall do what he does not do himself. It is strictly this right, which is indispensable for giving the body politic life and movement, that the Sovereign, in instituting the government, confers upon the prince.

It has been held that this act of establishment was a contract between the people and the rulers it sets over itself—a contract in which conditions were laid down between the two parties binding the one to command and the other to obey. It will be admitted, I am sure, that this is an odd kind of contract to enter into. But let us see if this view can be upheld.

First, the supreme authority can no more be modified than it can be alienated; to limit it is to destroy it. It is absurd and contradictory for the Sovereign to set a superior over itself; to bind itself to obey a master would be to return to absolute liberty.

Moreover, it is clear that this contract between the people and such and such persons would be a particular act; and from this it follows that it can be neither a law nor an act of Sovereignty, and that consequently it would be illegitimate.

It is plain too that contracting parties in relation to each other would be under the law of nature alone and wholly without guarantees of their mutual undertakings, a position wholly at variance with the civil state. He who has force at his command being always in a position to control execution, it would come to the same thing if the name "contract" were given to the act of one man who said to another: "I give you all my goods, on condition that you give me back as much of them as you please."

There is only one contract in the State, and that is the act of association, which in itself excludes the existence of a second. It is impossible to conceive of any public contract that would not be a violation of the first.

XVII

THE INSTITUTION OF GOVERNMENT

UNDER what general idea then should the act by which government is instituted be conceived as falling? I will begin by stating that the act is complex, as being composed of two others—the establishment of the law and its execution.

By the former, the Sovereign decrees that there shall be a governing body established in this or that form; this act is clearly a law.

By the latter, the people nominates the rulers who are to be entrusted with the government that has been established. This nomination, being a particular act, is clearly not a second law, but merely a consequence of the first and a function of government.

The difficulty is to understand how there can be a governmental act before government exists, and how the people, which is only Sovereign or subject, can, under certain circumstances, become a prince or magistrate.

It is at this point that there is revealed one of the astonishing properties of the body politic, by means of which it reconciles apparently contradictory operations; for this is accomplished by a sudden converion of Sovereignty into democracy, so that, without sensible change, and merely by virtue of a new relation of all to all, the citizens become magistrates and pass from general to particular acts, from legislation to the execution of the law.

This changed relation is no speculative subtlety without instances in practice: it happens every day in the English Parliament, where, on certain occasions, the Lower House resolves itself into Grand Committee, for the better discussion of affairs, and thus, from being at one moment a sovereign court, becomes at the next a mere commission; so that subsequently it reports to itself, as House of Commons, the result of its proceedings in Grand Committee, and debates over again under one name what it has already settled under another.

It is, indeed, the peculiar advantage of democratic government that it can be established in actuality by a simple act of the general will. Subsequently, this provisional government remains in power, if this form is adopted, or else establishes in the name of the Sovereign the government that is prescribed by law; and thus the whole proceeding is regular. It is impossible to set up government in any other manner legitimately and in accordance with the principles so far laid down.

XVIII

HOW TO CHECK THE USURPATIONS OF GOVERNMENT

WHAT we have just said confirms Chapter XVI, and makes it clear that the institution of government is not a contract, but a law; that the depositaries of the executive power are not the people's masters, but its officers; that it can set them up and pull them down when it likes; that for them there is no question of contract, but of obedience; and that in taking charge of the functions the State imposes on them they are doing no more than fulfilling their duty as citizens, without having the remotest right to argue about the conditions.

When therefore the people sets up an hereditary government, whether it be monarchical and confined to one family, or aristocratic and confined to a class, what it enters into is not an undertaking; the administration is given a provisional form, until the people chooses to order it otherwise.

It is true that such changes are always dangerous, and that the established government should never be touched except when it comes to be incompatible with the public good; but the circumspection this involves is a maxim of policy and not a rule of right, and the State is no more bound to leave civil authority in the hands of its rulers than military authority in the hands of its generals.

It is also true that it is impossible to be too careful to observe, in such cases, all the formalities necessary to distinguish a regular and legitimate act from a seditious tumult, and the will of a whole people from the clamor of a faction. Here above all no further concession should be made to the untoward possibility that cannot, in the strictest logic, be refused it.

From this obligation the prince derives a great advantage in preserving his power despite the people, without its being possible to say he has usurped it; for, seeming to avail himself only of his rights, he finds it very easy to extend them, and to prevent, under the pretext of keeping the peace, assemblies that are destined to the re-establishment in order; with the result that he takes advantage of a silence he does not allow to be broken, or of irregularities he causes to be committed, to assume that he has the support of those whom fear prevents from speaking, and to punish those who dare to speak. Thus it was that the decemvirs, first elected for one year and then kept on in office for a second, tried to perpetuate their power by forbidding the comitia to assemble; and by this easy method every government in the world, once clothed with the public power, sooner or later usurps the sovereign authority.

The periodical assemblies of which I have already spoken are designed to prevent or postpone this calamity, above all when they need no formal summoning; for in that case, the prince cannot stop them without openly declaring himself a law-breaker and an enemy of the State.

The opening of these assemblies, whose sole object is the maintenance of the social treaty, should always take the form of putting two propositions that may not be suppressed, which should be voted on separately.

The first is: "Does it please the Sovereign to preserve the present form of government?"

The second is: "Does it please the people to leave its administration in the hands of those who are actually in charge of it?"

I am here assuming what I think I have shown; that there is in the State no fundamental law that cannot be revoked, not excluding the social compact itself; for if all the citizens assembled of one accord to break the compact, it is impossible to doubt that it would be very legitimately broken. Grotius even thinks that each man can renounce his membership of his own State, and recover his natural liberty and his goods on leaving the country.[1] It would be indeed absurd if all the citizens in assembly could not do what each can do by himself.

BOOK IV

I

THAT THE GENERAL WILL IS INDESTRUCTIBLE

As long as several men in assembly regard themselves as a single body, they have only a single will which is concerned with their common preservation and general well-being. In this case, all the springs of the State are vigorous and simple and its rules clear and luminous; there are no embroilments or conflicts of interests; the common good is everywhere clearly apparent, and only good sense is needed to perceive it. Peace, unity, and equality are the enemies of political subtleties. Men who are upright and simple are difficult to deceive because of their simplicity; lures and pretexts fail to impose upon them, and they are not even subtle enough to be dupes. When, among the happiest people in the world, bands of peasants are seen regulating affairs of State under an oak, and always acting wisely, can we help scorning the ingenious methods of other nations, which make themselves illustrious and wretched with so much art and mystery?

A State so governed needs very few laws; and, as it becomes necessary to issue new ones, the necessity is universally seen. The first man to propose them merely says what all have already felt, and there is no question of factions or intrigues or eloquence in order to secure the passage into law of what everyone has already decided to do, as soon as he is sure that the rest will act with him.

Theorists are led into error because, seeing only States that have been from the beginning wrongly constituted, they are struck by the impossibility of applying such a policy to them. They make great game of all the absurdities a clever rascal or an insinuating speaker might get the people of Paris or London to believe. They do not know that Cromwell would have been put to "the bells" by the people of Berne, and the Duc de Beaufort on the treadmill by the Genevese.

But when the social bond begins to be relaxed and the State to grow weak, when particular interests begin to make themselves felt and the smaller societies to exercise an influence over the larger, the common interest changes and finds opponents: opinion is no longer unanimous; the general will ceases to be the will of all; contradictory views and debates arise; and the best advice is not taken without question.

Finally, when the State, on the eve of ruin, maintains only a vain, illusory, and formal existence, when in every heart the social bond is broken, and the meanest interest brazenly lays hold of the sacred name of "public good," the general will becomes mute: all men, guided by secret motives, no more give their views as citizens than if the State had never been; and iniquitous decrees directed solely to private interest get passed under the name of laws.

Does it follow from this that the general will is exterminated or corrupted? Not at all: it is always constant, unalterable, and pure; but it is subordinated to other wills which encroach upon its sphere. Each man, in detaching his interest from the common interest, sees clearly that he cannot entirely separate them; but his share in the public mishaps seems to him negligible beside the exclusive good he aims at making his own. Apart from this particular good, he wills the general good in his own interest, as strongly as any one else. Even in selling his vote for money, he does not extinguish in himself the general will, but only eludes it. The fault he commits is that of changing the state of the question, and answering something different from what he is asked. Instead of saying, by his vote, "It is to the advantage of the State," he says, "It is of advantage to this or that man or party that this or that view should prevail." Thus the law of public order in assemblies is not so much to maintain in them the general will as to secure that the question be always put to it, and the answer always given by it.

I could here set down many reflections on the simple right of voting in every act of Sovereignty—a right which no one can take from the citizens—and also on the right of stating views, making proposals, dividing and discussing, which the government is always most careful to leave solely to ts members; but this important subject would need a treatise to itself, and it is impossible to say everything in a single work.

II

VOTING

It may be seen, from the last chapter, that the way in which general business is managed may give a clear enough indication of the actual state of morals and the health of the body politic. The more concert reigns in the assemblies, that is, the nearer opinion approaches unanimity, the greater is the dominance of the general will. On the other hand, long debates, discussions, and tumult proclaim the ascendancy of particular interests and the decline of the State.

This seems less clear when two or more orders enter into the constitution, as patricians and plebeians did at Rome; for quarrels between these two orders often disturbed the comitia, even in the best days of the Republic. But the exception is rather apparent than real; for then, through the defect that is inherent in the body politic, there were, so to speak, two States in one, and what is not true of the two together is true of either separately. Indeed, even in the most stormy times, the *plebiscita* of the people, when the senate did not interfere with them, always went through quietly and by large majorities. The citizens having but one interest, the people had but a single will.

At the other extremity of the circle, unanimity recurs; this is the case when the citizens, having fallen into servitude, have lost both liberty and will. Fear and flattery then change votes into acclamation; deliberation ceases, and only worship or malediction is left. Such was the vile manner in which the senate expressed its views under the emperors. It did so sometimes with absurd precautions. Tacitus observes that, under Otho, the senators, while they heaped curses on Vitellius, contrived at the same time to make a deafening noise, in order that, should he ever become their master, he might not know what each of them had said.

On these various considerations depend the rules by which the methods of counting votes and comparing opinions should be regulated, according as the general will is more or less easy to discover, and the State more or less in its decline.

There is but one law which, from its nature, needs unanimous consent. This is the social compact; for civil association is the most voluntary of all acts. Every man being born free and his own master, no one, under any pretext whatsoever, can make any man subject without his consent. To decide that the son of a slave is born a slave is to decide that he is not born a man.

If then there are opponents when the social compact is made, their opposition does not invalidate the contract, but merely prevents them from being included in it. They are foreigners among citizens. When the State is instituted, residence constitutes consent; to dwell within its territory is to submit to the Sovereign.[1]

Apart from this primitive contract, the vote of the majority always binds all the rest. This follows from the contract itself. But it is asked how a man can be both free and forced to conform to wills that are not his own. How are the opponents at once free and subject to laws they have not agreed to?

I retort that the question is wrongly put. The citizen gives his consent to all the laws, including those which are passed in spite of his opposition, and even those which punish him when he dares to break any of them. The constant will of all the members of the State is the general will; by virtue of it they are citizens and free.[2] When in the popular assembly a law is proposed, what the people is asked is not exactly whether it approves or rejects the proposal, but whether it is in conformity with the general will, which is their will. Each man, in giving his vote, states his opinion on that point; and the general will is found by counting votes. When therefore the opinion that is contrary to my own prevails, this proves neither more nor less than I was mistaken, and that what I thought to be the general will was not so. If my particular opinion had carried the day I should have achieved the opposite of what was my will; and it is in that case that I should not have been free.

This presupposes, indeed, that all the qualities of the general will still reside in the majority: when they cease to do so, whatever side a man may take, liberty is no longer possible.

In my earlier demonstration of how particular wills are substituted for the general will in public deliberation, I have adequately pointed out the practicable methods of avoiding this abuse; and I shall have more to say of them later on. I have also given the principles for determining the proportional number of votes for declaring that will. A difference of one vote destroys equality; a single opponent destroys unanimity; but between equality and unanimity, there are several grades of unequal division, at each of which this proportion may be fixed in accordance with the condition and the needs of the body politic.

There are two general rules that may serve to regulate this relation. First, the more grave and important the questions discussed, the nearer should the opinion that is to prevail approach unanimity. Secondly, the more the matter in hand calls for speed, the smaller the prescribed difference in the numbers of votes may be allowed to become: where an instant decision has to be reached, a majority of one vote should be enough. The first of these two rules seems more in harmony with the laws, and the second with practical affairs. In any case, it is the combination of them that gives the best proportions for determining the majority necessary.

III

ELECTIONS

In the elections of the prince and the magistrates, which are, as I have said, complex acts, there are two possible methods of procedure, choice and lot. Both have been employed in various republics, and a highly complicated mixture of the two still survives in the election of the Doge at Venice.

"Election by lot," says Montesquieu, "is democratic in nature." I agree that it is so; but in what sense? "The lot," he goes on, "is a way of making choice that is unfair to nobody; it leaves each citizen a reasonable hope of serving his country." These are not reasons.

If we bear in mind that the election of rulers is a function of government, and not of Sovereignty, we shall see why the lot is the method more natural to democracy, in which the administration is better in proportion as the number of its acts is small.

In every real democracy, magistracy is not an advantage, but a burdensome charge which cannot justly be imposed on one individual rather than another. The law alone can lay the charge on him on whom the lot falls. For, the conditions being then the same for all, and the choice not depending on any human will, there is no particular application to alter the universality of the law.

In an aristocracy, the prince chooses the prince, the government is preserved by itself, and voting is rightly ordered.

The instance of the election of the Doge of Venice confirms, instead of destroying, this distinction; the mixed form suits a mixed government. For it is an error to take the government of Venice for a real aristocracy. If the people has no share in the government, the nobility is itself the people. A host of poor Barnabites never gets near any magistracy, and its nobility consists merely in the empty title of Excellency, and in the right to sit in the Great Council. As this Great Council is as numerous as our General Council at Geneva, its illustrious members have no more privileges than our plain citizens. It is indisputable that, apart from the extreme disparity between the two republics, the *bourgeoisie* of Geneva is exactly equivalent to the *patriciate* of Venice; our *natives* and *inhabitants* correspond to the *townsmen* and the *people* of Venice; our *peasants* correspond to the *subjects* on the mainland; and, however that republic be regarded, if its size be left out of account, its government is no more aristocratic than our own. The whole difference is that, having no life-ruler, we do not, like Venice, need to use the lot.

Election by lot would have few disadvantages in a real democracy, in which, as equality would everywhere exist in morals and talents as well as in principles and fortunes, it would become almost a matter of indifference who was chosen. But I have already said that a real democracy is only an ideal.

When choice and lots are combined, positions that require special terms, such as military posts, should be filled by the former; the latter does for cases, such as judicial offices, in which good sense, justice, and integrity are enough, because in a State that is well constituted, these qualities are common to all the citizens.

Neither lot nor vote has any place in monarchical government. The monarch being by right sole prince and only magistrate, the choice of his lieutenants belongs to none but him. When the Abbé de Saint-Pierre proposed that the Councils of the King of France should be multiplied, and their members elected by ballot, he did not see that he was proposing to change the form of government.

I should now speak of the methods of giving and counting opinions in the assembly of the people; but perhaps an account of this aspect of the Roman constitution will more forcibly illustrate all the rules I could lay down. It is worth the while of a judicious reader to follow in some detail the working of public and private affairs in a Council consisting of two hundred thousand men.

IV

THE ROMAN COMITIA

We are without well-certified records of the first period of Rome's existence; it even appears very probable that most of the stories told about it are fables; indeed, generally speaking, the most instructive part of the history of peoples, that which deals with their foundation, is what we have least of. Experience teaches us every day what causes lead to the revolutions of empires; but, as no new peoples are now formed, we have almost nothing beyond conjecture to go upon in explaining how they were created.

The customs we find established show at least that these customs had an origin. The traditions that go back to those origins, that have the greatest authorities behind them, and that are confirmed by the strongest proofs, should pass for the most certain. These are the rules I have tried to follow in inquiring how the freest and most powerful people on earth exercised its supreme power.

After the foundation of Rome, the new-born republic, that is, the army of its founder, composed of Albans, Sabines, and foreigners, was divided into three classes, which, from this division, took the name of *tribes.* Each of these tribes was subdivided into ten *curiae,* and each *curia* into *decuriae,* headed by leaders called *curiones* and *decuriones.*

Besides this, out of each tribe was taken a body of one hundred *Equites* or Knights, called a *century,* which shows that these divisions, being unnecessary in a town, were at first merely military. But an instinct for greatness seems to have led the little township of Rome to provide itself in advance with a political system suitable for the capital of the world.

Out of this original division an awkward situation soon arose. The tribes of the Albans (Ramnenses) and the Sabines (Tatienses) remained always in the same condition, while that of the foreigners (Luceres) continually grew as more and more foreigners came to live at Rome, so that it soon surpassed the others in strength. Servius remedied this dangerous fault by changing the principle of cleavage, and substituting for the racial division, which he abolished, a new one based on the quarter of the town inhabited by each tribe. Instead of three tribes he created four, each occupying and named after one of the hills of Rome. Thus, while redressing the inequality of the moment, he also provided for the future; and in order that the division might be one of persons as well as localities, he forbade the inhabitants of one quarter to migrate to another, and so prevented the mingling of the races.

He also doubled the three old centuries of Knights and added twelve more, still keeping the old names, and by this simple and prudent method, succeeded in making a distinction between the body of Knights and the people, without a murmur from the latter.

To the four urban tribes Servius added fifteen others called rural tribes, because they consisted of those who lived in the country, divided into fifteen cantons. Subsequently, fifteen more were created, and the Roman people finally found itself divided into thirty-five tribes, as it remained down to the end of the Republic.

The distinction between urban and rural tribes had one effect which is worth mention, both because it is without parallel elsewhere, and because to it Rome owed the preservation of her morality and the enlargement of her empire. We should have expected that the urban tribes would soon monopolize power and honors, and lose no time in bringing the rural tribes into disrepute; but what happened was exactly the reverse. The taste of the early Romans for country life is well known. This taste they owed to their wise founder, who made rural and military labors go along with liberty, and, so to speak, relegated to the town arts, crafts, intrigue, fortune, and slavery.

Since therefore all Rome's most illustrious citizens lived in the fields and tilled the earth, men grew used to seeking there alone the mainstays of the republic. This condition, being that of the best patricians, was honored by all men; the simple and laborious life of the villager was preferred to the slothful and idle life of the *bourgeoisie* of Rome; and he who, in the town, would have been but a wretched proletarian, became, as a laborer in the fields, a respected citizen. Not without reason, says Varro, did our great-souled ancestors establish in the village the nursery of the sturdy and valiant men who defended them in time of war and provided for their sustenance in time of peace. Pliny states positively that the country tribes were honored because of the men of whom they were composed; while cowards men wished to dishonor were transferred, as a public disgrace, to the town tribes. The Sabine Appius Claudius, when he had come to settle in Rome, was loaded with honors and enrolled in a rural tribe, which subsequently took his family name. Lastly, freedmen always entered the urban, and never the rural tribes: nor is there a single example, throughout the Republic, of a freedman, though he had become a citizen, reaching any magistracy.

This was an excellent rule; but it was carried so far that in the end it led to a change and certainly to an abuse in the political system.

First the censors, after having for a long time claimed the right of transferring citizens arbitrarily from one tribe to another, allowed most persons to enroll themselves in whatever tribe they pleased. This permission certainly did no good, and further robbed the censorship of one of its greatest resources. Moreover, as the great and powerful all got themselves enrolled in the country tribes, while the freedmen who had become citizens remained with the populace in the town tribes, both soon ceased to have any local or territorial meaning, and all were so confused that the members of one could not be told from those of another except by the registers; so that the idea of the word "tribe" became personal instead of real, or rather came to be little more than a chimera.

It happened in addition that the town tribes, being more on the spot, were soon the stronger in the comitia and sold the State to those who stooped to buy the votes of the rabble composing them.

As the founder had set up ten *curiae* in each tribe, the whole Roman people, which was then contained within the walls, consisted of thirty *curiae,* each with its temples, its gods, its officers, its priests, and its festivals, which were called *compitalia* and corresponded to the *paganalia,* held in later times by the rural tribes.

When Servius made his new division, as the thirty *curiae* could not be shared equally between his four tribes, and as he was unwilling to interfere with them, they became a further division of the inhabitants of Rome, quite independent of the tribes: but in the case of the rural tribes and their members there was no question of *curiae,* as the tribes had then become a purely civil institution, and, a new system of levying troops having been introduced, the military divisions of Romulus were superfluous. Thus, although every citizen was enrolled in a tribe, there were very many who were not members of a *curia.*

Servius made yet a third division, quite distinct from the two we have mentioned, which became, in its effects, the most important of all. He distributed the whole Roman people into six classes, distinguished neither by place nor by person, but by wealth; the first classes included the rich, the last the poor, and those between persons of moderate means. These six classes were subdivided into one hundred and ninety-three other bodies, called centuries, which were so divided that the first class alone comprised more than half of them, while the last comprised only one. Thus the class that had the smallest number of members had the largest number of centuries, and the whole of the last class only counted as a single subdivision, although it alone included more than half the inhabitants of Rome.

In order that the people might have the less insight into the results of this arrangement, Servius tried to give it a military tone: in the second class he inserted two centuries of armorers, and in the fourth two of makers of instruments of war: in each class, except the last, he distinguished young and old, that is, those who were under an obligation to bear arms and those whose age gave them legal exemption. It was this distinction, rather than that of wealth, which required frequent repetition of the census or counting. Lastly, he ordered that the assembly should be held in the Campus Martius, and that all who were of age to serve should come there armed.

The reason for his not making in the last class also the division of young and old was that the populace, of whom it was composed, was not given the right to bear arms for its country: a man had to possess a hearth to acquire the right to defend it, and of all the troops of beggars who today lend lustre to the armies of kings, there is perhaps not one who would not have been driven with scorn out of a Roman cohort, at a time when soldiers were the defenders of liberty.

In this last class, however, *proletarians* were distinguished from *capite unsi.* The former, not quite reduced to nothing, at least gave the State citizens, and sometimes, when the need was pressing, even soldiers. Those who had nothing at all, and could be numbered only by counting heads, were regarded as of absolutely no account, and Marius was the first who stooped to enroll them.

Without deciding now whether this third arrangement was good or bad in itself, I think I may assert that it could have been made practicable only by the simple morals, the disinterestedness, the liking for agriculture and the scorn for commerce and for love of gain which characterized the early Romans. Where is the modern people among whom consuming greed, unrest, intrigue, continual removals, and perpetual changes of fortune, could let such a system last for twenty years without turning the State upside down? We must indeed observe that morality and the censorship, being stronger than this institution, corrected its defects at Rome, and that the rich man found himself degraded to the class of the poor for making too much display of his riches.

From all this it is easy to understand why only five classes are almost always mentioned, although there were really six.

The sixth, as it furnished neither soldiers to the army nor votes in the Campus Martius,[1] and was almost without function in the State, was seldom regarded as of any account.

These were the various ways in which the Roman people was divided. Let us now see the effect on the assemblies. When lawfully summoned, these were called *comitia:* they were usually held in the public square at Rome or in the Campus Martius, and were distinguished as *Comitia Curiata, Comitia Centuriata,* and *Comitia Tributa,* according to the form under which they were convoked. The *Comitia Curiata* were founded by Romulus; the *Centuriata* by Servius; and the *Tributa* by the tribunes of the people. No law received its sanction and no magistrate was elected, save in the comitia; and as every citizen was enrolled in a *curia,* a century, or a tribe, it follows that no citizen was excluded from the right of voting, and that the Roman people was truly sovereign both *de jure* and *de facto.*

For the comitia to be lawfully assembled, and for their acts to have the force of law, three conditions were necessary. First, the body or magistrate convoking them had to possess the necessary authority; secondly, the assembly had to be held on a day allowed by law; and thirdly, the auguries had to be favorable.

The reason for the first regulation needs no explanation; the second is a matter of policy. Thus, the comitia might not be held on festivals or market-days, when the countryfolk, coming to Rome on business, had not time to spend the day in the public square. By means of the third, the senate held in check the proud and restive people, and meetly restrained the ardour of seditious tribunes, who, however, found more than one way of escaping this hindrance.

Laws and the election of rulers were not the only questions submitted to the judgment of the comitia: as the Roman people had taken on itself the most important functions of government, it may be said that the lot of Europe was regulated in its assemblies. The variety of their objects gave rise to the various forms these took, according to the matters on which they had to pronounce.

In order to judge of these various forms, it is enough to compare them. Romulus, when he set up *curiae,* had in view the checking of the senate by the people, and of the people by the senate, while maintaining his ascendancy over both alike. He therefore gave the people, by means of this assembly, all the authority of members to balance that of power and riches, which he left to the patricians. But, after the spirit of monarchy, he left all the same a greater advantage to the patricians in the influence of their clients on the majority of votes. This excellent institution of patron and client was a masterpiece of statesmanship and humanity without which the patriciate, being flagrantly in contradiction to the republican spirit, could not have survived. Rome alone has the honor of having given to the world this great example, which never led to any abuse, and yet has never been followed.

As the assemblies by *curiae* persisted under the kings till the time of Servius, and the reign of the later Tarquin was not regarded as legitimate, royal laws were called generally *leges curiatae.*

Under the Republic, the *curiae,* still confined to the four urban tribes, and including only the populace of Rome, suited neither the senate, which led the patricians, nor the tribunes, who, though plebeians, were at the head of the well-to-do citizens. They therefore fell into disrepute, and their degradation was such, that thirty lictors used to assemble and do what the *Comitia Curiata* should have done.

The division by centuries was so favorable to the aristocracy that it is hard to see at first how the senate ever failed to carry the day in the comitia bearing their name, by which the consuls, the censors, and the other curule magistrates were elected. Indeed, of the hundred and ninety-three centuries into which the six classes of the whole Roman people were divided, the first class contained ninety-eight; and, as voting went solely by centuries, this class alone had a majority over all the rest. When all these centuries were taken in agreement, the rest of the votes were not even taken; the decision of the smaller number passed for that of the multitude, and it may be said that, in the *Comitia Centuriata,* decisions were regulated far more by depth of purses than by the number of votes.

But this extreme authority was modified in two ways. First, the tribunes as a rule, and always a great number of plebeians, belonged to the class of the rich, and so counter-balanced the influence of the patricians in the first class.

The second way was this. Instead of causing the centuries to vote throughout in order, which would have meant beginning always with the first, the Romans always chose one by lot which proceeded alone to the election; after this all the centuries were summoned another day according to their rank, and the same election was repeated, and as a rule confirmed. Thus the authority of example was taken away from rank, and given to the lot on a democratic principle.

From this custom resulted a further advantage. The citizens from the country had time, between the two elections, to inform themselves of the merits of the candidate who had been provisionally nominated, and did not have to vote without knowledge of the case. But, under the pretext of hastening matters, the abolition of this custom was achieved, and both elections were held on the same day.

The *Comitia Tributa* were properly the council of the Roman people. They were convoked by the tribunes alone; at them the tribunes were elected and passed their *plebiscita.* The senate not only had no standing in them, but even no right to be present; and the senators, being forced to obey laws on which they could not vote, were in this respect less free than the meanest citizens. This injustice was altogether ill-conceived, and was alone enough to invalidate the decrees of a body to which all its members were not admitted. Had all the patricians attended the comitia by virtue of the right they had as citizens, they would not, as mere private individuals, have had any considerable influence on a vote reckoned by counting heads, where the meanest proletarian was as good as the *princeps senatus.*

It may be seen, therefore, that besides the order which was achieved by these various ways of distributing so great a people and taking its votes, the various methods were not reducible to forms indifferent in themselves, but the results of each were relative to the objects which caused it to be preferred.

Without going here into further details, we may gather from what has been said above that the *Comitia Tributa* were the most favorable to popular government, and the *Comitia Centuriata* to aristocracy. The *Comitia Curiata,* in which the populace of Rome formed the majority, being fitted only to further tyranny and evil designs, naturally fell into disrepute, and even seditious persons abstained from using a method which too clearly revealed their projects. It is indisputable that the whole majesty of the Roman people lay solely in the *Comitia Centuriata,* which alone included all; for the *Comitia Curiata* excluded the rural tribes, and the *Comitia Tributa* the senate and the patricians.

As for the method of taking the vote, it was among the ancient Romans as simple as their morals, although not so simple as at Sparta. Each man declared his vote aloud, and a clerk duly wrote it down; the majority in each tribe determined the vote of the tribe, the majority of the tribes that of the people, and so with *curiae* and centuries. This custom was good as long as honesty was triumphant among the citizens, and each man was ashamed to vote publicly in favor of an unjust proposal or an unworthy subject; but, when the people grew corrupt and votes were bought, it was fitting that voting should be secret in order that purchasers might be restrained by mistrust, and rogues be given the means of not being traitors.

I know that Cicero attacks this change, and attributes partly to it the ruin of the Republic. But though I feel the weight Cicero's authority must carry on such a point, I cannot agree with him; I hold, on the contrary, that, for want of enough such changes, the destruction of the State must be hastened. Just as the regimen of health does not suit the sick, we should not wish to govern a people that has been corrupted by the laws that a good people requires. There is no better proof of this rule than the long life of the Republic of Venice, of which the shadow still exists, solely because its laws are suitable only for men who are wicked.

The citizens were provided, therefore, with tablets by means of which each man could vote without anyone knowing how he voted: new methods were also introduced for collecting the tablets, for counting voices, for comparing numbers, etc.; but all these precautions did not prevent the good faith of the officers charged with these functions[2] from being often suspect. Finally, to prevent intrigues and trafficking in votes, edicts were issued; but their very number proves how useless they were.

Towards the close of the Republic, it was often necessary to have recourse to extraordinary expedients in order to supplement the inadequacy of the laws. Sometimes miracles were supposed; but this method, while it might impose on the people, could not impose on those who governed. Sometimes an assembly was hastily called together, before the candidates had time to form their factions: sometimes a whole sitting was occupied with talk, when it was seen that the people had been won over and was on the point of taking up a wrong position. But in the end ambition eluded all attempts to check it; and the most incredible fact of all is that, in the midst of all these abuses, the vast people, thanks to its ancient regulations, never ceased to elect magistrates, to pass laws, to judge cases, and to carry through business both public and private, almost as easily as the senate itself could have done.

V

THE TRIBUNATE

WHEN an exact proportion cannot be established between the constituent parts of the State, or when causes that cannot be removed continually alter the relation of one part to another, recourse is had to the institution of a peculiar magistracy that enters into no corporate unity with the rest. This restores to each term its right relation to the others, and provides a link or middle term between either prince and people, or prince and Sovereign, or, if necessary, both at once.

This body, which I shall call the *tribunate,* is the preserver of the laws and of the legislative power. It serves sometimes to protect the Sovereign against the government, as the tribunes of the people did at Rome; sometimes to uphold the government against the people, as the Council of Ten now does at Venice; and sometimes to maintain the balance between the two, as the Ephors did at Sparta.

The tribunate is not a constituent part of the city, and should have no share in either legislative or executive power; but this very fact makes its own power the greater: for, while it can do nothing, it can prevent anything from being done. It is more sacred and more revered, as the defender of the laws, than the prince who executes them, or than the Sovereign which ordains them. This was seen very clearly at Rome, when the proud patricians, for all their scorn of the people, were forced to bow before one of its officers, who had neither auspices nor jursidiction.

The tribunate, wisely tempered, is the strongest support a good constitution can have; but if its strength is ever so little excessive, it upsets the whole State. Weakness, on the other hand, is not natural to it: provided it is something, it is never less than it should be.

It degenerates into tyranny when it usurps the executive power, which it should confine itself to restraining, and when it tries to dispense with the laws, which it should confine itself to protecting. The immense power of the Ephors, harmless as long as Sparta preserved its morality, hastened corruption when once it had begun. The blood of Agis, slaughtered by these tyrants, was avenged by his successor; the crime and punishment of the Ephors alike hastened the destruction of the republic, and after Cleomenes Sparta ceased to be of any account. Rome perished in the same way: the excessive power of the tribunes, which they had usurped by degrees, finally served, with the help of laws made to secure liberty, as a safeguard for the emperors who destroyed it. As for the Venetian Council of Ten, it is a tribunal of blood, an object of horror to patricians and people alike; and, so far from giving a lofty protection to the laws, it does nothing, now they have become degraded, but strike in the darkness blows of which no one dare take note.

The tribunate, like the government, grows weak as the number of its members increases. When the tribunes of the Roman people, who first numbered only two, and then five, wished to double that number, the senate let them do so, in the confidence that it could use one to check another, as indeed it afterwards freely did.

The best method of preventing usurpations by so formidable a body, though no government has yet made use of it, would be not to make it permanent, but to regulate the periods during which it should remain in abeyance. These intervals, which should not be long enough to give abuses time to grow strong, may be so fixed by law that they can easily be shortened at need by extraordinary commissions.

This method seems to me to have no disadvantages, because, as I have said, the tribunate, which forms no part of the constitution, can be removed without the constitution being affected. It seems to be also efficacious, because a newly restored magistrate starts not with the power his predecessor exercised, but with that which the law allows him.

VI

THE DICTATORSHIP

THE inflexibility of the laws, which prevents them from adapting themselves to circumstances, may, in certain cases, render them disastrous, and make them bring about, at a time of crisis, the ruin of the State. The order and slowness of the forms they enjoin require a space of time which circumstances sometimes withhold. A thousand cases against which the legislator has made no provision may present themselves, and it is a highly necessary part of foresight to be conscious that everything cannot be foreseen.

It is wrong therefore to wish to make political institutions so strong as to render it impossible to suspend their operation. Even Sparta allowed its laws to lapse.

However, none but the greatest dangers can counterbalance that of changing the public order, and the sacred power of the laws should never be arrested save when the existence of the country is at stake. In these rare and obvious cases, provision is made for the public security by a particular act entrusting it to him who is most worthy. This commitment may be carried out in either of two ways, according to the nature of the danger.

If increasing the activity of the government is a sufficient remedy, power is concentrated in the hands of one or two of its members: in this case the change is not in the authority of the laws, but only in the form of administering them. If, on the other hand, the peril is of such a kind that the paraphernalia of the laws are an obstacle to their preservation, the method is to nominate a supreme ruler, who shall silence all the laws and suspend for a moment the sovereign authority. In such a case, there is no doubt about the general will, and it is clear that the people's first intention is that the state shall not perish. Thus the suspension of the legislative authority is in no sense its abolition; the magistrate who silences it cannot make it speak; he dominates it, but cannot represent it. He can do anything, except make laws.

The first method was used by the Roman senate when, in a consecrated formula, it changed the consuls to provide for the safety of the Republic. The second was employed when one of the two consuls nominated a dictator:[1] a custom Rome borrowed from Alba.

During the first period of the Republic, recourse was very often had to the dictatorship, because the State had not yet a firm enough basis to be able to maintain itself by the strength of its constitution alone. As the state of morality then made superfluous many of the precautions which would have been necessary at other times, there was no fear that a dictator would abuse his authority, or try to keep it beyond his term of office. On the contrary, so much power appeared to be burdensome to him who was clothed with it, and he made all speed to lay it down, as if taking the place of the laws had been too troublesome and too perilous a position to retain.

It is therefore the danger not of its abuse, but of its cheapening, that makes me attack the indiscreet use of this supreme magistracy in the earliest times. For as long as it was freely employed at elections, dedications, and purely formal functions, there was danger of its becoming less formidable in time of need, and of men growing accustomed to regarding as empty a title that was used only on occasions of empty ceremonial.

Towards the end of the Republic, the Romans, having grown more circumspect, were as unreasonably sparing in the use of the dictatorship as they had formerly been lavish. It is easy to see that their fears were without foundation, that the weakness of the capital secured it against the magistrates who were in its midst; that a dictator might, in certain cases, defend the public liberty, but could never endanger it; and that the chains of Rome would be forged, not in Rome itself, but in her armies. The weak resistance offered by Marius to Sulla, and by Pompey to Caesar, clearly showed what was to be expected from authority at home against force from abroad.

This misconception led the Romans to make great mistakes; such, for example, as the failure to nominate a dictator in the Catilinarian conspiracy. For, as only the city itself, with at most some province in Italy, was concerned, the unlimited authority the laws gave to the dictator would have enabled him to make short work of the conspiracy, which was, in fact, stifled only by a combination of lucky chances human prudence had no right to expect.

Instead, the senate contented itself with entrusting its whole power to the consuls, so that Cicero, in order to take effective action, was compelled on a capital point to exceed his powers; and if, in the first transports of joy, his conduct was approved, he was justly called, later on, to account for the blood of citizens spilt in violation of the laws. Such a reproach could never have been levelled at a dictator. But the consul's eloquence carried the day; and he himself, Roman though he was, loved his own glory better than his country, and sought, not so much the most lawful and secure means of saving the State, as to get for himself the whole honor of having done so.[2] He was therefore justly honored as the liberator of Rome, and also justly punished as a law-breaker. However brilliant his recall may have been, it was undoubtedly an act of pardon.

However this important trust be conferred, it is important that its duration should be fixed at a very brief period, incapable of being ever prolonged. In the crises which lead to its adoption, the state is either soon lost, or soon saved; and, the present need passed, the dictatorship becomes either tyrannical or idle. At Rome, where dictators held office for six months only, most of them abdicated before their time was up. If their term had been longer, they might well have tried to prolong it still further, as the decemvirs did when chosen for a year. The dictator had only time to provide against the need that had caused him to be chosen; he had none to think of further projects.

VII

THE CENSORSHIP

As the law is the declaration of the general will, the censorship is the declaration of the public judgment: public opinion is the form of law which the censor administers, and, like the prince, only applies to particular cases.

The censorial tribunal, so far from being the arbiter of the people's opinion, only declares it, and, as soon as the two part company, its decisions are null and void.

It is useless to distinguish the morality of a nation from the object of its esteem; both depend on the same principle and are necessarily indistinguishable. There is no people on earth the choice of whose pleasures is not decided by opinion rather than nature. Right men's opinions, and their morality will purge itself. Men always love what is good or what they find good; it is in judging what is good that they go wrong. This judgment, therefore, is what must be regulated. He who judges of morality judges of honor; and he who judges of honor finds his law in opinion.

The opinions of a people are derived from its constitution; although the law does not regulate morality, it is legislation that gives it birth. When legislation grows weak, morality degenerates; but in such cases the judgment of the censors will not do what the force of the laws has failed to effect.

From this it follows that the censorship may be useful for the preservation of morality, but can never be so for its restoration. Set up censors while the laws are vigorous; as soon as they have lost their vigor, all hope is gone; no legitimate power can retain force when the laws have it.

The censorship upholds morality by preventing opinion from growing corrupt, by preserving its rectitude by means of wise applications, and sometimes even by fixing it when it is still uncertain. The employment of seconds in duels, which had been carried to wild extremes in the kingdom of France, was done away with merely by these words in a royal edict: "As for those who are cowards enough to call upon seconds." This judgment, in anticipating that of the public, suddenly decided it. But when edicts from the same source tried to pronounce duelling itself an act of cowardice, as indeed it is, then, since common opinion does not regard it as such, the public took no notice of a decision on a point on which its mind was already made up.

I have stated elsewhere[1] that as public opinion is not subject to any constraint, there need be no trace of it in the tribunal set up to represent it. It is impossible to admire too much the art with which this resource, which we moderns have wholly lost, was employed by the Romans, and still more by the Lacedaemonians.

A man of bad morals having made a good proposal in the Spartan Council, the Ephors neglected it, and caused the same proposal to be made by a virtuous citizen. What an honor for the one, and what a disgrace for the other, without praise or blame of either! Certain drunkards from Samos[2] polluted the tribunal of the Ephors: the next day, a public edict gave Samians permission to be filthy. An actual punishment would not have been so severe as such an impunity. When Sparta has pronounced on what is or is not right, Greece makes no appeal from her judgments.

VIII

CIVIL RELIGION

AT first men had no kings save the gods, and no government save theocracy. They reasoned like Caligula, and, at that period, reasoned aright. It takes a long time for feeling so to change that men can make up their minds to take their equals as masters, in the hope that they will profit by doing so.

From the mere fact that God was set over every political society, it followed that there were as many gods as peoples. Two peoples that were strangers the one to the other, and almost always enemies, could not long recognize the same master: two armies giving battle could not obey the same leader. National divisions thus led to polytheism, and this in turn gave rise to theological and civil intolerance, which, as we shall see hereafter, are by nature the same.

The fancy the Greeks had for rediscovering their gods among the barbarians arose from the way they had of regarding themselves as the natural Sovereigns of such peoples. But there is nothing so absurd as the erudition which in our days identifies and confuses gods of different nations. As if Moloch, Saturn, and Chronos could be the same god! As if the Phoenician Baal, the Greek Zeus, and the Latin Jupiter could be the same! As if there could still be anything common to imaginary beings with different names!

If it is asked how in pagan times, where each State had its cult and its gods, there were no wars of religion, I answer that it was precisely because each State, having its own cult as well as its own government, made no distinction between its gods and its laws. Political war was also theological; the provinces of the gods were, so to speak, fixed by the boundaries of nations. The god of one people had no right over another.

The gods of the pagans were not jealous gods; they shared among themselves the empire of the world: even Moses and the Hebrews sometimes lent themselves to this view by speaking of the God of Israel. It is true, they regarded as powerless the gods of the Canaanites, a proscribed people condemned to destruction, whose place they were to take; but remember how they spoke of the divisions of the neighboring peoples they were forbidden to attack! "Is not the possession of what belongs to your god Chamos lawfully your due?" said Jephthah to the Ammonites. "We have the same title to the lands our conquering God has made his own."[3] Here, I think, there is a recognition that the rights of Chamos and those of the God of Israel are of the same nature.

But when the Jews, being subject to the kings of Babylon, and, subsequently, to those of Syria, still obstinately refused to recognize any god save their own, their refusal was regarded as rebellion against their conqueror, and drew down on them the persecutions we read of in their history, which are without parallel till the coming of Christianity.[4]

Every religion, therefore, being attached solely to the laws of the State which prescribed it, there was no way of converting a people except by enslaving it, and there could be no missionaries save conquerors. The obligation to change cults being the law to which the vanquished yielded, it was necessary to be victorious before suggesting such a change. So far from men fighting for the gods, the gods, as in Homer, fought for men; each asked his god for victory, and repaid him with new altars. The Romans, before taking a city, summoned its gods to quit it; and in leaving the Tarentines their outraged gods, they regarded them as subject to their own and compelled to do them homage. They left the vanquished their gods as they left them their laws. A wreath to the Jupiter of the Capitol was often the only tribute they imposed.

Finally, when, along with their emperor, the Romans had spread their cult and their gods, and had themselves often adopted those of the vanquished, by granting to both alike the rights of the city, the peoples of that vast empire insensibly found themselves with multitudes of gods and cults, everywhere almost the same; and thus paganism throughout the known world finally came to be one and the same religion.

It was in these circumstances that Jesus came to set up on earth a spiritual kingdom, which, by separating the theological from the political system, made the state no longer one, and brought about the internal divisions which have never ceased to trouble Christian peoples. As the new idea of a kingdom of the other world could never have occurred to pagans, they always looked on the Christians as really rebels, who, while feigning to submit, were only waiting for the chance to make themselves independent and their masters, and to usurp by guile the authority they pretended in their weakness to respect. This was the cause of the persecutions.

What the pagans had feared took place. Then everything changed its aspect: the humble Christians changed their language, and soon this so-called kingdom of the other world turned, under a visible leader, into the most violent of earthly despotisms.

However, as there have always been a prince and civil laws, this double power and conflict of jurisdiction have made all good polity impossible in Christian States; and men have never succeeded in finding out whether they were bound to obey the master or the priest.

Several peoples, however, even in Europe and its neighborhood, have desired without success to preserve or restore the old system: but the spirit of Christianity has everywhere prevailed. The sacred cult has always remained or again become independent of the Sovereign, and there has been no necessary link between it and the body of the State. Mahomet held very sane views, and linked his political system well together; and as long as the form of his government continued under the caliphs who succeeded him, that government was indeed one, and so far good. But the Arabs, having grown prosperous, lettered, civilized, slack, and cowardly, were conquered by barbarians: the division between the two powers began again; and, although it is less apparent among the Mahometans than among the Christians, it none the less exists, especially in the sect of Ali, and there are States, such as Persia, where it is continually making itself felt.

Among us, the Kings of England have made themselves heads of the Church, and the Czars have done the same: but this title has made them less its masters than its ministers; they have gained not so much the right to change it, as the power to maintain it: they are not its legislators, but only its princes. Wherever the clergy is a corporate body,[5] it is master and legislator in its own country. There are thus two powers, two Sovereigns, in England and in Russia, as well as elsewhere.

Of all Christian writers, the philosopher Hobbes alone has seen the evil and how to remedy it, and has dared to propose the reunion of the two heads of the eagle, and the restoration throughout of political unity, without which no State or government will ever be rightly constituted. But he should have seen that the masterful spirit of Christianity is incompatible with his system, and that the priestly interest would always be stronger than that of the State. It is not so much what is false and terrible in his political theory, as what is just and true, that has drawn down hatred on it.[6]

I believe that if the study of history were developed from this point of view, it would be easy to refute the contrary views of Bayle and Warburton, one of whom holds that religion can be of no use to the body politic, while the other, on the contrary, maintains that Christianity is its strongest support. We should demonstrate to the former that no State has ever been founded without a religious basis, and to the latter, that the law of Christianity at bottom does more harm by weakening than good by strengthening the constitution of the State. To make myself understood, I have only to make a little more exact the too vague ideas of religion as relating to this subject.

Religion, considered in relation to society, which is either general or particular, may also be divided into two kinds: the religion of man, and that of the citizen. The first, which has neither temples, nor altars, nor rites, and is confined to the purely internal cult of the supreme God and the eternal obligations of morality, is the religion of the Gospel pure and simple, the true theism, what may be called natural divine right or law. The other, which is codified in a single country, gives it its gods, its own tutelary patrons; it has its dogmas, its rites, and its external cult prescribed by law; outside the single nation that follows it, all the world is in its sight infidel, foreign, and barbarous; the duties and rights of man extend for it only as far as its own altars. Of this kind were all the religions of early peoples, which we may define as civil or positive divine right or law.

There is a third sort of religion of a more singular kind, which gives men two codes of legislation, two rulers, and two countries, renders them subject to contradictory duties, and makes it impossible for them to be faithful both to religion and to citizenship. Such are the religions of the Lamas and of the Japanese, and such is Roman Christianity, which may be called the religion of the priest. It leads to a sort of mixed and anti-social code which has no name.

In their political aspect, all three kinds of religion have their defects. The third is so clearly bad, that it is waste of time to stop to prove it such. All that destroys social unity is worthless; all institutions that set man in contradiction to himself are worthless.

The second is good in that it unites the divine cult with love of the laws, and, making country the object of the citizens' adoration, teaches them that service done to the State is service done to its tutelary god. It is a form of theocracy, in which there can be no pontiff save the prince, and no priests save the magistrates. To die for one's country than becomes martyrdom; violation of its laws, impiety; and to subject one who is guilty to public execration is to condemn him to the anger of the gods: *Sacer estod.*

On the other hand, it is bad in that, being founded on lies and error, it deceives men, makes them credulous and superstitious, and drowns the true cult of the Divinity in empty ceremonial. It is bad, again, when it becomes tyrannous and exclusive, and makes a people bloodthirsty and intolerant, so that it breathes fire and slaughter, and regards as a sacred act the killing of everyone who does not believe in its gods. The result is to place such a people in a natural state of war with all others, so that its security is deeply endangered.

There remains therefore the religion of man or Christianity—not the Christianity of to-day, but that of the Gospel, which is entirely different. By means of this holy, sublime, and real religion all men, being children of one God, recognize one another as brothers, and the society that unites them is not dissolved even at death.

But this religion, having no particular relation to the body politic, leaves the laws in possession of the force they have in themselves without making any addition to it; and thus one of the great bonds that unite society considered in severally fails to operate. Nay, more, so far from binding the hearts of the citizens to the State, it has the effect of taking them away from all earthly things. I know of nothing more contrary to the social spirit.

We are told that a people of true Christians would form the most perfect society imaginable. I see in this supposition only one great difficulty: that a society of true Christians would not be a society of men.

I say further that such a society, with all its perfection, would be neither the strongest nor the most lasting: the very fact that it was perfect would rob it of its bond of union; the flaw that would destroy it would lie in its very perfection.

Every one would do his duty; the people would be law-abiding, the rulers just and temperate; the magistrates upright and incorruptible; the soldiers would scorn death; there would be neither vanity nor luxury. So far so good; but let us hear more.

Christianity as a religion is entirely spiritual, occupied solely with heavenly things; the country of the Christian is not of this world. He does his duty, indeed, but does it with profound indifference to the good or ill success of his cares. Provided he has nothing to reproach himself with, it matters little to him whether things go well or ill here on earth. If the State is prosperous, he hardly dares to share in the public happiness, for fear he may grow proud of his country's glory; if the State is languishing he blesses the hand of God that is hard upon His people.

For the State to be peaceable and for harmony to be maintained, all the citizens without exception would have to be good Christians; if by ill hap there should be a single self-seeker or hypocrite, a Catiline or a Cromwell, for instance, he would certainly get the better of his pious compatriots. Christian charity does not readily allow a man to think hardly of his neighbors. As soon as, by some trick, he has discovered the art of imposing on them and getting hold of a share in the public authority, you have a man established in dignity; it is the will of God that he be respected: very soon you have a power; it is God's will that it be obeyed: and if the power is abused by him who wields it, it is the scourge wherewith God punishes His children. There would be scruples about driving out the usurper: public tranquillity would have to be disturbed, violence would have to be employed, and blood spilt; all this accords ill with Christian meekness; and after all, in this vale of sorrows, what does it matter whether we are free men or serfs? The essential thing is to get to heaven, and resignation is only an additional means of doing so.

If war breaks out with another State, the citizens march readily out to battle; not one of them thinks of flight; they do their duty, but they have no passion for victory; they know better how to die than how to conquer. What does it matter whether they win or lose? Does not providence know better than they what is meet for them? Only think to what account a proud, impetuous, and passionate enemy could turn their stoicism! Set over against them those generous people who were devoured by ardent love of glory and of their country, imagine your Christian republic face to face with Sparta or Rome: the pious Christians will be beaten, crushed, and destroyed, before they know where they are, or will owe their safety only to the contempt their enemy will conceive for them. It was to my mind a fine oath that was taken by the soldiers of Fabius, who swore, not to conquer or die, but to come back victorious—and kept their oath. Christians would never have taken such an oath; they would have looked on it as tempting God.

But I am mistaken in speaking of a Christian republic; the terms are mutually exclusive. Christianity preaches only servitude and dependence. Its spirit is so favorable to tyranny that it always profits by such a regime. True Christians are made to be slaves, and they know it and do not much mind: this short life counts for too little in their eyes.

I shall be told that Christian troops are excellent. I deny it. Show me an instance. For my part, I know of no Christian troops. I shall be told of the Crusades. Without disputing the valor of the Crusaders, I answer that, so far from being Christians, they were the priests' soldiery, citizens of the Church. They fought for their spiritual country, which the Church had, somehow or other, made temporal. Well understood, this goes back to paganism: as the Gospel sets up no national religion, a holy war is impossible among Christians.

Under the pagan emperors, the Christian soldiers were brave; every Christian writer affirms it, and I believe it: it was a case of honorable emulation of the pagan troops. As soon as the emperors were Christian, this emulation no longer existed, and, when the Cross had driven out the eagle, Roman valor wholly disappeared.

But, setting aside political considerations, let us come back to what is right, and settle our principles on this important point. The right which the social compact gives the Sovereign over the subjects does not, we have seen, exceed the limits of public expediency.[7] The subjects then owe the Sovereign an account of their opinions only to such an extent as they matter to the community. Now, it matters very much to the community that each citizen should have a religion. That will make him love his duty; but the dogmas of that religion concern the State and its members only so far as they have reference to morality and to the duties which he who professes them is bound to do to others. Each man may have, over and above, what opinions he pleases, without its being the Sovereign's business to take cognizance of them; for, as the Sovereign has no authority in the other world, whatever the lot of its subjects may be in the life to come, that is not its business, provided they are good citizens in this life.

There is therefore a purely civil profession of faith of which the Sovereign should fix the articles, not exactly as religious dogmas, but as social sentiments without which a man cannot be a good citizen or a faithful subject.[8] While it can compel no one to believe them, it can banish from the State whoever does not believe them—it can banish him, not from impiety, but as an anti-social being, incapable of truly loving the laws and justice, and of sacrificing, at need, his life to his duty. If anyone, after publicly recognizing these dogmas, behaves as if he does not believe them, let him be punished by death: he has committed the worst of all crimes, that of lying before the law.

The dogmas of civil religion ought to be few, simple, and exactly worded, without explanation or commentary. The existence of a mighty, intelligent, and beneficent divinity, possessed of foresight and providence, the life to come, the happiness of the just, the punishment of the wicked, the sanctity of the social contract and the law: these are its positive dogmas. Its negative dogmas I confine to one, intolerance, which is a part of the cults we have rejected.

Those who distinguish civil from theological intolerance are, to my mind, mistaken. The two forms are inseparable. It is impossible to live at peace with those we regard as damned; to love them would be to hate God who punishes them: we positively must either reclaim or torment them. Wherever theological intolerance is admitted, it must inevitably have some civil effect;[9] and as soon as it has such an effect, the Sovereign is no longer Sovereign even in the temporal sphere: thenceforth priests are the real masters, and kings only their ministers.

Now that there is and can be no longer an exclusive national religion, tolerance should be given to all religions that tolerate others, so long as their dogmas contain nothing contrary to the duties of citizenship. But whoever dares to say: "Outside the Church is no salvation," ought to be driven from the State, unless the State is the Church, and the prince the pontiff. Such a dogma is good only in a theocratic government; in any other, it is fatal. The reason for which Henry IV is said to have embraced the Roman religion ought to make every honest man leave it, and still more any prince who knows how to reason.

IX

CONCLUSION

Now that I have laid down the true principles of political right, and tried to give the State a basis of its own to rest on, I ought next to strengthen it by its external relations, which would include the law of nations, commerce, the right of war and conquest, public right, leagues, negotiations, treaties, etc. But all this forms a new subject that is far too vast for my narrow scope. I ought throughout to have kept to a more limited sphere.

ENDNOTES

BOOK I

II

[1] "Learned inquiries into public right are often only the history of past abuses; and troubling to study them too deeply is a profitless infatuation" (*Essay on the Interests of France in Relation to its Neighbours,* by the Marquis d'Argenson). This is exactly what Grotius has done.

[2] See a short treatise of Plutarch's entitled "That Animals Reason."

IV

[1] The Romans, who understood and respected the right of war more than any other nation on earth, carried their scruples on this head so far that a citizen was not allowed to serve as a volunteer without engaging himself expressly against the enemy, and against such and such an enemy by name. A legion in which the younger Cato was seeing his first service under Popilius having been reconstructed, the elder Cato wrote to Popilius that, if he wished his son to continue serving under him, he must administer to him a new military oath, because, the first having been annulled, he was no longer able to bear arms against the enemy. The same Cato wrote to his son telling him to take great care not go to into battle before taking this new oath. I know that the siege of Clusium and other isolated events can be quoted against me; but I am citing laws and customs. The Romans are the people that least often transgressed in laws; and no other people has had such good ones.

VI

[1] The real meaning of this word has been almost wholly lost in modern times; most people mistake a town for a city, and a townsman for a citizen. They do not know that houses make a town, but citizens a city. The same mistake long ago cost the Carthaginians dear. I have never read of the title of citizens being given to the subjects of any prince, not even the ancient Macedonians or the English of to-day, though they are nearer liberty than any one else. The French alone everywhere familiarly adopt the name of citizens, because, as can be seen from their dictionaries, they have no idea of its meaning; otherwise they would be

guilty in usurping it, of the crime of *lèse-majesté:* among them, the name expresses a virtue, and not a right. When Bodin spoke of our citizens and townsmen, he fell into a bad blunder in taking the one class for the other. M. d'Alembert has avoided the error, and, in his article on Geneva, has clearly distinguished the four orders of men (or even five, counting mere foreigners) who dwell in our town, of which only two compose the Republic. No other French writer, to my knowledge, has understood the real meaning of the word citizen.

IX

[1] Under bad governments, this equality is only apparent and illusory; it serves only to keep the pauper in his poverty and the rich man in the position he has usurped. In fact, laws are always of use to those who possess and harmful to those who have nothing: from which it follows that the social state is advantageous to men only when all have something and none too much.

BOOK II

II

[1] To be general, a will need not always be unanimous; but every vote must be counted: andy exclusion is a breach of generality.

III

[1] "Every interest," says the Marquis d'Argenson, "has different principles. The agreement of two particular interests is formed by opposition to a third." He might have added that the agreement of all interests is formed by opposition to that of each. If there were no different interests, the common interest would be barely felt, as it would encounter no obstacle; all would go on of its own accord, and politics would cease to be an art.

[2] "In fact," says Machiavelli, "there are some divisions that are harmful to a Republic and some that are advantageous. Those which stir up sects and parties are harmful; those attended by neither are advantageous. Since, then, the founder of a Republic cannot help enmities arising, he ought at least to prevent them from growing into sects" (*History of Florence,* Book VII). [Rousseau quotes the Italian.]

IV

[1] Attentive readers, do not, I pray, be in a hurry to charge me with contradicting myself. The terminology made it unavoidable, considering the poverty of the language; but wait and see.

VI

[1] I understand by this word, not merely an aristocracy or a democracy, but generally any government directed by the general will, which is the law. To be legitimate, the government must be, not one with the Sovereign, but its minister. In such a case even a monarchy is a Republic. This will be made clearer in the following book.

VII

[1] A people becomes famous only when its legislation begins to decline. We do not know for how many centuries the system of Lycurgus made the Spartans happy before the rest of Greece took any notice of it.

[2] Montesquieu, *The Greatness and Decadence of the Romans,* ch. i.

[3] Those who know Calvin only as a theologian much underestimate the extent of his genius. The codification of our wise edicts, in which he played a large part, does him no less honor than his *Institute.* Whatever revolution time may bring in our religion, so long as the spirit of patriotism and liberty still lives among us, the memory of this great man will be for ever blessed.

[4] "In truth," says Machiavelli, "there has never been, in any country, an extraordinary legislator who has not had, recourse to God; for otherwise his laws would not have been accepted; there are, in fact, many useful truths of which a wise man may have knowledge without their having in themselves such clear reasons for their being so as to be able to convince others" (*Discourses on Livy,* Bk V, ch. xi). [Rousseau quotes the Italian.]

X

[1] If there were two neighboring peoples, one of which could not do without the other, it would be very hard on the former, and very dangerous for the latter. Every wise nation, in such a case, would make haste to free the other from dependence. The Republic of Thlascala, enclosed by the Mexican Empire, preferred doing without salt to buying from the Mexicans, or even getting it from them as a gift. The Thlascalans were wise enough to see the snare hidden under such liberality. They kept their freedom, and that little State, shut up in that great Empire, was finally the instrument of its ruin.

XI

[1] If the object is to give the State consistency, bring the two extremes as near to each other as possible; allow neither rich men nor beggars. These two estates, which are naturally inseparable, are equally fatal to the common good; from the one come the friends of tyranny, and from the other tyrants. It is always between them that public liberty is put up to auction; the one buys, and the other sells.

[2] "Any branch of foreign commerce," says M. d'Argenson, "creates on the whole only apparent advantage for the kingdom in general; it may enrich some individuals, or even some towns; but the nation as a whole gains nothing by it, and the people is no better off."

BOOK III

III

[1] Thus at Venice the College, even in the absence of the Doge, is called "Most Serence Prince."

IV

[1] The Palatine of Posen, father of the King of Poland, Duke of Lorraine. [I prefer liberty with danger to peace with slavery.]

V

[1] It is clear that the word *optimates* meant, among the ancients, not the best, but the most powerful.

[2] It is of great importance that the form of the election of magistrates should be regulated by law; for if it is left at the discretion of the prince, it is impossible to avoid falling into hereditary aristocracy, as the Republics of Venice and Berne actually did. The first of these has therefore long been a State dissolved; the second, however, is maintained by the extreme wisdom of the senate, and forms an honorable and highly dangerous exception.

VI

[1] Machiavelli was a proper man and a good citizen; but, being attached to the court of the Medici, he could not help veiling his love of liberty in the midst of his country's oppression. The choice of his detestable hero, Caesar Borgia, clearly enough shows his hidden aim; and the contradiction between the teaching of the *Prince* and that of the *Discourses on Livy* and the *History of Florence* shows that this profound political thinker has so far been studied only by superficial or corrupt readers. The court of Rome sternly prohibited his book. I can well believe it; for it is that court it most clearly portrays.

[2] Tacitus, *Histories,* I. 16. "For the best, and also the shortest way of finding out what is good and what is bad is to consider what you would have wished to happen or not to happen, had another than you been Emperior."

[3] In the *Politicus.*

VIII

[1] This does not contradict what I said before (bk. ii, ch. ix) about the disadvantages of great States; for we were then dealing with the authority of the government over the members, while here we are dealing with its force against the subjects. Its scattered members serve it as rallying-points for action against the people at a distance, but it has no rallying-point for direct action on its members themselves. Thus the length of the lever is its weakness in the one case, and its strength in the other.

IX

[1] On the same principle it should be judged what centuries deserve the preference for human prosperity. Those in which letters and arts have flourished have been too much admired, because the hidden object of their culture has not been fathomed, and their fatal effects not taken into account. "Idque apud imperitos humanitas vocabatur, cum pars servitutis esset." ["Fools called 'humanity' what was a part of slavery," Tacitus *Agricola,* 31.] Shall we never see in the maxims books lay down the vulgar interest that makes their writers speak? No, whatever they may say, when, despite its renown, a country is depopulated, it is not true that all is well, and it is not enough that a poet should have an income of 100,000 francs to make his age the best of all. Less attention should be paid to the apparent repose and tranquillity of the rulers than to the well-being of their nations as wholes, and above all

of the most numerous States. A hail-storm lays several cantons waste, but it rarely makes a famine. Outbreaks and civil wars give rulers rude shocks, but they are not the real ills of peoples, who may even get a respite, while there is a dispute as to who shall tyrannize over them. Their true prosperity and calamities come from their permanent condition: it is when the whole remains crushed beneath the yoke, that decay sets in, and that the rulers destroy them at will, and "ubi solitudinem faciunt, pacem appellant." ["Where they create solitude, they call it peace," Tacitus, *Agricola,* 31.] When the bickerings of the great disturbed the kingdom of France, and the Coadjutor of Paris took a dagger in his pocket to the Parliament, these things did not prevent the people of France from prospering and multiplying in dignity, ease, and freedom. Long ago Greece flourished in the midst of the most savage wars; blood ran in torrents, and yet the whole country was covered with inhabitants. It appeared, says Machiavelli, that in the midst of murder, proscription, and civil war, our republic only throve: the virtue, morality, and independence of the citizens did more to strengthen it than all their dissensions had done to enfeeble it. A little disturbance gives the soul elasticity; what makes the race truly prosperous is not so much peace as liberty.

X

[1] The slow formation and the progress of the Republic of Venice in its lagoons are a notable instance of this sequence; and it is most astonishing that, after more than twelve hundred years' existence, the Venetians seem to be still at the second stage, which they reached with the *Serrar di Consiglio* in 1198. As for the ancient Dukes who are brought up against them, it is proved, whatever the *Squittinio della libetà veneta* may say of them, that they were in no sense Sovereigns.

A case certain to be cited against my view is that of the Roman Republic, which, it will be said, followed exactly the opposite course, and passed from monarchy to aristocracy and from aristocracy to democracy. I by no means take this view of it.

What Romulus first set up was a mixed government, which soon deteriorated into despotism. From special causes, the State died an untimely death, as new-born children sometimes perish without reaching manhood. The expulsion of the Tarquins was the real period of the birth of the Republic. But at first it took on no constant form, because, by not abolishing the patriciate, it left half its works undone. For, by this means, hereditary aristocracy, the worst of all legitimate forms of administration, remained in conflict with democracy, and the form of the government, as Machiavelli has proved, was only fixed on the establishment of the tribunate: only then was there a true government and a veritable democracy. In fact, the people was then not only Sovereign, but also magistrate and judge; the senate was only a subordinate tribunal, to temper and concentrate the government, and the consuls themselves, though they were patricians, first magistrates, and absolute generals in war, were in Rome itself no more than presidents of the people.

From that point, the government followed its natural tendency, and inclined strongly to aristocracy. The patriciate, we may say, abolished itself, and the aristocracy was found no longer in the body of patricians as at Venice and Genoa, but in the body of the senate, which was composed of patricians and plebeians, and even in the body of tribunes when they began to usurp an active function: for names do not affect facts, and, when the people has rulers who govern for it, whatever name they bear, the government is an aristocracy.

The abuse of aristocracy led to the civil wars and the triumvirate. Sulla, Julius Caesar, and Augustus became in fact real monarchs; and finally, under the despotism of Tiberius, the State was dissolved. Roman history then confirms, instead of invalidating, the principle I have laid down.

[2] "Omnes enim et habentur et dicuntur tyranni, qui potestate utuntur perpetua in ea civitate quae libertate usa est" (Cornelius Nepos, *Life of Miltiades*). ["For all those are called and considered tyrants, who hold perpetual power in a State that has known liberty."] It is true that Aristotle (*Nicomachean Ethics,* Bk. viii, ch. x) distinguishes the tyrant from the king by the fact that the former governs in his own interest, and the latter only for the good of his subjects; but not only did all Greek authors in general use the word "tyrant" in a different sense, as appears most clearly in Xenophon's *Hiero,* but also it would follow from Aristotle's distinction that, from the very beginning of the world, there has not yet been a single king.

XIV

[1] In nearly the same sense as this word has in the English Parliament. The similarity of these functions would have brought the consuls and the tribunes into conflict, even had all jursidiction been suspended.

XV

[1] To adopt in cold countries the luxury and effeminacy of the East is to desire to submit to its chains; it is indeed to bow to them far more inevitably in our case than in theirs.

[2] I had intended to do this in the sequel to this work, when in dealing with external relations I came to the subject of confederations. The subject is quite new, and its principles have still to be laid down.

XVIII

[1] Provided, of course, he does not leave to escape his obligations and avoid having to serve his country in the hour of need. Flight in such a case would be criminal and punishable, and would be, not withdrawal, but desertion.

BOOK IV

II

[1] This should of course be understood as applying to a free State; for elsewhere family, goods, lack of a refuge, necessity, or violence may detain a man in a country against his will; and then his dwelling there no longer by itself implies his consent to the contract or to its violation.

[2] At Genoa, the word "Liberty" may be read over the front of the prisons and on the chains of the galley-slaves. This application of the device is good and just. It is indeed only malefactors of all estates who prevent the citizen from being free. In the country in which all such men were in the galleys, the most perfect liberty would be enjoyed.

IV

[1] I say "in the Campus Martius" because it was there that the comitia assembled by centuries; in its two other forms the people assembled in the *forum* or elsewhere; and then the *capite unsi* had as much influence and authority as the foremost citizens.

[2] *Custodes, diribitores, rogatores suffragiorum.*

VI

[1] The nomination was made secretly by night, as if there were something shameful in setting a man above the laws.

[2] That is what he could not be sure of, if he proposed a dictator; for he dared not nominate himself, and could not be certain that his colleague would nominate him.

VII

[1] I merely call attention in this chapter to a subject with which I have dealt at greater length in my *Letter to M. d'Alembert.*

[2] They were from another island, which the delicacy of our language forbids me to name on this occasion.

[3] "Nonne ea quae possidet Chamos deus tuus, tibi jure debentur?" (Judges xi. 24). Such is the text in the Vulgate. Father de Carrières translates: "Do you not regard yourselves as having a right to what your god possesses?" I do not know the force of the Hebrew text: but I perceive that, in the Vulgate, Jephthah positively recognizes the right of the god Chamos, and that the French translator weakened this admission by inserting an "according to you," which is not in the Latin.

[4] It is quite clear that the Phocian war, which was called "the Sacred War," was not a war of religion. Its object was the punishment of acts of sacrilege, and not the conquest of unbelievers.

[5] It should be noted that the clergy find their bond of union not so much in formal assemblies, as in the communion of Churches. Communion and excommunication are the social compact of the clergy, a compact which will always make them masters of people and kings. All priests who communicate together are fellow citizens, even if they come from opposite ends of the earth. This invention is a masterpiece of statesmanship: there is nothing like it among pagan priests; who have therefore never formed a clerical corporate body.

[6] See, for instance, in a letter from Grotius to his brother (April 18, 1643) what that learned man found to praise and to blame in the *De Cive.* It is true that, with a bent for indulgence, he seems to pardon the writer the good for the sake of the bad; but all men are not so forgiving.

[7] "In the republic," says the Marquis d'Argenson, "each man is prefectly free in what does not harm others." This is the invariable limitation, which it is impossible to define more exactly. I have not been able to deny myself the pleasure of occasionally quoting from this manuscrpt, though it is unknown to the public, in order to do honor to the memory of a good and illustrious man, who had kept even in the Ministry the heart of a good citizen, and views on the government of his country that were sane and right.

[8] Caesar, pleading for Catiline, tried to establish the dogma that the soul is mortal: Cato and Cicero, in refutation, did not waste time in philosophizing. They were content to show that Caesar spoke like a bad citizen, and brought forward a doctrine that would have a bad effect on the State. This, in fact, and not a problem of theology, was what the Roman senate had to judge.

[9] Marriage, for instance, being a civil contract, has civil effects without which society cannot even subsist. Suppose a body of clergy should claim the sole right of permitting this act, a right which every intolerant religion must out of necessity claim, is it not clear that in establishing the authority of the Church in this respect, it will be destroying that of the prince, who will have thenceforth only as many subjects as the clergy choose to allow him? Being in a position to marry or not to marry people, according to their acceptance of such and such a doctrine, their admission or rejection of such and such a formula, their greater or less piety, the Church alone, by the exercise of prudence and firmness, will dispose of all inheritances, offices, and citizens, and even of the state itself, which could not subsist if it were composed entirely of bastards. But, I shall be told, there will be appeals on the ground of abuse, summonses, and decrees; the temporalities will be seized. How sad! The clergy, however little, I will not say courage, but sense it has, will take no notice and go its way: it will quietly allow appeals, summonses, decrees, and seizures, and, in the end, will remain the master. It is not, I think, a great sacrifice to give up a part, when one is sure of securing all.

RIGHTS OF MAN

Thomas Paine

PART I

To

GEORGE WASHINGTON,
President of the United States of America

SIR,

I present you a small Treatise in defence of those Principles of Freedom which your exemplary Virtue hath so eminently contributed to establish.— That the Rights of Man may become as universal as your Benevolence can wish, and that you may enjoy the Happiness of seeing the New World regenerate the Old, is the Prayer of

SIR,

Your much obliged, and

Obedient humble Servant,

THOMAS PAINE

PREFACE

FROM the part Mr Burke took in the American Revolution, it was natural that I should consider him a friend to mankind; and as our acquaintance commenced on that ground, it would have been more agreeable to me to have had cause to continue in that opinion, than to change it.

At the time Mr Burke made his violent speech last winter in the English Parliament against the French Revolution and the National Assembly, I was in Paris, and had written him, but a short time before, to inform him how prosperously matters were going on. Soon after this, I saw his advertisement of the Pamphlet he intended to publish: As the attack was to be made in a language but little studied, and less understood, in France, and as every thing suffers by translation, I promised some of the friends of the Revolution in that country, that whenever Mr Burke's Pamphlet came forth, I would answer it. This appeared to me the more necessary to be done, when I saw the flagrant misrepresentations which Mr Burke' Pamphlet contains; and that while it is an outrageous abuse on the French Revolution, and the principles of Liberty, it is an imposition on the rest of the world.

I am the more astonished and disappointed at this conduct in Mr Burke, as (from the circumstance I am going to mention), I had formed other expectations.

I had seen enough of the miseries of war, to wish it might never more have existence in the world, and that some other mode might be found out to settle the differences that should occasionally arise in the neighbourhood of nations. This certainly might be done if Courts were disposed to set honestly about it, or if countries were enlightened enough not to be made the dupes of Courts. The people of America had been bred up in the same prejudices against France, which at that time characterized the people of England; but experience and an acquaintance with the French Nation have most effectually shown to the Americans the falsehood of those prejudices; and I do not believe that a more cordial and confidential intercourse exists between any two countries than between America and France.

When I came to France in the Spring of 1787, the Archbishop of Toulouse was then Minister, and at that time highly esteemed. I became much acquainted with the private Secretary of that Minister, a man of an enlarged benevolent heart; and found, that his sentiments and my own perfectly agreed with respect to the madness of war, and the wretched impolicy of two nations, like England and France, continually worrying each other, to no other end than that of a mutual increase of burdens and taxes. That I might be assured I had not misunderstood him, nor he me, I put the substance of our opinions into writing, and sent it to him; subjoining a request, that if I should see among the people of England, any disposition to cultivate a better understanding between the two nations than had hitherto prevailed, how far I might be authorized to say that the same disposition prevailed on the part of France? He answered me by letter in the most unreserved manner, and that not for himself only, but for the Minister, with whose knowledge the letter was declared to be written.

I put this letter into the hands of Mr Burke almost three years ago, and left it with him, where it still remains; hoping, and at the same time naturally expecting, from the opinion I had conceived of him, that he would find some opportunity of making a good use of it, for the purpose of removing those errors and prejudices, which two neighbouring nations, from the want of knowing each other, had entertained, to the injury of both.

When the French Revolution broke out, it certainly afforded to Mr Burke an opportunity of doing some good, had he been disposed to it; instead of which, no sooner did he see the old prejudices wearing away, than he immediately began sowing the seeds of a new inveteracy, as if he were afraid that England and France would cease to be enemies. That there are men in all countries who get their living by war, and by keeping up the quarrels of Nations, is as shocking as it is true; but when those who are concerned in the government of a country, make it their study to sow discord, and cultivate prejudices between Nations, it becomes the more unpardonable.

With respect to a paragraph in this Work alluding to Mr Burke's having a pension, the report has been some time in circulation, at least two months; and as a person is often the last to hear what concerns him the most to know, I have mentioned it, that Mr Burke may have an opportunity of contradicting the rumour, if he thinks proper.

THOMAS PAINE

RIGHTS OF MAN

&c. &c.

AMONG the incivilities by which nations or individuals provoke and irritate each other, Mr Burke's pamphlet on the French Revolution is an extraordinary instance. Neither the People of France, nor the National Assembly, were troubling themselves about the affairs of England, or the English Parliament; and why Mr Burke should commence an unprovoked attack upon them, both in parliament and in public, is a conduct that cannot be pardoned on the score of manners, nor justified on that of policy.

There is scarcely an epithet of abuse to be found in the English language, with which Mr Burke has not loaded the French Nation and the National Assembly. Everything which rancour, prejudice, ignorance, or knowledge could suggest, are poured forth in the copious fury of near four hundred pages. In the strain and on the plan Mr Burke was writing, he might have written on to as many thousands. When the tongue or the pen is let loose in a frenzy of passion, it is the man, and not the subject, that becomes exhausted.

Hitherto Mr Burke has been mistaken and disappointed in the opinions he had formed of the affairs of France; but such is the ingenuity of his hope, or the malignancy of his despair, that it furnishes him with new pretences to go on. There was a time when it was impossible to make Mr Burke believe there would be any revolution in France. His opinion then was, that the French had neither spirit to undertake it, nor fortitude to support it; and now that there is one, he seeks an escape, by condemning it.

Not sufficiently content with abusing the National Assembly, a great part of his work is taken up with abusing Dr Price (one of the best-hearted men that lives), and the two societies in England known by the name of the Revolution Society, and the Society for Constitutional Information.

Dr Price had preached a sermon on the 4th of November 1789, being the anniversary of what is called in England, the Revolution which took place 1688. Mr Burke, speaking of this sermon, says, 'The Political Divine proceeds dogmatically to assert, that, by the principles of the Revolution, the people of England have acquired three fundamental rights:

'1. To choose our own governors.

2. To cashier them for misconduct.

3. To frame a government for ourselves.'

Dr Price does not say that the right to do these things exists in this or in that person, or in this or in that description of persons, but that it exists in the *whole*; that it is a right resident in the nation.—Mr Burke, on the contrary, denies that such a right exists in the nation, either in whole or in part, or that it exists anywhere; and, what is still more strange and marvellous, he says, 'that the people of England utterly disclaim such a right, and that they will resist the practical assertion of it with their lives and fortunes.' That men should take up arms, and spend their lives and fortunes, *not* to maintain their rights, but to maintain they have *not* rights, is an entirely new species of discovery, and suited to the paradoxical genius of Mr Burke.

The method which Mr Burke takes to prove that the people of England have no such rights, and that such rights do not now exist in the nation, either in whole or in part, or anywhere at all, is of the same marvellous and monstrous kind with what he has already said; for his arguments are, that the persons, or the generation of persons, in whom they did exist, are dead, and with them the right is dead also. To prove this, he quotes a declaration made by parliament about a hundred years ago, to William and Mary, in these words: 'The Lords Spiritual and Temporal, and Commons, do, in the name of the people aforesaid,'—(meaning the people of England then living)—'most humbly and faithfully *submit* themselves, their *heirs* and *posterities*, for EVER.' He also quotes a clause of another act of parliament made in the same reign, the terms of which, he says, 'bind us'—(meaning the people of that day)—'our *heirs*, and our *posterity*, to *them*, their *heirs* and *posterity*, to the end of time.'

Mr Burke conceives his point sufficiently established by producing those clauses, which he enforces by saying that they exclude the right of the nation for *ever:* And not yet content with making such declarations, repeated over and over again, he farther says, 'that if the people of

England possessed such a right before the Revolution,' (which he acknowledges to have been the case, not only in England, but throughout Europe, at an early period), 'yet that the *English nation* did, at the time of the Revolution, most solemnly renounce and abdicate it, for themselves, and for *all their posterity, for ever.*'

As Mr Burke occasionally applies the poison drawn from his horrid principles, not only to the English nation, but to the French Revolution and the National Assembly, and charges that august, illuminated and illuminating body of men with the epithet of *usurpers,* I shall, *sans ceremonie,* place another system of principles in opposition to his.

The English Parliament of 1688 did a certain thing, which, for themselves and their constituents, they had a right to do, and which it appeared right should be done: But, in addition to this right, which they possessed by delegation, *they setup another right by assumption,* that of binding and controlling posterity to the end of time. The case, therefore, divides itself into two parts; the right which they possessed by delegation, and the right which they set up by assumption. The first is admitted; but, with respect to the second, I reply —

There never did, there never will, and there never can exist a parliament, or any description of men, or any generation of men, in any country, possessed of the right or the power of binding and controlling posterity to the '*end of time,*' or of commanding for ever how the world shall be governed, or who shall govern it; and therefore, all such clauses, acts or declarations, by which the makers of them attempt to do what they have neither the right nor the power to do, nor the power to execute, are in themselves null and void.—Every age and generation must be as free to act for itself, *in all cases,* as the ages and generations which preceded it. The vanity and presumption of governing beyond the grave, is the most ridiculous and insolent of all tyrannies. Man has no property in man; neither has any generation a property in the generations which are to follow. The parliament or the people of 1688, or of any other period, has no more right to dispose of the people of the present day, or to bind or to control them *in any shape whatever,* than the parliament or the people of the present day have to dispose of, bind or control those who are to live a hundred or a thousand years hence. Every generation is, and must be, competent to all the purposes which its occasions require. It is the living, and not the dead, that are to be accommodated. When man ceases to be, his power and his wants cease with him; and having no longer any participation in the concerns of this world, he has no longer any authority in directing who shall be its governors, or how its government shall be organized, or how administered.

I am not contending for nor against any form of government, nor for nor against any party here or elsewhere. That which a whole nation chooses to do, it has a right to do. Mr Burke says, No. Where then *does* the right exist? I am contending for the rights of the *living*, and against their being willed away, and controlled and contracted for, by the manuscript assumed authority of the dead; and Mr Burke is contending for the authority of the dead over the rights and freedom of the living. There was a time when kings disposed of their crowns by will upon their deathbeds, and consigned the people, like beasts of the field, to whatever successor they appointed. This is now so exploded as scarcely to be remembered, and so monstrous as hardly to be believed: But the parliamentary clauses upon which Mr Burke builds his political church, are of the same nature.

The laws of every country must be analogous to some common principle. In England, no parent or master, nor all the authority of parliament, omnipotent as it has called itself, can bind or control the personal freedom even of an individual beyond the age of twenty-one years: On what ground of right, then, could the parliament of 1688, or any other parliament, bind all posterity for ever?

Those who have quitted the world, and those who are not yet arrived at it, are as remote from each other, as the utmost stretch of mortal imagination can conceive: What possible obligation, then, can exist between them; what rule or principle can be laid down, that of two non-entities, the one out of existence, and the other not in, and who never can meet in this world, the one should control the other to the end of time?

In England, it is said that money cannot be taken out of the pockets of the people without their consent: But who authorized, or who could authorize the parliament of 1688 to control and take away the freedom of posterity, (who were not in existence to give or to withhold their consent,) and limit and confine their right of acting in certain cases for ever?

A greater absurdity cannot present itself to the understanding of man, than what Mr Burke offers to his readers. He tells them, and he tells the world to come, that a certain body of men, who existed a hundred years ago, made a law; and that there does not now exist in the nation, nor ever will, nor ever can, a power to alter it. Under how many subtleties, or absurdities, has the divine right to govern been imposed on the credulity of mankind! Mr Burke has discovered a new one, and he has shortened his journey to Rome, by appealing to the power of this infallible parliament of former days; and he produces what it has done, as of divine authority: for that power must certainly be more than human, which no human power to the end of time can alter.

But Mr Burke has done some service, not to his cause, but to his country, by bringing those clauses into public view. They serve to demonstrate how necessary it is at all times to watch against the attempted encroachment of power, and to prevent its running to excess. It is somewhat extraordinary, that the offence for which James II was expelled, that of setting up power by *assumption*, should be re-acted, under another shape and form, by the parliament that expelled him. It shows, that the rights of man were but imperfectly understood at the Revolution; for, certain it is, that the right which that parliament set up by *assumption* (for by delegation it had it not, and could not have it, because none could give it) over the persons and freedom of posterity for ever, was of the same tyrannical unfounded kind which James attempted to set up over the parliament and the nation, and for which he was expelled. The only difference is, (for in principle they differ not), that the one was an usurper over the living, and the other over the unborn; and as the one has no better authority to stand upon than the other, both of them must be equally null and void, and of no effect.

From what, or from whence, does Mr Burke prove the right of any human power to bind posterity for ever? He has produced his clauses; but he must produce also his proofs, that such a right existed, and show how it existed. If it ever existed, it must now exist; for whatever appertains to the nature of man, cannot be annihilated by man. It is the nature of man to die, and he will continue to die as long as he continues to be born. But Mr Burke has set up a sort of political Adam, in whom all posterity are bound for ever, he must therefore prove that his Adam possessed such a power, or such a right.

The weaker any cord is, the less will it bear to be stretched, and the worse is the policy to stretch it, unless it is intended to break it. Had any one purposed the overthrow of Mr Burke's positions, he would have proceeded as Mr Burke has done. He would have magnified the authorities, on purpose to have called the *right* of them into question; and the instant the question of right was started, the authorities must have been given up.

It requires but a very small glance of thought to perceive, that although laws made in one generation often continue in force through succeeding generations, yet that they continue to derive their force from the consent of the living. A law not repealed continues in force, not because it *cannot* be repealed, but because it *is not* repealed; and the non-repealing passes for consent.

But Mr Burke's clauses have not even this qualification in their favour. They become null, by attempting to become immortal. The nature of them precludes consent. They destroy the right which they *might* have, by grounding it on a right which they *cannot* have. Immortal power is not a human right, and therefore cannot be a right of parliament. The parliament of 1688 might as well have passed an act to have authorized themselves to live for ever, as to make their authority live for ever. All therefore that can be said of those clauses is, that they are a formality of words, of as much import, as if those who used them had addressed a congratulation to themselves, and, in the oriental style of antiquity, had said, O Parliament, live for ever!

The circumstances of the world are continually changing, and the opinions of men change also; and as government is for the living, and not for the dead, it is the living only that has any right in it. That which may be thought right and found convenient in one age, may be thought wrong and found inconvenient in another. In such cases, Who is to decide, the living, or the dead?

As almost one hundred pages of Mr Burke's book are employed upon these clauses, it will consequently follow, that if the clauses themselves, so far as they set up an *assumed, usurped* dominion over posterity for ever, are unauthoritative, and in their nature null and void; that all his voluminous inferences and declamation drawn therefrom, or founded thereon, are null and void also: and on this ground I rest the matter.

We now come more particularly to the affairs of France. Mr Burke's book has the appearance of being written as instruction to the French nation; but if I may permit myself the use of an extravagant metaphor, suited to the extravagance of the case, It is darkness attempting to illuminate light.

While I am writing this, there are accidentally before me some proposals for a declaration of rights by the Marquis de Lafayette (I ask his pardon for using his former address, and do it only for distinction's sake) to the National Assembly, on the 11th of July 1789, three days before the taking of the Bastille; and I cannot but remark with astonishment how opposite the sources are from which that Gentleman and Mr Burke draw their principles. Instead of referring to musty records and mouldy parchments to prove that the rights of the living are lost, 'renounced and abdicated for ever,' by those who are now no more, as Mr Burke has done, M. de Lafayette applies to the living world, and emphatically says, 'Call to mind the sentiments which Nature has engraved in the heart of every citizen, and which take a new force when they are solemnly recognized by all:—For a nation to love liberty, it is sufficient that she knows it; and to be free, it is sufficient that she wills it.' How dry, barren, and obscure, is the source from which Mr Burke labours! and how ineffectual, though gay with flowers, are all his declamation and his arguments, compared with these clear, concise, and soul-animating sentiments! Few and short as they are, they lead on to a vast field of generous and manly thinking, and do not finish, like Mr Burke's periods, with music in the ear, and nothing in the heart.

As I have introduced M. de Lafayette, I will take the liberty of adding an anecdote respecting his farewell address to the Congress of America in 1783, and which occurred fresh to my mind when I saw Mr Burke's thundering attack on the French Revolution.—M. de Lafayette went to America at an early period of the war, and continued a volunteer in her service to the end. His conduct through the whole of that enterprise is one of the most extraordinary that is to be found in the history of a young man, scarcely then twenty years of age. Situated in a country that was like the lap of sensual pleasure, and with the means of enjoying it, how few are there to be found who would exchange such a scene for the woods and wildernesses of America, and pass the flowery years of youth in unprofitable danger and hardship! but such is the fact. When the war ended, and he was on the point of taking his final departure, he presented himself to Congress, and contemplating, in his affectionate farewell, the revolution he had seen, expressed himself in these words: '*May this great monument, raised to Liberty, serve as a lesson to the oppressor, and an example to the oppressed!*'—When this address came to the hands of Dr Franklin, who was then in France, he applied to Count Vergennes to have it inserted in the French Gazette, but never could obtain his consent. The fact was, that Count Vergennes was an aristocratical despot at home, and dreaded the example of the American revolution in France, as certain other persons now dread the example of the French revolution in England; and Mr Burke's tribute of fear (for in this light his book must be considered) runs parallel with Count Vergennes' refusal. But, to return more particularly to his work — 'We have seen' (says Mr Burke) 'the French rebel against a mild and lawful Monarch, with more fury, outrage, and insult, than any people has been known to rise against the most illegal usurper, or the most sanguinary tyrant.' — This is one among a thousand other instances, in which Mr Burke shows that he is ignorant of the springs and principles of the French revolution.

It was not against Louis the XVIth, but against the despotic principles of the government, that the nation revolted. These principles had not their origin in him, but in the original establishment, many centuries back; and they were become too deeply rooted to be removed, and the augean stable of parasites and plunderers too abominably filthy to be cleansed, by anything short of a complete and universal revolution. When it becomes necessary to do a thing, the whole heart and soul should go into the measure, or not attempt it. That crisis was then arrived, and there remained no choice but to act with determined vigour, or not to act at all. The King was known to be the friend of the nation, and this circumstance was favourable to the enterprise. Perhaps no man bred up in the style of an absolute King, ever possessed a heart so little disposed to the exercise of that species of power as the present King of France. But the principles of the government itself still remained the same. The Monarch and the Monarchy were distinct and separate things; and it was against the established despotism of the latter, and not against the person or principles of the former, that the revolt commenced, and the revolution has been carried.

Mr Burke does not attend to the distinction between *men* and *principles*; and therefore, he does not see that a revolt may take place against the despotism of the latter, while there lies no charge of despotism against the former.

The natural moderation of Louis XVI contributed nothing to alter the hereditary despotism of the monarchy. All the tyrannies of former reigns, acted under that hereditary despotism, were still liable to be revived in the hands of a successor. It was not the respite of a reign that would satisfy France, enlightened as she was then become. A casual discontinuance of the *practice* of despotism, is not a discontinuance of its *principles*; the former depends on the virtue of the individual who is in immediate possession of the power; the latter, on the virtue and fortitude of the nation. In the case of Charles I and James II of England, the revolt was against the personal despotism of the men; whereas in France, it was against the hereditary despotism of the established government. But men who can consign over the rights of posterity for ever on the authority of a mouldy parchment, like Mr Burke, are not qualified to judge of this revolution. It takes in a field too vast for their views to explore, and proceeds with a mightiness of reason they cannot keep pace with.

But there are many points of view in which this revolution may be considered. When despotism has established itself for ages in a country, as in France, it is not in the person of the King only that it resides. It has the appearance of being so in show, and in nominal authority; but it is not so in practice, and in fact. It has its standard everywhere. Every office and department has its despotism, founded upon custom and usage. Every place has its Bastille, and every Bastille its despot. The original hereditary despotism resident in the person of the King, divides and subdivides itself into a thousand shapes and forms, till at last the whole of it is acted by deputation. This was the case in France; and against this species of despotism, proceeding on through an endless labyrinth of office till the source of it is scarcely perceptible, there is no mode of redress. It strengthens itself by assuming the appearance of duty, and tyrannizes under the pretence of obeying.

When a man reflects on the condition which France was in from the nature of her government, he will see other causes for revolt than those which immediately connect themselves with the person or character of Louis XVI. There were, if I may so express it, a thousand despotisms to be reformed in France, which had grown up under the hereditary despotism of the monarchy, and became so rooted as to be in a great measure independent of it. Between the monarchy, the parliament, and the church, there was a *rivalship* of despotism, besides the feudal despotism operating locally, and the ministerial despotism operating everywhere. But Mr Burke, by considering the King as the only possible object of a revolt, speaks as if France was a village, in which everything that passed must be known to its commanding officer, and no oppression could be acted but what he could immediately control. Mr Burke might have been in the Bastille his whole life, as well under Louis XVI as Louis XIV and neither the one nor the other have known that such a man as Mr Burke existed. The despotic principles of the government were the same in both reigns, though the dispositions of the men were as remote as tyranny and benevolence.

What Mr Burke considers as a reproach to the French Revolution, (that of bringing it forward under a reign more mild than the preceding ones), is one of its highest honours. The revolutions that have taken place in other European countries, have been excited by personal hatred. The rage was against the man, and he became the victim. But, in the instance of France, we see a revolution generated in the rational contemplation of the rights of man, and distinguishing from the beginning between persons and principles.

But Mr Burke appears to have no idea of principles, when he is contemplating governments. 'Ten years ago' (says he) 'I could have felicitated France on her having a government, without inquiring what the nature of that government was, or how it was administered.' Is this the language of a rational man? Is it the language of a heart feeling as it ought to feel for the rights and happiness of the human race? On this ground, Mr Burke must compliment all the governments in the world, while the victims who suffer under them, whether sold into slavery, or tortured out of existence, are wholly forgotten. It is power, and not principles, that Mr Burke venerates; and under this abominable depravity, he is disqualified to judge between them.—Thus much for his opinion as to the occasions of the French Revolution. I now proceed to other considerations.

I know a place in America called Point-no-Point; because as you proceed along the shore, gay and flowery as Mr Burke's language, it continually recedes and presents itself at a distance before you; but when you have got as far as you can go, there is no point at all. Just thus it is with Mr Burke's three hundred and fifty-six pages. It is therefore difficult to reply to him. But as the points he wishes to establish, may be inferred from what he abuses, it is in his paradoxes that we must look for his arguments.

As to the tragic paintings by which Mr Burke has outraged his own imagination, and seeks to work upon that of his readers, they are very well calculated for theatrical representation, where facts are manufactured for the sake of show, and accommodated to produce, through the weakness of sympathy, a weeping effect. But Mr Burke should recollect that he is writing History, and not *Plays*; and that his readers will expect truth, and not the spouting rant of high-toned exclamation.

When we see a man dramatically lamenting in a publication intended to be believed, that, '*The age of chivalry is gone*!' that '*The glory of Europe is extinguished forever!*' that '*The unbought grace of life*' (if any one knows what it is), '*the cheap defence of nations, the nurse of manly sentiment and heroic enterprise, is gone!*' and all this because the Quixote age of chivalry nonsense is gone, what opinion can we form of his judgement, or what regard can we pay to his facts? In the rhapsody of his imagination, he has discovered a world of windmills, and his sorrows are, that there are no Quixotes to attack them. But if the age of aristocracy, like that of chivalry, should fall, (and they had originally some connexion), Mr Burke, the trumpeter of the Order, may continue his parody to the end, and finish with exclaiming, '*Othello's occupation's gone!*'

Notwithstanding Mr Burke's horrid paintings, when the French Revolution is compared with the revolutions of other countries, the astonishment will be, that it is marked with so few sacrifices; but this astonishment will cease when we reflect that *principles*, and not *persons*, were the meditated objects of destruction. The mind of the nation was acted upon by a higher stimulus than what the consideration of persons could inspire, and sought a higher conquest than could be produced by the downfall of an enemy. Among the few who fell, there do not appear to be any that were intentionally singled out. They all of them had their fate in the circumstances of the moment, and were not pursued with that long, cold-blooded, unabated revenge which pursued the unfortunate Scotch in the affair of 1745.

Through the whole of Mr Burke's book I do not observe that the Bastille is mentioned more than once, and that with a kind of implication as if he were sorry it was pulled down, and wished it were built up again. 'We have rebuilt Newgate' (says he), 'and tenanted the mansion; and we have prisons almost as strong as the Bastille for those who dare to libel the Queens of France.'[1] As to what a madman, like the person called Lord G—G—, might say, and to whom Newgate is rather a bedlam than a prison, it is unworthy a rational consideration. It was a madman that libelled—and that is sufficient apology; and it afforded an opportunity for confining him, which was the thing that was wished for: But certain it is that Mr Burke, who does not call himself a madman, (whatever other people may do), has libelled, in the most unprovoked manner, and in the grossest style of the most vulgar abuse, the whole representative authority of France; and yet Mr Burke takes his seat in the British House of Commons! From his violence and his grief, his silence on some points, and his excess on others, it is difficult not to believe that Mr Burke is sorry, extremely sorry, that arbitrary power, the power of the Pope, and the Bastille, are pulled down.

Not one glance of compassion, not one commiserating reflection, that I can find throughout his book, has he bestowed on those who lingered out the most wretched of lives, a life without hope, in the most miserable of prisons. It is painful to behold a man employing his talents to corrupt himself. Nature has been kinder to Mr Burke than he is to her. He is not affected by the reality of distress touching his heart, but by the showy resemblance of it striking his imagination. He pities the plumage, but forgets the dying bird. Accustomed to kiss the aristocratical hand that hath purloined him from himself, he degenerates into a composition of art, and the genuine soul of nature forsakes him. His hero or his heroine must be a tragedy-victim expiring in show, and not the real prisoner of misery, sliding into death in the silence of a dungeon.

As Mr Burke has passed over the whole transaction of the Bastille (and his silence is nothing in his favour), and has entertained his readers with reflections on supposed facts distorted into real falsehoods, I will give, since he has not, some account of the circumstances which preceded that transaction. They will serve to show, that less mischief could scarcely have accompanied such an event, when considered with the treacherous and hostile aggravations of the enemies of the Revolution.

The mind can hardly picture to itself a more tremendous scene than what the city of Paris exhibited at the time of taking the Bastille, and for two days before and after, nor conceive the possibility of its quieting so soon. At a distance, this transaction has appeared only as an act of heroism, standing on itself; and the close political connexion it had with the Revolution is lost in the brilliancy of the achievement. But we are to consider it as the strength of the parties, brought man to man, and contending for the issue. The Bastille was to be either the prize or the prison of the assailants. The downfall of it included the idea of the downfall of Despotism; and this compounded image was become as figuratively united as Bunyan's Doubting Castle and Giant Despair.

The National Assembly, before and at the time of taking the Bastille, was sitting at Versailles, twelve miles distant from Paris. About a week before the rising of the Parisians, and their taking the Bastille, it was discovered that a plot was forming, at the head of which was the Count d'Artois, the King's youngest brother, for demolishing the National Assembly, seizing its members, and thereby crushing, by a *coup de main*, all hopes and prospects of forming a free government. For the sake of humanity, as well as of freedom, it is well this plan did not succeed. Examples are not wanting to show how dreadfully vindictive and cruel are all old governments, when they are successful against what they call a revolt.

This plan must have been some time in contemplation; because, in order to carry it into execution, it was necessary to collect a large military force round Paris, and to cut off the communication between that city and the National Assembly at Versailles. The troops destined for this service were chiefly the foreign troops in the pay of France, and who, for this particular purpose, were drawn from the distant provinces where they were then stationed. When they were collected, to the amount of between twenty-five and thirty thousand, it was judged time to put the plan in execution. The ministry who were then in office, and who were friendly to the Revolution, were instantly dismissed, and a new ministry formed of those who had concerted the project;—among whom was Count de Broglio, and to his share was given the command of those troops. The character of this man, as described to me in a letter which I communicated to Mr Burke before he began to write his book, and from an authority which Mr Burke well knows was good, was that of 'an high-flying aristocrat, cool, and capable of every mischief.'

While these matters were agitating, the National Assembly stood in the most perilous and critical situation that a body of men can be supposed to act in. They were the devoted victims, and they knew it. They had the hearts and wishes of their country on their side, but military authority they had none. The guards of Broglio surrounded the hall where the assembly sat, ready, at the word of command, to seize their persons, as had been done the year before to the parliament of Paris. Had the National Assembly deserted their trust, or had they exhibited signs of weakness or fear, their enemies had been encouraged, and the country depressed. When the situation they stood in, the cause they were engaged in, and the crisis then ready to burst (which was to determine their personal and political fate, and that of their country, and probably of Europe) are taken into one view, none but a heart callous with prejudice, or corrupted by dependence, can avoid interesting itself in their success.

The archbishop of Vienne was at this time president of the National Assembly; a person too old to undergo the scene that a few days, or a few hours, might bring forth. A man of more activity, and greater fortitude, was necessary; and the National Assembly chose under the form of a vice-president, (for the presidency still resided in the archbishop) M. de

Lafayette; and this is the only instance of a vice-president being chosen. It was at the moment that this storm was pending (July 11) that a declaration of rights was brought forward by M. de Lafayette, and is the same which is alluded to in page 289. It was hastily drawn up, and makes only a part of a more extensive declaration of rights, agreed upon and adopted afterwards by the National Assembly. The particular reason for bringing it forward at this moment, (M. de Lafayette has since informed me) was, that if the National Assembly should fall in the threatened destruction that then surrounded it, some traces of its principles might have the chance of surviving the wreck.

Everything now was drawing to a crisis. The event was to be freedom or slavery. On one side, an army of nearly thirty thousand men; on the other, an unarmed body of citizens: for the citizens of Paris, on whom the National Assembly must then immediately depend, were as unarmed and as undisciplined as the citizens of London are now.—The French guards had given strong symptoms of their being attached to the national cause; but their numbers were small, not a tenth part of the force that Broglio commanded, and their officers were in the interest of Broglio.

Matters being now ripe for execution, the new ministry made their appearance in office. The reader will carry in his mind, that the Bastille was taken the 14th of July: the point of time I am now speaking to, is the 12th. Immediately on the news of the change of ministry reaching Paris, in the afternoon, all the playhouses and places of entertainment, shops and houses, were shut up. The change of ministry was considered as the prelude of hostilities, and the opinion was rightly founded.

The foreign troops began to advance towards the city. The Prince de Lambesc, who commanded a body of German cavalry, approached by the Palace of Louis XV which connects itself with some of the streets. In his march, he insulted and struck an old man with his sword. The French are remarkable for their respect to old age, and the insolence with which it appeared to be done, uniting with the general fermentation they were in, produced a powerful effect, and a cry of *To arms! to arms!* spread itself in a moment over the city.

Arms they had none, nor scarcely any who knew the use of them: but desperate resolution, when every hope is at stake, supplies, for a while, the want of arms. Near where the Prince de Lambesc was drawn up, were large piles of stones collected for building the new bridge, and with these the people attacked the cavalry. A party of the French guards, upon hearing the firing, rushed from their quarters and joined the people; and the night coming on, the cavalry retreated.

The streets of Paris, being narrow, are favourable for defence; and the loftiness of the houses, consisting of many stories, from which great annoyance might be given, secured them against nocturnal enterprises; and the night was spent in providing themselves with every sort of weapon they could make or procure: Guns, swords, blacksmiths' hammers, carpenters' axes, iron crows, pikes, halberts, pitchforks, spits, clubs, &c. &c. The incredible numbers in which they assembled the next morning, and the still more incredible resolution they exhibited, embarrassed and astonished their enemies. Little did the new ministry expect such a salute. Accustomed to slavery themselves, they had no idea that Liberty was capable of such inspiration, or that a body of unarmed citizens would dare to face the military force of thirty thousand men. Every moment of this day was employed in collecting arms, concerting plans, and arranging themselves into the best order which such an instantaneous movement could afford. Broglio continued lying round the city, but made no farther advances this day, and the succeeding night passed with as much tranquillity as such a scene could possibly admit.

But defence only was not the object of the citizens. They had a cause at stake, on which depended their freedom or their slavery. They every moment expected an attack, or to hear of one made on the National Assembly; and in such a situation, the most prompt measures are sometimes the best. The object that now presented itself was the Bastille; and the eclat of carrying such a fortress in the face of such an army, could not fail to strike a terror into the new ministry, who had scarcely yet had time to meet. By some intercepted correspondence this morning, it was discovered, that the Mayor of Paris, M. Defflesselles, who appeared to be in the interest of the citizens, was betraying them; and from this discovery, there remained no doubt that Broglio would reinforce the Bastille the ensuing evening. It was therefore necessary to attack it that day; but before this could be done, it was first necessary to procure a better supply of arms than they were then possessed of.

There was adjoining to the city a large magazine of arms deposited at the Hospital of the Invalids, which the citizens summoned to surrender; and as the place was not defensible, nor attempted much defence, they soon succeeded. Thus supplied, they marched to attack the Bastille; a vast mixed multitude of all ages, and of all degrees, and armed with all sorts of weapons. Imagination would fail in describing to itself the appearance of such a procession, and of the anxiety for the events which a few hours or a few minutes might produce. What plans the ministry was forming, were as unknown to the people within the city, as what the citizens were doing was unknown to the ministry; and what movements Broglio might make for the support or relief of the place, were to the citizens equally as unknown. All was mystery and hazard.

That the Bastille was attacked with an enthusiasm of heroism, such only as the highest animation of liberty could inspire, and carried in the space of a few hours, is an event which the world is fully possessed of. I am not undertaking a detail of the attack; but bringing into view the conspiracy against the nation which provoked it, and which fell with the Bastille. The prison to which the new ministry were dooming the National Assembly, in addition to its being the high altar and castle of despotism, became the proper object to begin with. This enterprise broke up the new ministry, who began now to fly from the ruin they had prepared for others. The troops of Broglio dispersed, and himself fled also.

Mr Burke has spoken a great deal about plots, but he has never once spoken of this plot against the National Assembly, and the liberties of the nation; and that he might not, he has passed over all the circumstances that might throw it in his way. The exiles who have fled from France, whose case he so much interests himself in, and from whom he has had his lesson, fled in consequence of the miscarriage of this plot. No plot was formed against them: they were plotting against others; and those who fell, met, not unjustly, the punishment they were preparing to execute. But will Mr Burke say, that if this plot, contrived with the subtlety of an ambuscade, had succeeded, the successful party would have restrained their wrath so soon? Let the history of all old governments answer the question.

Whom has the National Assembly brought to the scaffold? None. They were themselves the devoted victims of this plot, and they have not retaliated; why then are they charged with revenge they have not acted? In the tremendous breaking forth of a whole people, in which all degrees, tempers and characters are confounded, and delivering themselves, by a miracle of exertion, from the destruction meditated against them, is it to be expected that nothing will happen? When men are sore with the sense of oppressions, and menaced with the prospect of new ones, is the calmness of philosophy, or the palsy of insensibility, to be looked for? Mr Burke exclaims against outrage; yet the greatest is that which himself has committed. His book is a volume of outrage, not apologized for by the impulse of a moment, but cherished through a space often months; yet Mr Burke had no provocation—no life, no interest at stake.

More of the citizens fell in this struggle than of their opponents: but four or five persons were seized by the populace, and instantly put to death; the Governor of the Bastille, and the Mayor of Paris, who was detected in the act of betraying them; and afterwards Foulon, one of the new ministry, and Berthier his son-in-law, who had accepted the office of Intendant of Paris. Their heads were stuck upon spikes, and carried about the city; and it is upon this mode of punishment that Mr Burke builds a great part of his tragic scene. Let us therefore examine how men came by the idea of punishing in this manner.

They learn it from the governments they live under, and retaliate the punishments they have been accustomed to behold. The heads stuck upon spikes, which remained for years upon Temple-bar, differed nothing in the horror of the scene from those carried about upon spikes at Paris: yet this was done by the English government. It may perhaps be said, that it signifies nothing to a man what is done to him after he is dead; but it signifies much to the living: it either tortures their feelings, or hardens their hearts; and in either case, it instructs them how to punish when power falls into their hands.

Lay then the axe to the root, and teach governments humanity. It is their sanguinary punishments which corrupt mankind. In England, the punishment in certain cases, is by *hanging*, *drawing*, and *quartering*, the heart of the sufferer is cut out, and held up to the view of the populace. In France, under the former government, the punishments were not less barbarous. Who does not remember the execution of Damien, torn to pieces by horses? The effect of those cruel spectacles exhibited to the populace, is to destroy tenderness, or excite revenge; and by the base and false idea of governing men by terror, instead of reason, they become precedents. It is over the lowest class of mankind that government by terror is intended to operate, and it is on them that it operates to the worst effect. They have sense enough to feel they are the objects aimed at; and they inflict in their turn the examples of terror they have been instructed to practise.

There is in all European countries, a large class of people of that description which in England is called the '*mob*'. Of this class were those who committed the burnings and devastations in London in 1780, and of this class were those who carried the heads upon spikes in Paris. Foulon and Berthier were taken up in the country, and sent to Paris, to undergo their examination at the Hotel de Ville; for the National Assembly, immediately on the new ministry coming into office, passed a decree, which they communicated to the King and Cabinet, that they (the National Assembly) would hold the ministry, of which Foulon was one, responsible for the measures they were advising and pursuing; but the mob, incensed at the appearance of Foulon and Berthier, tore them from their conductors before they were carried to the Hotel de Ville, and executed them on the spot. Why then does Mr Burke charge outrages of this kind on a whole people? As well may he charge the riots and outrages of 1780 on all the people of London, or those in Ireland on all his countrymen.

But everything we see or hear offensive to our feelings, and derogatory to the human character, should lead to other reflections than those of reproach. Even the beings who commit them have some claim to our consideration. How then is it that such vast classes of mankind as are distinguished by the appellation of the vulgar, or the ignorant mob, are so numerous in all old countries? The instant we ask ourselves this question, reflection feels an answer. They arise, as an unavoidable consequence, out of the ill construction of all old governments in Europe, England included with the rest. It is by distortedly exalting some men, that others are distortedly debased, till the whole is out of nature. A vast mass of mankind are degradedly thrown into the background of the human picture, to bring forward with greater glare, the puppet-show of state and aristocracy. In the commencement of a Revolution, those men are rather the followers of the *camp* than of the *standard* of liberty, and have yet to be instructed how to reverence it.

I give to Mr Burke all his theatrical exaggerations for facts, and I then ask him, if they do not establish the certainty of what I here lay down? Admitting them to be true, they show the necessity of the French Revolution, as much as any one thing he could have asserted. These outrages were not the effect of the principles of the Revolution, but of the degraded mind that existed before the Revolution, and which the Revolution is calculated to reform. Place them then to their proper cause, and take the reproach of them to your own side.

It is to the honour of the National Assembly, and the city of Paris, that during such a tremendous scene of arms and confusion, beyond the control of all authority, they have been able, by the influence of example and exhortation, to restrain so much. Never were more pains taken to instruct and enlighten mankind, and to make them see that their interest consisted in their virtue, and not in their revenge, than have been displayed in the Revolution of France. I now proceed to make some remarks on Mr Burke's account of the expedition to Versailles, October the 5th and 6th.

I cannot consider Mr Burke's book in scarcely any other light than a dramatic performance; and he must, I think, have considered it in the same light himself, by the poetical liberties he has taken of omitting some facts, distorting others, and making the whole machinery bend to produce a stage effect. Of this kind is his account of the expedition to Versailles. He begins this account by omitting the only facts which as causes are known to be true; everything beyond these is conjecture even in Paris: and he then works up a tale accommodated to his own passions and prejudices.

It is to be observed throughout Mr Burke's book, that he never speaks of plots *against the* Revolution; and it is from those plots that all the mischiefs have arisen. It suits his purpose to exhibit the consequences without their causes. It is one of the arts of the drama to do so. If the crimes of men were exhibited with their sufferings, stage effect would sometimes be lost, and the audience would be inclined to approve where it was intended they should commiserate.

After all the investigations that have been made into this intricate affair, (the expedition to Versailles), it still remains enveloped in all that kind of mystery which ever accompanies events produced more from a concurrence of awkward circumstances, than from fixed design. While the characters of men are forming, as is always the case in revolutions, there is a reciprocal suspicion, and a disposition to misinterpret each other; and even parties directly opposite in principle, will sometimes concur in pushing forward the same movement with very different views, and with the hopes of its producing very different consequences. A great deal of this may be discovered in this embarrassed affair, and yet the issue of the whole was what nobody had in view.

The only things certainly known, are, that considerable uneasiness was at this time excited at Paris, by the delay of the King in not sanctioning and forwarding the decrees of the National Assembly, particularly that of the *Declaration of the Rights of Man*, and the decrees of the *fourth of August*, which contained the foundation principles on which the constitution was to be erected. The kindest, and perhaps the fairest conjecture upon this matter is, that some of the ministers intended to make remarks and observations upon certain parts of them, before they were finally sanctioned and sent to the provinces; but be this as it may, the enemies of the revolution derived hope from the delay, and the friends of the revolution, uneasiness.

During this state of suspense, the *Garde du Corps*, which was composed, as such regiments generally are, of persons much connected with the Court, gave an entertainment at Versailles (Oct. 1) to some foreign regiments then arrived; and when the entertainment was at the height, on a signal given, the *Garde du Corps* tore the national cockade from their hats, trampled it under foot, and replaced it with a counter cockade prepared for the purpose. An indignity of this kind amounted to defiance. It was like declaring war; and if men will give challenges, they must expect consequences. But all this Mr Burke has carefully kept out of sight. He begins his account by saying, 'History will record, that on the morning of the 6th of October 1789, the King and Queen of France, after a day of confusion, alarm, dismay, and slaughter, lay down under the pledged security of public faith, to indulge nature in a few hours of respite, and troubled melancholy repose.' This is neither the sober style of history, nor the intention of it. It leaves everything to be guessed at, and mistaken. One would at least think there had been a battle; and a battle there would have been, had it not been for the moderating prudence of those whom Mr Burke involves in his censures. By his keeping the *Garde du Corps* out of sight, Mr Burke has afforded himself the dramatic licence of putting the King and Queen in their places, as if the object of the expedition was against them.—But, to return to my account—

This conduct of the *Garde du Corps*, as might well be expected, alarmed and enraged the Parisians. The colours of the cause, and the cause itself, were become too united to mistake the intention of the insult, and the Parisians were determined to call the *Garde du Corps* to an account. There was certainly nothing of the cowardice of assassination in marching in the face of day to demand satisfaction, if such a phrase may be used, of a body of armed men who had voluntarily given defiance. But the circumstance which serves to throw this affair into embarrassment is, that the enemies of the revolution appear to have encouraged it, as well as its friends. The one hoped to prevent a civil war by checking it in time, and the other to make one. The hopes of those opposed to the revolution, rested in making the King of their party, and getting him from Versailles to Metz, where they expected to collect a force, and set up a standard. We have therefore two different objects presenting themselves at the same time, and to be accomplished by the same means: the one, to chastise the *Garde du Corps,* which was the object of the Parisians; the other, to render the confusion of such a scene an inducement to the King to set off for Metz.

On the 5th of October, a very numerous body of women, and men in the disguise of women, collected round the Hotel de Ville or town-hall at Paris, and set off for Versailles. Their professed object was the *Garde du Corps*; but prudent men readily recollect that mischief is more easily begun than ended; and this impressed itself with the more force, from the suspicions already stated, and the irregularity of such a cavalcade. As soon therefore as a sufficient force could be collected, M. de Lafayette, by orders from the civil authority of Paris, set off after them at the head of twenty thousand of the Paris militia. The revolution could derive no benefit from confusion, and its opposers might. By an amiable and spirited manner of address, he had hitherto been fortunate in calming disquietudes, and in this he was extraordinarily successful; to frustrate, therefore, the hopes of those who might seek to improve this scene into a sort of justifiable necessity for the King's quitting Versailles and withdrawing to Metz, and to prevent at the same time the consequences that might ensue between the *Garde du Corps* and this phalanx of men and women, he forwarded expresses to the King, that he was on his march to Versailles, by the orders of the civil authority of Paris, for the purpose of peace and protection, expressing at the same time the necessity of restraining the *Garde du Corps* from firing upon the people.[2]

He arrived at Versailles between ten and eleven at night. The *Garde du Corps* was drawn up, and the people had arrived some time before, but everything had remained suspended. Wisdom and policy now consisted in changing a scene of danger into a happy event. M. de Lafayette became the mediator between the enraged parties; and the King, to remove the uneasiness which had arisen from the delay already stated, sent for the President of the National Assembly, and signed the *Declaration of the Rights of Man,* and such other parts of the constitution as were in readiness.

It was now about one in the morning. Everything appeared to be composed, and a general congratulation took place. By the beat of drum a proclamation was made, that the citizens of Versailles would give the hospitality of their houses to their fellow-citizens of Paris. Those who could not be accommodated in this manner, remained in the streets, or took up their quarters in the churches; and at two o'clock the King and Queen retired.

In this state matters passed till the break of day, when a fresh disturbance arose from the censurable conduct of some of both parties, for such characters there will be in all such scenes. One of the *Garde du Corps* appeared at one of the windows of the palace, and the people who had remained during the night in the streets accosted him with reviling and provocative language. Instead of retiring, as in such a case prudence would have dictated, he presented his musket, fired, and killed one of the Paris militia. The peace being thus broken, the people rushed into the palace in quest of the offender. They attacked the quarters of the *Garde du Corps* within the palace, and pursued them throughout the avenues of it, and to the apartments of the King. On this tumult, not the Queen only, as Mr Burke has represented it, but every person in the palace, was awakened and alarmed; and M. de Lafayette had a second time to interpose between the parties, the event of which was, that the *Garde du Corps* put on the national cockade, and the matter ended as by oblivion, after the loss of two or three lives.

During the latter part of the time in which this confusion was acting, the King and Queen were in public at the balcony, and neither of them concealed for safety's sake, as Mr Burke insinuates. Matters being thus appeased, and tranquillity restored, a general acclamation broke forth, of *Le Roi à Paris*—*Le Roi à Paris*—The King to Paris. It was the shout of peace, and immediately accepted on the part of the King. By this measure, all future projects of trepanning the King to Metz, and setting up the standard of opposition to the constitution, were prevented, and the suspicions extinguished. The King and his family reached Paris in the evening, and were congratulated on their arrival by M. Bailley the Mayor of Paris, in the name of the citizens. Mr Burke, who throughout his book confounds things, persons, and principles, has in his remarks on M. Bailley's address, confounded time also. He censures M. Bailley for calling it, '*un bon jour,*' a good day. Mr Burke should have informed himself, that this scene took up the space of two days, the day on which it began with every appearance of danger and mischief, and the day on which it terminated without the mischiefs that threatened; and that it is to this peaceful termination that M. Bailley alludes, and to the arrival of the King at Paris. Not less than three hundred thousand persons arranged themselves in the procession from Versailles to Paris, and not an act of molestation was committed during the whole march.

Mr Burke, on the authority of M. Lally Tollendal, a deserter from the National Assembly, says, that on entering Paris, the people shouted, '*Tous les évêques à la lanterne.*' All Bishops to be hanged at the lantern or lamp-posts.—It is surprising that nobody could hear this but Lally Tollendal, and that nobody should believe it but Mr Burke. It has not the least connexion with any part of the transaction, and is totally foreign to every circumstance of it. The bishops had never been introduced before into any scene of Mr Burke's drama; Why then are they, all at once, and altogether, *tout à coup et tous ensemble,* introduced now? Mr Burke brings forward his bishops and his lantern like figures in a magic lantern, and raises his scenes by contrast instead of connexion. But it serves to show, with the rest of his book, what little credit ought to be given, where even probability is set at defiance, for the purpose of defaming; and with this reflection, instead of a soliloquy in praise of chivalry, as Mr Burke has done, I close the account of the expedition to Versailles.[3]

I have now to follow Mr Burke through a pathless wilderness of rhapsodies, and a sort of descant upon governments, in which he asserts whatever he pleases, on the presumption of its being believed, without offering either evidence or reasons for so doing.

Before anything can be reasoned upon to a conclusion, certain facts, principles, or data, to reason from, must be established, admitted, or denied. Mr Burke, with his usual outrage, abuses the *Declaration of the Rights of Man,* published by the National Assembly of France as the basis on which the constitution of France is built. This he calls 'paltry and blurred sheets of paper about the rights of man.'—Does Mr Burke mean to deny that *man* has any rights? If he does, then he must mean that there are no such things as rights anywhere, and that he has none himself; for who is there in the world but man? But if Mr Burke means to admit that man has rights, the question then will be, What are those rights, and how came man by them originally?

The error of those who reason by precedents drawn from antiquity, respecting the rights of man, is, that they do not go far enough into antiquity. They do not go the whole way. They stop in some of the intermediate stages of an hundred or a thousand years, and produce what was then done, as a rule for the present day. This is no authority at all. If we travel still farther into antiquity, we shall find a direct contrary opinion and practice prevailing; and if antiquity is to be authority, a thousand such authorities may be produced, successively contradicting each other: But if we proceed on, we shall at last come out right; we shall come to the time when man came from the hand of his Maker. What was he then? Man. Man was his high and only title, and a higher cannot be given him.—But of titles I shall speak hereafter.

We are now got at the origin of man, and at the origin of his rights. As to the manner in which the world has been governed from that day to this, it is no further any concern of ours than to make a proper use of the errors or the improvements which the history of it presents. Those who lived a hundred or a thousand years ago, were then moderns, as we are now. They had *their* ancients, and those ancients had others, and we also shall be ancients in our turn. If the mere name of antiquity is to govern in the affairs of life, the people who are to live an hundred or a thousand years hence, may as well take us for a precedent, as we make a precedent of those who lived an hundred or a thousand years ago. The fact is, that portions of antiquity, by proving everything, establish nothing. It is authority against authority all the way, till we come to the divine origin of the rights of man at the creation. Here our inquiries find a resting-place, and our reason finds a home. If a dispute about the rights of man had arisen at the distance of an hundred years from the creation, it is to this source of authority they must have referred, and it is to the same source of authority that we must now refer.

Though I mean not to touch upon any sectarian principle of religion, yet it may be worth observing, that the genealogy of Christ is traced to Adam. Why then not trace the rights of man to the creation of man? I will answer the question. Because there have been upstart governments, thrusting themselves between, and presumptuously working to *un-make* man.

If any generation of men ever possessed the right of dictating the mode by which the world should be governed for ever, it was the first generation that existed; and if that generation did it not, no succeeding generation can show any authority for doing it, nor can set any up. The illuminating and divine principle of the equal rights of man, (for it has its origin from the Maker of man) relates, not only to the living individuals, but to generations of men succeeding each other. Every generation is equal in rights to the generations which preceded it, by the same rule that every individual is born equal in rights with his contemporary.

Every history of the creation, and every traditionary account, whether from the lettered or unlettered world, however they may vary in their opinion or belief of certain particulars, all agree in establishing one point, *the unity of man*; by which I mean, that men are all of *one degree*, and consequently that all men are born equal, and with equal natural right, in the same manner as if posterity had been continued by *creation* instead of *generation*, the latter being only the mode by which the former is carried forward; and consequently, every child born into the world must be considered as deriving its existence from God. The world is as new to him as it was to the first man that existed, and his natural right in it is of the same kind.

The Mosaic account of the creation, whether taken as divine authority, or merely historical, is full to this point, *the unity or equality of man*. The expressions admit of no controversy. 'And God said, Let us make man in our own image. In the image of God created he him; male and female created he them.' The distinction of sexes is pointed out, but no other distinction is even implied. If this be not divine authority, it is at least historical authority, and shows that the equality of man, so far from being a modern doctrine, is the oldest upon record.

It is also to be observed, that all the religions known in the world are founded, so far as they relate to man, on the *unity of man*, as being all of one degree. Whether in heaven or in hell, or in whatever state man may be supposed to exist hereafter, the good and the bad are the only distinctions. Nay, even the laws of governments are obliged to slide into this principle, by making degrees to consist in crimes, and not in persons.

It is one of the greatest of all truths, and of the highest advantage to cultivate. By considering man in this light, and by instructing him to consider himself in this light, it places him in a close connexion with all his duties, whether to his Creator, or to the creation, of which he is a part; and it is only when he forgets his origin, or, to use a more fashionable phrase, his *birth and family*, that he becomes dissolute. It is not among the least of the evils of the present existing governments in all parts of Europe, that man, considered as man, is thrown back to a vast distance from his Maker, and the artificial chasm filled up by a succession of barriers, or sort of turnpike gates, through which he has to pass. I will quote Mr Burke's catalogue of barriers that he has set up between man and his Maker. Putting himself in the character of a herald, he says—'We fear God—we look with *awe* to kings—with affection to parliaments—with duty to magistrates—with reverence to priests, and with respect to nobility.' Mr Burke has forgotten to put in '*chivalry*'. He has also forgotten to put in Peter.

The duty of man is not a wilderness of turnpike gates, through which he is to pass by tickets from one to the other. It is plain and simple, and consists but of two points. His duty to God, which every man must feel; and with respect to his neighbour, to do as he would be done by. If those to whom power is delegated do well, they will be respected; if not, they will be despised: and with regard to those to whom no power is delegated, but who assume it, the rational world can know nothing of them.

Hitherto we have spoken only (and that but in part) of the natural rights of man. We have now to consider the civil rights of man, and to show how the one originates from the other. Man did not enter into society to become *worse* than he was before, nor to have fewer rights than he had before, but to have those rights better secured. His natural rights are the foundation of all his civil rights. But in order to pursue this distinction with more precision, it will be necessary to mark the different qualities of natural and civil rights.

A few words will explain this. Natural rights are those which appertain to man in right of his existence. Of this kind are all the intellectual rights, or rights of the mind, and also all those rights of acting as an individual for his own comfort and happiness, which are not injurious to the natural rights of others.—Civil rights are those which appertain to man in right of his being a member of society. Every civil right has for its foundation, some natural right pre-existing in the individual, but to the enjoyment of which his individual power is not, in all cases, sufficiently competent. Of this kind are all those which relate to security and protection.

From this short review, it will be easy to distinguish between that class of natural rights which man retains after entering into society, and those which he throws into the common stock as a member of society.

The natural rights which he retains, are all those in which the *power* to execute is as perfect in the individual as the right itself. Among this class, as is before mentioned, are all the intellectual rights, or rights of the mind: consequently, religion is one of those rights. The natural rights which are not retained, are all those in which, though the right is perfect in the individual, the power to execute them is defective. They answer not his purpose. A man, by natural right, has a right to judge in his own cause; and so far as the right of mind is concerned, he never surrenders it: But what availeth it him to judge, if he has not power to redress? He therefore deposits this right in the common stock of society, and takes the arm of society, of which he is a part, in preference and in addition to his own. Society *grants* him nothing. Every man is a proprietor in society, and draws on the capital as a matter of right.

From these premises, two or three certain conclusions will follow.

First, That every civil right grows out of a natural right; or, in other words, is a natural right exchanged.

Secondly, That civil power, properly considered as such, is made up of the aggregate of that class of the natural rights of man, which becomes defective in the individual in point of power, and answers not his purpose; but when collected to a focus, becomes competent to the purpose of every one.

Thirdly, That the power produced from the aggregate of natural rights, imperfect in power in the individual, cannot be applied to invade the natural rights which are retained in the individual, and in which the power to execute is as perfect as the right itself.

We have now, in a few words, traced man from a natural individual to a member of society, and shown, or endeavoured to show, the quality of the natural rights retained, and of those which are exchanged for civil rights. Let us now apply these principles to governments.

In casting our eyes over the world, it is extremely easy to distinguish the governments which have arisen out of society, or out of the social compact, from those which have not: but to place this in a clearer light than what a single glance may afford, it will be proper to take a review of the several sources from which governments have arisen, and on which they have been founded.

They may be all comprehended under three heads. First, Superstition. Secondly, Power. Thirdly, The common interest of society, and the common rights of man.

The first was a government of priestcraft, the second of conquerors, and the third of reason.

When a set of artful men pretended, through the medium of oracles, to hold intercourse with the Deity, as familiarly as they now march up the back-stairs in European courts, the world was completely under the government of superstition. The oracles were consulted, and whatever they were made to say, became the law; and this sort of government lasted as long as this sort of superstition lasted.

After these a race of conquerors arose, whose government, like that of William the Conqueror, was founded in power, and the sword assumed the name of a sceptre. Governments thus established, last as long as the power to support them lasts; but that they might avail themselves of every engine in their favour, they united fraud to force, and set up an idol which they called *Divine Right*, and which, in imitation of the Pope, who affects to be spiritual and temporal, and in contradiction to the Founder of the Christian religion, twisted itself afterwards into an idol of another shape, called *Church and State.* The key of St Peter, and the key of the Treasury, became quartered on one another, and the wondering cheated multitude worshipped the invention.

When I contemplate the natural dignity of man; when I feel (for Nature has not been kind enough to me to blunt my feelings) for the honour and happiness of its character, I become irritated at the attempt to govern mankind by force and fraud, as if they were all knaves and fools, and can scarcely avoid disgust at those who are thus imposed upon.

We have now to review the governments which arise out of society, in contradistinction to those which arose out of superstition and conquest.

It has been thought a considerable advance towards establishing the principles of Freedom, to say, that government is a compact between those who govern and those who are governed: but this cannot be true, because it is putting the effect before the cause; for as man must have existed before governments existed, there necessarily was a time when governments did not exist, and consequently there could originally exist no governors to form such a compact with. The fact therefore must be, that the *individuals themselves,* each in his own personal and sovereign right, *entered into a compact with each other* to produce a government: and this is the only mode in which governments have a right to arise, and the only principle on which they have a right to exist.

To possess ourselves of a clear idea of what government is, or ought to he, we must trace it to its origin. In doing this, we shall easily discover that governments must have arisen, either *out* of the people, or *over* the people. Mr Burke has made no distinction. He investigates nothing to its source, and therefore he confounds everything: but he has signified his intention of undertaking at some future opportunity, a comparison between the constitutions of England and France. As he thus renders it a subject of controversy by throwing the gauntlet, I take him up on his own ground. It is in high challenges that high truths have the right of appearing; and I accept it with the more readiness, because it affords me, at the same time, an opportunity of pursuing the subject with respect to governments arising out of society.

But it will be first necessary to define what is meant by a *constitution.* It is not sufficient that we adopt the word; we must fix also a standard signification to it.

A constitution is not a thing in name only, but in fact. It has not an ideal, but a real existence; and wherever it cannot be produced in a visible form, there is none. A constitution is a thing *antecedent* to a government, and a government is only the creature of a constitution. The constitution of a country is not the act of its government, but of the people constituting a government. It is the body of elements, to which you can refer, and quote article by article; and which contains the principles on which the government shall be established, the manner in which it shall be organized, the powers it shall have, the mode of elections, the duration of parliaments, or by what other name such bodies may be called; the powers which the executive part of the government shall have; and, in fine, everything that relates to the complete organization of a civil government, and the principles on which it shall act, and by which it shall be bound. A constitution, therefore, is to a government, what the laws made afterwards by that government are to a court of judicature. The court of judicature does not make the laws, neither can it alter them; it only acts in conformity to the laws made: and the government is in like manner governed by the constitution.

Can then Mr Burke produce the English Constitution? If he cannot, we may fairly conclude, that though it has been so much talked about, no such thing as a constitution exists, or ever did exist, and consequently that the people have yet a constitution to form.

Mr Burke will not, I presume, deny the position I have already advanced; namely, that governments arise, either *out* of the people, or *over* the people. The English government is one of those which arose out of a conquest, and not out of society, and, consequently it arose over the people; and though it has been much modified from the opportunity of circumstances since the time of William the Conqueror, the country has never yet regenerated itself, and is therefore without a constitution.

I readily perceive the reason why Mr Burke declined going into the comparison between the English and French constitutions, because he could not but perceive, when he sat down to the task, that no such thing as a constitution existed on his side the question. His book is certainly bulky enough to have contained all he could say on this subject, and it would have been the best manner in which people could have judged of their separate merits. Why then has he declined the only thing that was worth while to write upon? It was the strongest ground he could take, if the advantages were on his side; but the weakest, if they were not: and his declining to take it, is either a sign that he could not possess it, or could not maintain it.

Mr Burke said in a speech last winter in parliament. That when the National Assembly first met in three Orders, (the Tiers Etats, the Clergy, and the Noblesse), France had then a good constitution. This shows, among numerous other instances, that Mr Burke does not understand what a constitution is. The persons so met, were not a *constitution,* but a *convention,* to make a constitution.

The present National Assembly of France is, strictly speaking, the personal social compact.—The members of it are the delegates of the nation in its *original* character; future assemblies will be the delegates of the nation in its *organized* character. The authority of the present Assembly is different to what the authority of future Assemblies will be. The authority of the present one is to form a constitution: the authority of future Assemblies will be to legislate according to the principles and forms prescribed in that constitution; and if experience should hereafter show that alterations, amendments, or additions, are necessary, the constitution will point out the mode by which such things shall be done, and not leave it to the discretionary power of the future government.

A government on the principles on which constitutional governments arising out of society are established, cannot have the right of altering itself. If it had, it would be arbitrary. It might make itself what it pleased; and wherever such a right is set up, it shows there is no constitution. The act by which the English Parliament empowered itself to sit seven years, shows there is no constitution in England. It might, by the same self-authority, have sat any greater number of years, or for life. The Bill which the present Mr Pitt brought into parliament some years ago, to reform parliament, was on the same erroneous principle. The right to reform is in the nation in its original character, and the constitutional method would be by a general convention elected for the purpose. There is, moreover, a paradox in the idea of vitiated bodies reforming themselves.

From these preliminaries I proceed to draw some comparisons. I have already spoken of the declaration of rights; and as I mean to be as concise as possible, I shall proceed to other parts of the French constitution.

The constitution of France says, That every man who pays a tax of sixty *sous per annum*, (2s. and 6d. English), is an elector.—What article will Mr Burke place against this? Can anything be more limited, and at the same time more capricious, than the qualifications of electors are in England? Limited—because not one man in an hundred (I speak much within compass) is admitted to vote: Capricious—because the lowest character that can be supposed to exist, and who has not so much as the visible means of an honest livelihood, is an elector in some places; while, in other places, the man who pays very large taxes, and has a known fair character, and the farmer who rents to the amount of three or four hundred pounds a year, with a property on that farm to three or four times that amount, is not admitted to be an elector. Everything is out of nature, as Mr Burke says on another occasion, in this strange chaos, and all sorts of follies are blended with all sorts of crimes. William the Conqueror and his descendants parcelled out the country in this manner, and bribed some parts of it by what they called Charters, to hold the other parts of it the better subjected to their will. This is the reason why so many of those charters abound in Cornwall; the people were averse to the government established at the Conquest, and the towns were garrisoned and bribed to enslave the country. All the old charters are the badges of this conquest, and it is from this source that the capriciousness of elections arises.

The French constitution says, That the number of representatives for any place shall be in a ratio to the number of taxable inhabitants or electors. What article will Mr Burke place against this? The county of Yorkshire, which contains near a million of souls, sends two county members; and so does the county of Rutland, which contains not an hundredth part of that number. The town of old Sarum, which contains not three houses, sends two members; and the town of Manchester, which contains upwards of sixty thousand souls, is not admitted to send any. Is there any principle in these things? Is there anything by which you can trace the marks of freedom, or discover those of wisdom? No wonder, then, Mr Burke has declined the comparison, and endeavoured to lead his readers from the point by a wild unsystematical display of paradoxical rhapsodies.

The French constitution says, That the National Assembly shall be elected every two years.—What article will Mr Burke place against this? Why, that the nation has no right at all in the case: that the government is perfectly arbitrary with respect to this point; and he can quote for his authority, the precedent of a former parliament.

The French constitution says, There shall be no game laws; that the farmer on whose lands wild game shall be found (for it is by the produce of his lands they are fed) shall have a right to what he can take: That there shall be no monopolies of any kind—that all trade shall be free, and every man free to follow any occupation by which he can procure an honest livelihood, and in any place, town or city throughout the nation. —What will Mr Burke say to this? In England, game is made the property of those at whose expense it is not fed; and with respect to monopolies, the country is cut up into monopolies. Every chartered town is an aristocratical monopoly in itself, and the qualification of electors proceeds out of those chartered monopolies. Is this freedom? Is this what Mr Burke means by a constitution?

In these chartered monopolies, a man coming from another part of the country, is hunted from them as if he were a foreign enemy. An Englishman is not free of his own country: every one of those places presents a barrier in his way, and tells him he is not a freeman—that he has no rights. Within these monopolies, are other monopolies. In a city, such for instance as Bath, which contains between twenty and thirty thousand inhabitants, the right of electing representatives to parliament is monopolized by about thirty-one persons. And within these monopolies are still others. A man even of the same town, whose parents were not in circumstances to give him an occupation, is debarred, in many cases, from the natural right of acquiring one, be his genius or industry what it may.

Are these things examples to hold out to a country regenerating itself from slavery, like France?—Certainly they are not; and certain am I, that when the people of England come to reflect upon them, they will, like France, annihilate those badges of ancient oppression, those traces of a conquered nation.—Had Mr Burke possessed talents similar to the author of 'On the Wealth of Nations', he would have comprehended all the parts which enter into, and, by assemblage, form a constitution. He would have reasoned from minutiae to magnitude. It is not from his prejudices only, but from the disorderly cast of his genius, that he is unfitted for the subject he writes upon. Even his genius is without a constitution. It is a genius at random, and not a genius constituted. But he must say something—He has therefore mounted in the air like a balloon, to draw the eyes of the multitude from the ground they stand upon.

Much is to be learned from the French constitution. Conquest and tyranny transplanted themselves with William the Conqueror from Normandy into England, and the country is yet disfigured with the marks. May then the example of all France contribute to regenerate the freedom which a province of it destroyed!

The French constitution says, That to preserve the national representation from being corrupt, no member of the National Assembly shall be an officer of the government, a place-man, or a pensioner.—What will Mr Burke place against this? I will whisper his answer: *Loaves* and *fishes.* Ah! this government of loaves and fishes has more mischief in it than people have yet reflected on. The National Assembly has made the discovery, and it holds out the example to the world. Had governments agreed to quarrel on purpose to fleece their countries by taxes, they could not have succeeded better than they have done.

Many things in the English government appear to me the reverse of what they ought to be, and of what they are said to be. The Parliament, imperfectly and capriciously elected as it is, is nevertheless *supposed to* hold the national purse in *trust* for the nation: but in the manner in which an English parliament is constructed, it is like a man being both mortgager and mortgagee; and in the case of misapplication of trust, it is the criminal sitting in judgement upon himself. If those who vote the supplies are the same persons who receive the supplies when voted, and are to account for the expenditure of those supplies to those who voted them, it is *themselves accountable to themselves*, and the Comedy of Errors concludes with the Pantomime of HUSH. Neither the ministerial party, nor the opposition, will touch upon this case. The national purse is the common hack which each mounts upon. It is like what the country people call, 'Ride and tie—You ride a little way, and then I[4]'—They order these things better in France.

The French constitution says, That the right of war and peace is in the nation. Where else should it reside, but in those who are to pay the expense?

In England, this right is said to reside in a *metaphor*, shown at the Tower for sixpence or a shilling apiece: So are the lions; and it would be a step nearer to reason to say it resided in them, for any inanimate metaphor is no more than a hat or a cap. We can all see the absurdity of worshipping Aaron's molten calf, or Nebuchadnezzar's golden image; but why do men continue to practise themselves the absurdities they despise in others?

It may with reason be said, that in the manner the English nation is represented, it signifies not where this right resides, whether in the Crown, or in the Parliament. War is the common harvest of all those who participate in the division and expenditure of public money, in all countries. It is the art of *conquering at home*: the object of it is an increase of revenue; and as revenue cannot be increased without taxes, a pretence must be made for expenditures. In reviewing the history of the English Government, its wars and its taxes, a bystander, not blinded by prejudice, nor warped by interest, would declare, that taxes were not raised to carry on wars, but that wars were raised to carry on taxes.

Mr Burke, as a Member of the House of Commons, is a part of the English Government; and though he professes himself an enemy to war, he abuses the French Constitution, which seeks to explode it. He holds up the English Government as a model in all its parts, to France; but he should first know the remarks which the French make upon it. They contend, in favour of their own, that the portion of liberty enjoyed in England, is just enough to enslave a country by, more productively than by despotism; and that as the real object of all despotism is revenue, a Government so formed obtains more than it could do either by direct despotism, or in a full state of freedom, and is therefore, on the ground of interest, opposed to both. They account also for the readiness which always appears in such governments for engaging in wars, by remarking on the different motives which produce them. In despotic governments, wars are the effect of pride; but in those governments in which they become the means of taxation, they acquire thereby a more permanent promptitude.

The French Constitution, therefore, to provide against both these evils, has taken away the power of declaring war from kings and ministers, and placed the right where the expense must fall.

When the question on the right of war and peace was agitating in the National Assembly, the people of England appeared to be much interested in the event, and highly to applaud the decision.—As a principle, it applies as much to one country as to another. William the Conqueror, *as a conqueror*, held this power of war and peace in himself, and his descendants have ever since claimed it under him as a right.

Although Mr Burke has asserted the right of the parliament at the Revolution to bind and control the nation and posterity for *ever,* he denies, at the same time, that the parliament or the nation had any right to alter what he calls the succession of the crown, in anything but in part; or by a sort of modification. By his taking this ground, he throws the case back to the *Norman Conquest,* and by thus running a line of succession springing from William the Conqueror to the present day, he makes it necessary to inquire who and what William the Conqueror was, and where he came from; and into the origin, history, and nature of what are called prerogatives. Everything must have had a beginning, and the fog of time and antiquity should be penetrated to discover it. Let then Mr Burke bring forward his William of Normandy, for it is to this origin that his argument goes. It also unfortunately happens, in running this line of succession, that another line, parallel thereto, presents itself, which is, that if the succession runs in the line of the conquest, the nation runs in the line of being conquered, and it ought to rescue itself from this reproach.

But it will perhaps be said, that though the power of declaring war descends in the heritage of the conquest, it is held in check by the right of the parliament to withhold the supplies. It will always happen, when a thing is originally wrong, that amendments do not make it right; and it often happens, that they do as much mischief one way, as good the other: and such is the case here; for if the one rashly declares war as a matter of right, and the other peremptorily withholds the supplies as a matter of right, the remedy becomes as bad, or worse than the disease. The one forces the nation to a combat, and the other ties its hands: but the more probable issue is, that the contest will end in a collusion between the parties, and be made a screen to both.

On this question of war, three things are to be considered. First, the right of declaring it: Secondly, the expense of supporting it: Thirdly, the mode of conducting it after it is declared. The French constitution places the *right* where the *expense* must fall, and this union can be only in the nation. The mode of conducting it after it is declared, it consigns to the executive department.—Were this the case in all countries, we should hear but little more of wars.

Before I proceed to consider other parts of the French constitution, and by way of relieving the fatigue of argument, I will introduce an anecdote which I had from Dr Franklin.—

While the Doctor resided in France as minister from America during the war, he had numerous proposals made to him by projectors of every country and of every kind, who wished to go to the land that floweth with milk and honey, America; and among the rest, there was one who offered himself to be King. He introduced his proposal to the Doctor by letter, which is now in the hands of M. Beaumarchais, of Paris —stating, first, that as the Americans had dismissed or sent away[5] their King, that they would want another. Secondly, that himself was a Norman. Thirdly, that he was of a more ancient family than the Dukes of Normandy, and of a more honourable descent, his line having never been bastardized. Fourthly, that there was already a precedent in England, of Kings coming out of Normandy: and on these grounds he rested his offer, *enjoining* that the Doctor would forward it to America. But as the Doctor neither did this, nor yet sent him an answer, the projector wrote a second letter; in which he did not, it is true, threaten to go over and conquer America, but only with great dignity proposed, that if his offer was not accepted, an acknowledgement of about £30,000 might be made to him for his generosity!—Now, as all arguments respecting succession must necessarily connect that succession with some beginning, Mr Burke's arguments on this subject go to show, that there is no English origin of kings, and that they are descendants of the Norman line in right of the Conquest. It may, therefore, be of service to his doctrine to make this story known, and to inform him, that in case of that natural extinction to which all mortality is subject, Kings may again be had from Normandy, on more reasonable terms than William the Conqueror; and consequently, that the good people of England, at the Revolution of 1688, *might have done much better*, had such a generous Norman as *this* known *their* wants, and they had known *his*. The chivalric character which Mr Burke so much admires, is certainly much easier to make a bargain with, than a *hard-dealing Dutchman.*—But, to return to the matters of the constitution —

The French constitution says, *There shall be no titles*; and of consequence, all that class of equivocal generation, which in some countries is called '*aristocracy*,' and in others '*nobility*,' is done away, and the *peer* is exalted into MAN.

Titles are but nick-names, and every nick-name is a title. The thing is perfectly harmless in itself; but it marks a sort of foppery in the human character, which degrades it. It reduces man into the diminutive of man in things which are great, and the counterfeit of woman in things which are little. It talks about its fine *blue ribbon* like a girl, and shows its new *garter* like a child. A certain writer of some antiquity, says, 'When I was a child, I thought as a child; but when I became a man, I put away childish things.'

It is, properly, from the elevated mind of France, that the folly of titles has fallen. It has outgrown the baby-clothes of *Count* and *Duke*, and breeched itself in manhood. France has not levelled; it has exalted. It has put down the dwarf, to set up the man. The punyism of a senseless word like *Duke*, or *Count*, or *Earl*, has ceased to please. Even those who possessed them have disowned the gibberish, and as they outgrew the rickets, have despised the rattle. The genuine mind of man, thirsting for its native home, society, condemns the gewgaws that separate him from it. Titles are like circles drawn by the magician's wand, to contract the sphere of man's felicity. He lives immured within the Bastille of a word, and surveys at a distance the envied life of man.

Is it then any wonder that titles should fall in France? Is it not a greater wonder they should be kept up anywhere? What are they? What is their worth, and 'what is their amount?' When we think or speak of a *Judge* or a *General*, we associate with it the ideas of office and character; we think of gravity in the one, and bravery in the other: but when we use a word *merely as a title*, no ideas associate with it. Through all the vocabulary of Adam, there is not such an animal as a Duke or a Count; neither can we connect any certain idea with the words. Whether they mean strength or weakness, wisdom or folly, a child or a man, or the rider or the horse, is all equivocal. What respect then can be paid to that which describes nothing, and which means nothing? Imagination has given figure and character to centaurs, satyrs, and down to all the fairy tribe; but titles baffle even the powers of fancy, and are a chimerical nondescript.

But this is not all.—If a whole country is disposed to hold them in contempt, all their value is gone, and none will own them. It is common opinion only that makes them anything, or nothing, or worse than nothing. There is no occasion to take titles away, for they take themselves away when society concurs to ridicule them. This species of imaginary consequence has visibly declined in every part of Europe, and it hastens to its exit as the world of reason continues to rise. There was a time when the lowest class of what are called nobility was more thought of than the highest is now, and when a man in armour riding throughout Christendom in quest of adventures was more stared at than a modern

Duke. The world has seen this folly fall, and it has fallen by being laughed at, and the farce of titles will follow its fate.—The patriots of France have discovered in good time, that rank and dignity in society must take a new ground. The old one has fallen through.—It must now take the substantial ground of character, instead of the chimerical ground of titles; and they have brought their titles to the altar, and made of them a burnt-offering to Reason.

If no mischief had annexed itself to the folly of titles, they would not have been worth a serious and formal destruction, such as the National Assembly have decreed them: and this makes it necessary to inquire farther into the nature and character of aristocracy.

That, then, which is called aristocracy in some countries, and nobility in others, arose out of the governments founded upon conquest. It was originally a military order, for the purpose of supporting military government, (for such were all governments founded in conquest); and to keep up a succession of this order for the purpose for which it was established, all the younger branches of those families were disinherited, and the law of *primogenitureship* set up.

The nature and character of aristocracy shows itself to us in this law. It is a law against every law of nature, and Nature herself calls for its destruction. Establish family justice, and aristocracy falls. By the aristocratical law of primogenitureship, in a family of six children, five are exposed. Aristocracy has never more than *one* child. The rest are begotten to be devoured. They are thrown to the cannibal for prey, and the natural parent prepares the unnatural repast.

As everything which is out of nature in man, affects, more or less, the interest of society, so does this. All the children which the aristocracy disowns (which are all, except the eldest) are, in general, cast like orphans on a parish, to be provided for by the public, but at a greater charge.—Unnecessary offices and places in governments and courts are created at the expense of the public, to maintain them.

With what kind of parental reflections can the father or mother contemplate their younger offspring. By nature they are children, and by marriage they are heirs; but by aristocracy they are bastards and orphans. They are the flesh and blood of their parents in one line, and nothing akin to them in the other. To restore, therefore, parents to their children, and children to their parents—relations to each other, and man to society—and to exterminate the monster Aristocracy, root and branch—the French constitution has destroyed the law of PRIMOGENITURESHIP. Here then lies the monster; and Mr Burke, if he pleases, may write its epitaph.

Hitherto we have considered aristocracy chiefly in one point of view. We have now to consider it in another. But whether we view it before or behind, or sideways, or any way else, domestically or publicly, it is still a monster.

In France, aristocracy had one feature less in its countenance, than what it has in some other countries. It did not compose a body of hereditary legislators. It was not '*a corporation of aristocracy*,' for such I have heard M. de Lafayette describe an English House of Peers. Let us then examine the grounds upon which the French constitution has resolved against having such a House in France.

Because, in the first place, as is already mentioned, aristocracy is kept up by family tyranny and injustice.

Secondly, Because there is an unnatural unfitness in an aristocracy to be legislators for a nation. Their ideas of *distributive justice* are corrupted at the very source. They begin life by trampling on all their younger brothers and sisters, and relations of every kind, and are taught and educated so to do. With what ideas of justice or honour can that man enter a house of legislation, who absorbs in his own person the inheritance of a whole family of children, or doles out to them some pitiful portion with the insolence of a gift?

Thirdly, Because the idea of hereditary legislation is as inconsistent as that of hereditary judges, or hereditary juries; and as absurd as an hereditary mathematician, or an hereditary wise man; and as ridiculous as an hereditary poet-laureate.

Fourthly, Because a body of men holding themselves accountable to nobody, ought not to be trusted by anybody.

Fifthly, Because it is continuing the uncivilized principle of governments founded in conquest, and the base idea of man having property in man, and governing him by personal right.

Sixthly, Because aristocracy has a tendency to degenerate the human species.—By the universal economy of nature it is known, and by the instance of the Jews it is proved, that the human species has a tendency to degenerate, in any small number of persons, when separated from the general stock of society, and intermarrying constantly with each other. It defeats even its pretended end, and becomes in time the opposite of what is noble in man. Mr Burke talks of nobility; let him show what it is. The greatest characters the world have known, have risen on the democratic floor. Aristocracy has not been able to keep a proportionate pace with democracy. The artificial NOBLE shrinks into a dwarf before the NOBLE of Nature; and in the few instances of those (for there are some in all countries) in whom nature, as by a miracle, has survived in aristocracy, THOSE MEN DESPISE IT.—But it is time to proceed to a new subject.

The French constitution has reformed the condition of the clergy. It has raised the income of the lower and middle classes, and taken from the higher. None is now less than twelve hundred livres (fifty pounds sterling), nor any higher than about two or three thousand pounds. What will Mr Burke place against this? Hear what he says.

He says, 'That the people of England can see without pain or grudging, an archbishop precede a duke; they can see a bishop of Durham, or a bishop of Winchester, in possession of £10,000 a year; and cannot see why it is in worse hands than estates to the like amount in the hands of this earl or that 'squire.' And Mr Burke offers this as an example to Prance.

As to the first part, whether the archbishop precedes the duke, or the duke the bishop, it is, I believe, to the people in general, somewhat like *Sternhold* and *Hopkins*, or *Hopkins* and *Sternhold*; you may put which you please first: and as I confess that I do not understand the merits of this case, I will not contend it with Mr Burke.

But with respect to the latter, I have something to say.—Mr Burke has not put the case right.—The comparison is out of order, by being put between the bishop and the earl or the 'squire. It ought to be put between the bishop and the curate, and then it will stand thus:—*The people of England can see without pain or grudging, a bishop of Durham, or a bishop of Winchester, in possession of ten thousand pounds a year, and a curate on thirty or forty pounds a year, or less.*—No, Sir, they certainly do not see those things without great pain or grudging. It is a case that applies itself to every man's sense of justice, and is one among many that calls aloud for a constitution.

In France, the cry of '*the church! the church!*' was repeated as often as in Mr Burke's book, and as loudly as when the dissenters' bill was before the English parliament; but the generality of the French clergy were not to be deceived by this cry any longer. They knew, that whatever the pretence might be, it was themselves who were one of the principal objects of it. It was the cry of the high beneficed clergy, to prevent any regulation of income taking place between those often thousand pounds a year and the parish priest. They, therefore, joined their case to those of every other oppressed class of men, and by this union obtained redress.

The French constitution has abolished tithes, that source of perpetual discontent between the tithe-holder and the parishioner. When land is held on tithe, it is in the condition of an estate held between two parties; the one receiving one-tenth, and the other nine-tenths of the produce: and, consequently, on principles of equity, if the estate can be improved, and made to produce by that improvement double or treble what it did before, or in any other ratio, the expense of such improvement ought to be borne in like proportion between the parties who are to share the produce. But this is not the case in tithes; the farmer bears the whole expense, and the tithe-holder takes a tenth of the improvement, in addition to the original tenth, and by this means gets the value of two-tenths instead of one. This is another case that calls for a constitution.

The French constitution hath abolished or renounced *Toleration*, and *Intolerance* also, and hath established UNIVERSAL RIGHT OF CONSCIENCE.

Toleration is not the *opposite* of Intolerance, but is the *counterfeit* of it. Both are despotisms. The one assumes to itself the right of withholding Liberty of Conscience, and the other of granting it. The one is the pope armed with fire and faggot, and the other is the pope selling or granting indulgences. The former is church and state, and the latter is church and traffic.

But Toleration may be viewed in a much stronger light. Man worships not himself, but his Maker; and the liberty of conscience which he claims, is not for the service of himself, but of his God. In this case, therefore, we must necessarily have the associated idea of two beings; the *mortal* who renders the worship, and the IMMORTAL BEING who is worshipped. Toleration, therefore, places itself, not between man and man, nor between church and church, nor between one denomination of religion and another, but between God and Man; between the being who worships, and the BEING who is worshipped; and by the same act of assumed authority by which it tolerates man to pay his worship, it presumptuously and blasphemously sets itself up to tolerate the Almighty to receive it.

Were a Bill brought into any parliament, entitled 'AN ACT to tolerate or grant liberty to the Almighty to receive the worship of a Jew or a Turk,' or 'to prohibit the Almighty from receiving it,' all men would startle, and call it blasphemy. There would be an uproar. The presumption of toleration in religious matters would then present itself unmasked: but the presumption is not the less because the name of 'Man' only appears to those laws, for the associated idea of the *worshipper* and the *worshipped* cannot be separated.—Who, then, an thou, vain dust and ashes! by whatever name thou art called, whether a King, a Bishop, a Church or a State, a Parliament, or anything else, that obtrudest thine insignificance between the soul of man and its Maker? Mind thine own concerns. If he believes not as thou believest, it is a proof that thou believest not as he believeth, and there is no earthly power can determine between you.

With respect to what are called denominations of religion, if everyone is left to judge of his own religion, there is no such thing as a religion that is wrong; but if they are to judge of each other's religion, there is no such thing as a religion that is right; and therefore, all the world is right, or all the world is wrong. But with respect to religion itself, without regard to names, and as directing itself from the universal family of mankind to the Divine object of all adoration, *it is man bringing to his Maker the fruits of his heart,* and though those fruits may differ from each other like the fruits of the earth, the grateful tribute of everyone is accepted.

A Bishop of Durham, or a Bishop of Winchester, or the Archbishop who heads the Dukes, will not refuse a tithe-sheaf of wheat, because it is not a cock of hay; nor a cock of hay, because it is not a sheaf of wheat; nor a pig, because it is neither one nor the other: but these same persons, under the figure of an established church, will not permit their Maker to receive the varied tithes of man's devotion.

One of the continual choruses of Mr Burke's book is, 'Church and State.' He does not mean some one particular church, or some one particular state, but any church and state; and he uses the term as a general figure to hold forth the political doctrine of always uniting the church with the state in every country, and he censures the National Assembly for not having done this in France.—Let us bestow a few thoughts on this subject.

All religions are in their nature kind and benign, and united with principles of morality. They could not have made proselytes at first, by professing anything that was vicious, cruel, persecuting, or immoral. Like everything else, they had their beginning; and they proceeded by persuasion, exhortation, and example. How then is it that they lose their native mildness, and become morose and intolerant?

It proceeds from the connexion which Mr Burke recommends. By engendering the church with the state, a sort of mule-animal, capable only of destroying, and not of breeding up, is produced, called *The Church established by Law.* It is a stranger, even from its birth, to any parent mother on which it is begotten, and whom in time it kicks out and destroys.

The inquisition in Spain docs not proceed from the religion originally professed, but from this mule-animal, engendered between the church and the state. The burnings in Smithfield proceeded from the same heterogeneous production; and it was the regeneration of this strange animal in England afterwards, that renewed rancour and irreligion among the inhabitants, and that drove the people called Quakers and Dissenters to America. Persecution is not an original feature in *any* religion; but it is always the strongly marked feature of all law-religions, or religions established by law. Take away the law-establishment, and every religion reassumes its original benignity. In America, a Catholic Priest is a good citizen, a good character, and a good neighbour; an Episcopalian Minister is of the same description: and this proceeds, independently of the men, from there being no law-establishment in America.

If also we view this matter in a temporal sense, we shall see the ill effects it has had on the prosperity of nations. The union of church and state has impoverished Spain. The revoking the edict of Nantes drove the silk manufacture from France into England; and church and state are now driving the cotton manufacture from England to America and France. Let then Mr Burke continue to preach his antipolitical doctrine of Church and State. It will do some good. The National Assembly will not follow his advice, but will benefit by his folly. It was by observing the ill effects of it in England, that America has been warned against it; and it is by experiencing them in France, that the National Assembly have abolished it, and, like America, have established UNIVERSAL RIGHT OF CONSCIENCE, AND UNIVERSAL RIGHT OF CITIZENSHIP.[6]

I will here cease the comparison with respect to the principles of the French constitution, and conclude this part of the subject with a few observations on the organization of the formal parts of the French and English governments.

The executive power in each country is in the hands of a person styled the King; but the French constitution distinguishes between the King and the Sovereign: It considers the station of King as official, and places Sovereignty in the nation.

The representatives of the nation, who compose the National Assembly, and who are the legislative power, originate in and from the people by election, as an inherent right in the people.—In England it is otherwise; and this arises from the original establishment of what is called its monarchy; for, as by the conquest all the rights of the people or the nation were absorbed into the hands of the Conqueror, and who added the title of King to that of Conqueror, those same matters which in France are now held as rights in the people, or in the nation, are held in England as grants from what is called the Crown. The Parliament in England, in both its branches, was erected by patents from the descendants of the Conqueror. The House of Commons did not originate as a matter of right in the people to delegate or elect, but as a grant or boon.

By the French constitution, the Nation is always named before the King. The third article of the Declaration of rights says, '*The nation is essentially the source*' (or fountain) '*of all sovereignty.*' Mr Burke argues, that, in England, a King is the fountain—that he is the fountain of all honour. But as this idea is evidently descended from the Conquest, I shall make no other remark upon it, than that it is the nature of conquest to turn everything upside down; and as Mr Burke will not be refused the privilege of speaking twice, and as there are but two parts in the figure, *the fountain* and the *spout,* he will be right the second time.

The French constitution puts the legislative before the executive; the Law before the King; *La Loi, Le Roi.* This also is in the natural order of things; because laws must have existence, before they can have execution.

A King in France does not, in addressing himself to the National Assembly, say, 'My assembly,' similar to the phrase used in England of *my* 'Parliament;' neither can he use it consistently with the constitution, nor could it be admitted. There may be propriety in the use of it in England, because, as is before mentioned, both Houses of Parliament originated from what is called the Crown by patent or boon—and not from the inherent rights of the people, as the National Assembly does in France, and whose name designates its origin.

The President of the National Assembly does not ask the King *to grant to the Assembly liberty of speech,* as is the case with the English House of Commons. The constitutional dignity of the National Assembly cannot debase itself. Speech is, in the first place, one of the natural rights of man always retained; and with respect to the National Assembly, the use of it is their *duty,* and the nation is their *authority.* They were elected by the greatest body of men exercising the right of election the European world ever saw. They sprung not from the filth of rotten boroughs, nor are they the vassal representatives of aristocratical ones. Feeling the proper dignity of their character, they support it. Their parliamentary language, whether for or against a question, is free, bold, and manly, and extends to all the parts and circumstances of the case. If any matter or subject respecting the executive department, or the person who presides in it, (the King), comes before them, it is debated on with the spirit of men, and the language of gentlemen; and their answer, or their address, is returned in the same style. They stand not aloof with the gaping vacuity of vulgar ignorance, nor bend with the cringe of sycophantic insignificance. The graceful pride of truth knows no extremes, and preserves, in every latitude of life, the right-angled character of man.

Let us now look to the other side of the question.—In the addresses of the English Parliaments to their Kings, we see neither the intrepid spirit of the old Parliaments of France, nor the serene dignity of the present National Assembly; neither do we see in them anything of the style of English manners, which border somewhat on bluntness. Since then they are neither of foreign extraction, nor naturally of English production, their origin must be sought for elsewhere, and that origin is the Norman Conquest. They are evidently of the vassalage class of manners, and emphatically mark the prostrate distance that exists in no other condition of men than between the conqueror and the conquered. That this vassalage idea and style of speaking was not got rid of even at the Revolution of 1688, is evident from the declaration of Parliament to William and Mary, in these words: 'We do most humbly and faithfully *submit* ourselves, our heirs and posterities, for ever.' Submission is wholly a vassalage term, repugnant to the dignity of Freedom, and an echo of the language used at the Conquest.

As the estimation of all things is by comparison, the Revolution of 1688, however from circumstances it may have been exalted beyond its value, will find its level. It is already on the wane, eclipsed by the enlarging orb of reason, and the luminous revolutions of America and France. In less than another century, it will go, as well as Mr Burke's labours, 'to the family vault of all the Capulets.' Mankind will then scarcely believe that a country calling itself free, would send to Holland fora man, and clothe him with power, on purpose to put themselves in fear of him, and give him almost a million sterling a year for leave to *submit* themselves and their posterity, like bond-men and bondwomen, for ever.

But there is a truth that ought to be made known: I have had the opportunity of seeing it; which is, *that, notwithstanding appearances, there is not any description of men that despise monarchy so much as courtiers.* But they well know, that if it were seen by others, as it is seen by them, the juggle could not be kept up. They are in the condition of men who get their living by a show, and to whom the folly of that show is so familiar that they ridicule it; but were the audience to be made as wise in this respect as themselves, there would be an end to the show and the profits with it. The difference between a republican and a courtier with respect to monarchy, is, that the one opposes monarchy, believing it to be something; and the other laughs at it, knowing it to be nothing.

As I used sometimes to correspond with Mr Burke, believing him then to be a man of sounder principles than his book shows him to be, I wrote to him last winter from Paris, and gave him an account how prosperously matters were going on. Among other subjects in that letter, I referred to the happy situation the National Assembly were placed in; that they had taken a ground on which their moral duty and their political interest were united. They have not to hold out a language which they do not themselves believe, for the fraudulent purpose of making others believe it. Their station requires no artifice to support it, and can only be maintained by enlightening mankind. It is not their interest to cherish ignorance, but to dispel it. They are not in the case of a ministerial or an opposition party in England, who, though they are opposed, are still united to keep up the common mystery. The National Assembly must throw open a magazine of light. It must show man the proper character of man; and the nearer it can bring him to that standard, the stronger the National Assembly becomes.

In contemplating the French constitution, we see in it a rational order of things. The principles harmonize with the forms, and both with their origin. It may perhaps be said as an excuse for bad forms, that they are nothing more than forms; but this is a mistake. Forms grow out of principles, and operate to continue the principles they grow from. It is impossible to practise a bad form on anything but a bad principle. It cannot be ingrafted on a good one; and wherever the forms in any government are bad, it is a certain indication that the principles are bad also.

I will here finally close this subject. I began it by remarking that Mr Burke had *voluntarily* declined going into a comparison of the English and French constitutions. He apologizes (in page 241) for not doing it, by saying that he had not time. Mr Burke's book was upwards of eight months in hand, and is extended to a volume of three hundred and sixty-six pages. As his omission does injury to his cause, his apology makes it worse; and men on the English side of the water will begin to consider, whether there is not some radical defect in what is called the English constitution, that made it necessary for Mr Burke to suppress the comparison, to avoid bringing it into view.

As Mr Burke has not written on constitutions, so neither has he written on the French revolution. He gives no account of its commencement or its progress. He only expresses his wonder. 'It looks,' says he, 'to me, as if I were in a great crisis, not of the affairs of France alone, but of all Europe, perhaps of more than Europe. All circumstances taken together, the French revolution is the most astonishing that has hitherto happened in the world.'

As wise men are astonished at foolish things, and other people at wise ones, I know not on which ground to account for Mr Burke's astonishment; but certain it is, that he does not understand the French revolution. It has apparently burst forth like a creation from a chaos, but it is no more than the consequence of a mental revolution priorily existing in France. The mind of the nation had changed beforehand, and the new order of things has naturally followed the new order of thoughts.—I will here, as concisely as I can, trace out the growth of the French revolution, and mark the circumstances that have contributed to produce it.

The despotism of Louis XIV united with the gaiety of his Court, and the gaudy ostentation of his character, had so humbled, and at the same time so fascinated the mind of France, that the people appeared to have lost all sense of their own dignity, in contemplating that of their Grand Monarch: and the whole reign of Louis XV, remarkable only for weakness and effeminacy, made no other alteration than that of spreading a sort of lethargy over the nation, from which it showed no disposition to rise.

The only signs which appeared of the spirit of Liberty during those periods, are to be found in the writings of the French philosophers. Montesquieu, president of the Parliament of Bordeaux, went as far as a writer under a despotic government could well proceed; and being obliged to divide himself between principle and prudence, his mind often appears under a veil, and we ought to give him credit for more than he has expressed.

Voltaire, who was both the flatterer and the satirist of despotism, took another line. His forte lay in exposing and ridiculing the superstitions which priestcraft united with statecraft had interwoven with governments. It was not from the purity of his principles, or his love of mankind, (for satire and philanthropy are not naturally concordant), but from his strong capacity of seeing folly in its true shape, and his irresistible propensity to expose it, that he made those attacks. They were however as formidable as if the motives had been virtuous; and he merits the thanks, rather than the esteem of mankind.

On the contrary, we find in the writings of Rousseau, and the Abbé Raynal, a loveliness of sentiment in favour of Liberty, that excites respect, and elevates the human faculties; but having raised this animation, they do not direct its operations, and leave the mind in love with an object, without describing the means of possessing it.

The writings of Quesnay, Turgot, and the friends of those authors, are of the serious kind; but they laboured under the same disadvantage with Montesquieu: their writings abound with moral maxims of government, but are rather directed to economize and reform the administration of the government, than the government itself.

But all those writings and many others had their weight; and by the different manner in which they treated the subject of government, Montesquieu by his judgement and knowledge of laws, Voltaire by his wit, Rousseau and Raynal by their animation, and Quesnay and Turgot by their moral maxims and systems of economy, readers of every class met with something to their taste, and a spirit of political inquiry began to diffuse itself through the nation at the time the dispute between England and the then colonies of America broke out.

In the war which France afterwards engaged in, it is very well known that the nation appeared to be beforehand with the French ministry. Each of them had its view: but those views were directed to different objects; the one fought liberty, and the other retaliation on England. The French officers and soldiers who after this went to America, were eventually placed in the school of Freedom, and learned the practice as well as the principles of it by heart.

As it was impossible to separate the military events which took place in America from the principles of the American revolution, the publication of those events in France necessarily connected themselves with the principles which produced them. Many of the facts were in themselves principles; such as the declaration of American independence, and the treaty of alliance between France and America, which recognized the natural right of man, and justified resistance to oppression.

The then Minister of France, Count Vergennes, was not the friend of America; and it is both justice and gratitude to say, that it was the Queen of France who gave the cause of America a fashion at the French Court.

Count Vergennes was the personal and social friend of Dr Franklin; and the Doctor had obtained, by his sensible gracefulness, a sort of influence over him; but with respect to principles, Count Vergennes was a despot.

The situation of Dr Franklin as Minister from America to France, should be taken into the chain of circumstances. The diplomatic character is of itself the narrowest sphere of society that man can act in. It forbids intercourse by a reciprocity of suspicion; and a diplomatic is a sort of unconnected atom, continually repelling and repelled. But this was not the case with Dr Franklin. He was not the diplomatic of a Court, but of MAN. His character as a philosopher had been long established, and his circle of society in France was universal.

Count Vergennes resisted for a considerable time the publication in France of the American constitutions, translated into the French language; but even in this he was obliged to give way to public opinion, and a sort of propriety in admitting to appear what he had undertaken to defend. The American constitutions were to liberty, what a grammar is to language: they define its parts of speech, and practically construct them into syntax.

The peculiar situation of the then Marquis de Lafayette is another link in the great chain. He served in America as an American officer under a commission of Congress, and by the universality of his acquaintance, was in close friendship with the civil government of America, as well as with the military line. He spoke the language of the country, entered into the discussions on the principles of government, and was always a welcome friend at any election.

When the war closed, a vast reinforcement to the cause of Liberty spread itself over France, by the return of the French officers and soldiers. A knowledge of the practice was then joined to the theory; and all that was wanting to give it real existence, was opportunity. Man cannot, properly speaking, make circumstances for his purpose, but he always has it in his power to improve them when they occur; and this was the case in France.

M. Necker was displaced in May 1781; and by the ill management of the finances afterwards, and particularly during the extravagant administration of M. Calonne, the revenue of France, which was nearly twenty-four millions sterling *per* year, was become unequal to the expenditure, not because the revenue had decreased, but because the expenses had increased; and this was the circumstance which the nation laid hold of to bring forward a revolution. The English Minister, Mr Pitt, has frequently alluded to the state of the French finances in his budgets, without understanding the subject. Had the French Parliaments been as ready to register edicts for new taxes, as an English Parliament is to grant them, there had been no derangement in the finances, nor yet any revolution; but this will better explain itself as I proceed.

It will be necessary here to show how taxes were formerly raised in France. The King, or rather the Court or Ministry acting under the use of that name, framed the edicts for taxes at their own discretion, and sent them to the Parliaments to be registered; for until they were registered by the Parliaments, they were not operative. Disputes had long existed between the Court and the Parliaments with respect to the extent of the Parliament's authority on this head. The Court insisted that the authority of Parliaments went no farther than to remonstrate or show reasons against the tax, reserving to itself the right of determining whether the reasons were well or ill-founded; and in consequence thereof, either to withdraw the edict as a matter of choice, or to *order* it to be enregistered as a matter of authority. The Parliaments on their part insisted, that they had not only a right to remonstrate, but to reject; and on this ground they were always supported by the Nation.

But, to return to the order of my narrative—M. Calonne wanted money; and as he knew the sturdy disposition of the Parliaments with respect to new taxes, he ingeniously sought either to approach them by a more gentle means than that of direct authority, or to get over their heads by a manoeuvre: and, for this purpose, he revived the project of assembling a body of men from the several provinces, under the style of an 'Assembly of the Notables,' or Men of Note, who met in 1787, and who were either to recommend taxes to the Parliaments, or to act as a Parliament themselves. An Assembly under this name had been called in 1617.

As we are to view this as the first practical step towards the revolution, it will be proper to enter into some particulars respecting it. The Assembly of the Notables has in some places been mistaken for the States-General, but was wholly a different body; the States-General being always by election. The persons who composed the Assembly of the Notables were all nominated by the King, and consisted of one hundred and forty members. But as M. Calonne could not depend upon a majority of this Assembly in his favour, he very ingeniously arranged them in such a manner as to make forty-four a majority of one hundred and forty: to effect this, he disposed of them into seven separate committees, of twenty members each. Every general question was to be decided, not by a majority of persons, but by a majority of committees; and as eleven votes would make a majority in a committee, and four committees a majority of seven, M. Calonne had good reason to conclude, that as forty-four would determine any general question, he could not be outvoted. But all his plans deceived him, and in the event became his overthrow.

The then Marquis de Lafayette was placed in the second committee, of whom Count D'Artois was president: and as money-matters was the object, it naturally brought into view every circumstance connected with it. M. de Lafayette made a verbal charge against Calonne, for selling crown-lands to the amount of two millions of livres, in a manner that appeared to be unknown to the King. The Count D'Artois (as if to intimidate, for the Bastille was then in being) asked the Marquis, if he would render the charge in writing? He replied, that he would.—The Count D'Artois did not demand it, but brought a message from the King to that purport. M. de Lafayette then delivered in his charge in writing, to be given to the King, undertaking to support it. No farther proceedings were had upon this affair; but M. Calonne was soon after dismissed by the King, and set off to England.

As M. de Lafayette, from the experience of what he had seen in America, was better acquainted with the science of civil government than the generality of the members who composed the Assembly of the Notables could then be, the brunt of the business fell considerably to his share. The plan of those who had a constitution in view, was to contend with the Court on the ground of taxes, and some of them openly professed their object. Disputes frequently arose between Count D'Artois and M. de Lafayette, upon various subjects. With respect to the arrears already incurred, the latter proposed to remedy them, by accommodating the expenses to the revenue, instead of the revenue to the expenses; and as objects of reform, he proposed to abolish the Bastille, and all the State-prisons throughout the nation, (the keeping of which was attended with great expense), and to suppress *Lettres de Cachet:* But those matters were not then much attended to; and with respect to *Lettres de Cachet, a majority of the Nobles appeared to be in favour of them.*

On the subject of supplying the Treasury by new taxes, the Assembly declined taking the matter on themselves, concurring in the opinion that they had not authority. In a debate on this subject, M. de Lafayette said, that raising money by taxes could only be done by a National Assembly, freely elected by the people, and acting as their representatives. Do you mean, said the Count D'Artois, the *States General*? M. de Lafayette replied, that he did. Will you, said the Count D'Artois, sign what you say, to be given to the King? The other replied, that he not only would do this, but that he would go farther, and say, that the effectual mode would be, for the King to agree to the establishment of a Constitution.

As one of the plans had thus failed, that of getting the Assembly to act as a Parliament, the other came into view, that of recommending. On this subject, the Assembly agreed to recommend two new taxes to be enregistered by the Parliament: The one a stamp tax, and the other a territorial tax, or sort of land tax. The two have been estimated at about five millions sterl. *per ann.* We have now to turn our attention to the Parliaments, on whom the business was again devolving.

The Archbishop of Toulouse (since Archbishop of Sens, and now a Cardinal) was appointed to the administration of the finances, soon after the dismission of Calonne. He was also made Prime Minister, an office that did not always exist in France. When this office did not exist, the Chief of each of the principal departments transacted business immediately with the King; but when a Prime Minister was appointed, they did business only with him. The Archbishop arrived to more State-authority than any Minister since the Duke de Choiseul, and the nation was strongly disposed in his favour; but by a line of conduct scarcely to be accounted for, he perverted every opportunity, turned out a despot, and sunk into disgrace, and a Cardinal.

The Assembly of the Notables having broken up, the new Minister sent the edicts for the two new taxes recommended by the Assembly to the Parliaments, to be enregistered. They of course came first before the parliament of Paris, who returned for answer. *That with such a revenue as the Nation then supported, the name of taxes ought not to be mentioned, but for the purpose of reducing them*; and threw both the edicts out.[7]

On this refusal, the Parliament was ordered to Versailles, where, in the usual form, the King held, what under the old government was called, a Bed of Justice; and the two edicts were enregistered in presence of the Parliament, by an order of State, in the manner mentioned in page 66. On this, the Parliament immediately returned to Paris, renewed their session in form, and ordered the enregistering to be struck out, declaring that everything done at Versailles was illegal. All the members of the Parliament were then served with Lettres de

Cachet, and exiled to Trois; but as they continued as inflexible in exile as before, and as vengeance did not supply the place of taxes, they were after a short time recalled to Paris.

The edicts were again tendered to them, and the Count D'Artois undertook to act as representative of the King. For this purpose, he came from Versailles to Paris, in a train of procession; and the Parliament were assembled to receive him. But show and parade had lost their influence in France; and whatever ideas of importance he might set off with, he had to return with those of mortification and disappointment. On alighting from his carriage to ascend the steps of the Parliament House, the crowd (which was numerously collected) threw out trite expressions, saying 'This is Monsieur D'Artois, who wants more of our money to spend.' The marked disapprobation which he saw, impressed him with apprehensions; and the word *Aux armes!* (*To arms!*) was given out by the officer of the guard who attended him. It was so loudly vociferated, that it echoed through the avenues of the House, and produced a temporary confusion: I was then standing in one of the apartments through which he had to pass, and could not avoid reflecting how wretched was the condition of a disrespected man.

He endeavoured to impress the Parliament by great words, and opened his authority by saying, 'The King, our Lord and Master.' The Parliament received him very coolly, and with their usual determination not to register the taxes: and in this manner the interview ended.

After this a new subject took place: In the various debates and contests which arose between the Court and the Parliaments on the subject of taxes, the Parliament of Paris at last declared, that although it had been customary for Parliaments to enregister edicts for taxes as a matter of convenience, the right belonged only to the *States-General*; and that, therefore, the Parliament could no longer with propriety continue to debate on what it had not authority to act. The King after this came to Paris, and held a meeting with the Parliament, in which he continued from ten in the morning till about six in the evening; and, in a manner that appeared to proceed from him, as if unconsulted upon with the cabinet or the ministry, gave his word to the Parliament, that the States-General should be convened.

But after this another scene arose, on a ground different from all the former. The minister and the cabinet were averse to calling the States-General: They well knew, that if the States-General were assembled, themselves must fall; and as the King had not mentioned *any time*, they hit on a project calculated to elude, without appearing to oppose.

For this purpose, the Court set about making a sort of constitution itself: It was principally the work of M. Lamoignon, Keeper of the Seals, who afterwards shot himself. This new arrangement consisted in establishing a body under the name of a *Cour plénière*, or full Court, in which were invested all the powers that the government might have occasion to make use of. The persons composing this Court were to be nominated by the King; the contended right of taxation was given up on the part of the King, and a new criminal code of laws, and law proceedings, was substituted in the room of the former. The thing, in many points, contained better principles than those upon which the government had hitherto been administered: but with respect to the *Cour plénière*, it was no other than a medium through which despotism was to pass, without appearing to act directly from itself.

The Cabinet had high expectations from their new contrivance. The persons who were to compose the *Cour plénière*, were already nominated; and as it was necessary to carry a fair appearance, many of the best characters in the nation were appointed among the number. It was to commence on the 8th of May 1788: But an opposition arose to it, on two grounds—the one as to principle, the other as to form.

On the ground of Principle it was contended. That government had not a right to alter itself; and that if the practice was once admitted, it would grow into a principle, and be made a precedent for any future alterations the government might wish to establish: That the right of altering the government was a national right, and not a right of government.—And on the ground of Form, it was contended, That the *Cour plénière* was nothing more than a larger Cabinet.

The then Duke de la Rochefoucault, Luxembourg, De Noailles, and many others, refused to accept the nomination, and strenuously opposed the whole plan. When the edict for establishing this new Court was sent to the Parliaments to be enregistered, and put into execution, they resisted also. The Parliament of Paris not only refused, but denied the authority; and the contest renewed itself between the Parliament and the Cabinet more strongly than ever. While the Parliament were sitting in debate on this subject, the Ministry ordered a regiment of soldiers to surround the House, and form a blockade. The Members sent out for beds and provision, and lived as in a besieged citadel: and as this had no effect, the commanding officer was ordered to enter the Parliament house and seize them; which he did, and some of the principal members were shut up in different prisons. About the same time a deputation of persons arrived from the province of Brittany, to remonstrate against the establishment of the *Cour plénière*; and those the Archbishop sent to the Bastille. But the spirit of the Nation was not to be overcome; and it was so fully sensible of the strong ground it had taken, that of withholding taxes, that it contented itself with keeping up a sort of quiet resistance, which effectually overthrew all the plans at that time formed against it. The project of the *Cour plénière* was at last obliged to be given up, and the Prime Minister not long afterwards followed its fate; and M. Necker was recalled into office.

The attempt to establish the *Cour plénière* had an effect upon the Nation which itself did not perceive. It was a sort of new form of government, that insensibly served to put the old one out of sight, and to unhinge it from the superstitious authority of antiquity. It was government dethroning government; and the old one, by attempting to make a new one, made a chasm.

The failure of this scheme renewed the subject of convening the States-General; and this gave rise to a new series of politics. There was no settled form for convening the States-General: all that it positively meant, was a deputation from what was then called the Clergy, the Noblesse, and the Commons; but their numbers, or their proportions, had not been always the same. They had been convened only on extraordinary occasions, the last of which was in 1614; their numbers were then in equal proportions, and they voted by orders.

It could not well escape the sagacity of M. Necker, that the mode of 1614 would answer neither the purpose of the then government, nor of the nation. As matters were at that time circumstanced, it would have been too contentious to agree upon anything. The debates would have been endless upon privileges and exemptions, in which neither the wants of the government, nor the wishes of the nation for a constitution, would have been attended to. But as he did not choose to take the decision upon himself, he summoned again the *Assembly of the Notables*, and referred it to them. This body was in general interested in the decision, being chiefly of the aristocracy and the high-paid-clergy; and they decided in favour of the mode of 1614. This decision was against the sense of the Nation, and also against the wishes of the Court; for the aristocracy opposed itself to both, and contended for privileges independent of either. The subject was then taken up by the Parliament, who recommended, that the number of the Commons should be equal to the other two; and that they should all sit in one house, and vote in one body. The number finally determined on was twelve hundred: six hundred to be chosen by the Commons, (and this was less than their proportion ought to have been when their worth and consequence is considered on a national scale), three hundred by the Clergy, and three hundred by the Aristocracy; but with respect to the mode of assembling themselves, whether together or apart, or the manner in which they should vote, those matters were referred.[8]

The election that followed, was not a contested election, but an animated one. The candidates were not men, but principles. Societies were formed in Paris, and committees of correspondence and communication established throughout the nation, for the purpose of enlightening the people, and explaining to them the principles of civil government; and so orderly was the election conducted, that it did not give rise even to the rumour of tumult.

The States-General were to meet at Versailles in April 1789, but did not assemble till May. They situated themselves in three separate chambers, or rather the Clergy and the Aristocracy withdrew each into a separate chamber. The majority of the aristocracy claimed what they called the privilege of voting as a separate body, and of giving their consent or their negative in that manner; and many of the bishops and the high-beneficed clergy claimed the same privilege on the part of their Order.

The *Tiers Etat* (as they were then called) disowned any knowledge of artificial Orders and artificial privileges; and they were not only resolute on this point, but somewhat disdainful. They began to consider aristocracy as a kind of fungus growing out of the corruption of society, that could not be admitted even as a branch of it; and from the disposition the aristocracy had shown by upholding Lettres de Cachet, and in sundry other instances, it was manifest that no constitution could be formed by admitting men in any other character than as National Men.

After various altercations on this head, the Tiers Etat or Commons (as they were then called) declared themselves (on a motion made for that purpose by the Abbé Sieyès) 'THE REPRESENTATIVES OF THE NATION; *and that the two Orders could be considered hut as deputies of corporations, and could only have a deliberative voice when they assembled in a national character with the national representatives.*' This proceeding extinguished the style of *Etats Généraux*, or States-General, and erected it into the style it now bears, that of L'Assemblée Nationale, or National Assembly.

This motion was not made in a precipitate manner: It was the result of cool deliberation, and concerted between the national representatives and the patriotic members of the two chambers, who saw into the folly, mischief, and injustice of artificial privileged distinctions. It was become evident, that no constitution, worthy of being called by that name, could be established on any thing less than a national ground. The aristocracy had hitherto opposed the despotism of the Court, and affected the language of patriotism; but it opposed it as its rival (as the English Barons opposed King John), and it now opposed the nation from the same motives.

On carrying this motion, the national representatives, as had been concerted, sent an invitation to the two chambers, to unite with them in a national character, and proceed to business. A majority of the clergy, chiefly of the parish priests, withdrew from the clerical chamber, and joined the nation; and forty-five from the other chamber joined in like manner. There is a sort of secret history belonging to this last circumstance, which is necessary to its explanation: It was not judged prudent that all the patriotic members of the chamber styling itself the Nobles, should quit it at once; and in consequence of this arrangement, they drew off by degrees, always leaving some, as well to reason the case, as to watch the suspected. In a little time, the numbers increased from forty-five to eighty, and soon after to a greater number; which, with a majority of the clergy, and the whole of the national representatives, put the malcontents in a very diminutive condition.

The King, who, very different from the general class called by that name, is a man of a good heart, showed himself disposed to recommend an union of the three chambers, on the ground the National Assembly had taken; but the malcontents exerted themselves to prevent it, and began now to have another project in view. Their numbers consisted of a majority of the aristocratical chamber, and a minority of the clerical chamber, chiefly of bishops and high-beneficed clergy; and these men were determined to put everything to issue, as well by strength as by stratagem. They had no objection to a constitution; but it must be such a one as themselves should dictate, and suited to their own views and particular situations. On the other hand, the Nation disowned knowing anything of them but as citizens, and was determined to shut out all such upstart pretensions. The more aristocracy appeared, the more it was despised; there was a visible imbecility and want of intellects in the majority, a sort of *je ne sais quoi*, that while it affected to be more than citizen, was less than man. It lost ground from contempt more than from hatred; and was rather jeered at as an ass, than dreaded as a lion. This is the general character of aristocracy, or what are called Nobles or Nobility, or rather No-ability, in all countries.

The plan of the malcontents consisted now of two things; either to deliberate and vote by chambers, (or orders), more especially on all questions respecting a constitution, (by which the aristocratical chamber would have had a negative on any article of the constitution); or, in case they could not accomplish this object, to overthrow the National Assembly entirely.

To effect one or other of these objects, they began now to cultivate a friendship with the despotism they had hitherto attempted to rival, and the Count D'Artois became their chief. The King (who has since declared himself deceived into their measures) held, according to the old form, *a Bed of Justice*, in which he accorded to the deliberation and vote *par tête* (by head) upon several subjects; but reserved the deliberation and vote upon all questions respecting a constitution, to the three chambers separately. This declaration of the King was made against the advice of M. Necker, who now began to perceive that he was growing out of fashion at Court, and that another minister was in contemplation.

As the form of sitting in separate chambers was yet apparently kept up, though essentially destroyed, the national representatives, immediately after this declaration of the King, resorted to their own chambers to consult on a protest against it; and the minority of the chamber (calling itself the Nobles), who had joined the national cause, retired to a private house to consult in like manner. The malcontents had by this time concerted their measures with the Court, which Count D'Artois undertook to conduct; and as they saw from the discontent which the declaration excited, and the opposition making against it, that they could not obtain a control over the intended constitution by a separate vote, they prepared themselves for their final object—that of conspiring against the National Assembly, and overthrowing it.

The next morning, the door of the chamber of the National Assembly was shut against them, and guarded by troops; and the Members were refused admittance. On this, they withdrew to a tennis ground in the neighbourhood of Versailles, as the most convenient place they could find, and, after renewing their session, took an oath never to separate from each other, under any circumstance whatever, death excepted, until they had established a constitution. As the experiment of shutting up the house had no other effect than that of producing a closer connexion in the Members, it was opened again the next day, and the public business recommenced in the usual place.

We now are to have in view the forming of the new Ministry, which was to accomplish the overthrow of the National Assembly. But as force would be necessary, orders were issued to assemble thirty thousand troops, the command of which was given to Broglio, one of the new-intended Ministry, who was recalled from the country for this purpose. But as some management was necessary to keep this plan concealed till the moment it should be ready for execution, it is to this policy that a declaration made by Count D'Artois must be attributed, and which is here proper to be introduced.

It could not but occur, that while the malcontents continued to resort to their chambers separate from the National Assembly, that more jealousy would be excited than if they were mixed with it, and that the plot might be suspected. But as they had taken their ground, and now wanted a pretence for quitting it, it was necessary that one should be devised. This was effectually accomplished by a declaration made by Count D'Artois, '*That if they took not a part in the National Assembly, the life of the King would be endangered*:' on which they quitted their chambers, and mixed with the Assembly in one body.

At the time this declaration was made, it was generally treated as a piece of absurdity in Count D'Artois, and calculated merely to relieve the outstanding Members of the two chambers from the diminutive situation they were put in; and if nothing more had followed, this conclusion would have been good. But as things best explain themselves by their events, this apparent union was only a cover to the machinations which were secretly going on; and the declaration accommodated itself to answer that purpose. In a little time the National Assembly found itself surrounded by troops, and thousands more were daily arriving. On this a very strong declaration was made by the National Assembly to the King, remonstrating on the impropriety of the measure, and demanding the reason. The King, who was not in the secret of this business, as himself afterwards declared, gave substantially for answer, that he had no other object in view than to preserve the public tranquillity, which appeared to be much disturbed.

But in a few days from this time, the plot unravelled itself. M. Necker and the Ministry were displaced, and a new one formed, of the enemies of the Revolution; and Broglio, with between twenty-five and thirty thousand foreign troops, was arrived to support them. The mask was now thrown off, and matters were come to a crisis. The event was, that in the space of three days, the new Ministry and their abettors found it prudent to fly the nation; the Bastille was taken, and Broglio and his foreign troops dispersed; as is already related in the former part of this work.

There are some curious circumstances in the history of this short-lived ministry, and this short-lived attempt at a counter-revolution. The palace of Versailles, where the Court was sitting, was not more than four hundred yards distant from the hall where the National Assembly was sitting. The two places were at this moment like the separate headquarters of two combatant armies; yet the Court was as perfectly ignorant of the information which had arrived from Paris to the National Assembly, as if it had resided at an hundred miles distance. The then Marquis de Lafayette, who (as has been already mentioned) was chosen to preside in the National Assembly on this particular occasion, named, by order of the Assembly, three successive deputations to the King, on the day, and up to the evening on which the Bastille was taken, to inform and confer with him on the state of affairs: but the ministry, who knew not so much as that it was attacked, precluded all communication, and were solacing themselves how dexterously they had succeeded; but in a few hours the accounts arrived so thick and fast, that they had to start from their desks and run. Some set off in one disguise, and some in another, and none in their own character. Their anxiety now was to outride the news lest they should be stopped, which, though it flew fast, flew not so fast as themselves.

It is worth remarking, that the National Assembly neither pursued those fugitive conspirators, nor took any notice of them, nor sought to retaliate in any shape whatever. Occupied with establishing a constitution founded on the Rights of Man and the Authority of the People, the only authority on which Government has a right to exist in any country, the National Assembly felt none of those mean passions which mark the character of impertinent governments, founding themselves on their own authority, or on the absurdity of hereditary succession. It is the faculty of the human mind to become what it contemplates, and to act in unison with its object.

The conspiracy being thus dispersed, one of the first works of the National Assembly, instead of vindictive proclamations, as has been the case with other governments, published a Declaration of the Rights of Man, as the basis on which the new constitution was to be built, and which is here subjoined.

DECLARATION OF THE RIGHTS OF MAN AND OF CITIZENS

By the National Assembly of France

'THE representatives of the people of FRANCE, formed into a NATIONAL ASSEMBLY, considering that ignorance, neglect, or contempt of human rights, are the sole causes of public misfortunes and corruptions of Government, have resolved to set forth, in a solemn declaration, these natural, imprescriptible, and inalienable rights: that this declaration being constantly present to the minds of the members of the body social, they may be ever kept attentive to their rights and their duties: that the acts of the legislative and executive powers of Government, being capable of being every moment compared with the end of political institutions, may be more respected: and also, that the future claims of the citizens, being directed by simple and incontestible principles, may always tend to the maintenance of the Constitution, and the general happiness.

'For these reasons, the NATIONAL ASSEMBLY doth recognize and declare, in the presence of the Supreme Being, and with the hope of his blessing and favour, the following *sacred* rights of men and of citizens:

'I. *Men are born, and always continue, free, and equal in respect of their rights. Civil distinctions, therefore, can be founded only on public utility.*

'II. *The end of all political associations, is, the preservation of the natural and imprescriptible rights of man; and these rights are liberty, property, security, and resistance of oppression.*

'III. *The nation is essentially the source of all sovereignty; nor can any* INDIVIDUAL, *or* ANY BODY OF MEN, *be entitled to any authority which is not expressly derived from it.*

'IV. Political Liberty consists in the power of doing whatever does not injure another. The exercise of the natural rights of every man, has no other limits than those which are necessary to secure to every *other* man the free exercise of the same rights; and these limits are determinable only by the law.

'V. The law ought to prohibit only actions hurtful to society. What is not prohibited by the law, should not be hindered; nor should any one be compelled to that which the law does not require.

'VI. The law is an expression of the will of the community. All citizens have a right to concur, either personally, or by their representatives, in its formation. It should be the same to all, whether it protects or punishes; and *all being equal in its sight, are equally eligible to all honours, places, and employments, according to their different abilities, without any other distinction than that created by their virtues and talents.*

'VII. No man should be accused, arrested, or held in confinement, except in cases determined by the law, and according to the forms which it has prescribed. All who promote, solicit, execute, or cause to be executed, arbitrary orders, ought to be punished; and every citizen called upon, or apprehended by virtue of the law, ought immediately to obey, and renders himself culpable by resistance.

'VIII. The law ought to impose no other penalties but such as are absolutely and evidently necessary: and no one ought to be punished, but in virtue of a law promulgated before the offence, and legally applied.

'IX. Every man being presumed innocent till he has been convicted, whenever his detention becomes indispensable, all rigour to him, more than is necessary to secure his person, ought to be provided against by the law.

'X. No man ought to be molested on account of his opinions, not even on account of his *religious* opinions, provided his avowal of them does not disturb the public order established by the law.

'XI. The unrestrained communication of thoughts and opinions being one of the most precious rights of man, every citizen may speak, write, and publish freely, provided he is responsible for the abuse of this liberty in cases determined by the law.

'XII. A public force being necessary to give security to the rights of men and of citizens, that force is instituted for the benefit of the community, and not for the particular benefit of the persons with whom it is entrusted.

'XIII. A common contribution being necessary for the support of the public force, and for defraying the other expenses of government, it ought to be divided equally among the members of the community, according to their abilities.

'XIV. Every citizen has a right, either by himself or his representative, to a free voice in determining the necessity of public contributions, the appropriation of them, and their amount, mode of assessment, and duration.

'XV. Every community has a right to demand of all its agents, an account of their conduct.

'XVI. Every community in which a separation of powers and a security of rights is not provided for, wants a constitution.

'XVII. The right to property being inviolable and sacred, no one ought to be deprived of it, except in cases of evident public necessity, legally ascertained, and on condition of a previous just indemnity.'

OBSERVATIONS ON THE DECLARATION OF RIGHTS

THE three first articles comprehend in general terms, the whole of a Declaration of Rights: All the succeeding articles either originate from them, or follow as elucidations. The 4th, 5th, and 6th, define more particularly what is only generally expressed in the 1st, 2nd, and 3rd.

The 7th, 8th, 9th, 10th, and 11th articles, are declaratory of *principles* upon which laws shall be constructed, conformable to *rights* already declared. But it is questioned by some very good people in France, as well as in other countries, whether the 10th article sufficiently guarantees the right it is intended to accord with: besides which, it takes off from the divine dignity of religion, and weakens its operative force upon the mind, to make it a subject of human laws. It then presents itself to Man, like light intercepted by a cloudy medium, in which the source of it is obscured from his sight, and he sees nothing to reverence in the dusky ray.[9]

The remaining articles, beginning with the twelfth, are substantially contained in the principles of the preceding articles; but, in the particular situation which France then was, having to undo what was wrong, as well as to set up what was right, it was proper to be more particular than what in another condition of things would be necessary.

While the Declaration of Rights was before the National Assembly, some of its members remarked, that if a Declaration of Rights was published, it should be accompanied by a Declaration of Duties. The observation discovered a mind that reflected, and it only erred by not reflecting far enough. A Declaration of Rights is, by reciprocity, a Declaration of Duties also. Whatever is my right as a man, is also the right of another; and it becomes my duty to guarantee, as well as to possess.

The three first articles are the basis of Liberty, as well individual as national; nor can any country be called free, whose government does not take its beginning from the principles they contain, and continue to preserve them pure; and the whole of the Declaration of Rights is of more value to the world, and will do more good, than all the laws and statutes that have yet been promulgated.

In the declaratory exordium which prefaces the Declaration of Rights, we see the solemn and majestic spectacle of a Nation opening its commission, under the auspices of its Creator, to establish a Government; a scene so new, and so transcendently unequalled by anything in the European world, that the name of a Revolution is diminutive of its character, and it rises into a Regeneration of man. What are the present Governments of Europe, but a scene of iniquity and oppression? What is that of England? Do not its own inhabitants say. It is a market where every man has his price, and where corruption is common traffic, at the expense of a deluded people? No wonder, then, that the French Revolution is traduced. Had it confined itself merely to the destruction of flagrant despotism, perhaps Mr Burke and some others had been silent. Their cry now is, 'It has gone too far:' that is, it has gone too far for them. It stares corruption in the face, and the venal tribe are all alarmed. Their fear discovers itself in their outrage, and they are but publishing the groans of a wounded vice. But from such opposition, the French Revolution, instead of suffering, receives an homage. The more it is struck, the more sparks it will emit; and the fear is, it will not be struck enough. It has nothing to dread from attacks: Truth has given it an establishment; and Time will record it with a name as lasting as his own.

Having now traced the progress of the French Revolution through most of its principal stages, from its commencement, to the taking of the Bastille, and its establishment by the Declaration of Rights, I will close the subject with the energetic apostrophe of M. de Lafayette—*May this great monument raised to Liberty, serve as a lesson to the oppressor, and an example to the oppressed!*[10]

MISCELLANEOUS CHAPTER

To prevent interrupting the argument in the preceding part of this work, or the narrative that follows it, I reserved some observations to be thrown together into a Miscellaneous Chapter; by which variety might not be censured for confusion. Mr Burke's Book is *all* Miscellany. His intention was to make an attack on the French Revolution; but instead of proceeding with an orderly arrangement, he has stormed it with a mob of ideas tumbling over and destroying one another.

But this confusion and contradiction in Mr Burke's Book is easily accounted for.—When a man in a long cause attempts to steer his course by anything else than some polar truth or principle, he is sure to be lost. It is beyond the compass of his capacity to keep all the parts of an argument together, and make them unite in one issue, by any other means than having this guide always in view. Neither memory nor invention will supply the want of it. The former fails him, and the latter betrays him.

Notwithstanding the nonsense, for it deserves no better name, that Mr Burke has asserted about hereditary rights, and hereditary succession, and that a Nation has not a right to form a Government for itself; it happened to fall in his way to give some account of what Government is. '*Government,* says he, *is a contrivance of human wisdom.*'

Admitting that Government is a contrivance of human *wisdom,* it must necessarily follow, that hereditary succession, and hereditary rights (as they are called), can make no part of it, because it is impossible to make wisdom hereditary; and on the other hand, *that* cannot be a wise contrivance, which in its operation may commit the government of a nation to the wisdom of an idiot. The ground which Mr Burke now takes, is fatal to every part of his cause. The argument changes from hereditary rights to hereditary wisdom; and the question is, Who is the wisest man? He must now show that everyone in the line of hereditary succession was a Solomon, or his title is not good to be a king.—What a stroke has Mr Burke now made! To use a sailor's phrase, he has *swabbed the deck,* and scarcely left a name legible in the list of Kings; and he has mowed down and thinned the House of Peers, with a scythe as formidable as Death and Time.

But Mr Burke appears to have been aware of this retort; and he has taken care to guard against it, by making government to be not only a *contrivance* of human wisdom, but a *monopoly* of wisdom. He puts the nation as fools on one side, and places his government of wisdom, all wise men of Gotham, on the other side; and he then proclaims, and says, that '*Men have a* RIGHT *that their* WANTS *should be provided for by this wisdom.*' Having thus made proclamation, he next proceeds to explain to them what their *wants* are, and also what their *rights* are. In this he has succeeded dexterously, for he makes their wants to be a *want* of wisdom; but as this is but cold comfort, he then informs them, that they have a *right* (*not* to any of the wisdom) but to be governed by it: and in order to impress them with a solemn reverence for this monopoly-government of wisdom, and of its vast capacity for all purposes, possible or impossible, right or wrong, he proceeds with astrological mysterious importance, to tell to them its powers, in these words —'The Rights of men in government are their advantages; and these are often in balances between differences of good; and in compromises sometimes between *good* and *evil,* and sometimes between *evil* and *evil.* Political reason is a *computing principle*; adding—subtracting—multiplying—and dividing, morally, and not metaphysically or mathematically, true moral demonstrations.'

As the wondering audience, whom Mr Burke supposes himself talking to, may not understand all this learned jargon, I will undertake to be its interpreter. The meaning then, good people, of all this, is, *That government is governed by no principle whatever; that it can make evil good, or good evil, just as it pleases. In short, that government is arbitrary power.*

But there are some things which Mr Burke has forgotten. *First,* He has not shown where the wisdom originally came from: and *secondly,* he has not shown by what authority it first began to act. In the manner he introduces the matter, it is either government stealing wisdom, or wisdom stealing government. It is without an origin, and its powers without authority. In short, it is usurpation.

Whether it be from a sense of shame, or from a consciousness of some radical defect in a government necessary to be kept out of sight, or from both, or from any other cause, I undertake not to determine; but so it is, that a monarchical reasoner never traces government to its source, or from its source. It is one of the *shibboleths* by which he may be known. A thousand years hence, those who shall live in America or in France, will look back with contemplative pride on the origin of their governments, and say, *This was the work of our glorious ancestors!* But what can a monarchical talker say? What has he to exult in? Alas! he has nothing. A certain something forbids him to look back to a beginning, lest some robber or some Robin Hood should rise from the long obscurity of time, and say, *I am the origin!* Hard as Mr Burke laboured the Regency Bill and Hereditary Succession two years ago, and much as he dived for precedents, he still had not boldness enough to bring up William of Normandy, and say, *There is the head of the list! there is the fountain of honour!* the son of a prostitute, and the plunderer of the English nation.

The opinions of men with respect to government are changing fast in all countries. The revolutions of America and France have thrown a beam of light over the world, which reaches into man. The enormous expense of governments have provoked people to think, by making them feel: and when once the veil begins to rend, it admits not of repair. Ignorance is of a peculiar nature: and once dispelled, and it is impossible to re-establish it. It is not originally a thing of itself, but is only the absence of knowledge; and though man may be *kept* ignorant, he cannot be *made* ignorant. The mind, in discovering truth, acts in the same manner as it acts through the eye in discovering objects; when once any object has been seen, it is impossible to put the mind back to the same condition it was in before it saw it. Those who talk of a counter-revolution in France, show how little they understand of man. There does not exist in the compass of language, an arrangement of words to express so much as the means of effecting a counter-revolution. The means must be an obliteration of knowledge; and it has never yet been discovered, how to make man *unknow* his knowledge, or *unthink* his thoughts.

Mr Burke is labouring in vain to stop the progress of knowledge; and it comes with the worse grace from him, as there is a certain transaction known in the city, which renders him suspected of being a pensioner in a fictitious name. This may account for some strange doctrine he has advanced in his book, which, though he points it at the Revolution Society, is effectually directed against the whole Nation.

'The King of England,' says he, 'holds *his* Crown' (for it does not belong to the Nation, according to Mr Burke) 'in *contempt* of the choice of the Revolution Society, who have not a single vote for a King among them either *individually* or *collectively*, and his Majesty's heirs, each in their time and order, will come to the Crown *with the same contempt* of their choice, with which his Majesty has succeeded to that which he now wears.'

As to who is King in England or elsewhere, or whether there is any King at all, or whether the people choose a Cherokee Chief, or a Hessian Hussar for a King, it is not a matter that I trouble myself about—be that to themselves; but with respect to the doctrine, so far as it relates to the Rights of Men and Nations, it is as abominable as anything ever uttered in the most enslaved country under heaven. Whether it sounds worse to my ear, by not being accustomed to hear such despotism, than what it does to the ear of another person, I am not so well a judge of; but of its abominable principle I am at no loss to judge.

It is not the Revolution Society that Mr Burke means; it is the Nation, as well in its *original*, as in its *representative character*; and he has taken care to make himself understood, by saying that they have not a vote either *collectively* or *individually*. The Revolution Society is composed of citizens of all denominations, and of members of both the Houses of Parliament; and consequently, if there is not a right to vote in any of the characters, there can be no right to any, either in the nation, or in its parliament. This ought to be a caution to every country, how it imports foreign families to be kings. It is somewhat curious to observe, that although the people of England have been in the habit of talking about kings, it is always a Foreign House of kings; hating Foreigners, yet governed by them.—It is now the House of Brunswick, one of the petty tribes of Germany.

It has hitherto been the practice of the English Parliaments, to regulate what was called the succession, (taking it for granted, that the Nation then continued to accord to the form of annexing a monarchical branch to its government; for without this, the Parliament could not have had authority to have sent either to Holland or to Hanover, or to impose a King upon the Nation against its will). And this must be the utmost limit to which Parliament can go upon the case; but the right of the Nation goes to the *whole* case, because it has the right of changing its *whole* form of government. The right of a Parliament is only a right in trust, a right by delegation, and that but from a very small part of the Nation; and one of its Houses has not even this. But the right of the Nation is an original right, as universal as taxation. The Nation is the paymaster of everything, and everything must conform to its general will.

I remember taking notice of a speech in what is called the English House of Peers, by the then Earl of Shelburne, and I think it was at the time he was Minister, which is applicable to this case. I do not directly charge my memory with every particular; but the words and the purport, as nearly as I remember, were these: *That the form of a Government was a matter wholly at the will of a Nation, at all times; that if it chose a monarchical form, it had a right to have it so; and if it afterwards chose to be a Republic, it had a right to be a Republic, and to say to a King, 'We have no longer any occasion for you.'*

When Mr Burke says that 'His Majesty's heirs and successors, each in their time and order, will come to the crown with the *same contempt* of their choice with which His Majesty has succeeded to that he wears,' it is saying too much even to the humblest individual in the country; part of whose daily labour goes towards making up the million sterling a year, which the country gives the person it styles a King. Government with insolence, is despotism; but when contempt is added, it becomes worse; and to pay for contempt, is the excess of slavery. This species of Government comes from Germany; and reminds me of what one of the Brunswick soldiers told me, who was taken prisoner by the Americans in the late war: 'Ah!' said he, 'America is a fine free country, it is worth the people's fighting for; I know the difference by knowing my own: in my country, if the prince says, Eat straw, we eat straw.' God help that country, thought I, be it England or elsewhere, whose liberties are to be protected by German principles of government, and Princes of Brunswick!

As Mr Burke sometimes speaks of England, sometimes of France, and sometimes of the world, and of government in general, it is difficult to answer his book without apparently meeting him on the same ground. Although principles of Government are general subjects, it is next to impossible in many cases to separate them from the idea of place and circumstance; and the more so when circumstances are put for arguments, which is frequently the case with Mr Burke.

In the former part of his book, addressing himself to the people of France, he says, 'No experience has taught us,' (meaning the English), 'that in any other course or method than that of an *hereditary crown*, can our liberties be regularly perpetuated and preserved sacred as our *hereditary right.*' I ask Mr Burke, who is to take them away?—M. de Lafayette, in speaking to France, says, '*For a Nation to be free, it is sufficient that she wills it.*' But Mr Burke represents England as wanting capacity to take care of itself, and that its liberties must be taken care of by a King holding it in 'contempt.' If England is sunk to this, it is preparing itself to eat straw, as in Hanover or in Brunswick. But besides the folly of the declaration, it happens that the facts are all against Mr Burke. It was by the Government *being hereditary*, that the liberties of the people were endangered. Charles I and James II are instances of this truth; yet neither of them went so far as to hold the Nation in contempt.

As it is sometimes of advantage to the people of one country, to hear what those of other countries have to say respecting it, it is possible that the people of France may learn something from Mr Burke's book, and that the people of England may also learn something from the answers it will occasion. When Nations fall out about freedom, a wide field of debate is opened. The argument commences with the rights of war, without its evils; and as knowledge is the object contended for, the party that sustains the defeat obtains the prize.

Mr Burke talks about what he calls an hereditary crown, as if it were some production of Nature; or as if, like Time, it had a power to operate, not only independently, but in spite of man; or as if it were a thing or a subject universally consented to. Alas! it has none of those properties, but is the reverse of them all. It is a thing in imagination, the propriety of which is more than doubted, and the legality of which in a few years will be denied.

But, to arrange this matter in a clearer view than what general expressions can convey, it will be necessary to state the distinct heads under which (what is called) an hereditary crown, or, more properly speaking, an hereditary succession to the Government of a Nation, can be considered; which are,

First, The right of a particular Family to establish itself.

Secondly, The right of a Nation to establish a particular Family.

With respect to the *first* of these heads, that of a Family establishing itself with hereditary powers on its own authority, and independent of the consent of a Nation, all men will concur in calling it despotism; and it would be trespassing on their understanding to attempt to prove it.

But the *second* head, that of a Nation establishing a particular Family with *hereditary powers,* does not present itself as despotism on the first reflection; but if men will permit a second reflection to take place, and carry that reflection forward but one remove out of their own persons to that of their offspring, they will then see that hereditary succession becomes in its consequences the same despotism to others, which they reprobated for themselves. It operates to preclude the consent of the succeeding generation; and the preclusion of consent is despotism. When the person who at any time shall be in possession of a Government, or those who stand in succession to him, shall say to a Nation, I hold this power in 'contempt' of you, it signifies not on what authority he pretends to say it. It is no relief, but an aggravation to a person in slavery, to reflect that he was sold by his parent; and as that which heightens the criminality of an act cannot be produced to prove the legality of it, hereditary succession cannot be established as a legal thing.

In order to arrive at a more perfect decision on this head, it will be proper to consider the generation which undertakes to establish a Family with *hereditary powers,* apart and separate from the generations which are to follow; and also to consider the character in which the *first* generation acts with respect to succeeding generations.

The generation which first selects a person, and puts him at the head of its Government, either with the title of King, or any other distinction, acts its *own choice,* be it wise or foolish, as a free agent for itself. The person so set up is not hereditary, but selected and appointed; and the generation who sets him up, does not live under an hereditary government, but under a government of its own choice and establishment. Were the generation who sets him up, and the person so set up, to live for ever, it never could become hereditary succession; and of consequence, hereditary succession can only follow on the death of the first parties.

As therefore hereditary succession is out of the question with respect to the *first* generation, we have now to consider the character in which *that* generation acts with respect to the commencing generation, and to all succeeding ones.

It assumes a character, to which it has neither right nor title. It changes itself from a *Legislator* to a *Testator,* and affects to make its Will, which is to have operation after the demise of the makers, to bequeath the Government; and it not only attempts to bequeath, but to establish on the succeeding generation, a new and different form of government under which itself lived. Itself, as is already observed, lived not under an hereditary Government, but under a Government of its own choice and establishment; and it now attempts, by virtue of a will and testament, (and which it has not authority to make), to take from the commencing generation, and all future ones, the rights and free agency by which itself acted.

But, exclusive of the right which any generation has to act collectively as a testator, the objects to which it applies itself in this case, are not within the compass of any law, or of any will or testament.

The rights of men in society, are neither devisable, nor transferable, nor annihilable, but are descendable only; and it is not in the power of any generation to intercept finally, and cut off the descent. If the present generation, or any other, are disposed to be slaves, it does not lessen the right of the succeeding generation to be free: wrongs cannot have a legal descent. When Mr Burke attempts to maintain, that the *English Nation did at the Revolution of* 1688, *most solemnly renounce and abdicate their rights for themselves, and for all their posterity for ever,* he speaks a language that merits not reply, and which can only excite contempt for his prostitute principles, or pity for his ignorance.

In whatever light hereditary succession, as growing out of the will and testament of some former generation, presents itself, it is an absurdity. A cannot make a will to take from B the property of B, and give it to C; yet this is the manner in which (what is called) hereditary succession by law operates. A certain former generation made a will, to take away the rights of the commencing generation, and all future ones, and convey those rights to a third person, who afterwards comes forward, and tells them, in Mr Burke's language, that they have *no rights,* that their rights are already bequeathed to him, and that he will govern in *contempt* of them. From such principles, and such ignorance, Good Lord deliver the world!

But, after all, what is this metaphor called a crown, or rather what is monarchy? Is it a thing, or is it a name, or is it a fraud? Is it 'a contrivance of human wisdom,' or of human craft to obtain money from a nation under specious pretences? Is it a thing necessary to a nation? If it is, in what does that necessity consist, what services does it perform, what is its business, and what are its merits? Doth the virtue consist in the metaphor, or in the man? Doth the goldsmith that makes the crown, make the virtue also? Doth it operate like Fonunatus's wishing-cap, or Harlequin's wooden sword? Doth it make a man a conjuror? In fine, what is it? It appears to be a something going much out of fashion, falling into ridicule, and rejected in some countries both as unnecessary and expensive. In America it is considered as an absurdity; and in France it has so far declined, that the goodness of the man, and the respect for his personal character, are the only things that preserve the appearance of its existence.

If Government be what Mr Burke describes it, 'a contrivance of human wisdom,' I might ask him, if wisdom was at such a low ebb in England, that it was become necessary to import it from Holland and from Hanover? But I will do the country the justice to say, that was not the case; and even if it was, it mistook the cargo. The wisdom of every country, when properly exerted, is sufficient for all its purposes; and there could exist no more real occasion in England to have sent for a Dutch Stadtholder, or a German Elector, than there was in America to have done a similar thing. If a country does not understand its own affairs, how is a foreigner to understand them, who knows neither its laws, its manners, nor its language? If there existed a man so transcendently wise above all others, that his wisdom was necessary to instruct a nation, some reason might be offered for monarchy; but when we cast our eyes about a country, and observe how every part understands its own affairs; and when we look around the world, and see that of all men in it, the race of kings are the most insignificant in capacity, our reason cannot fail to ask us—What are those men kept for?

If there is anything in monarchy which we people of America do not understand, I wish Mr Burke would be so kind as to inform us. I see in America, a government extending over a country ten times as large as England, and conducted with regularity, for a fortieth part of the expense which government costs in England. If I ask a man in America, if he wants a King? he retorts, and asks me if I take him for an idiot? How is it that this difference happens? are we more or less wise than others? I see in America, the generality of people living in a style of plenty unknown in monarchical countries; and I see that the principle of its government, which is that of the *equal Rights of Man*, is making a rapid progress in the world.

If monarchy is a useless thing, why is it kept up anywhere? and if a necessary thing, how can it be dispensed with? That *civil government* is necessary, all civilized nations will agree; but civil government is republican government. All that part of the government of England which begins with the office of constable, and proceeds through the department of magistrate, quarter-session, and general assize, including trial by jury, is republican government. Nothing of monarchy appears in any part of it, except the name which William the Conqueror imposed upon the English, that of obliging them to call him 'Their Sovereign Lord the King.'

It is easy to conceive, that a band of interested men, such as Placemen, Pensioners, Lords of the bed-chamber, Lords of the kitchen, Lords of the necessary-house, and the Lord knows what besides, can find as many reasons for monarchy as their salaries, paid at the expense of the country, amount to; but if I ask the farmer, the manufacturer, the merchant, the tradesman, and down through all the occupations of life to the common labourer, what service monarchy is to him? he can give me no answer. If I ask him what monarchy is, he believes it is something like a sinecure.

Notwithstanding the taxes of England amount to almost seventeen millions a year, said to be for the expenses of Government, it is still evident that the sense of the Nation is left to govern itself, and does govern itself by magistrates and juries, almost at its own charge, on republican principles, exclusive of the expense of taxes. The salaries of the Judges are almost the only charge that is paid out of the revenue. Considering that all the internal Government is executed by the people, the taxes of England ought to be the lightest of any nation in Europe; instead of which, they are the contrary. As this cannot be accounted for on the score of civil government, the subject necessarily extends itself to the monarchical part.

When the people of England sent for George the First, (and it would puzzle a wiser man than Mr Burke to discover for what he could be wanted, or what service he could render), they ought at least to have conditioned for the abandonment of Hanover. Besides the endless German intrigues that must follow from a German Elector being King of England, there is a natural impossibility of uniting in the same person the principles of Freedom and the principles of Despotism, or, as it is usually called in England, Arbitrary Power. A German Elector is in his electorate a despot: How then could it be expected that he should be attached to principles of liberty in one country, while his interest in another was to be supported by despotism? The union cannot exist; and it might easily have been foreseen, that German Electors would make German Kings, or, in Mr Burke's words, would assume government with 'contempt.' The English have been in the habit of considering a King of England only in the character in which he appears to them: whereas the same person, while the connexion lasts, has a home-seat in another country, the interest of which is different to their own, and the principles of the governments in opposition to each other—To such a person England will appear as a town-residence, and the Electorate as the estate. The English may wish, as I believe they do, success to the principles of Liberty in France, or in Germany; but a German Elector trembles for the fate of despotism in his electorate: and the Duchy of Mecklenburgh, where the present Queen's family governs, is under the same wretched state of arbitrary power, and the people in slavish vassalage.

There never was a time when it became the English to watch continental intrigues more circumspectly than at the present moment, and to distinguish the politics of the Electorate from the politics of the Nation. The revolution of France has entirely changed the ground with respect to England and France, as nations: but the German despots, with Prussia at their head, are combining against Liberty; and the fondness of Mr Pitt for office, and the interest which all his family-connexions have obtained, do not give sufficient security against this intrigue.

As everything which passes in the world becomes matter for history, I will now quit this subject, and take a concise review of the state of parties and politics in England, as Mr Burke has done in France.

Whether the present reign commenced with contempt, I leave to Mr Burke: certain however it is, that it had strongly that appearance. The animosity of the English Nation, it is very well remembered, ran high; and, had the true principles of Liberty been as well understood then as they now promise to be, it is probable the Nation would not have patiently submitted to so much. George the First and Second were sensible of a rival in the remains of the Stuarts; and as they could not but consider themselves as standing on their good behaviour, they had prudence to keep their German principles of Government to themselves; but as the Stuart family wore away, the prudence became less necessary.

The contest between rights, and what were called prerogatives, continued to heat the Nation till some time after the conclusion of the American War, when all at once it fell a calm—Execration exchanged itself for applause, and Court popularity sprang up like a mushroom in a night.

To account for this sudden transition, it is proper to observe, that there are two distinct species of popularity; the one excited by merit, the other by resentment. As the Nation had formed itself into two parties, and each was extolling the merits of its parliamentary champions for and against prerogative, nothing could operate to give a more general shock than an immediate coalition of the champions themselves. The partisans of each being thus suddenly left in the lurch, and mutually heated with disgust at the measure, felt no other relief than uniting in a common execration against both. A higher stimulus of resentment being thus excited, than what the contest on prerogatives had occasioned, the Nation quitted all former objects of rights and wrongs, and sought only that of gratification. The indignation at the Coalition, so effectually superseded the indignation against the Court, as to extinguish it; and without any change of principles on the part of the Court, the same people who had reprobated its despotism, united with it, to revenge themselves on the Coalition Parliament. The case was not, which they liked best,—but, which they hated most; and the least hated passed for love. The dissolution of the Coalition Parliament, as it afforded the means of gratifying the resentment of the Nation, could not fail to be popular; and from hence arose the popularity of the Court.

Transitions of this kind exhibit a Nation under the government of temper, instead of a fixed and steady principle; and having once committed itself, however rashly, it feels itself urged along to justify by continuance its first proceeding.—Measures which at other times it would censure, it now approves, and acts persuasion upon itself to suffocate its judgement.

On the return of a new Parliament, the new Minister, Mr Pitt, found himself in a secure majority: and the nation gave him credit, not out of regard to himself, but because it had resolved to do it out of resentment to another. He introduced himself to public notice by a proposed Reform of Parliament, which in its operation would have amounted to a public justification of corruption. The Nation was to be at the expense of buying up the rotten boroughs, whereas it ought to punish the persons who deal in the traffic.

Passing over the two bubbles, of the Dutch business, and the million a year to sink the national debt, the matter which most presents itself, is the affair of the Regency. Never, in the course of my observation, was delusion more successfully acted, nor a nation more completely deceived.—But, to make this appear, it will be necessary to go over the circumstances.

Mr Fox had stated in the House of Commons, that the Prince of Wales, as heir in succession, had a right in himself to assume the government. This was opposed by Mr Pitt; and, so far as the opposition was confined to the doctrine, it was just. But the principles which Mr Pitt maintained on the contrary side, were as bad, or worse in their extent, than those of Mr Fox; because they went to establish an aristocracy over the Nation, and over the small representation it has in the House of Commons.

Whether the English form of Government be good or bad, is not in this case the question; but, taking it as it stands, without regard to its merits or demerits, Mr Pitt was farther from the point than Mr Fox.

It is supposed to consist of three parts:—while therefore the Nation is disposed to continue this form, the parts have a *national standing*, independent of each other, and are not the creatures of each other. Had Mr Fox passed through Parliament, and said, that the person alluded to claimed on the ground of the Nation, Mr Pitt must then have contended (what he called) the right of the Parliament, against the right of the Nation.

By the appearance which the contest made, Mr Fox took the hereditary ground, and Mr Pitt the parliamentary ground; but the fact is, they both took hereditary ground, and Mr Pitt took the worst of the two.

What is called the Parliament, is made up of two Houses; one of which is more hereditary, and more beyond the control of the Nation, than what the Crown (as it is called) is supposed to be. It is an hereditary aristocracy, assuming and asserting indefeasible, irrevocable rights and authority, wholly independent of the Nation. Where then was the merited popularity of exalting this hereditary power over another hereditary power less independent of the Nation than what itself assumed to be, and of absorbing the rights of the Nation into a House over which it has neither election nor control?

The general impulse of the Nation was right; but it acted without reflection. It approved the opposition made to the right set up by Mr Fox, without perceiving that Mr Pitt was supporting another indefeasible right, more remote from the Nation, in opposition to it.

With respect to the House of Commons, it is elected but by a small part of the Nation; but were the election as universal as taxation, which it ought to be, it would still be only the organ of the Nation, and cannot possess inherent rights.—When the National Assembly of France resolves a matter, the resolve is made in right of the Nation; but Mr Pitt, on all national questions, so far as they refer to the House of Commons, absorbs the rights of the Nation into the organ, and makes the organ into a Nation, and the Nation itself into a cypher.

In a few words, the question on the Regency was a question of a million a year, which is appropriated to the executive department: and Mr Pitt could not possess himself of any management of this sum, without setting up the supremacy of Parliament; and when this was accomplished, it was indifferent who should be Regent, as he must be Regent at his own cost. Among the curiosities which this contentious debate afforded, was that of making the Great Seal into a King; the affixing of which to an act, was to be royal authority. If, therefore. Royal Authority is a Great Seal, it consequently is in itself nothing; and a good Constitution would be of infinitely more value to the Nation, than what the three Nominal Powers, as they now-stand, are worth.

The continual use of the word *Constitution* in the English Parliament, shows there is none; and that the whole is merely a form of Government without a Constitution, and constituting itself with what powers it pleases. If there were a Constitution, it certainly could be referred to; and the debate on any constitutional point, would terminate by producing the Constitution. One member says, This is Constitution; and another says, That is Constitution—Today it is one thing; and tomorrow, it is something else—while the maintaining the debate proves there is none. Constitution is now the cant word of Parliament, turning itself to the ear of the Nation. Formerly it was the *universal supremacy of Parliament*—the *omnipotence of Parliament*: But since the progress of Liberty in France, those phrases have a despotic harshness in their note; and the English Parliament have caught the fashion from the National Assembly, but without the substance, of speaking of *Constitution.*

As the present generation of people in England did not make the Government, they are not accountable for any of its defects; but that sooner or later it must come into their hands to undergo a constitutional reformation, is as certain as that the same thing has happened in France. If France, with a revenue of nearly twenty-four millions sterling, with an extent of rich and fertile country above four times larger than England, with a population of twenty-four millions of inhabitants to support taxation, with upwards of ninety millions sterling of gold and silver circulating in the nation, and with a debt less than the present debt of England—still found it necessary, from whatever cause, to come to a settlement of its affairs, it solves the problem of funding for both countries.

It is out of the question to say how long what is called the English constitution has lasted, and to argue from thence how long it is to last; the question is, how long can the funding system last? It is a thing but of modern invention, and has not yet continued beyond the life of a man; yet in that short space it has so far accumulated, that, together with the current expenses, it requires an amount of taxes at least equal to the whole landed rental of the nation in acres to defray the annual expenditure. That a government could not always have gone on by the same system which has been followed for the last seventy years, must be evident to every man; and for the same reason it cannot always go on.

The funding system is not money; neither is it, properly speaking, credit. It in effect creates upon paper the sum which it appears to borrow, and lays on a tax to keep the imaginary capital alive by the payment of interest, and sends the annuity to market, to be sold for paper already in circulation. If any credit is given, it is to the disposition of the people to pay the tax, and not to the government which lays it on. When this disposition expires, what is supposed to be the credit of Government expires with it. The instance of France under the former Government, shows, that it is impossible to compel the payment of taxes by force, when a whole nation is determined to take its stand upon that ground.

Mr Burke, in his review of the finances of France, states the quantity of gold and silver in France, at about eighty-eight millions sterling. In doing this, he has, I presume, divided by the difference of exchange, instead of the standard of twenty-four livres to a pound sterling; for M. Necker's statement, from which Mr Burke's is taken, is *two thousand two hundred millions of livres*, which is upwards of ninety-one millions and a half sterling.

M. Necker in France, and Mr George Chalmers of the Office of Trade and Plantation in England, of which Lord Hawkesbury is president, published nearly about the same time (1786) an account of the quantity of money in each nation, from the returns of the Mint of each nation. Mr Chalmers, from the returns of the English Mint at the Tower of London, states the quantity of money in England, including Scotland and Ireland, to be twenty millions sterling.[11]

M. Necker[12] says, that the amount of money in France, recoined from the old coin which was called in, was two thousand five hundred millions of livres, (upwards of one hundred and four millions sterling); and, after deducting for waste, and what may be in the West Indies, and other possible circumstances, states the circulation quantity at home, to be ninety-one millions and a half sterling, but, taking it as Mr Burke has put it, it is sixty-eight millions more than the national quantity in England.

That the quantity of money in France cannot be under this sum, may at once be seen from the state of the French Revenue, without referring to the records of the French Mint for proofs. The revenue of France prior to the Revolution, was nearly twenty-four millions sterling; and as paper had then no existence in France, the whole revenue was collected upon gold and silver; and it would have been impossible to have collected such a quantity of revenue upon a less national quantity than M. Necker has stated. Before the establishment of paper in England, the revenue was about a fourth part of the national amount of gold and silver, as may be known by referring to the revenue prior to King William, and the quantity of money stated to be in the nation at that time, which was nearly as much as it is now.

It can be of no real service to a Nation, to impose upon itself, or to permit itself to be imposed upon; but the prejudices of some, and the imposition of others, have always represented France as a nation possessing but little money—whereas the quantity is not only more than four times what the quantity is in England, but is considerably greater on a proportion of numbers. To account for this deficiency on the part of England, some reference should be had to the English system of funding. It operates to multiply paper, and to substitute it in the room of money, in various shapes; and the more paper is multiplied, the more opportunities are afforded to export the specie; and it admits of a possibility (by extending it to small notes) of increasing paper till there is no money left.

I know this is not a pleasant subject to English readers; but the matters I am going to mention, are so important in themselves, as to require the attention of men interested in money-transactions of a public nature.—There is a circumstance stated by M. Necker, in his treatise on the administration of the finances, which has never been attended to in England, but which forms the only basis whereon to estimate the quantity of money (gold and silver) which ought to be in every nation in Europe, to preserve a relative proportion with other nations.

Lisbon and Cadiz are the two ports into which (money) gold and silver from South America are imported, and which afterwards divides and spreads itself over Europe by means of commerce, and increases the quantity of money in all parts of Europe. If, therefore, the amount of the annual importation into Europe can be known, and the relative proportion of the foreign commerce of the several nations by which it is distributed can be ascertained, they give a rule, sufficiently true, to ascertain the quantity of money which ought to be found in any nation, at any given time.

M. Necker shows from the registers of Lisbon and Cadiz, that the importation of gold and silver into Europe, is five millions sterling annually. He has not taken it on a single year, but on an average of fifteen succeeding years, from 1763 to 1777, both inclusive; in which time, the amount was one thousand eight hundred million livres, which is seventy-five millions sterling.[13]

From the commencement of the Hanover succession in 1714, to the time Mr Chalmers published, is seventy-two years; and the quantity imported into Europe, in that time, would be three hundred and sixty millions sterling.

If the foreign commerce of Great Britain be stated at a sixth part of what the whole foreign commerce of Europe amounts to, (which is probably an inferior estimation to what the gentlemen at the Exchange would allow) the proportion which Britain should draw by commerce of this sum, to keep herself on a proportion with the rest of Europe, would be also a sixth part, which is sixty millions sterling; and if the same allowance for waste and accident be made for England which M. Necker makes for France, the quantity remaining after these deductions would be fifty-two millions; and this sum ought to have been in the nation (at the time Mr Chalmcrs published) in addition to the sum which was in the nation at the commencement of the Hanover succession, and to have made in the whole at least sixty-six millions sterling; instead of which, there were but twenty millions, which is forty-six millions below its proportionate quantity.

As the quantity of gold and silver imported into Lisbon and Cadiz, is more exactly ascertained than that of any commodity imported into England; and as the quantity of money coined at the Tower of London, is still more positively known; the leading facts do not admit of controversy. Either, therefore, the commerce of England is unproductive of profit, or the gold and silver which it brings in, leak continually away by unseen means, at the average rate of about three quarters of a million a year, which, in the course of seventy-two years, accounts for the deficiency; and its absence is supplied by paper.[14]

The Revolution of France is attended with many novel circumstances, not only in the political sphere, but in the circle of money transactions. Among others, it shows that a Government may be in a state of insolvency, and a Nation rich. So far as the fact is confined to the late Government of France, it was insolvent; because the Nation would no longer support its extravagance, and therefore it could no longer support itself—but with respect to the Nation, all the means existed. A Government may be said to be insolvent, every time it applies to a Nation to discharge its arrears. The insolvency of the late Government of France, and the present Government of England, differed in no other respect than as the disposition of the people differ. The people of France refused their aid to the old Government; and the people of England submit to taxation without inquiry. What is called the Crown in England, has been insolvent several times; the last of which, publicly known, was in May 1777, when it applied to the Nation to discharge upwards of £600,000, private debts, which otherwise it could not pay.

It was the error of Mr Pitt, Mr Burke, and all those who were unacquainted with the affairs of France, to confound the French Nation with the French Government, The French Nation, in effect, endeavoured to render the late Government insolvent, for the purpose of taking Government into its own hands; and it reserved its means for the support of the new Government. In a country of such vast extent and population as France, the natural means cannot be wanting; and the political means appear the instant the Nation is disposed to permit them. When Mr Burke, in a speech last Winter in the British Parliament, *cast his eyes over the map of Europe, and saw a chasm that once was France*, he talked like a dreamer of dreams. The same natural France existed as before, and all the natural means existed with it. The only chasm was that which the extinction of despotism had left, and which was to be filled up with a constitution more formidable in resources than the power which had expired.

Although the French Nation rendered the late Government insolvent, it did not permit the insolvency to act towards the creditors; and the creditors considering the Nation as the real paymaster, and the Government only as the agent, rested themselves on the Nation, in preference to the Government. This appears greatly to disturb Mr Burke, as the precedent is fatal to the policy by which Governments have supposed themselves secure. They have contracted debts, with a view of attaching what is called the monied interest of a Nation to their support; but the example in France shows, that the permanent security of the creditor is in the Nation, and not in the Government; and that in all possible revolutions that may happen in Governments, the means are always with the Nation, and the Nation always in existence. Mr Burke argues, that the creditors ought to have abided the fate of the Government which they trusted; but the National Assembly considered them as the creditors of the Nation, and not of the Government-of the master, and not of the steward.

Notwithstanding the late Government could not discharge the current expenses, the present Government has paid off a great part of the capital. This has been accomplished by two means; the one by lessening the expenses of Government, and the other by the sale of the monastic and ecclesiastical landed estates. The devotees and penitent debauchees, extortioners and misers of former days, to ensure themselves a better world than that which they were about to leave, had bequeathed immense property in trust to the priesthood, for *pious uses*; and the priesthood kept it for themselves. The National Assembly has ordered it to be sold for the good of the whole Nation, and the priesthood to be decently provided for.

Inconsequence of the Revolution, the annual interest of the debt of France will be reduced at least six millions sterling, by paying off upwards of one hundred millions of the capital; which, with lessening the former expenses of Government at least three millions, will place France in a situation worthy the imitation of Europe.

Upon a whole review of the subject, how vast is the contrast! While Mr Burke has been talking of a general bankruptcy in France, the National Assembly has been paying off the capital of its debt; and while taxes have increased near a million a year in England, they have lowered several millions a year in France. Not a word has either Mr Burke or Mr Pitt said about French affairs, or the state of the French finances, in the present Session of Parliament. The subject begins to be too well understood, and imposition serves no longer.

There is a general enigma running through the whole of Mr Burke's book. He writes in a rage against the National Assembly; but what is he enraged about? If his assertions were as true as they are groundless, and that France, by her Revolution, had annihilated her power, and become what he calls a *chasm*, it might excite the grief of a Frenchman, (considering himself as a national man), and provoke his rage against the National Assembly; but why should it excite the rage of Mr Burke?—Alas! it is not the Nation of France that Mr Burke means, but the COURT; and every Court in Europe, dreading the same fate, is in mourning. He writes neither in the character of a Frenchman nor an Englishman, but in the fawning character of that creature known in all countries, and a friend to none, a COURTIER. Whether it be the Court of Versailles, or the Court of

St James or Carlton House, or the Court in expectation, signifies not; for the caterpillar principle of all Courts and Courtiers are alike. They form a common policy throughout Europe, detached and separate from the interest of Nations: and while they appear to quarrel, they agree to plunder. Nothing can be more terrible to a Court or a Courtier, than the Revolution of France. That which is a blessing to Nations, is bitterness to them; and as their existence depends on the duplicity of a country, they tremble at the approach of principles, and dread the precedent that threatens their overthrow.

CONCLUSION

REASON and Ignorance, the opposites of each other, influence the great bulk of mankind. If either of these can be rendered sufficiently extensive in a country, the machinery of Government goes easily on. Reason obeys itself; and Ignorance submits to whatever is dictated to it.

The two modes of Government which prevail in the world, are, *first,* Government by election and representation: *Secondly,* Government by hereditary succession. The former is generally known by the name of republic; the latter by that of monarchy and aristocracy.

Those two distinct and opposite forms, erect themselves on the two distinct and opposite bases of Reason and Ignorance.—As the exercise of Government requires talents and abilities, and as talents and abilities cannot have hereditary descent, it is evident that hereditary succession requires a belief from man, to which his reason cannot subscribe, and which can only be established upon his ignorance; and the more ignorant any country is, the better it is fitted for this species of Government.

On the contrary, Government in a well-constituted republic, requires no belief from man beyond what his reason can give. He sees the *rationale* of the whole system, its origin and its operation; and as it is best supported when best understood, the human faculties act with boldness, and acquire, under this form of Government, a gigantic manliness.

As, therefore, each of those forms acts on a different base, the one moving freely by the aid of reason, the other by ignorance; we have next to consider, what it is that gives motion to that species of Government which is called mixed Government, or, as it is sometimes ludicrously styled, a Government of *this, that,* and *t'other.*

The moving power in this species of Government, is of necessity, Corruption. However imperfect election and representation may be in mixed Governments, they still give exercise to a greater portion of reason than is convenient to the hereditary part; and therefore it becomes necessary to buy the reason up. A mixed Government is an imperfect everything, cementing and soldering the discordant parts together by corruption, to act as a whole. Mr Burke appears highly disgusted, that France, since she had resolved on a revolution, did not adopt what he calls '*A British Constitution*'; and the regretful manner in which he expresses himself on this occasion, implies a suspicion, that the British Constitution needed something to keep its defects in countenance.

In mixed Governments there is no responsibility: the parts cover each other till responsibility is lost; and the corruption which moves the machine, contrives at the same time its own escape. When it is laid down as a maxim, that *a King can do no wrong*, it places him in a state of similar security with that of idiots and persons insane, and responsibility is out of the question with respect to himself. It then descends upon the Minister, who shelters himself under a majority in Parliament, which, by places, pensions, and corruption, he can always command; and that majority justifies itself by the same authority with which it protects the Minister. In this rotatory motion, responsibility is thrown off from the parts, and from the whole.

When there is a part in a Government which can do no wrong, it implies that it does nothing; and is only the machine of another power, by whose advice and direction it acts. What is supposed to be the King in mixed Governments, is the Cabinet; and as the Cabinet is always a part of the Parliament, and the members justifying in one character what they advise and act in another, a mixed Government becomes a continual enigma; entailing upon a country, by the quantity of corruption necessary to solder the parts, the expense of supporting all the forms of Government at once, and finally resolving itself into a Government by committee; in which the advisers, the actors, the approvers, the justifiers, the persons responsible, and the persons not responsible, are the same persons.

By this pantomimical contrivance, and change of scene and character, the parts help each other out in matters which neither of them singly would assume to act. When money is to be obtained, the mass of variety apparently dissolves, and a profusion of parliamentary praises passes between the parts. Each admires with astonishment, the wisdom, the liberality, the disinterestedness of the other; and all of them breathe a pitying sigh at the burdens of the Nation.

But in a well-constituted republic, nothing of this soldering, praising, and pitying, can take place; the representation being equal throughout the country, and complete in itself, however it may be arranged into legislative and executive, they have all one and the same natural source. The parts are not foreigners to each other, like democracy, aristocracy, and monarchy. As there are no discordant distinctions, there is nothing to corrupt by compromise, nor confound by contrivance. Public measures appeal of themselves to the understanding of the Nation, and, resting on their own merits, disown any flattering application to vanity. The continual whine of lamenting the burden of taxes, however successfully it may be practised in mixed Governments, is inconsistent with the sense and spirit of a republic. If taxes are necessary, they are of course advantageous; but if they require an apology, the apology itself implies an impeachment. Why then is man thus imposed upon, or why does he impose upon himself?

When men are spoken of as kings and subjects, or when Government is mentioned under the distinct or combined heads of monarchy, aristocracy, and democracy, what is it that *reasoning* man is to understand by the terms? If there really existed in the world two or more distinct and separate *elements* of human power, we should then see the several origins to which those terms would descriptively apply: but as there is but one species of man, there can be but one element of human power; and that element is man himself. Monarchy, aristocracy, and democracy, are but creatures of imagination; and a thousand such may be contrived, as well as three.

From the Revolutions of America and France, and the symptoms that have appeared in other countries, it is evident that the opinion of the world is changed with respect to systems of Government, and that revolutions arc not within the compass of political calculations. The progress of time and circumstances, which men assign to the accomplishment of great changes, is too mechanical to measure the force of the mind, and the rapidity of reflection, by which revolutions are generated: All the old Governments have received a shock from those that already appear, and which were once more improbable, and are a greater subject of wonder, than a general revolution in Europe would be now.

When we survey the wretched condition of man under the monarchical and hereditary systems of Government, dragged from his home by one power, or driven by another, and impoverished by taxes more than by enemies, it becomes evident that those systems are bad, and that a general revolution in the principle and construction of Governments is necessary.

What is government more than the management of the affairs of a Nation? It is not, and from its nature cannot be, the property of any particular man or family, but of the whole community, at whose expense it is supported; and though by force or contrivance it has been usurped into an inheritance, the usurpation cannot alter the right of things. Sovereignty, as a matter of right, appertains to the Nation only, and not to any individual; and a Nation has at all times an inherent indefeasible right to abolish any form of Government it finds inconvenient, and establish such as accords with its interest, disposition, and happiness. The romantic and barbarous distinction of men into Kings and subjects, though it may suit the condition of courtiers, cannot that of citizens; and is exploded by the principle upon which Governments are now founded. Every citizen is a member of the Sovereignty, and, as such, can acknowledge no personal subjection; and his obedience can be only to the laws.

When men think of what Government is, they must necessarily suppose it to possess a knowledge of all the objects and matters upon which its authority is to be exercised. In this view of Government, the republican system, as established by America and France, operates to embrace the whole of a Nation; and the knowledge necessary to the interest of all the parts, is to be found in the centre, which the parts by representation form: But the old Governments are on a construction that excludes knowledge as well as happiness; Government by monks, who know nothing of the world beyond the walls of a convent, is as consistent as government by Kings.

What were formerly called Revolutions, were little more than a change of persons, or an alteration of local circumstances. They rose and fell like things of course, and had nothing in their existence or their fate that could influence beyond the spot that produced them. But what we now see in the world, from the Revolutions of America and France, are a renovation of the natural order of things, a system of principles as universal as truth and the existence of man, and combining moral with political happiness and national prosperity.

'I. *Men are born and always continue free, and equal in respect of their rights. Civil distinctions, therefore, can be founded only on public utility.*

'II. *The end of all political associations is the preservation of the natural and imprescriptible rights of man; and these rights are liberty, property, security, and resistance of oppression.*

'III. *The Nation is essentially the source of all Sovereignty; nor can any* INDIVIDUAL, *or* ANY BODY OF MEN, *be entitled to any authority which is not expressly derived from it.*'

In these principles, there is nothing to throw a Nation into confusion by inflaming ambition. They are calculated to call forth wisdom and abilities, and to exercise them for the public good, and not for the emolument or aggrandizement of particular descriptions of men or families. Monarchical sovereignty, the enemy of mankind, and the source of misery, is abolished; and sovereignty itself is restored to its natural and original place, the Nation. Were this the case throughout Europe, the cause of wars would be taken away.

It is attributable to Henry the Fourth of France, a man of an enlarged and benevolent heart, that he proposed, about the year 1610, a plan for abolishing war in Europe. The plan consisted in constituting an European Congress, or as the French Authors style it, a Pacific Republic; by appointing delegates from the several Nations, who were to act as a Court of arbitration in any disputes that might arise between nation and nation.

Had such a plan been adopted at the time it was proposed, the taxes of England and France, as two of the parties, would have been at least ten millions sterling annually to each Nation less than they were at the commencement of the French Revolution.

To conceive a cause why such a plan has not been adopted, (and that instead of a Congress for the purpose of *preventing* war, it has been called only to *terminate* a war, after a fruitless expense of several years), it will be necessary to consider the interest of Governments as a distinct interest to that of Nations.

Whatever is the cause of taxes to a Nation, becomes also the means of revenue to a Government. Every war terminates with an addition of taxes, and consequently with an addition of revenue; and in any event of war, in the manner they are now commenced and concluded, the power and interest of Governments are increased. War, therefore, from its productiveness, as it easily furnishes the pretence of necessity for taxes and appointments to places and offices, becomes a principal part of the system of old Governments; and to establish any mode to abolish war, however advantageous it might be to Nations, would be to take from such Government the most lucrative of its branches. The frivolous matters upon which war is made, show the disposition and avidity of Governments to uphold the system of war, and betray the motives upon which they act.

Why are not Republics plunged into war, but because the nature of their Government does not admit of an interest distinct from that of the Nation? Even Holland, though an ill-constructed Republic, and with a commerce extending over the world, existed nearly a century without war: and the instant the form of Government was changed in France, the republican principles of peace and domestic prosperity and economy arose with the new Government; and the same consequences would follow the same causes in other Nations.

As war is the system of Government on the old construction, the animosity which Nations reciprocally entertain, is nothing more than what the policy of their Governments excites, to keep up the spirit of the system. Each Government accuses the other of perfidy, intrigue, and ambition, as a means of heating the imagination of their respective Nations, and incensing them to hostilities. Man is not the enemy of man, but through the medium of a false system of Government. Instead, therefore, of exclaiming against the ambition of Kings, the exclamation should be directed against the principle of such Governments; and instead of seeking to reform the individual, the wisdom of a Nation should apply itself to reform the system.

Whether the forms and maxims of Governments which are still in practice, were adapted to the condition of the world at the period they were established, is not in this case the question. The older they are, the less correspondence can they have with the present state of things. Time, and change of circumstances and opinions, have the same progressive effect in rendering modes of Government obsolete, as they have upon customs and manners.—Agriculture, commerce, manufactures, and the tranquil arts, by which the prosperity of Nations is best promoted, require a different system of Government, and a different species of knowledge to direct its operations, than what might have been required in the former condition of the world.

As it is not difficult to perceive, from the enlightened state of mankind, that hereditary Governments are verging to their decline, and that Revolutions on the broad basis of national sovereignty, and

Government by representation, are making their way in Europe, it would be an act of wisdom to anticipate their approach, and produce Revolutions by reason and accommodation, rather than commit them to the issue of convulsions.

From what we now see, nothing of reform in the political world ought to be held improbable. It is an age of Revolutions, in which everything may be looked for. The intrigue of Courts, by which the system of war is kept up, may provoke a confederation of Nations to abolish it: and an European Congress, to patronize the progress of free Government, and promote the civilization of Nations with each other, is an event nearer in probability, than once were the Revolutions and Alliance of France and America.

FINIS

PART II

To
M. DE LAFAYETTE

AFTER an acquaintance of nearly fifteen years, in difficult situations in America, and various consultations in Europe, I feel a pleasure in presenting to you this small treatise, in gratitude for your services to my beloved America, and as a testimony of my esteem for the virtues, public and private, which I know you to possess.

The only point upon which I could ever discover that we differed, was not as to principles of Government, but as to time. For my own part, I think it equally as injurious to good principles to permit them to linger, as to push them on too fast. That which you suppose accomplishable in fourteen or fifteen years, I may believe practicable in a much shorter period. Mankind, as it appears to me, are always ripe enough to understand their true interest, provided it be presented clearly to their understanding, and that in a manner not to create suspicion by anything like self-design, nor offend by assuming too much. Where we would wish to reform we must not reproach.

When the American revolution was established, I felt a disposition to sit serenely down and enjoy the calm. It did not appear to me that any object could afterwards arise great enough to make me quit tranquillity, and feel as I had felt before. But when principle, and not place, is the energetic cause of action, a man, I find, is everywhere the same.

I am now once more in the public world; and as I have not a right to contemplate on so many years of remaining life as you have, I am resolved to labour as fast as I can; and as I am anxious for your aid and your company, I wish you to hasten your principles, and overtake me.

If you make a campaign the ensuing spring, which it is most probable there will be no occasion for, I will come and join you. Should the campaign commence, I hope it will terminate in the extinction of German despotism, and in establishing the freedom of all Germany. When France shall be surrounded with revolutions, she will be in peace and safety, and her taxes, as well as those of Germany, will consequently become less.

Your sincere,

Affectionate Friend,

THOMAS PAINE

London, Feb. 9, 1792.

PREFACE

WHEN I began the chapter entitled the 'Conclusion' in the former part of the *Rights of Man*, published last year, it was my intention to have extended it to a greater length; but in casting the whole matter in my mind which I wished to add, I found that I must either make the work too bulky, or contract my plan too much. I therefore brought it to a close as soon as the subject would admit, and reserved what I had further to say to another opportunity.

Several other reasons contributed to produce this determination. I wished to know the manner in which a work, written in a style of thinking and expression different to what had been customary in England, would be received before I proceeded farther. A great field was opening to the view of mankind by means of the French Revolution. Mr Burke's outrageous opposition thereto brought the controversy into England. He attacked principles which he knew (from information) I would contest with him, because they are principles I believe to be good, and which I have contributed to establish, and conceive myself bound to defend. Had he not urged the controversy, I had most probably been a silent man.

Another reason for deferring the remainder of the work was, that Mr Burke promised in his first publication to renew the subject at another opportunity, and to make a comparison of what he called the English and French Constitutions. I therefore held myself in reserve for him. He has published two works since, without doing this; which he certainly would not have omitted, had the comparison been in his favour.

In his last work, '*His appeal from the new to the old Whigs,*' he has quoted about ten pages from the *Rights of Man*, and having given himself the trouble of doing this, says, 'he shall not attempt in the smallest degree to refute them,' meaning the principles therein contained. I am enough acquainted with Mr Burke to know, chat he would if he could. But instead of contesting them, he immediately after consoles himself with saying, that 'he has done his part.'—He has not done his part. He has not performed his promise of a comparison of constitutions. He started the controversy, he gave the challenge, and has fled from it; and he is now a *case in point* with his own opinion, that, '*the age of chivalry is gone!*'

The title, as well as the substance of his last work, his '*Appeal,*' is his condemnation. Principles must stand on their own merits, and if they are good they certainly will. To put them under the shelter of other men's authority, as Mr Burke has done, serves to bring them into suspicion. Mr Burke is not very fond of dividing his honours, but in this case he is artfully dividing the disgrace.

But who are those to whom Mr Burke has made his appeal? A set of childish thinkers and half-way politicians born in the last century; men who went no farther with any principle than as it suited their purpose as a party; the nation was always left out of the question; and this has been the character of every party from that day to this. The nation sees nothing in such works, or such politics worthy its attention. A little matter will move a party, but it must be something great that moves a nation.

Though I see nothing in Mr Burke's Appeal worth taking much notice of, there is, however, one expression upon which I shall offer a few remarks. —After quoting largely from the *Rights of Man,* and declining to contest the principles contained in that work, he says, 'This will most probably be done (*if such writings shall be thought to deserve any other refutation than that of criminal justice*) by others, who may think with Mr Burke and with the same zeal.'

In the first place, it has not yet been done by anybody. Not less, I believe, than eight or ten pamphlets intended as answers to the former part of the '*Rights of Man*' have been published by different persons, and not one of them, to my knowledge, has extended to a second edition, nor are even the titles of them so much as generally remembered. As I am averse to unnecessarily multiplying publications, I have answered none of them. And as I believe that a man may write himself out of reputation when nobody else can do it, I am careful to avoid that rock.

But as I would decline unnecessary publications on the one hand, so would I avoid everything that might appear like sullen pride on the other. If Mr Burke, or any person on his side the question, will produce an answer to the *Rights of Man,* that shall extend to an half, or even to a fourth part of the number of copies to which the *Rights of Man* extended,

I will reply to his work. But until this be done, I shall so far take the sense of the public for my guide (and the world knows I am not a flatterer) that what they do not think worth while to read, is not worth mine to answer. I suppose the number of copies to which the first part of the *Rights of Man* extended, taking England, Scotland, and Ireland, is not less than between forty and fifty thousand.

I now come to remark on the remaining part of the quotation I have made from Mr Burke.

'If,' says he, 'such writings shall be thought to deserve any other refutation than that of *criminal* justice.'

Pardoning the pun, it must be *criminal* justice indeed that should condemn a work as a substitute for not being able to refute it. The greatest condemnation that could be passed upon it would be a refutation. But in proceeding by the method Mr Burke alludes to, the condemnation would, in the final event, pass upon the criminality of the process and not upon the work, and in this case, I had rather be the author, than be either the judge, or the jury, that should condemn it.

But to come at once to the point. I have differed from some professional gentlemen on the subject of prosecutions, and I since find they are falling into my opinion, which I will here state as fully, but as concisely as I can.

I will first put a case with respect to any law, and then compare it with a government, or with what in England is, or has been, called a constitution.

It would be an act of despotism, or what in England is called arbitrary power, to make a law to prohibit investigating the principles, good or bad, on which such a law, or any other is founded.

If a law be bad, it is one thing to oppose the practice of it, but it is quite a different thing to expose its errors, to reason on its defects, and to show cause why it should be repealed, or why another ought to be substituted in its place. I have always held it an opinion (making it also my practice) that it is better to obey a bad law, making use at the same time of every argument to show its errors and procure its repeal, than forcibly to violate it; because the precedent of breaking a bad law might weaken the force, and lead to a discretionary violation, of those which are good.

The case is the same with respect to principles and forms of government, or to what are called constitutions and the parts of which they are composed.

It is for the good of nations, and not for the emolument or aggrandizement of particular individuals, that government ought to be established, and that mankind are at the expense of supporting it. The defects of every government and constitution, both as to principle and form must, on a parity of reasoning, be as open to discussion as the defects of a law, and it is a duty which every man owes to society to point them out. When those defects, and the means of remedying them are generally seen by a nation, that nation will reform its government or its constitution in the one case, as the government repealed or reformed the law in the other. The operation of government is restricted to the making and the administering of laws; but it is to a nation that the right of forming or reforming, generating or regenerating constitutions and governments belong; and consequently those subjects, as subjects of investigation, are always before a country *as a matter of right,* and cannot, without invading the general rights of that country, be made subjects for prosecution. On this ground I will meet Mr Burke whenever he please. It is better that the whole argument should come out, than to seek to stifle it. It was himself that opened the controversy, and he ought not to desert it.

I do not believe that monarchy and aristocracy will continue seven years longer in any of the enlightened countries in Europe. If better reasons can be shown for them than against them, they will stand; if the contrary, they will not. Mankind are not now to be told they shall not think, or they shall not read; and publications that go no further than to investigate principles of government, to invite men to reason and to reflect, and to show the errors and excellences of different systems, have a right to appear. If they do not excite attention, they are not worth the trouble of a prosecution; and if they do, the prosecution will amount to nothing, since it cannot amount to a prohibition of reading. This would be a sentence on the public, instead of the author, and would also be the most effectual mode of making or hastening revolutions.

On all cases that apply universally to a nation, with respect to systems of government, a jury of *twelve* men is not competent to decide. Where there are no witnesses to be examined, no facts to be proved, and where the whole matter is before the whole public, and the merits or demerits of it resting on their opinion; and where there is nothing to be known in a court, but what everybody knows out of it, every twelve men is equally as good a jury as the other, and would most probably reverse each other's verdict; or from the variety of their opinions, not be able to form one. It is one case, whether a nation approve a work, or a plan; but it is quite another case, whether it will commit to any such jury the power of determining whether that nation have a right to, or shall reform its government, or not. I mention those cases, that Mr Burke may see I have not written on Government without reflecting on what is Law, as well as on what are Rights.—The only effectual jury in such cases would be, a convention of the whole nation fairly elected; for in all such cases the whole nation is the vicinage. If Mr Burke will propose such a jury, I will waive all privileges of being the citizen of another country, and, defending its principles, abide the issue, provided he will do the same; for my opinion is, that his work and his principles would be condemned instead of mine.

As to the prejudices which men have from education and habit, in favour of any particular form or system of government, those prejudices have yet to stand the test of reason and reflection. In fact, such prejudices are nothing. No man is prejudiced in favour of a thing, knowing it to be wrong. He is attached to it on the belief of its being right; and when he sees it is not so, the prejudice will be gone. We have but a defective idea of what prejudice is. It might be said, that until men think for themselves the whole is prejudice, and *not opinion*; for that only is opinion which is the result of reason and reflection. I offer this remark, that Mr Burke may not confide too much in what has been the customary prejudices of the country.

I do not believe that the people of England have ever been fairly and candidly dealt by. They have been imposed upon by parties, and by men assuming the character of leaders. It is time that the nation should rise above those trifles. It is time to dismiss that inattention which has so long been the encouraging cause of stretching taxation to excess. It is time to dismiss all those songs and toasts which are calculated to enslave, and operate to suffocate reflection. On all such subjects men have but to think, and they will neither act wrong nor be misled. To say that any people are not fit for freedom, is to make poverty their choice, and to say they had rather be loaded with taxes than not. If such a case could be proved, it would equally prove, that those who govern are not fit to govern them, for they are a part of the same national mass.

But admitting governments to be changed all over Europe; it certainly may be done without convulsion or revenge. It is not worth making changes or revolutions, unless it be for some great national benefit; and when this shall appear to a nation, the danger will be, as in America and France, to those who oppose; and with this reflection I close my Preface.

THOMAS PAINE

London, Feb. 9, 1792.

INTRODUCTION

WHAT Archimedes said of the mechanical powers, may be applied to Reason and Liberty: '*Had we,*' said he, '*a place to stand upon, we might raise the world.*'

The revolution of America presented in politics what was only theory in mechanics. So deeply rooted were all the governments of the old world, and so effectually had the tyranny and the antiquity of habit established itself over the mind, that no beginning could be made in Asia, Africa, or Europe, to reform the political condition of man. Freedom had been hunted round the globe; reason was considered as rebellion; and the slavery of fear had made men afraid to think.

But such is the irresistible nature of truth, that all it asks, and all it wants, is the liberty of appearing. The sun needs no inscription to distinguish him from darkness; and no sooner did the American governments display themselves to the world, than despotism felt a shock, and man began to contemplate redress.

The independence of America, considered merely as a separation from England, would have been a matter but of little importance, had it not been accompanied by a revolution in the principles and practice of governments. She made a stand, not for herself only, but for the world, and looked beyond the advantages herself could receive. Even the Hessian, though hired to fight against her, may live to bless his defeat; and England, condemning the viciousness of its government, rejoice in its miscarriage.

As America was the only spot in the political world, where the principles of universal reformation could begin, so also was it the best in the natural world. An assemblage of circumstances conspired, not only to give birth, but to add gigantic maturity to its principles. The scene which that country presents to the eye of a spectator, has something in it which generates and encourages great ideas. Nature appears to him in magnitude. The mighty objects he beholds, act upon his mind by enlarging it, and he partakes of the greatness he contemplates.—Its first settlers were emigrants from different European nations, and of diversified professions of religion, retiring from the governmental persecutions of the old world, and meeting in the new, not as enemies, but as brothers. The wants which necessarily accompany the cultivation of a wilderness produced among them a state of society, which countries, long harassed by the quarrels and intrigues of governments, had neglected to cherish. In such a situation man becomes what he ought. He sees his species, not with the inhuman idea of a natural enemy, but as kindred; and the example shows to the artificial world, that man must go back to Nature for information.

From the rapid progress which America makes in every species of improvement, it is rational to conclude, that if the governments of Asia, Africa, and Europe, had begun on a principle similar to that of America, or had not been very early corrupted therefrom, that those countries must, by this time, have been in a far superior condition to what they are. Age after age has passed away, for no other purpose than to behold their wretchedness.—Could we suppose a spectator who knew nothing of the world, and who was put into it merely to make his observations, he would take a great part of the old world to be new, just struggling with the difficulties and hardships of an infant settlement. He could not suppose that the hordes of miserable poor, with which old countries abound, could be any other than those who had not yet had time to provide for themselves. Little would he think they were the consequence of what in such countries is called government.

If, from the more wretched parts of the old world, we look at those which are in an advanced stage of improvement, we still find the greedy hand of government thrusting itself into every corner and crevice of industry, and grasping the spoil of the multitude. Invention is continually exercised, to furnish new pretences for revenue and taxation. It watches prosperity as its prey, and permits none to escape without a tribute.

As revolutions have begun, (and as the probability is always greater against a thing beginning, than of proceeding after it has begun), it is natural to expect that other revolutions will follow. The amazing and still increasing expenses with which old governments are conducted, the numerous wars they engage in or provoke, the embarrassments they throw in the way of universal civilization and commerce, and the oppression and usurpation they practise at home, have wearied out the patience, and exhausted the property of the world. In such a situation, and with the examples already existing, revolutions are to be looked for. They are become subjects of universal conversation, and may be considered as the *Order of the day.*

If systems of government can be introduced, less expensive, and more productive of general happiness, than those which have existed, all attempts to oppose their progress will in the end be fruitless. Reason, like time, will make its own way, and prejudice will fall in a combat with interest. If universal peace, civilization, and commerce, are ever to be the happy lot of man, it cannot be accomplished but by a revolution in the system of governments. All the monarchical governments are military. War is their trade, plunder and revenue their objects. While such governments continue, peace has not the absolute security of a day. What is the history of all monarchical governments, but a disgustful picture of human wretchedness, and the accidental respite of a few years' repose? Wearied with war, and tired with human butchery, they sat down to rest, and called it peace. This certainly is not the condition that Heaven intended for man; and if*this be monarchy*, well might monarchy be reckoned among the sins of the Jews.

The revolutions which formerly took place in the world, had nothing in them that interested the bulk of mankind. They extended only to a change of persons and measures, but not of principles, and rose or fell among the common transactions of the moment. What we now behold, may not improperly be called a '*counter-revolution.*' Conquest and tyranny, at some early period, dispossessed man of his rights, and he is now recovering them. And as the tide of all human affairs has its ebb and flow in directions contrary to each other, so also is it in this. Government founded on a *moral theory, on a system of universal peace, on the indefeasible hereditary Rights of Man*, is now revolving from west to cast, by a stronger impulse than the government of the sword revolved from east to west. It interests not particular individuals, but nations, in its progress, and promises a new era to the human race.

The danger to which the success of revolutions is most exposed, is that of attempting them before the principles on which they proceed, and the advantages to result from them, are sufficiently seen and understood.

Almost everything appertaining to the circumstances of a nation, has been absorbed and confounded under the general and mysterious word *government.* Though it avoids taking to its account the errors it commits, and the mischiefs it occasions, it fails not to arrogate to itself whatever has the appearance of prosperity. It robs industry of its honours, by pedantically making itself the cause of its effects; and purloins from the general character of man, the merits that appertain to him as a social being.

It may therefore be of use, in this day of revolutions, to discriminate between those things which are the effect of government, and those which are not. This will best be done by taking a review of society and civilization, and the consequences resulting therefrom, as things distinct from what are called governments. By beginning with this investigation, we shall be able to assign effects to their proper cause, and analyse the mass of common errors.

CHAPTER I

OF SOCIETY AND CIVILIZATION

GREAT part of that order which reigns among mankind is not the effect of government. It has its origin in the principles of society and the natural constitution of man. It existed prior to government, and would exist if the formality of government was abolished. The mutual dependence and reciprocal interest which man has upon man, and all the parts of a civilized community upon each other, create that great chain of connexion which holds it together. The landholder, the farmer, the manufacturer, the merchant, the tradesman, and every occupation, prospers by the aid which each receives from the other, and from the whole. Common interest regulates their concerns, and forms their law; and the laws which common usage ordains, have a greater influence than the laws of government. In fine, society performs for itself almost everything which is ascribed to government.

To understand the nature and quantity of government proper for man, it is necessary to attend to his character. As Nature created him for social life, she fitted him for the station she intended. In all cases she made his natural wants greater than his individual powers. No one man is capable, without the aid of society, of supplying his own wants; and those wants, acting upon every individual, impel the whole of them into society, as naturally as gravitation acts to a centre.

But she has gone further. She has not only forced man into society, by a diversity of wants, which the reciprocal aid of each other can supply, but she has implanted in him a system of social affections, which, though not necessary to his existence, are essential to his happiness. There is no period in life when this love for society ceases to act. It begins and ends with our being.

If we examine, with attention, into the composition and constitution of man, the diversity of his wants, and the diversity of talents in different men for reciprocally accommodating the wants of each other, his propensity to society, and consequently to preserve the advantages resulting from it, we shall easily discover, that a great part of what is called government is mere imposition.

Government is no farther necessary than to supply the few cases to which society and civilization are not conveniently competent; and instances are not wanting to show, that everything which government can usefully add thereto, has been performed by the common consent of society, without government.

For upwards of two years from the commencement of the American war, and to a longer period in several of the American States, there were no established forms of government. The old governments had been abolished, and the country was too much occupied in defence, to employ its attention in establishing new governments; yet during this interval, order and harmony were preserved as inviolate as in any country in Europe. There is a natural aptness in man, and more so in society, because it embraces a greater variety of abilities and resource, to accommodate itself to whatever situation it is in. The instant formal government is abolished, society begins to act. A general association takes place, and common interest produces common security.

So far is it from being true, as has been pretended, that the abolition of any formal government is the dissolution of society, that it acts by a contrary impulse, and brings the latter the closer together. All that part of its organization which it had committed to its government, devolves again upon itself, and acts through its medium. When men, as well from natural instinct, as from reciprocal benefits, have habituated themselves to social and civilized life, there is always enough of its principles in practice to carry them through any changes they may find necessary or convenient to make in their government. In short, man is so naturally a creature of society, that it is almost impossible to put him out of it.

Formal government makes but a small part of civilized life; and when even the best that human wisdom can devise is established, it is a thing more in name and idea, than in fact. It is to the great and fundamental principles of society and civilization—to the common usage universally consented to, and mutually and reciprocally maintained—to the unceasing circulation of interest, which, passing through its million channels, invigorates the whole mass of civilized man—it is to these things, infinitely more than to anything which even the best instituted government can perform, that the safety and prosperity of the individual and of the whole depends.

The more perfect civilization is, the less occasion has it for government, because the more does it regulate its own affairs, and govern itself; but so contrary is the practice of old governments to the reason of the case, that the expenses of them increase in the proportion they ought to diminish. It is but few general laws that civilized life requires, and those of such common usefulness, that whether they are enforced by the forms of government or not, the effect will be nearly the same. If we consider what the principles are that first condense men into society, and what the motives that regulate their mutual intercourse afterwards, we shall find, by the time we arrive at what is called government, that nearly the whole of the business is performed by the natural operation of the parts upon each other.

Man, with respect to all those matters, is more a creature of consistency than he is aware, or than governments would wish him to believe. All the great laws of society are laws of nature. Those of trade and commerce, whether with respect to the intercourse of individuals, or of nations, are laws of mutual and reciprocal interest. They are followed and obeyed, because it is the interest of the parties so to do, and not on account of any formal laws their governments may impose or interpose.

But how often is the natural propensity to society disturbed or destroyed by the operations of government! When the latter, instead of being ingrafted on the principles of the former, assumes to exist for itself, and acts by partialities of favour and oppression, it becomes the cause of the mischiefs it ought to prevent.

If we look back to the riots and tumults, which at various times have happened in England, we shall find, that they did not proceed from the want of a government, but that government was itself the generating cause; instead of consolidating society it divided it; it deprived it of its natural cohesion, and engendered discontents and disorders, which otherwise would not have existed. In those associations which men promiscuously form for the purpose of trade, or of any concern, in which government is totally out of the question, and in which they act merely on the principles of society, we see how naturally the various parties unite; and this shows, by comparison, that governments, so far from being always the cause or means of order, are often the destruction of it. The riots of 1780 had no other source than the remains of those prejudices, which the government itself had encouraged. But with respect to England there are also other causes.

Excess and inequality of taxation, however disguised in the means, never fail to appear in their effects. As a great mass of the community are thrown thereby into poverty and discontent, they are constantly on the brink of commotion; and deprived, as they unfortunately are, of the means of information, are easily heated to outrage. Whatever the apparent cause of any riots may be, the real one is always want of happiness. It shows that something is wrong in the system of government, that injures the felicity by which society is to be preserved.

But as fact is superior to reasoning, the instance of America presents itself to confirm these observations.—If there is a country in the world, where concord, according to common calculation, would be least expected, it is America. Made up, as it is, of people from different nations,[1] accustomed to different forms and habits of government, speaking different languages, and more different in their modes of worship, it would appear that the union of such a people was impracticable; but by the simple operation of constructing government on the principles of society and the rights of man, every difficulty retires, and all the parts are brought into cordial unison. There, the poor are not oppressed, the rich are not privileged. Industry is not mortified by the splendid extravagance of a court rioting at its expense. Their taxes are few, because their government is just; and as there is nothing to render them wretched, there is nothing to engender riots and tumults.

A metaphysical man, like Mr Burke, would have tortured his invention to discover how such a people could be governed. He would have supposed that some must be managed by fraud, others by force, and all by some contrivance; that genius must be hired to impose upon ignorance, and show and parade to fascinate the vulgar. Lost in the abundance of his researches, he would have resolved and re-resolved, and finally overlooked the plain and easy road that lay directly before him.

One of the great advantages of the American Revolution has been, that it led to a discovery of the principles, and laid open the imposition, of governments. All the revolutions till then had been worked within the atmosphere of a court, and never on the great floor of a nation. The parties were always of the class of courtiers; and whatever was their rage for reformation, they carefully preserved the fraud of the profession.

In all cases they took care to represent government as a thing made up of mysteries, which only themselves understood; and they hid from the understanding of the nation, the only thing that was beneficial to know, namely, *That government is nothing more than a national association acting on the principles of society.*

Having thus endeavoured to show, that the social and civilized state of man is capable of performing within itself, almost everything necessary to its protection and government, it will be proper, on the other hand, to take a review of the present old governments, and examine whether their principles and practice are correspondent thereto.

CHAPTER II

OF THE ORIGIN OF THE PRESENT OLD GOVERNMENTS

It is impossible that such governments as have hitherto existed in the world, could have commenced by any other means than a total violation of every principle sacred and moral. The obscurity in which the origin of all the present old governments is buried, implies the iniquity and disgrace with which they began. The origin of the present government of America and France will ever be remembered, because it is honourable to record it; but with respect to the rest, even Flattery has consigned them to the tomb of time, without an inscription.

It could have been no difficult thing in the early and solitary ages of the world, while the chief employment of men was that of attending flocks and herds, for a banditti of ruffians to overrun a country, and lay it under contributions. Their power being thus established, the chief of the band contrived to lose the name of Robber in that of Monarch; and hence the origin of Monarchy and Kings.

The origin of the government of England, so far as relates to what is called its line of monarchy, being one of the latest, is perhaps the best recorded. The hatred which the Norman invasion and tyranny begat, must have been deeply rooted in the nation, to have outlived the contrivance to obliterate it. Though not a courtier will talk of the curfew-bell, not a village in England has forgotten it.

Those bands of robbers having parcelled out the world, and divided it into dominions, began, as is naturally the case, to quarrel with each other. What at first was obtained by violence, was considered by others as lawful to be taken, and a second plunderer succeeded the first. They alternately invaded the dominions which each had assigned to himself, and the brutality with which they treated each other explains the original character of monarchy. It was ruffian torturing ruffian. The conqueror considered the conquered, not as his prisoner, hut his property. He led him in triumph rattling in chains, and doomed him, at pleasure, to slavery or death. As time obliterated the history of their beginning, their successors assumed new appearances, to cut off the entail of their disgrace, but their principles and objects remained the same. What at first was plunder, assumed the foster name of revenue; and the power originally usurped, they affected to inherit.

From such beginning of governments, what could be expected, but a continual system of war and extortion? It has established itself into a trade. The vice is not peculiar to one more than to another, but is the common principle of all. There does not exist within such governments sufficient stamina whereon to ingraft reformation; and the shortest, easiest, and most effectual remedy, is to begin anew on the ground of the oration.

What scenes of horror, what perfection of iniquity, present themselves in contemplating the character, and reviewing the history of such governments! If we would delineate human nature with a baseness of heart, and hypocrisy of countenance, that reflection would shudder at and humanity disown, it is kings, courts, and cabinets, that must sit for the portrait. Man, naturally as he is, with all his faults about him, is not up to the character.

Can we possibly suppose that if governments had originated in a right principle, and had not an interest in pursuing a wrong one, that the world could have been in the wretched and quarrelsome condition we have seen it? What inducement has the farmer, while following the plough, to lay aside his peaceful pursuit, and go to war with the farmer of another country? or what inducement has the manufacturer? What is dominion to them, or to any class of men in a nation? Does it add an acre to any man's estate, or raise its value? Are not conquest and defeat each of the same price, and taxes the never-failing consequence?—Though this reasoning may be good to a nation, it is not so to a government. War is the Faro table of governments, and nations the dupes of the games.

If there is anything to wonder at in this miserable scene of governments, more than might be expected, it is the progress which the peaceful arts of agriculture, manufacture and commerce have made, beneath such a long accumulating load of discouragement and oppression. It serves to show, that instinct in animals does not act with stronger impulse, than the principles of society and civilization operate in man. Under all discouragements, he pursues his object, and yields to nothing but impossibilities.

CHAPTER III

OF THE OLD AND NEW SYSTEMS OF GOVERNMENT

NOTHING can appear more contradictory than the principles on which the old governments began, and the condition to which society, civilization, and commerce, are capable of carrying mankind. Government on the old system, is an assumption of power, for the aggrandizement of itself; on the new, a delegation of power, for the common benefit of society. The former supports itself by keeping up a system of war; the latter promotes a system of peace, as the true means of enriching a nation. The one encourages national prejudices; the other promotes universal society, as the means of universal commerce. The one measures its prosperity, by the quantity of revenue it extorts; the other proves its excellence, by the small quantity of taxes it requires.

Mr Burke has talked of old and new whigs. If he can amuse himself with childish names and distinctions, I shall not interrupt his pleasure. It is not to him, but to the Abbé Sieyès, that I address this chapter. I am already engaged to the latter gentleman, to discuss the subject of monarchical government; and as it naturally occurs in comparing the old and new systems, I make this the opportunity of presenting to him my observations. I shall occasionally take Mr Burke in my way.

Though it might be proved that the system of government now called the NEW, is the most ancient in principle of all that have existed, being founded on the original inherent Rights of Man: yet, as tyranny and the sword have suspended the exercise of those rights for many centuries past, it serves better the purpose of distinction to call it the *new*, than to claim the right of calling it the old.

The first general distinction between those two systems, is, that the one now called the old is *hereditary*, either in whole or in part; and the new is entirely *representative*. It rejects all hereditary government:

First, As being an imposition on mankind.

Secondly, As inadequate to the purposes for which government is necessary.

With respect to the first of these heads—It cannot be proved by what right hereditary government could begin: neither docs there exist within the compass of mortal power, a right to establish it. Man has no authority over posterity in matters of personal right; and therefore, no man, or body of men, had, or can have, a right to set up hereditary government. Were even ourselves to come again into existence, instead of being succeeded by posterity, we have not now the right of taking from ourselves the rights which would then be ours. On what ground, then, do we pretend to take them from others?

All hereditary government is in its nature tyranny. An heritable crown, or an heritable throne, or by what other fanciful name such things may be called, have no other significant explanation than that mankind are heritable property. To inherit a government, is to inherit the people, as if they were flocks and herds.

With respect to the second head, that of being inadequate to the purposes for which government is necessary, we have only to consider what government essentially is, and compare it with the circumstances to which hereditary succession is subject.

Government ought to be a thing always in full maturity. It ought to be so constructed as to be superior to all the accidents to which individual man is subject; and therefore, hereditary succession, by being *subject to them all*, is the most irregular and imperfect of all the systems of government.

We have heard the *Rights of Man* called a *levelling* system; but the only system to which the word *levelling* is truly applicable is the hereditary monarchical system. It is a system of *mental levelling*. It indiscriminately admits every species of character to the same authority. Vice and virtue, ignorance and wisdom, in short, every quality, good or bad, is put on the same level. Kings succeed each other, not as rationals, but as animals. It signifies not what their mental or moral characters are. Can we then be surprised at the abject state of the human mind in monarchical countries, when the government itself is formed on such an abject levelling system?—It has no fixed character. Today it is one thing; tomorrow it is something else. It changes with the temper of every succeeding individual, and is subject to all the varieties of each. It is government through the medium of passions and accidents. It appears under all the various characters of childhood, decrepitude, dotage, a thing at nurse, in leading-strings, or in crutches. It reverses the wholesome order of nature. It occasionally puts children over men, and the conceits of nonage over wisdom and experience. In short, we cannot conceive a more ridiculous figure of government, than hereditary succession, in all its cases, presents.

Could it be made a decree in nature, or an edict registered in heaven, and man could know it, that virtue and wisdom should invariably appertain to hereditary succession, the objections to it would be removed; but when we see that nature acts as if she disowned and sported with the hereditary system; that the mental characters of successors, in all countries, are below the average of human understanding; that one is a tyrant, another an idiot, a third insane, and some all three together, it is impossible to attach confidence to it, when reason in man has power to act.

It is not to the Abbé Sieyès that I need apply this reasoning; he has already saved me that trouble, by giving his own opinion upon the case. 'If it be asked,' says he, 'what is my opinion with respect to hereditary right, I answer, without hesitation, That, in good theory, an hereditary transmission of any power or office, can never accord with the laws of a true representation. Hereditaryship is, in this sense, as much an attaint upon principle, as an outrage upon society. But let us,' continues he, 'refer to the history of all elective monarchies and principalities: Is there one in which the elective mode is not worse than the hereditary succession?'

As to debating on which is the worst of the two, it is admitting both to be bad; and herein we are agreed. The preference which the Abbé has given, is a condemnation of the thing that he prefers. Such a mode of reasoning on such a subject is inadmissible, because it finally amounts to an accusation upon Providence, as if she had left to man no other choice with respect to government than between two evils, the best of which he admits to be '*an attaint upon principle, and an outrage upon society.*'

Passing over, for the present, all the evils and mischiefs which monarchy has occasioned in the world, nothing can more effectually prove its uselessness in a state of *civil government,* than making it hereditary. Would we make any office hereditary that required wisdom and abilities to fill it? and where wisdom and abilities are not necessary, such an office, whatever it may be, is superfluous or insignificant.

Hereditary succession is a burlesque upon monarchy. It puts it in the most ridiculous light, by presenting it as an office which any child or idiot may fill. It requires some talents to be a common mechanic; but, to be a king, requires only the animal figure of man-a sort of breathing automaton. This sort of superstition may last a few years more, but it cannot long resist the awakened reason and interest of man.

As to Mr Burke, he is a stickler for monarchy, not altogether as a pensioner, if he is one, which I believe, but as a political man. He has taken up a contemptible opinion of mankind, who, in their turn, are taking up the same of him. He considers them as a herd of beings that must be governed by fraud, effigy and show; and an idol would be as good a figure of monarchy with him, as a man. I will, however, do him the justice to say, that, with respect to America, he has been very complimentary. He always contended, at least in my hearing, that the people of America were more enlightened than those of England, or of any country in Europe; and that therefore the imposition of show was not necessary in their governments.

Though the comparison between hereditary and elective monarchy, which the Abbé has made, is unnecessary to the case, because the representative system rejects both; yet, were I to make the comparison, I should decide contrary to what he has done.

The civil wars which have originated from contested hereditary claims, are more numerous, and have been more dreadful, and of longer continuance, than those which have been occasioned by election. All the civil wars in France arose from the hereditary system; they were either produced by hereditary claims, or by the imperfection of the hereditary form, which admits of regencies, or monarchy at nurse. With respect to England, its history is full of the same misfortunes. The contests for succession between the houses of York and Lancaster, lasted a whole century; and others of a similar nature, have renewed themselves since that period. Those of 1715 and 1745, were of the same kind. The succession war for the crown of Spain, embroiled almost half Europe. The disturbances in Holland are generated from the hereditaryship of the Stadtholder. A government calling itself free, with an hereditary office, is like a thorn in the flesh, that produces a fermentation which endeavours to discharge it.

But I might go further, and place also foreign wars, of whatever kind, to the same cause. It is by adding the evil of hereditary succession to that of monarchy, that a permanent family interest is created, whose constant objects are dominion and revenue. Poland, though an elective monarchy, has had fewer wars than those which are hereditary; and it is the only government that has made a voluntary essay, though but a small one, to reform the condition of the country.

Having thus glanced at a few of the defects of the old, or hereditary systems of government, let us compare it with the new, or representative system.

The representative system takes society and civilization for its basis; nature, reason, and experience, for its guide.

Experience, in all ages, and in all countries, has demonstrated, that it is impossible to control Nature in her distribution of mental powers. She gives them as she pleases. Whatever is the rule by which she, apparently to us, scatters them among mankind, that rule remains a secret to man. It would be as ridiculous to attempt to fix the hereditaryship of human beauty, as of wisdom. Whatever wisdom constituently is, it is like a seedless plant; it may be reared when it appears, but it cannot be voluntarily produced. There is always a sufficiency somewhere in the general mass of society for all purposes; but with respect to the parts of society, it is continually changing its place. It rises in one today, in another tomorrow, and has most probably visited in rotation every family of the earth, and again withdrawn.

As this is the order of nature, the order of government must necessarily follow it, or government will, as we see it does, degenerate into ignorance. The hereditary system, therefore, is as repugnant to human wisdom, as to human right; and is as absurd, as it is unjust.

As the republic of letters brings forward the best literary productions, by giving to genius a fair and universal chance; so the representative system of government is calculated to produce the wisest laws, by collecting wisdom from where it can be found. I smile to myself when I contemplate the ridiculous insignificance into which literature and all the sciences would sink, were they made hereditary; and I carry the same idea into governments. An hereditary governor is as inconsistent as an hereditary author. I know not whether Homer or Euclid had sons: but I will venture an opinion, that if they had, and had left their works unfinished, those sons could not have completed them.

Do we need a stronger evidence of the absurdity of hereditary government, than is seen in the descendants of those men, in any line of life, who once were famous? Is there scarcely an instance in which there is not a total reverse of the character? It appears as if the tide of mental faculties flowed as far as it could in certain channels, and then forsook its course, and arose in others. How irrational then is the hereditary system which establishes channels of power, in company with which wisdom refuses to flow! By continuing this absurdity, man is perpetually in contradiction with himself; he accepts, for a king, or a chief magistrate, or a legislator, a person whom he would not elect for a constable.

It appears to general observation, that revolutions create genius and talents; but those events do no more than bring them forward. There is existing in man, a mass of sense lying in a dormant state, and which, unless something excites it to action, will descend with him, in that condition, to the grave. As it is to the advantage of society that the whole of its faculties should be employed, the construction of government ought to be such as to bring forward, by a quiet and regular operation, all that extent of capacity which never fails to appear in revolutions.

This cannot take place in the insipid state of hereditary government, not only because it prevents, but because it operates to benumb. When the mind of a nation is bowed down by any political superstition in its government, such as hereditary succession is, it loses a considerable portion of its powers on all other subjects and objects. Hereditary succession requires the same obedience to ignorance, as to wisdom; and when once the mind can bring itself to pay this indiscriminate reverence, it descends below the stature of mental manhood. It is fit to be great only in little things. It acts a treachery upon itself, and suffocates the sensations that urge the detection.

Though the ancient governments present to us a miserable picture of the condition of man, there is one which above all others exempts itself from the general description. I mean the democracy of the Athenians. We see more to admire, and less to condemn, in that great, extraordinary people, than in any thing which history affords.

Mr Burke is so little acquainted with constituent principles of government, that he confounds democracy and representation together. Representation was a thing unknown in the ancient democracies. In those the mass of the people met and enacted laws (grammatically speaking) in the first person. Simple democracy was no other than the common-hall of the ancients. It signifies the *form*, as well as the public principle of the government. As these democracies increased in population, and the territory extended, the simple democratical form became unwieldy and impracticable; and as the system of representation was not known, the consequence was, they either degenerated convulsively into monarchies, or became absorbed into such as then existed. Had the system of representation been then understood, as it now is, there is no reason to believe that those forms of government, now called monarchical or aristocratical, would ever have taken place. It was the want of some method to consolidate the parts of society, after it became too populous, and too extensive for the simple democratical form, and also the lax and solitary condition of shepherds and herdsmen in other parts of the world, that afforded opportunities to those unnatural modes of government to begin.

As it is necessary to clear away the rubbish of errors, into which the subject of government has been thrown, I shall proceed to remark on some others.

It has always been the political craft of courtiers and court-governments, to abuse something which they called republicanism; but what republicanism was, or is, they never attempt to explain. Let us examine a little into this case.

The only forms of government are, the democratical, the aristocratical, the monarchical, and what is now called the representative.

What is called a *republic*, is not any *particular form* of government. It is wholly characteristical of the purport, matter, or object for which government ought to be instituted, and on which it is to be employed, RES-PUBLICA, the public affairs, or the public good; or, literally translated, the *public thing*. It is a word of a good original, referring to what ought to be the character and business of government; and in this sense it is naturally opposed to the word *monarchy*, which has a base original signification. It means arbitrary power in an individual person; in the exercise of which, *himself*, and not the *res-publica*, is the object.

Every government that does not act on the principle of a *Republic*, or in other words, that does not make the *res-publica* its whole and sole object, is not a good government. Republican government is no other than government established and conducted for the interest of the public, as well individually as collectively. It is not necessarily connected with any particular form, but it most naturally associates with the representative form, as being best calculated to secure the end for which a nation is at the expense of supporting it.

Various forms of government have affected to style themselves a republic. Poland calls itself a republic, which is an hereditary aristocracy, with what is called an elective monarchy. Holland calls itself a republic, which is chiefly aristocratical, with an hereditary stadtholdership. But the government of America, which is wholly on the system of representation, is the only real republic in character and in practice, that now exists. Its government has no other object than the public business of the nation, and therefore it is properly a republic; and the Americans have taken care that THIS, and no other, shall always be the object of their government, by their rejecting everything hereditary, and establishing government on the system of representation only.

Those who have said that a republic is not a *form* of government calculated for countries of great extent, mistook, in the first place, the *business* of a government, for a *form* of government; for the *res-publica* equally appertains to every extent of territory and population. And, in the second place, if they meant anything with respect to *form*, it was the simple democratical form, such as was the mode of government in the ancient democracies, in which there was no representation. The case, therefore, is not, that a republic cannot be extensive, but that it cannot be extensive on the simple democratical form; and the question naturally presents itself, *What is the best form of government for conducting the* RES-PUBLICA, *or the* PUBLIC BUSINESS *of a nation, after it becomes too extensive and populous for the simple democratical form?*

It cannot be monarchy, because monarchy is subject to an objection of the same amount to which the simple democratical form was subject.

It is possible that an individual may lay down a system of principles, on which government shall be constitutionally established to any extent of territory. This is no more than an operation of the mind, acting by its own powers. But the practice upon those principles, as applying to the various and numerous circumstances of a nation, its agriculture, manufacture, trade, commerce, &c. &c. requires a knowledge of a different kind, and which can be had only from the various parts of society. It is an assemblage of practical knowledge, which no one individual can possess; and therefore the monarchical form is as much limited, in useful practice, from the incompetency of knowledge, as was the democratical form, from the multiplicity of population. The one degenerates, by extension, into confusion; the other, into ignorance and incapacity, of which all the great monarchies are an evidence. The monarchical form, therefore, could not be a substitute for the democratical, because it has equal inconveniences.

Much less could it when made hereditary. This is the most effectual of all forms to preclude knowledge. Neither could the high democratical mind have voluntarily yielded itself to be governed by children and idiots, and all the motley insignificance of character, which attends such a mere animal system, the disgrace and the reproach of reason and of man.

As to the aristocratical form, it has the same vices and defects with the monarchical, except that the chance of abilities is better from the proportion of numbers, but there is still no security for the right use and application of them.[2]

Referring, then, to the original simple democracy, it affords the true data from which government on a large scale can begin. It is incapable of extension, not from its principle, but from the inconvenience of its form; and monarchy and aristocracy, from their incapacity. Retaining, then, democracy as the ground, and rejecting the corrupt systems of monarchy and aristocracy, the representative system naturally presents itself; remedying at once the defects of the simple democracy as to form, and the incapacity of the other two with respect to knowledge.

Simple democracy was society governing itself without the aid of secondary means. By ingrafting representation upon democracy, we arrive at a system of government capable of embracing and confederating all the various interests and every extent of territory and population; and that also with advantages as much superior to hereditary government, as the republic of letters is to hereditary literature.

It is on this system that the American government is founded. It is representation ingrafted upon democracy. It has fixed the form by a scale parallel in all cases to the extent of the principle. What Athens was in miniature, America will be in magnitude. The one was the wonder of the ancient world; the other is becoming the admiration and model of the present. It is the easiest of all the forms of government to be understood, and the most eligible in practice; and excludes at once the ignorance and insecurity of the hereditary mode, and the inconvenience of the simple democracy.

It is impossible to conceive a system of government capable of acting over such an extent of territory, and such a circle of interests, as is immediately produced by the operation of representation. France, great and populous as it is, is but a spot in the capaciousness of the system. It adapts itself to all possible cases. It is preferable to simple democracy even in small territories. Athens, by representation, would have outrivalled her own democracy.

That which is called government, or rather that which we ought to conceive government to be, is no more than some common centre, in which all the parts of society unite. This cannot be accomplished by any method so conducive to the various interests of the community, as by the representative system. It concentrates the knowledge necessary to the interest of the parts, and of the whole. It places government in a state of constant maturity. It is, as has been already observed, never young, never old. It is subject neither to nonage, nor dotage. It is never in the cradle, nor on crutches. It admits not of a separation between knowledge and power, and is superior, as government always ought to be, to all the accidents of individual man, and is therefore superior to what is called monarchy.

A nation is not a body, the figure of which is to be represented by the human body; but is like a body contained within a circle, having a common centre, in which every radius meets; and that centre is formed by representation. To connect representation with what is called monarchy, is eccentric government. Representation is of itself the delegated monarchy of a nation, and cannot debase itself by dividing it with another.

Mr Burke has two or three times, in his parliamentary speeches, and in his publications, made use of a jingle of words that convey no ideas. Speaking of government, he says, 'It is better to have monarchy for its basis, and republicanism for its corrective, than republicanism for its basis, and monarchy for its corrective.'—If he means that it is better to correct folly with wisdom, than wisdom with folly, I will no otherwise contend with him, than that it would be much better to reject the folly entirely.

But what is this thing which Mr Burke calls monarchy? Will he explain it? All men can understand what representation is; and that it must necessarily include a variety of knowledge and talents. But, what security is there for the same qualities on the part of monarchy? or, when this monarchy is a child, where then is the wisdom? What does it know about government? Who then is the monarch, or where is the monarchy? If it is to be performed by regency, it proves it to be a farce. A regency is a mock species of republic, and the whole of monarchy deserves no better description. It is a thing as various as imagination can paint. It has none of the stable character that government ought to possess. Every succession is a revolution, and every regency a counter-revolution. The whole of it is a scene of perpetual court cabal and intrigue, of which Mr Burke is himself an instance. To render monarchy consistent with government, the next in succession should not be born a child, but a man at once, and that man a Solomon. It is ridiculous that nations are to wait, and government be interrupted, till boys grow to be men.

Whether I have too little sense to see, or too much to be imposed upon; whether I have too much or too little pride, or of anything else, I leave out of the question; but certain it is, that what is called monarchy, always appears to me a silly, contemptible thing. I compare it to something kept behind a curtain, about which there is a great deal of bustle and fuss, and a wonderful air of seeming solemnity; but when, by any accident, the curtain happens to be open, and the company see what it is, they burst into laughter.

In the representative system of government, nothing of this can happen. Like the nation itself, it possesses a perpetual stamina, as well of body as of mind, and presents itself on the open theatre of the world in a fair and manly manner. Whatever are its excellences or its defects, they are visible to all. It exists not by fraud and mystery; it deals not in cant and sophistry; but inspires a language, that, passing from heart to heart, is felt and understood.

We must shut our eyes against reason, we must basely degrade our understanding, not to see the folly of what is called monarchy. Nature is orderly in all her works; but this is a mode of government that counteracts nature. It turns the progress of the human faculties upside down. It subjects age to be governed by children, and wisdom by folly.

On the contrary, the representative system is always parallel with the order and immutable laws of nature, and meets the reason of man in every part. For example:

In the American federal government, more power is delegated to the President of the United States, than to any other individual member of congress. He cannot, therefore, be elected to this office under the age of thirty-five years. By this time the judgement of man becomes matured, and he has lived long enough to be acquainted with men and things, and the country with him.—But on the monarchical plan, (exclusive of the numerous chances there are against every man born into the world, of drawing a prize in the lottery of human faculties), the next in succession, whatever he may be, is put at the head of a nation, and of a government, at the age of eighteen years. Does this appear like an act of wisdom? Is it consistent with the proper dignity and the manly character of a nation?

Where is the propriety of calling such a lad the father of the people?—In all other cases, a person is a minor until the age of twenty-one years. Before this period, he is not trusted with the management of an acre of land, or with the heritable property of a flock of sheep, or an herd of swine; but, wonderful to tell! he may, at the age of eighteen years, be trusted with a nation.

That monarchy is all a bubble, a mere court artifice to procure money, is evident, (at least to me), in every character in which it can be viewed. It would be impossible, on the rational system of representative government, to make out a bill of expenses to such an enormous amount as this deception admits. Government is not of itself a very chargeable institution. The whole expense of the federal government of America, founded, as I have already said, on the system of representation, and extending over a country nearly ten times as large as England, is but six hundred thousand dollars, or one hundred and thirty-five thousand pounds sterling.

I presume, that no man in his sober senses, will compare the character of any of the kings of Europe with that of General Washington. Yet, in France, and also in England, the expense of the civil list only, for the support of one man, is eight times greater than the whole expense of the federal government in America. To assign a reason for this, appears almost impossible. The generality of people in America, especially the poor, are more able to pay taxes, than the generality of people either in France or England.

But the case is, that the representative system diffuses such a body of knowledge throughout a nation, on the subject of government, as to explode ignorance and preclude imposition. The craft of courts cannot be acted on that ground. There is no place for mystery; nowhere for it to begin. Those who are not in the representation, know as much of the nature of business as those who are. An affectation of mysterious importance would there be scouted. Nations can have no secrets; and the secrets of courts, like those of individuals, are always their defects.

In the representative system, the reason for everything must publicly appear. Every man is a proprietor in government, and considers it a necessary part of his business to understand. It concerns his interest, because it affects his property. He examines the cost, and compares it with the advantages; and above all, he does not adopt the slavish custom of following what in other governments are called LEADERS.

It can only be by blinding the understanding of man, and making him believe that government is some wonderful mysterious thing, that excessive revenues are obtained. Monarchy is well calculated to ensure this end. It is the popery of government; a thing kept up to amuse the ignorant, and quiet them into taxes.

The government of a free country, properly speaking, is not in the persons, but in the laws. The enacting of those requires no great expense; and when they are administered, the whole of civil government is performed—the rest is all court contrivance.

CHAPTER IV

OF CONSTITUTIONS

THAT men mean distinct and separate things when they speak of constitutions and of governments, is evident; or, why are those terms distinctly and separately used? A constitution is not the act of a government, but of a people constituting a government; and government without a constitution, is power without a right.

All power exercised over a nation, must have some beginning. It must be either delegated, or assumed. There are no other sources. All delegated power is trust, and all assumed power is usurpation. Time does not alter the nature and quality of either.

In viewing this subject, the case and circumstances of America present themselves as in the beginning of a world; and our enquiry into the origin of government is shortened, by referring to the facts that have arisen in our own day. We have no occasion to roam for information into the obscure field of antiquity, nor hazard ourselves upon conjecture. We are brought at once to the point of seeing government begin, as if we had lived in the beginning of time. The real volume, not of history, but of facts, is directly before us, unmutilated by contrivance, or the errors of tradition.

I will here concisely state the commencement of the American constitutions; by which the difference between constitutions and governments will sufficiently appear.

It may not be improper to remind the reader, that the United States of America consist of thirteen separate states, each of which established a government for itself, after the declaration of independence, done the fourth of July 1776. Each state acted independently of the rest, in forming its government; but the same general principle pervades the whole. When the several state governments were formed, they proceeded to form the federal government, that acts over the whole in all matters which concern the interest of the whole, or which relate to the intercourse of the several states with each other, or with foreign nations. I will begin with giving an instance from one of the state governments, (that of Pennsylvania), and then proceed to the federal government.

The state of Pennsylvania, though nearly of the same extent of territory as England, was then divided into only twelve counties. Each of those counties had elected a committee at the commencement of the dispute with the English government; and as the city of Philadelphia, which also had its committee, was the most central for intelligence, it became the centre of communication to the several county committees. When it became necessary to proceed to the formation of a government, the committee of Philadelphia proposed a conference of all the county committees, to be held in that city, and which met the latter end of July 1776.

Though these committees had been elected by the people, they were not elected expressly for the purpose, nor invested with the authority of forming a constitution; and as they could not, consistently with the American idea of rights, assume such a power, they could only confer upon the matter, and put it into a train of operation. The conferees, therefore, did no more than state the case, and recommend to the several counties to elect six representatives for each county, to meet in convention at Philadelphia, with powers to form a constitution, and propose it for public consideration.

This convention, of which Benjamin Franklin was president, having met and deliberated, and agreed upon a constitution, they next ordered it to be published, not as a thing established, but for the consideration of the whole people, their approbation or rejection, and then adjourned to a stated time. When the time of adjournment was expired, the convention reassembled; and as the general opinion of the people in approbation of it was then known, the constitution was signed, sealed, and proclaimed on the *authority of the people* and the original instrument deposited as a public record. The convention then appointed a day for the general election of the representatives who were to compose the government, and the time it should commence; and having done this, they dissolved, and returned to their several homes and occupations.

In this constitution were laid down, first, a declaration of rights. Then followed the form which the government should have, and the powers it should possess—the authority of the courts of judicature, and of juries—the manner in which elections should be conducted, and the proportion of representatives to the number of electors—the time which each succeeding assembly should continue, which was one year—the mode of levying, and of accounting for the expenditure, of public money—of appointing public officers, &c. &c. &c.

No article of this constitution could be altered or infringed at the discretion of the government that was to ensue. It was to that government a law. But as it would have been unwise to preclude the benefit of experience, and in order also to prevent the accumulation of errors, if any should be found, and to preserve a unison of government with the circumstances of the state at all times, the constitution provided, that, at the expiration of every seven years, a convention should be elected, for the express purpose of revising the constitution, and making alterations, additions, or abolitions therein, if any such should be found necessary.

Here we see a regular process—a government issuing out of a constitution, formed by the people in their original character; and that constitution serving, not only as an authority, but as a law of control to the government. It was the political bible of the state. Scarcely a family was without it. Every member of the government had a copy; and nothing was more common, when any debate arose on the principle of a bill, or on the extent of any species of authority, than for the members to take the printed constitution out of their pocket, and read the chapter with which such matter in debate was connected.

Having thus given an instance from one of the states, I will show the proceedings by which the federal constitution of the United States arose and was formed.

Congress, at its two first meetings, in September 1774, and May 1775, was nothing more than a deputation from the legislatures of the several provinces, afterwards states; and had no other authority than what arose from common consent, and the necessity of its acting as a public body. In everything which related to the internal affairs of America, congress went no further than to issue recommendations to the several provincial assemblies, who at discretion adopted them or not. Nothing on the part of congress was compulsive; yet, in this situation, it was more faithfully and affectionately obeyed, than was any government in Europe. This instance, like that of the national assembly in France, sufficiently shows, that the strength of government does not consist in anything *within* itself, but in the attachment of a nation, and the interest which the people feel in supporting it. When this is lost, government is but a child in power; and though, like the old government of France, it may harass individuals for a while, it but facilitates its own fall.

After the declaration of independence, it became consistent with the principle on which representative government is founded, that the authority of congress should be defined and established. Whether that authority should be more or less than congress then discretionarily exercised, was not the question. It was merely the rectitude of the measure.

For this purpose, the act, called the act of confederation, (which was a sort of imperfect federal constitution), was proposed, and, after long deliberation, was concluded in the year 1781. It was not the act of congress, because it is repugnant to the principles of representative government that a body should give power to itself. Congress first informed the several states of the powers which it conceived were necessary to be invested in the union, to enable it to perform the duties and services required from it; and the states severally agreed with each other, and concentrated in congress those powers.

It may not be improper to observe, that in both those instances, (the one of Pennsylvania, and the other of the United States), there is no such thing as the idea of a compact between the people on one side, and the government on the other. The compact was that of the people with each other, to produce and constitute a government. To suppose that any government can be a party in a compact with the whole people, is to suppose it to have existence before it can have a right to exist. The only instance in which a compact can take place between the people and those who exercise the government, is, that the people shall pay them, while they choose to employ them.

Government is not a trade which any man or body of men has a right to set up and exercise for his own emolument, but is altogether a trust, in right of those by whom that trust is delegated, and by whom it is always resumable. It has of itself no rights; they are altogether duties.

Having thus given two instances of the original formation of a constitution, I will show the manner in which both have been changed since their first establishment.

The powers vested in the governments of the several states, by the state constitutions, were found, upon experience, to be too great; and those vested in the federal government, by the act of confederation, too little. The defect was not in the principle, but in the distribution of power,

Numerous publications, in pamphlets and in the newspapers, appeared, on the propriety and necessity of new modelling the federal government. After some time of public discussion, carried on through the channel of the press, and in conversations, the state of Virginia, experiencing some inconvenience with respect to commerce, proposed holding a continental conference; in consequence of which, a deputation from five or six of the state assemblies met at Annapolis in Maryland, in 1786. This meeting, not conceiving itself sufficiently authorized to go into the business of a reform, did no more than state their general opinions of the propriety of the measure, and recommend that a convention of all the states should be held the year following.

This convention met at Philadelphia in May 1787, of which General Washington was elected president. He was not at that time connected with any of the state governments, or with congress. He delivered up his commission when the war ended, and since then had lived a private citizen.

The convention went deeply into all the subjects; and having, after a variety of debate and investigation, agreed among themselves upon the several parts of a federal constitution, the next question was, the manner of giving it authority and practice.

For this purpose, they did not, like a cabal of courtiers, send for a Dutch Stadtholder, or a German Elector; but they referred the whole matter to the sense and interest of the country.

They first directed, that the proposed constitution should be published. Secondly, that each state should elect a convention, expressly for the purpose of taking it into consideration, and of ratifying or rejecting it; and that as soon as the approbation and ratification of any nine states should be given, that those states should proceed to the election of their proportion of members to the new federal government; and that the operation of it should then begin, and the former federal government cease.

The several states proceeded accordingly to elect their conventions. Some of those conventions ratified the constitution by very large majorities, and two or three unanimously. In others there were much debate and division of opinion. In the Massachusetts convention, which met at Boston, the majority was not above nineteen or twenty, in about three hundred members; but such is the nature of representative government, that it quietly decides all matters by majority. After the debate in the Massachusetts convention was closed, and the vote taken, the objecting members rose, and declared, '*That though they had argued and voted against it, because certain parts appeared to them in a different light to what they appeared to other members; yet, as the vote had decided in favour of the constitution as proposed, they should give it the same practical support as if they had voted for it.*'

As soon as nine states had concurred, (and the rest followed in the order their conventions were elected), the old fabric of the federal government was taken down, and the new one erected, of which General Washington is President.—In this place I cannot help remarking, that the character and services of this gentleman are sufficient to put all those men called kings to shame. While they are receiving from the sweat and labours of mankind, a prodigality of pay, to which neither their abilities nor their services can entitle them, he is rendering every service in his power, and refusing every pecuniary reward. He accepted no pay as commander in chief; he accepts none as President of the United States.

After the new federal constitution was established, the state of Pennsylvania, conceiving that some parts of its own constitution required to be altered, elected a convention for that purpose. The proposed alterations were published, and the people concurring therein, they were established.

In forming those constitutions, or in altering them, little or no inconvenience took place. The ordinary course of things was not interrupted, and the advantages have been much. It is always the interest of a far greater number of people in a nation to have things right, than to let them remain wrong; and when public matters are open to debate, and the public judgement free, it will not decide wrong, unless it decides too hastily.

In the two instances of changing the constitutions, the governments then in being were not actors either way. Government has no right to make itself a party in any debate respecting the principles or modes of forming, or of changing, constitutions. It is not for the benefit of those who exercise the powers of government, that constitutions, and the governments issuing from them, are established. In all those matters, the right of judging and acting are in those who pay, and not in those who receive.

A constitution is the property of a nation, and not of those who exercise the government. All the constitutions of America are declared to be established on the authority of the people. In France, the word nation is used instead of the people; but in both cases, a constitution is a thing antecedent to the government, and always distinct therefrom.

In England, it is not difficult to perceive that everything has a constitution, except the nation. Every society and association that is established, first agreed upon a number of original articles, digested into form, which are its constitution. It then appointed its officers, whose powers and authorities are described in that constitution, and the government of that society then commenced. Those officers, by whatever name they are called, have no authority to add to, alter, or abridge the original articles. It is only to the constituting power that this right belongs.

From the want of understanding the difference between a constitution and a government, Dr Johnson, and all writers of his description, have always bewildered themselves. They could not but perceive, that there must necessarily be a *controlling* power existing somewhere, and they placed this power in the discretion of the persons exercising the government, instead of placing it in a constitution formed by the nation. When it is in a constitution, it has the nation for its support, and the natural and the political controlling powers are together. The laws which are enacted by governments, control men only as individuals, but the nation, through its constitution, controls the whole government, and has a natural ability so to do. The final controlling power, therefore, and the original constituting power, are one and the same power.

Dr Johnson could not have advanced such a position in any country where there was a constitution; and he is himself an evidence, that no such thing as a constitution exists in England.—But it may be put as a question, not improper to be investigated, That if a constitution does not exist, how came the idea of its existence so generally established?

In order to decide this question, it is necessary to consider a constitution in both its cases:—First, as creating a government and giving it powers. Secondly, as regulating and restraining the powers so given.

If we begin with William of Normandy, we find that the government of England was originally a tyranny, founded on an invasion and conquest of the country. This being admitted, it will then appear, that the exertion of the nation, at different periods, to abate that tyranny, and render it less intolerable, has been credited for a constitution.

Magna Carta, as it was called, (it is now like an almanac of the same date,) was no more than compelling the government to renounce a part of its assumptions. It did not create and give powers to government in the manner a constitution does; but was, as far as it went, of the nature of re-conquest, and not of a constitution; for could the nation have totally expelled the usurpation, as France has done its despotism, it would then have had a constitution to form.

The history of the Edwards and the Henries, and up to the commencement of the Stuarts, exhibits as many instances of tyranny as could be acted within the limits to which the nation had restricted it. The Stuarts endeavoured to pass those limits, and their fate is well known. In all those instances we see nothing of a constitution, but only of restrictions on assumed power.

After this, another William, descended from the same stock, and claiming from the same origin, gained possession; and of the two evils, *James* and *William*, the nation preferred what it thought the least; since, from circumstances, it must take one. The act, called the Bill of Rights, comes here into view. What is it, but a bargain, which the parts of the government made with each other to divide powers, profits, and privileges? You shall have so much, and I will have the rest; and with respect to the nation, it said, for *your share*, YOU *shall have the right of petitioning*. This being the case, the bill of rights is more properly a bill of wrongs, and of insult. As to what is called the convention parliament, it was a thing that made itself, and then made the authority by which it acted. A few persons got together, and called themselves by that name. Several of them had never been elected, and none of them for the purpose.

From the time of William, a species of government arose, issuing out of this coalition bill of rights; and more so, since the corruption introduced at the Hanover succession, by the agency of Walpole; that can be described by no other name than a despotic legislation. Though the parts may embarrass each other, the whole has no bounds; and the only right it acknowledges out of itself, is the right of petitioning. Where then is the constitution either that gives or that restrains power?

It is not because a part of the government is elective, that makes it less a despotism, if the persons so elected possess afterwards, as a parliament, unlimited powers. Election, in this case, becomes separated from representation, and the candidates are candidates for despotism.

I cannot believe that any nation, reasoning on its own rights, would have thought of calling those things *a constitution*, if the cry of constitution had not been set up by the government. It has got into circulation like the words *bore* and *quoz*, by being chalked up in the speeches of parliament, as those words were on window shutters and door posts; but whatever the constitution may be in other respects, it has undoubtedly been *the most productive machine of taxation that was ever invented.* The taxes in France, under the new constitution, are not quite thirteen shillings per head,[3] and the taxes in England, under what is called its present constitution, are forty-eight shillings and sixpence per head, men, women, and children, amounting to nearly seventeen millions sterling, besides the expense of collection, which is upwards of a million more.

In a country like England, where the whole of the civil government is executed by the people of every town and county, by means of parish officers, magistrates, quarterly sessions, juries, and assize; without any trouble to what is called the government, or any other expense to the revenue than the salary of the judges, it is astonishing how such a mass of taxes can be employed. Not even the internal defence of the country is paid out of the revenue. On all occasions, whether real or contrived, recourse is continually had to new loans and new taxes. No wonder, then, that a machine of government so advantageous to the advocates of a court, should be so triumphantly extolled! No wonder, that St James's or St Stephen's should echo with the continual cry of constitution; No wonder, that the French revolution should be reprobated, and the *res-publica* treated with reproach! The *red book* of England, like the red book of France will explain the reason.[4]

I will now, by way of relaxation, turn a thought or two to Mr Burke. I ask his pardon for neglecting him so long.

'America,' says he, (in his speech on the Canada constitution bill) 'never dreamed of such absurd doctrine as the *Rights of Man*.'

Mr Burke is such a bold presumer, and advances his assertions and his premises with such a deficiency of judgement, that, without troubling ourselves about principles of philosophy or politics, the mere logical conclusions they produce, are ridiculous. For instance,

If governments, as Mr Burke asserts, are not founded on the Rights of MAN, and are founded on *any rights* at all, they consequently must be founded on the rights of *something* that is *not man*. What then is that something?

Generally speaking, we know of no other creatures that inhabit the earth than man and beast; and in all cases, where only two things offer themselves, and one must be admitted, a negation proved on anyone, amounts to an affirmative on the other; and therefore, Mr Burke, by proving against the Rights of *Man*, proves in behalf of the *beast*; and consequently, proves that government is a beast: and as difficult things sometimes explain each other, we now see the origin of keeping wild beasts in the Tower; for they certainly can be of no other use than to show the origin of the government. They are in the place of a constitution. O John Bull, what honours thou hast lost by not being a wild beast. Thou mightest, on Mr Burke's system, have been in the Tower for life.

If Mr Burke's arguments have not weight enough to keep one serious, the fault is less mine than his; and as I am willing to make an apology to the reader for the liberty I have taken, I hope Mr Burke will also make his for giving the cause.

Having thus paid Mr Burke the compliment of remembering him, I return to the subject.

From the want of a constitution in England to restrain and regulate the wild impulse of power, many of the laws are irrational and tyrannical, and the administration of them vague and problematical.

The attention of the government of England, (for I rather choose to call it by this name, than the English government) appears, since its political connexion with Germany, to have been so completely engrossed and absorbed by foreign affairs, and the means of raising taxes, that it seems to exist for no other purposes. Domestic concerns are neglected; and with respect to regular law, there is scarcely such a thing.

Almost every case now must be determined by some precedent, be that precedent good or bad, or whether it properly applies or not; and the practice is become so general, as to suggest a suspicion, that it proceeds from a deeper policy than at first sight appears.

Since the Revolution of America, and more so since that of France, this preaching up the doctrine of precedents, drawn from times and circumstances antecedent to those events, has been the studied practice of the English government. The generality of those precedents are founded on principles and opinions, the reverse of what they ought; and the greater distance of time they are drawn from, the more they are to be suspected. But by associating those precedents with a superstitious reverence for ancient things, as monks show relics and call them holy, the generality of mankind are deceived into the design. Governments now act as if they were afraid to awaken a single reflection in man. They are softly leading him to the sepulchre of precedents, to deaden his faculties and call his attention from the scene of revolutions. They feel that he is arriving at knowledge faster than they wish, and their policy of precedents is the barometer of their fears. This political popery, like the ecclesiastical popery of old, has had its day, and is hastening to its exit. The ragged relic and the antiquated precedent, the monk and the monarch, will moulder together.

Government by precedent, without any regard to the principle of the precedent, is one of the vilest systems that can be set up. In numerous instances, the precedent ought to operate as a warning, and not as an example, and requires to be shunned instead of imitated; but instead of this, precedents are taken in the lump, and put at once for constitution and for law.

Either the doctrine of precedents is policy to keep a man in a state of ignorance, or it is a practical confession that wisdom degenerates in governments as governments increase in age, and can only hobble along by the stilts and crutches of precedents. How is it that the same persons who would proudly be thought wiser than their predecessors, appear at the same time only as the ghosts of departed wisdom? How strangely is antiquity treated! To answer some purposes it is spoken of as the times of darkness and ignorance, and to answer others, it is put for the light of the world.

If the doctrine of precedents is to be followed, the expenses of government need not continue the same. Why pay men extravagantly, who have but little to do? If everything that can happen is already in precedent, legislation is at an end, and precedent, like a dictionary, determines every case. Either, therefore, government has arrived at its dotage, and requires to be renovated, or all the occasions for exercising its wisdom have occurred.

We now see all over Europe, and particularly in England, the curious phenomenon of a nation looking one way, and a government the other—the one forward and the other backward. If governments are to go on by precedent, while nations go on by improvement, they must at last come to a final separation; and the sooner, and the more civilly they determine this point, the better.[5]

Having thus spoken of constitutions generally, as things distinct from actual governments, let us proceed to consider the parts of which a constitution is composed.

Opinions differ more on this subject, than with respect to the whole. That a nation ought to have a constitution, as a rule for the conduct of its government, is a simple question in which all men, not directly courtiers, will agree. It is only on the component parts that questions and opinions multiply.

But this difficulty, like every other, will diminish when put into a train of being rightly understood.

The first thing is, that a nation has a right to establish a constitution.

Whether it exercises this right in the most judicious manner at first, is quite another case. It exercises it agreeably to the judgement it possesses; and by continuing to do so, all errors will at last be exploded.

When this right is established in a nation, there is no fear that it will be employed to its own injury. A nation can have no interest in being wrong.

Though all the constitutions of America are on one general principle, yet no two of them are exactly alike in their component parts, or in the distribution of the powers which they give to the actual governments. Some are more, and others less complex.

In forming a constitution, it is first necessary to consider what are the ends for which government is necessary? Secondly, what are the best means, and the least expensive, for accomplishing those ends?

Government is nothing more than a national association; and the object of this association is the good of all, as well individually as collectively. Every man wishes to pursue his occupation, and to enjoy the fruits of his labours, and the produce of his property in peace and safety, and with the least possible expense. When these things are accomplished, all the objects for which government ought to be established are answered.

It has been customary to consider government under three distinct general heads. The legislative, the executive, and the judicial.

But if we permit our judgement to act unencumbered by the habit of multiplied terms, we can perceive no more than two divisions of power, of which civil government is composed, namely, that of legislating or enacting laws, and that of executing or administering them. Everything, therefore, appertaining to civil government, classes itself under one or other of these two divisions.

So far as regards the execution of the laws, that which is called the judicial power, is strictly and properly the executive power of every country. It is that power to which every individual has appeal, and which causes the laws to be executed; neither have we any other clear idea with respect to the official execution of the laws. In England, and also in America and France, this power begins with the magistrate, and proceeds up through all the courts of judicature.

I leave to courtiers to explain what is meant by calling monarchy the executive power. It is merely a name in which acts of government are done; and any other, or none at all, would answer the same purpose. Laws have neither more nor less authority on this account. It must be from the justness of their principles, and the interest which a nation feels therein, that they derive support; if they require any other than this, it is a sign that something in the system of government is imperfect. Laws difficult to be executed cannot be generally good.

With respect to the organization of the *legislative power*, different modes have been adopted in different countries. In America it is generally composed of two houses. In France it consists but of one, but in both countries it is wholly by representation.

The case is, that mankind (from the long tyranny of assumed power) have had so few opportunities of making the necessary trials on modes and principles of government, in order to discover the best, *that government is but now beginning to be known*, and experience is yet wanting to determine many particulars.

The objections against two houses, are, first, that there is an inconsistency in any part of a whole legislature, coming to a final determination by vote on any matter, whilst *that matter*, with respect to *that whole*, is yet only in a train of deliberation, and consequently open to new illustrations.

Secondly, That by taking the vote on each, as a separate body, it always admits of the possibility, and is often the case in practice, that the minority governs the majority, and that, in some instances, to a degree of great inconsistency.

Thirdly, That two houses arbitrarily checking or controlling each other is inconsistent; because it cannot be proved, on the principles of just representation, that either should be wiser or better than the other. They may check in the wrong as well as in the right,—and therefore, to give the power where we cannot give the wisdom to use it, nor be assured of its being rightly used, renders the hazard at least equal to the precaution.[6]

The objection against a single house is, that it is always in a condition of committing itself too soon.—But it should at the same time be remembered, that when there is a constitution which defines the power, and establishes the principles within which a legislature shall act, there is already a more effectual check provided, and more powerfully operating, than any other check can be. For example.

Were a bill to be brought into any of the American legislatures, similar to that which was passed into an act by the English parliament, at the commencement of George the First, to extend the duration of the assemblies to a longer period than they now sit, the check is in the constitution, which in effect says, *Thus far shalt thou go and no further.*

But in order to remove the objection against a single house, (that of acting with too quick an impulse,) and at the same time to avoid the inconsistencies, in some cases absurdities, arising from two houses, the following method has been proposed as an improvement upon both.

First, To have but one representation.

Secondly, To divide that representation, by lot, into two or three parts.

Thirdly, That every proposed bill, shall be first debated in those parts by succession, that they may become the hearers of each other, but without taking any vote. After which the whole representation to assemble for a general debate and determination by vote.

To this proposed improvement has been added another, for the purpose of keeping the representation in a state of constant renovation; which is, that one-third of the representation of each county, shall go out at the expiration of one year, and the number be replaced by new elections.—Another third at the expiration of the second year replaced in like manner, and every third year to be a general election.[7]

But in whatever manner the separate parts of a constitution may be arranged, there is *one* general principle that distinguishes freedom from slavery, which is, that all *hereditary government over a people is to them a species of slavery, and representative government is freedom.*

Considering government in the only light in which it should be considered, that of a NATIONAL ASSOCIATION; it ought to be so constructed as not to be disordered by any accident happening among the parts; and, therefore, no extraordinary power, capable of producing such an effect, should be lodged in the hands of any individual. The death, sickness, absence, or defection, of any one individual in a government, ought to be a matter of no more consequence, with respect to the nation, than if the same circumstance had taken place in a member of the English Parliament, or the French National Assembly.

Scarcely anything presents a more degrading character of national greatness, than its being thrown into confusion by anything happening to, or acted by, an individual; and the ridiculousness of the scene is often increased by the natural insignificance of the person by whom it is occasioned. Were a government so constructed, that it could not go on unless a goose or a gander were present in the senate, the difficulties would be just as great and as real on the flight or sickness of the goose, or the gander, as if it were called a King. We laugh at individuals for the silly difficulties they make to themselves, without perceiving, that the greatest of all ridiculous things are acted in governments.[8]

All the constitutions of America are on a plan that excludes the childish embarrassments which occur in monarchical countries. No suspension of government can there take place for a moment, from any circumstance whatever. The system of representation provides for everything, and is the only system in which nations and governments can always appear in their proper character.

As extraordinary power ought not to be lodged in the hands of any individual, so ought there to be no appropriations of public money to any person, beyond what his services in a state may be worth. It signifies not whether a man be called a president, a king, an emperor, a senator, or by any other name, which propriety or folly may devise, or arrogance assume; it is only a certain service he can perform in the state; and the service of any such individual in the routine of office, whether such office be called monarchical, presidential, senatorial, or by any other name or title, can never exceed the value of ten thousand pounds a year. All the great services that are done in the world are performed by volunteer characters, who accept nothing for them; but the routine of office is always regulated to such a general standard of abilities as to be within the compass of numbers in every country to perform, and therefore cannot merit very extraordinary recompense. *Government*, says Swift, *is a plain thing, and fitted to the capacity of many heads.*

It is inhuman to talk of a million sterling a year, paid out of the public taxes of any country, for the support of any individual, whilst thousands who are forced to contribute thereto, are pining with want, and struggling with misery. Government does not consist in a contrast between prisons and palaces, between poverty and pomp; it is not instituted to rob the needy of his mite, and increase the wretchedness of the wretched.—But of this part of the subject I shall speak hereafter, and confine myself at present to political observations.

When extraordinary power and extraordinary pay are allotted to any individual in a government, he becomes the centre, round which every kind of corruption generates and forms. Give to any man a million a year, and add thereto the power of creating and disposing of places, at the expense of a country, and the liberties of that country are no longer secure. What is called the splendour of a throne is no other than the corruption of the state. It is made up of a band of parasites, living in luxurious indolence, out of the public taxes.

When once such a vicious system is established it becomes the guard and protection of all inferior abuses. The man who is in the receipt of a million a year is the last person to promote a spirit of reform, lest, in the event, it should reach to himself. It is always his interest to defend inferior abuses, as so many outworks to protect the citadel; and in this species of political fortification, all the parts have such a common dependence that it is never to be expected they will attack each other.[9]

Monarchy would not have continued so many ages in the world, had it not been for the abuses it protects. It is the master-fraud, which shelters all others. By admitting a participation of the spoil, it makes itself friends; and when it ceases to do this, it will cease to be the idol of courtiers.

As the principle on which constitutions are now formed rejects all hereditary pretensions to government, it also rejects all that catalogue of assumptions known by the name of prerogatives.

If there is any government where prerogatives might with apparent safety be entrusted to any individual, it is in the federal government of America. The President of the United States of America is elected only for four years. He is not only responsible in the general sense of the word, but a particular mode is laid down in the constitution for trying him. He cannot be elected under thirty-five years of age; and he must be a native of the country.

In a comparison of these cases with the government of England, the difference when applied to the latter amounts to an absurdity. In England the person who exercises prerogative is often a foreigner; always half a foreigner, and always married to a foreigner. He is never in full natural or political connexion with the country, is not responsible for anything, and becomes of age at eighteen years; yet such a person is permitted to form foreign alliances, without even the knowledge of the nation, and to make war and peace without its consent.

But this is not all. Though such a person cannot dispose of the government, in the manner of a testator, he dictates the marriage connexions, which, in effect, accomplishes a great part of the same end. He cannot directly bequeath half the government to Prussia, but he can form a marriage partnership that will produce almost the same thing. Under such circumstances, it is happy for England that she is not situated on the continent, or she might, like Holland, fall under the dictatorship of Prussia. Holland, by marriage, is as effectually governed by Prussia, as if the old tyranny of bequeathing the government had been the means.

The presidency in America, (or, as it is sometimes called, the executive) is the only office from which a foreigner is excluded, and in England it is the only one to which he is admitted. A foreigner cannot be a member of parliament, but he may be what is called a king. If there is any reason for excluding foreigners, it ought to be from those offices where mischief can most be acted, and where, by uniting every bias of interest and attachment, the trust is best secured.

But as nations proceed in the great business of forming constitutions, they will examine with more precision into the nature and business of that department which is called the executive. What the legislative and judicial departments are, everyone can see; but with respect to what, in Europe, is called the executive, as distinct from those two, it is either a political superfluity or a chaos of unknown things.

Some kind of official department to which reports shall be made from the different parts of a nation, or from abroad, to be laid before the national representatives, is all that is necessary; but there is no consistency in calling this the executive; neither can it be considered in any other light than as inferior to the legislative. The sovereign authority in any country is the power of making laws, and everything else is an official department.

Next to the arrangement of the principles and the organization of the several parts of a constitution, is the provision to be made for the support of the persons to whom the nation shall confide the administration of the constitutional powers.

A nation can have no right to the time and services of any person at his own expense, whom it may choose to employ or entrust in any department whatever; neither can any reason be given for making provision for the support of any one part of a government and not for the other.

But, admitting that the honour of being entrusted with any part of a government, is to be considered a sufficient reward, it ought to be so to every person alike. If the members of the legislature of any country are to serve at their own expense, that which is called the executive, whether monarchical, or by any other name, ought to serve in like manner. It is inconsistent to pay the one, and accept the service of the other gratis.

In America, every department in the government is decently provided for; but no one is extravagantly paid. Every member of Congress, and of the assemblies, is allowed a sufficiency for his expenses. Whereas in England, a most prodigal provision is made for the support of one part of the government, and none for the other, the consequence of which is, that the one is furnished with the means of corruption, and the other is put into the condition of being corrupted. Less than a fourth part of such expense, applied as it is in America, would remedy a great part of the corruption.

Another reform in the American constitution, is the exploding all oaths of personality. The oath of allegiance in America is to the nation only. The putting any individual as a figure for a nation is improper. The happiness of a nation is the superior object, and therefore the intention of an oath of allegiance ought not to be obscured by being figuratively taken, to, or in the name of, any person. The oath, called the civic oath, in France, viz. '*the nation, the law, and the king*,' is improper. If taken at all, it ought to be as in America, to the nation only. The law may or may not be good; but, in this place, it can have no other meaning, than as being conducive to the happiness of the nation, and therefore is included in it. The remainder of the oath is improper, on the ground, that all personal oaths ought to be abolished. They are the remains of tyranny on one part, and slavery on the other; and the name of the CREATOR ought not to be introduced to witness the degradation of his creation; or if taken, as is already mentioned, as figurative of the nation, it is in this place redundant. But whatever apology may be made for oaths at the first establishment of a government, they ought not to be permitted afterwards. If a government requires the support of oaths, it is a sign that it is not worth supporting, and ought not to be supported. Make government what it ought to be, and it will support itself.

To conclude this part of the subject:—One of the greatest improvements that has been made for the perpetual security and progress of constitutional liberty, is the provision which the new constitutions make for occasionally revising, altering, and amending them.

The principle upon which Mr Burke formed his political creed, that '*of binding and controlling posterity to the end of time, and of renouncing and abdicating the rights of all posterity, for ever,*' is now become too detestable to be made a subject of debate; and therefore, I pass it over with no other notice than exposing it.

Government is but now beginning to be known. Hitherto it has been the mere exercise of power, which forbade all effectual enquiry into rights, and grounded itself wholly on possession. While the enemy of liberty was its judge, the progress of its principles must have been small indeed.

The constitutions of America, and also that of France, have either affixed a period for their revision, or laid down the mode by which improvements shall be made. It is perhaps impossible to establish anything that combines principles with opinions and practice, which the progress of circumstances, through a length of years, will not in some measure derange, or render inconsistent; and, therefore, to prevent inconveniencies accumulating, till they discourage reformations or provoke revolutions, it is best to provide the means of regulating them as they occur. The Rights of Man are the rights of all generations of men, and cannot be monopolized by any. That which is worth following, will be followed for the sake of its worth; and it is in this that its security lies, and not in any conditions with which it may be encumbered. When a man leaves property to his heirs, he does not connect it with an obligation that they shall accept it. Why then should we do otherwise with respect to constitutions?

The best constitution that could now be devised, consistent with the condition of the present moment, may be far short of that excellence which a few years may afford. There is a morning of reason rising upon man on the subject of government, that has not appeared before. As the barbarism of the present old governments expires, the moral condition of nations with respect to each other will be changed. Man will not be brought up with the savage idea of considering his species as his enemy, because the accident of birth gave the individuals existence in countries distinguished by different names; and as constitutions have always some relation to external as well as to domestic circumstances, the means of benefiting by every change, foreign or domestic, should be a part of every constitution.

We already see an alteration in the national disposition of England and France towards each other, which, when we look back to only a few years, is itself a revolution. Who could have foreseen, or who would have believed, that a French National Assembly would ever have been a popular toast in England, or that a friendly alliance of the two nations should become the wish of either. It shows, that man, were he not corrupted by governments, is naturally the friend of man, and that human nature is not of itself vicious. That spirit of jealousy and ferocity, which the governments of the two countries inspired, and which they rendered subservient to the purpose of taxation, is now yielding to the dictates of reason, interest, and humanity. The trade of courts is beginning to be understood, and the affectation of mystery, with all the artificial sorcery by which they imposed upon mankind, is on the decline. It has received its death-wound; and though it may linger, it will expire.

Government ought to be as much open to improvement as anything which appertains to man, instead of which it has been monopolized from age to age, by the most ignorant and vicious of the human race. Need we any other proof of their wretched management, than the excess of debts and taxes with which every nation groans, and the quarrels into which they have precipitated the world?

Just emerging from such a barbarous condition, it is too soon to determine to what extent of improvement government may yet be carried. For what we can foresee, all Europe may form but one great republic, and man be free of the whole.

CHAPTER V

WAYS AND MEANS

of improving the condition of Europe, interspersed with Miscellaneous Observations

In contemplating a subject that embraces with equatorial magnitude the whole region of humanity, it is impossible to confine the pursuit in one single direction. It takes ground on every character and condition that appertains to man, and blends the individual, the nation, and the world.

From a small spark, kindled in America, a flame has arisen, not to be extinguished. Without consuming, like the *Ultima Ratio Regum*, it winds its progress from nation to nation, and conquers by a silent operation. Man finds himself changed, he scarcely perceives how. He acquires a knowledge of his rights by attending justly to his interest, and discovers in the event that the strength and powers of despotism consist wholly in the fear of resisting it, and that, in order '*to be free, it is sufficient that he wills it.*'

Having in all the preceding parts of this work endeavoured to establish a system of principles as a basis, on which governments ought to be erected, I shall proceed in this, to the ways and means of rendering them into practice. But in order to introduce this part of the subject with more propriety, and stronger effect, some preliminary observations, deducible from, or connected with, those principles, are necessary.

Whatever the form or constitution of government may be, it ought to have no other object than the *general* happiness. When, instead of this, it operates to create and increase wretchedness in any of the parts of society, it is on a wrong system, and reformation is necessary.

Customary language has classed the condition of man under the two descriptions of civilized and uncivilized life. To the one it has ascribed felicity and affluence; to the other hardship and want. But however our imagination may be impressed by painting and comparison, it is nevertheless true, that a great portion of mankind, in what are called civilized countries, are in a state of poverty and wretchedness, far below the condition of an Indian. I speak not of one country, but of all. It is so in England, it is so all over Europe. Let us enquire into the cause.

It lies not in any natural defect in the principles of civilization, but in preventing those principles having a universal operation; the consequence of which is, a perpetual system of war and expense, that drains the country, and defeats the general felicity of which civilization is capable.

All the European governments (France now excepted) are constructed not on the principle of universal civilization, but on the reverse of it. So far as those governments relate to each other, they are in the same condition as we conceive of savage uncivilized life; they put themselves beyond the law as well of God as of man, and are, with respect to principle and reciprocal conduct, like so many individuals in a state of nature.

The inhabitants of every country, under the civilization of laws, easily civilize together, but governments being yet in an uncivilized state, and almost continually at war, they pervert the abundance which civilized life produces to carry on the uncivilized part to a greater extent. By thus engrafting the barbarism of government upon the internal civilization of a country, it draws from the latter, and more especially from the poor, a great portion of those earnings, which should be applied to their own subsistence and comfort.—Apart from all reflections of morality and philosophy, it is a melancholy fact, that more than one fourth of the labour of mankind is annually consumed by this barbarous system.

What has served to continue this evil, is the pecuniary advantage which all the governments of Europe have found in keeping up this state of uncivilization. It affords to them pretences for power, and revenue, for which there would be neither occasion nor apology, if the circle of civilization were rendered complete. Civil government alone, or the government of laws, is not productive of pretences for many taxes; it operates at home, directly under the eye of the country, and precludes the possibility of much imposition. But when the scene is laid in the uncivilized contention of governments, the field of pretences is enlarged, and the country, being no longer a judge, is open to every imposition, which governments please to act.

Not a thirtieth, scarcely a fortieth, part of the taxes which are raised in England are either occasioned by, or applied to, the purposes of civil government. It is not difficult to see, that the whole which the actual government does in this respect, is to enact laws, and that the country administers and executes them, at its own expense, by means of magistrates, juries, sessions, and assize, over and above the taxes which it pays.

In this view of the case, we have two distinct characters of government; the one the civil government, or the government of laws, which operates at home, the other the court or cabinet government, which operates abroad, on the rude plan of uncivilized life; the one attended with little charge, the other with boundless extravagance; and so distinct are the two, that if the latter were to sink, as it were by a sudden opening of the earth, and totally disappear, the former would not be deranged. It would still proceed, because it is the common interest of the nation that it should, and all the means are in practice.

Revolutions, then, have for their object, a change in the moral condition of governments, and with this change the burden of public taxes will lessen, and civilization will be left to the enjoyment of that abundance, of which it is now deprived.

In contemplating the whole of this subject, I extend my views into the department of commerce. In all my publications, where the matter would admit, I have been an advocate for commerce, because I am a friend to its effects. It is a pacific system, operating to cordialize mankind, by rendering nations, as well as individuals, useful to each other. As to mere theoretical reformation, I have never preached it up. The most effectual process is that of improving the condition of man by means of his interest; and it is on this ground that I take my stand.

If commerce were permitted to act to the universal extent it is capable, it would extirpate the system of war, and produce a revolution in the uncivilized state of governments. The invention of commerce has arisen since those governments began, and is the greatest approach towards universal civilization, that has yet been made by any means not immediately flowing from moral principles.

Whatever has a tendency to promote the civil intercourse of nations, by an exchange of benefits, is a subject as worthy of philosophy as of politics. Commerce is no other than the traffic of two individuals, multiplied on a scale of numbers; and by the same rule that nature intended the intercourse of two, she intended that of all. For this purpose she has distributed the materials of manufactures and commerce, in various and distant parts of a nation and of the world; and as they cannot be procured by war so cheaply or so commodiously as by commerce, she has rendered the latter the means of extirpating the former.

As the two are nearly the opposites of each other, consequently, the uncivilized state of European governments is injurious to commerce. Every kind of destruction or embarrassment serves to lessen the quantity, and it matters but little in what part of the commercial world the reduction begins. Like blood, it cannot be taken from any of the parts, without being taken from the whole mass in circulation, and all partake of the loss. When the ability in any nation to buy is destroyed, it equally involves the seller. Could the government of England destroy the commerce of all other nations, she would most effectually ruin her own.

It is possible that a nation may be the carrier for the world, but she cannot be the merchant. She cannot be the seller and the buyer of her own merchandise. The ability to buy must reside out of herself; and, therefore, the prosperity of any commercial nation is regulated by the prosperity of the rest. If they are poor she cannot be rich, and her condition, be it what it may, is an index of the height of the commercial tide in other nations.

That the principles of commerce, and its universal operation may be understood, without understanding the practice, is a position that reason will not deny; and it is on this ground only that I argue the subject. It is one thing in the counting-house, in the world it is another. With respect to its operation it must necessarily be contemplated as a reciprocal thing; that only one half its powers resides within the nation, and that the whole is as effectually destroyed by destroying the half that resides without, as if the destruction had been committed on that which is within; for neither can act without the other.

When in the last, as well as in former wars, the commerce of England sunk, it was because the general quantity was lessened everywhere; and it now rises, because commerce is in a rising state in every nation. If England, at this day, imports and exports more than at any former period, the nations with which she trades must necessarily do the same; her imports are their exports, and *vice versa.*

There can be no such thing as a nation flourishing alone in commerce; she can only participate; and the destruction of it in any part must necessarily affect all. When, therefore, governments are at war, the attack is made upon the common stock of commerce, and the consequence is the same as if each had attacked his own.

The present increase of commerce is not to be attributed to ministers, or to any political contrivances, but to its own natural operations in consequence of peace. The regular markets had been destroyed, the channels of trade broken up, the high road of the seas infested with robbers of every nation, and the attention of the world called to other objects. Those interruptions have ceased, and peace has restored the deranged condition of things to their proper order.[10]

It is worth remarking, that every nation reckons the balance of trade in its own favour; and therefore something must be irregular in the common ideas upon this subject.

The fact, however, is true, according to what is called a balance; and it is from this cause that commerce is universally supported. Every nation feels the advantage, or it would abandon the practice: but the deception lies in the mode of making up the accounts, and in attributing what are called profits to a wrong cause.

Mr Pitt has sometimes amused himself, by showing what he called a balance of trade from the custom-house books. This mode of calculation, not only affords no rule that is true, but one that is false.

In the first place, every cargo that departs from the custom house, appears on the books as an export; and, according to the custom-house balance, the losses at sea, and by foreign failures, are all reckoned on the side of profit, because they appear as exports.

Secondly, Because the importation by the smuggling trade does not appear on the custom-house books, to arrange against the exports.

No balance, therefore, as applying to superior advantages, can be drawn from those documents; and if we examine the natural operation of commerce, the idea is fallacious; and if true, would soon be injurious. The great support of commerce consists in the balance being a level of benefits among all nations.

Two merchants of different nations trading together, will both become rich, and each makes the balance in his own favour; consequently, they do not get rich out of each other; and it is the same with respect to the nations in which they reside. The case must be, that each nation must get rich out of its own means, and increases that riches by something which it procures from another in exchange.

If a merchant in England sends an article of English manufacture abroad, which costs him a shilling at home, and imports something which sells for two, he makes a balance of one shilling in his own favour: but this is not gained out of the foreign nation or the foreign merchant, for he also does the same by the article he receives, and neither has a balance of advantage upon the other. The original value of the two articles in their proper countries were but two shillings; but by changing their places, they acquire a new idea of value, equal to double what they had at first, and that increased value is equally divided.

There is not otherwise a balance on foreign than on domestic commerce. The merchants of London and Newcastle trade on the same principles, as if they resided in different nations, and make their balances in the same manner: yet London docs not get rich out of Newcastle, any more than Newcastle out of London: but coals, the merchandise of Newcastle, have an additional value at London, and London merchandise has the same at Newcastle.

Though the principle of all commerce is the same, the domestic, in a national view, is the part the most beneficial; because the whole of the advantages, on both sides, rests within the nation; whereas, in foreign commerce, it is only a participation of one half.

The most unprofitable of all commerce is that connected with foreign dominion. To a few individuals it may be beneficial, merely because it is commerce; but to the nation it is a loss. The expense of maintaining dominion more than absorbs the profits of any trade. It does not increase the general quantity in the world, but operates to lessen it; and as a greater mass would be afloat by relinquishing dominion, the participation without the expense would be more valuable than a greater quantity with it.

But it is impossible to engross commerce by dominion; and therefore it is still more fallacious. It cannot exist in confined channels, and necessarily breaks out by regular or irregular means, that defeat the attempt: and to succeed would be still worse. France, since the revolution, has been more than indifferent as to foreign possessions; and other nations will become the same, when they investigate the subject with respect to commerce.

To the expense of dominion is to be added that of navies, and when the amount of the two are subtracted from the profits of commerce, it will appear, that what is called the balance of trade, even admitting it to exist, is not enjoyed by the nation, but absorbed by the government.

The idea of having navies for the protection of commerce is delusive. It is putting the means of destruction for the means of protection. Commerce needs no other protection than the reciprocal interest which every nation feels in supporting it—it is common stock—it exists by a balance of advantages to all, and the only interruption it meets, is from the present uncivilized state of governments, and which it is its common interest to reform.[11]

Quitting this subject, I now proceed to other matters.—As it is necessary to include England in the prospect of a general reformation, it is proper to enquire into the defects of its government. It is only by each nation reforming its own, that the whole can be improved, and the full benefit of reformation enjoyed. Only partial advantages can flow from partial reforms.

France and England are the only two countries in Europe where a reformation in government could have successfully begun. The one secure by the ocean, and the other by the immensity of its internal strength, could defy the malignancy of foreign despotism. But it is with revolutions as with commerce, the advantages increase by their becoming general, and double to either what each would receive alone.

As a new system is now opening to the view of the world, the European courts are plotting to counteract it. Alliances, contrary to all former systems, are agitating, and a common interest of courts is forming against the common interest of man. This combination draws a line that runs throughout Europe, and presents a cause so entirely new, as to exclude all calculations from former circumstances. While despotism warred with despotism, man had no interest in the contest; but in a cause that unites the soldier with the citizen, and nation with nation, the despotism of courts, though it feels the danger, and meditates revenge, is afraid to strike.

No question has arisen within the records of history that pressed with the importance of the present. It is not whether this or that party shall be in or not, or whig or tory, or high or low shall prevail; but whether man shall inherit his rights, and universal civilization take place? Whether the fruits of his labours shall be enjoyed by himself, or consumed by the profligacy of governments? Whether robbery shall be banished from courts, and wretchedness from countries?

When, in countries that are called civilized, we see age going to the workhouse and youth to the gallows, something must be wrong in the system of government. It would seem, by the exterior appearance of such countries, that all was happiness; but there lies hidden from the eye of common observation, a mass of wretchedness that has scarcely any other chance, than to expire in poverty or infamy. Its entrance into life is marked with the presage of its fate; and until this is remedied, it is in vain to punish.

Civil government does not consist in executions; but in making that provision for the instruction of youth, and the support of age, as to exclude, as much as possible, profligacy from the one, and despair from the other. Instead of this, the resources of a country are lavished upon kings, upon courts, upon hirelings, impostors, and prostitutes; and even the poor themselves, with all their wants upon them, are compelled to support the fraud that oppresses them.

Why is it, that scarcely any are executed but the poor? The fact is a proof, among other things, of a wretchedness in their condition. Bred up without morals, and cast upon the world without a prospect, they are the exposed sacrifice of vice and legal barbarity. The millions that are superfluously wasted upon governments, are more than sufficient to reform those evils, and to benefit the condition of every man in a nation, not included within the purlieus of a court. This I hope to make appear in the progress of this work.

It is the nature of compassion to associate with misfortune. In taking up this subject I seek no recompense—I fear no consequence. Fortified with that proud integrity, that disdains to triumph or to yield, I will advocate the Rights of Man.

It is to my advantage that I have served an apprenticeship to life. I know the value of moral instruction, and I have seen the danger of the contrary.

At an early period, little more than sixteen years of age, raw and adventurous, and heated with the false heroism of a master[12] who had served in a man of war, I began the carver of my own fortune, and entered on board the Terrible privateer, Capt. Death. From this adventure I was happily prevented by the affectionate and moral remonstrance of a good father, who, from his own habits of life, being of the Quaker profession, must begin to look upon me as lost. But the impression, much as it effected at the time, began to wear away, and I entered afterwards in the King of Prussia privateer, Capt. Mendez, and went with her to sea. Yet, from such a beginning, and with all the inconvenience of early life against me, I am proud to say, that with a perseverance undismayed by difficulties, a disinterested-ness that compelled respect, I have not only contributed to raise a new empire in the world, founded on a new system of government, but I have arrived at an eminence in political literature, the most difficult of all lines to succeed and excel in, which aristocracy, with all its aids, has not been able to reach or to rival.

Knowing my own heart, and feeling myself, as I now do, superior to all the skirmish of party, the inveteracy of interested or mistaken opponents, I answer not to falsehood or abuse, but proceed to the defects of the English government.[13]

I begin with charters and corporations.

It is a perversion of terms to say, that a charter gives rights. It operates by a contrary effect, that of taking rights away. Rights are inherently in all the inhabitants; but charters, by annulling those rights in the majority, leave the right by exclusion in the hands of a few. If charters were constructed so as to express in direct terms, '*that every inhabitant, who is not a member of a corporation, shall not exercise the right of voting,*' such charters would, in the face, be charters, not of the rights, but of exclusion. The effect is the same under the form they now stand; and the only persons on whom they operate, are the persons whom they exclude. Those whose rights are guaranteed, by not being taken away, exercise no other rights, than as members of the community they are entitled to without a charter; and, therefore, all charters have no other than an indirect negative operation. They do not give rights to A, but they make a difference in favour of A by taking away the right of B, and consequently are instruments of injustice.

But charters and corporations have a more extensive evil effect than what relates merely to elections. They are sources of endless contentions in the places where they exist; and they lessen the common rights of national society. A native of England, under the operation of these charters and corporations, cannot be said to be an Englishman in the full sense of the word. He is not free of the nation, in the same manner that a Frenchman is free of France, and an American of America. His rights are circumscribed to the town, and, in some cases, to the parish of his birth; and all other pares, though in his native land, are to him as a foreign country. To acquire a residence in these, he must undergo a local naturalization by purchase, or he is forbidden or expelled the place. This species of feudality is kept up to aggrandize the corporations at the ruin of towns; and the effect is visible.

The generality of corporation towns are in a state of solitary decay, and prevented from further ruin, only by some circumstance in their situation, such as a navigable river, or a plentiful surrounding country. As population is one of the chief sources of wealth, (for without it land itself has no value,) everything which operates to prevent it must lessen the value of property; and as corporations have not only this tendency, but directly this effect, they cannot but be injurious. If any policy were to be followed, instead of that of general freedom to every person to settle where he chose, (as in France or America,) it would be more consistent to give encouragement to newcomers, than to preclude their admission by exacting premiums from them.[14]

The persons most immediately interested in the abolition of corporations, are the inhabitants of the towns where corporations are established. The instances of Manchester, Birmingham, and Sheffield, show, by contrast, the injury which those Gothic institutions are to property and commerce. A few examples may be found, such as that of London, whose natural and commercial advantage, owing to its situation on the Thames, is capable of bearing up against the political evils of a corporation; but in almost all other cases the fatality is too visible to be doubted or denied.

Though the whole nation is not so directly affected by the depression of property in corporation towns as the inhabitants themselves, it partakes of the consequence. By lessening the value of property, the quantity of national commerce is curtailed. Every man is a customer in proportion to his ability; and as all parts of a nation trade with each other, whatever affects any of the parts, must necessarily communicate to the whole.

As one of the houses of the English parliament is, in a great measure, made up of elections from these corporations; and as it is unnatural that a pure stream should flow from a foul fountain, its vices are but a continuation of the vices of its origin. A man of moral honour and good political principles, cannot submit to the mean drudgery and disgraceful arts, by which such elections are carried. To be a successful candidate, he must be destitute of the qualities that constitute a just legislator: and being thus disciplined to corruption by the mode of entering into parliament, it is not to be expected that the representative should be better than the man.

Mr Burke, in speaking of the English representation, has advanced as bold a challenge as ever was given in the days of chivalry. 'Our representation,' says he, 'has been found *perfectly adequate to all the purposes* for which a representation of the people can be desired or devised. I defy,' continues he, 'the enemies of our constitution to show the contrary.'—This declaration from a man who has been in constant opposition to all the measures of parliament the whole of his political life, a year or two excepted, is most extraordinary; and, comparing him with himself, admits of no other alternative, than that he acted against his judgement as a member, or has declared contrary to it as an author.

But it is not in the representation only that the defects lie, and therefore I proceed in the next place to the aristocracy.

What is called the House of Peers, is constituted on a ground very similar to that, against which there is a law in other cases. It amounts to a combination of persons in one common interest. No reason can be given, why an house of legislation should be composed entirely of men whose occupation consists in letting landed property, than why it should be composed of those who hire, or of brewers, or bakers, or any other separate class of men.

Mr Burke calls this house, '*the great ground and pillar of security to the landed interest.*' Let us examine this idea.

What pillar of security does the landed interest require more than any other interest in the state, or what right has it to a distinct and separate representation from the general interest of a nation? The only use to be made of this power, (and which it has always made,) is to ward off taxes from itself, and throw the burden upon such articles of consumption by which itself would be least affected.

That this has been the consequence, (and will always be the consequence of constructing governments on combinations,) is evident with respect to England, from the history of its taxes.

Notwithstanding taxes have increased and multiplied upon every article of common consumption, the land-tax, which more particularly affects this 'pillar,' has diminished. In 1788, the amount of the land-tax was £1,950,000, which is half a million less than it produced almost a hundred years ago,[15] notwithstanding the rentals are in many instances doubled since that period.

Before the coming of the Hanoverians, the taxes were divided in nearly equal proportions between the land and articles of consumption, the land bearing rather the largest share: but since that era, nearly thirteen millions annually of new taxes have been thrown upon consumption. The consequence of which has been a constant increase in the number and wretchedness of the poor, and in the amount of the poor-rates. Yet here again the burden does not fall in equal proportions on the aristocracy with the rest of the community. Their residences, whether in town or country, are not mixed with the habitations of the poor. They live apart from distress, and the expense of relieving it. It is in manufacturing towns and labouring villages that those burdens press the heaviest; in many of which it is one class of poor supporting another.

Several of the most heavy and productive taxes are so contrived, as to give an exemption to this pillar, thus standing in its own defence. The tax upon beer brewed for sale does not affect the aristocracy, who brew their own beer free of this duty. It falls only on those who have not conveniency or ability to brew, and who must purchase it in small quantities. But what will mankind think of the justice of taxation, when they know that this tax alone, from which the aristocracy are from circumstances exempt, is nearly equal to the whole of the land-tax, being in the year 1788, and it is not less now, £1,666,152, and with its proportion of the taxes on malt and hops, it exceeds it. That a single article, thus partially consumed, and that chiefly by the working part, should be subject to a tax, equal to that on the whole rental of a nation, is, perhaps, a fact not to be paralleled in the histories of revenues.

This is one of the consequences resulting from an house of legislation, composed on the ground of a combination of common interest; for whatever their separate politics as to parties may be, in this they are united. Whether a combination acts to raise the price of any article for sale, or the rate of wages; or whether it acts to throw taxes from itself upon another class of the community, the principle and the effect are the same; and if the one be illegal, it will be difficult to show that the other ought to exist.

It is to no use to say that taxes are first proposed in the house of commons; for as the other house has always a negative, it can always defend itself; and it would be ridiculous to suppose that its acquiescence in the measures to be proposed were not understood beforehand. Besides which, it has obtained so much influence by borough-traffic, and so many of its relations and connexions are distributed on both sides of the commons, as to give it, besides an absolute negative in one house, a preponderancy in the other, in all matters of common concern.

It is difficult to discover what is meant by the *landed interest,* if it does not mean a combination of aristocratical land-holders, opposing their own pecuniary interest to that of the farmer, and every branch of trade, commerce, and manufacture. In all other respects it is the only interest that needs no partial protection. It enjoys the general protection of the world. Every individual, high or low, is interested in the fruits of the earth; men, women, and children, of all ages and degrees, will turn out to assist the farmer, rather than a harvest should not be got in; and they will not act thus by any other property. It is the only one for which the common prayer of mankind is put up, and the only one that can never fail from the want of means. It is the interest, not of the policy, but of the existence of man, and when it ceases, he must cease to be.

No other interest in a nation stands on the same united support. Commerce, manufactures, arts, sciences, and everything else, compared with this, are supported but in parts. Their prosperity or their decay has not the same universal influence. When the valleys laugh and sing, it is not the farmer only, but all creation that rejoice. It is a prosperity that excludes all envy; and this cannot be said of anything else.

Why then does Mr Burke talk of his house of peers, as the pillar of the landed interest? Were that pillar to sink into the earth, the same landed property would continue, and the same ploughing, sowing, and reaping would go on. The aristocracy are not the farmers who work the land, and raise the produce, but are the mere consumers of the rent; and when compared with the active world are the drones, a seraglio of males, who neither collect the honey nor form the hive, but exist only for lazy enjoyment.

Mr Burke, in his first essay, called aristocracy, '*the Corinthian capital of polished society*.' Towards completing the figure, he has now added the *pillar*; but still the base is wanting; and whenever a nation choose to act a Samson, not blind, but bold, down go the temple of Dagon, the Lords and the Philistines.

If a house of legislation is to be composed of men of one class, for the purpose of protecting a distinct interest, all the other interests should have the same. The inequality, as well as the burden of taxation, arises from admitting it in one case, and not in all. Had there been a house of farmers, there had been no game laws; or a house of merchants and manufacturers, the taxes had neither been so unequal nor so excessive. It is from the power of taxation being in the hands of those who can throw so great a part of it from their own shoulders, that it has raged without a check.

Men of small or moderate estates are more injured by the taxes being thrown on articles of consumption than they are eased by warding it from landed property, for the following reasons:

First, They consume more of the productive taxable articles, in proportion to their property, than those of large estates.

Secondly, Their residence is chiefly in towns, and their property in houses; and the increase of the poor-rates, occasioned by taxes on consumption, is in much greater proportion than the land-tax has been favoured. In Birmingham, the poor-rates are not less than seven shillings in the pound. From this, as already observed, the aristocracy are in a great measure exempt.

These are but a part of the mischiefs flowing from the wretched scheme of an house of peers.

As a combination, it can always throw a considerable portion of taxes from itself; and as an hereditary house, accountable to nobody, it resembles a rotten borough, whose consent is to be courted by interest. There are but few of its members who are not in some mode or other participators, or disposers of the public money. One turns a candle-holder, or a lord in waiting; another a lord of the bed-chamber, a groom of the stole, or any insignificant nominal office, to which a salary is annexed, paid out of the public taxes, and which avoids the direct appearance of corruption. Such situations are derogatory to the character of man; and where they can be submitted to, honour cannot reside.

To all these are to be added the numerous dependants, the long list of younger branches and distant relations, who are to be provided for at the public expense: in short, were an estimation to be made of the charge of aristocracy to a nation, it will be found nearly equal to that of supporting the poor. The Duke of Richmond alone (and there are cases similar to his) takes away as much for himself as would maintain two thousand poor and aged persons. Is it, then, any wonder, that under such a system of government, taxes and rates have multiplied to their present extent?

In stating these matters, I speak an open and disinterested language, dictated by no passion but that of humanity. To me, who have not only refused offers, because I thought them improper, but have declined rewards I might with reputation have accepted, it is no wonder that meanness and imposition appear disgustful. Independence is my happiness, and I view things as they are, without regard to place or person; my country is the world, and my religion is to do good.

Mr Burke, in speaking of the aristocratical law of primogeniture, says, 'it is the standing law of our landed inheritance; and which, without question, has a tendency, and I think,' continues he, 'a happy tendency, to preserve a character of weight and consequence.'

Mr Burke may call this law what he pleases, but humanity and impartial reflection will denounce it a law of brutal injustice. Were we not accustomed to the daily practice, and did we only hear of it as the law of some distant part of the world, we should conclude that the legislators of such countries had not yet arrived at a state of civilization.

As to its preserving a character of *weight and consequence*, the case appears to me directly the reverse. It is an attaint upon character; a sort of privateering of family property. It may have weight among dependent tenants, but it gives none on a scale of national, and much less of universal character. Speaking for myself, my parents were not able to give me a shilling, beyond what they gave me in education; and to do this they distressed themselves: yet, I possess more of what is called consequence in the world, than anyone in Mr Burke's catalogue of aristocrats.

Having thus glanced at some of the defects of the two houses of parliament, I proceed to what is called the crown, upon which I shall be very concise.

It signifies a nominal office of a million sterling a year, the business of which consists in receiving the money. Whether the person be wise or foolish, sane or insane, a native or a foreigner, matters not. Every ministry acts upon the same idea that Mr Burke writes, namely, that the people must be hoodwinked, and held in superstitious ignorance by some bugbear or other; and what is called the crown answers this purpose, and therefore it answers all the purposes to be expected from it. This is more than can be said of the other two branches.

The hazard to which this office is exposed in all countries, is not from anything that can happen to the man, but from what may happen to the nation—the danger of its coming to its senses.

It has been customary to call the crown the executive power, and the custom is continued, though the reason has ceased.

It was called the *executive*, because the person whom it signified used, formerly, to sit in the character of a judge, in administering or executing the laws. The tribunals were then a part of the court. The power, therefore, which is now called the judicial, is what was called the executive; and, consequently, one or other of the terms is redundant, and one of the offices useless. When we speak of the crown now, it means nothing; it signifies neither a judge nor a general: besides which it is the laws that govern, and not the man. The old terms are kept up, to give an appearance of consequence to empty forms; and the only effect they have is that of increasing expenses.

Before I proceed to the means of rendering governments more conducive to the general happiness of mankind than they are at present, it will not be improper to take a review of the progress of taxation in England.

It is a general idea, that when taxes are once laid on, they are never taken off. However true this may have been of late, it was not always so. Either, therefore, the people of former times were more watchful over government than those of the present, or government was administered with less extravagance.

It is now seven hundred years since the Norman conquest, and the establishment of what is called the crown. Taking this portion of time in seven separate periods of one hundred years each, the amount of the annual taxes, at each period, will be as follows: —

Annual amount of taxes levied by William the Conqueror, beginning in the year 1066 — — — — —	£400,000
Annual amount of taxes at one hundred years from the conquest, (1166) — — — — — —	200,000
Annual amount of taxes at two hundred years from the conquest, (1266) — — — — — —	150,000
Annual amount of taxes at three hundred years from the conquest, (1366) — — — — — —	130,000
Annual amount of taxes at four hundred years from the conquest, (1466) — — — — — —	100,000

These statements, and those which follow, are taken from Sir John Sinclair's History of the Revenue; by which it appears, that taxes continued decreasing for four hundred years, at the expiration of which time they were reduced three-fourths, viz. from four hundred thousand pounds to one hundred thousand. The people of England of the present day, have a traditionary and historical idea of the bravery of their ancestors; but whatever their virtues or their vices might have been, they certainly were a people who would not be imposed upon, and who kept government in awe as to taxation, if not as to principle. Though they were not able to expel the monarchical usurpation, they restricted it to a republican economy of taxes.

Let us now review the remaining three hundred years.

Annual amount of taxes at five hundred years from the conquest, (1566) — — — — — —	£500,000
Annual amount of taxes at six hundred years from the conquest, (1666) — — — — — —	1,800,000
Annual amount of taxes at the present time, (1791)	17,000,000

The difference between the first four hundred years and the last three, is so astonishing, as to warrant an opinion, that the national character of the English has changed. It would have been impossible to have dragooned the former English, into the excess of taxation that now exists; and when it is considered that the pay of the army, the navy, and of all the revenue officers, is the same now as it was above a hundred years ago, when the taxes were not above a tenth part of what they are at present, it appears impossible to account for the enormous increase in expenditure, on any other ground, than extravagance, corruption, and intrigue.[16]

With the revolution of 1688, and more so since the Hanover succession, came the destructive system of continental intrigues, and the rage for foreign wars and foreign dominion; systems of such secure mystery that the expenses admit of no accounts; a single line stands for millions. To what excess taxation might have extended, had not the French revolution contributed to break up the system, and put an end to pretences, is impossible to say. Viewed, as that revolution ought to be, as the fortunate means of lessening the load of taxes of both countries, it is of as much importance to England as to France; and, if properly improved to all the advantages of which it is capable, and to which it leads, deserve as much celebration in one country as the other.

In pursuing this subject, I shall begin with the matter that first presents itself, that of lessening the burden of taxes; and shall then add such matters and propositions, respecting the three countries of England, France, and America, as the present prospect of things appears to justify: I mean, an alliance of the three, for the purposes that will be mentioned in their proper place.

What has happened may happen again. By the statement before shown of the progress of taxation, it is seen, that taxes have been lessened to a fourth part of what they had formerly been. Though the present circumstances do not admit of the same reduction, yet it admits of such a beginning, as may accomplish that end in less time, than in the former case.

The amount of taxes for the year, ending at Michaelmas 1788, was as follows:

Land-tax, — — — — — —	£1,950,000
Customs, — — — — — —	3,789,274
Excise, (including old and new malt,) — —	6,751,727
Stamps, — — — — — —	1,278,214
Miscellaneous taxes and incidents, — — —	1,803,755
	£15,572,970

Since the year 1788, upwards of one million of new taxes have been laid on, besides the produce from the lotteries; and as the taxes have in general been more productive since than before, the amount may be taken, in round numbers, at £17,000,000.

N.B. The expense of collection and the drawbacks, which together amount to nearly two millions, are paid out of the gross amount; and the above is the net sum paid into the exchequer.

This sum of seventeen millions is applied to two different purposes; the one to pay the interest of the national debt, the other to the current expenses of each year. About nine millions are appropriated to the former; and the remainder, being nearly eight millions, to the latter. As to the million, said to be applied to the reduction of the debt, it is so much like paying with one hand and taking out with the other, as not to merit much notice.

It happened, fortunately for France, that she possessed national domains for paying off her debt, and thereby lessening her taxes: but as this is not the case in England, her reduction of taxes can only take place by reducing the current expenses, which may now be done to the amount of four or five millions annually, as will hereafter appear. When this is accomplished, it will more than counterbalance the enormous charge of the American war; and the saving will be from the same source from whence the evil arose.

As to the national debt, however heavy the interest may be in taxes; yet, as it serves to keep alive a capital, useful to commerce, it balances by its effects a considerable part of its own weight; and as the quantity of gold and silver in England is, by some means or other, short of its proper proportion,[17] (being not more than twenty millions, whereas it should be sixty,) it would, besides the injustice, be bad policy to extinguish a capital that serves to supply that defect. But with respect to the current expense, whatever is saved therefrom is gain. The excess may serve to keep corruption alive, but it has no reaction on credit and commerce, like the interest of the debt.

It is now very probable, that the English government (I do not mean the nation) is unfriendly to the French revolution. Whatever serves to expose the intrigue and lessen the influence of courts, by lessening taxation, will be unwelcome to those who feed upon the spoil. Whilst the clamour of French intrigue, arbitrary power, popery, and wooden shoes could be kept up, the nation was easily allured and alarmed into taxes. Those days are now past; deception, it is to be hoped, has reaped its last harvest, and better times are in prospect for both countries, and for the world.

Taking it for granted that an alliance may be formed between England, France, and America, for the purposes hereafter to be mentioned, the national expenses of France and England may consequently be lessened. The same fleets and armies will no longer be necessary to either, and the reduction can be made ship for ship on each side. But to accomplish these objects, the governments must necessarily be fitted to a common and correspondent principle. Confidence can never take place while an hostile disposition remains in either, or where mystery and secrecy on one side, is opposed to candour and openness on the other.

These matters admitted, the national expenses might be put back, *for the sake of a precedent,* to what they were at some period when France and England were not enemies. This, consequently, must be prior to the Hanover succession, and also to the Revolution of 1688.[18] The first instance that presents itself, antecedent to those dates, is in the very wasteful and profligate times of Charles the Second, at which time England and France acted as allies. If I have chosen a period of great extravagance, it will serve to show modern extravagance in a still worse light; especially as the pay of the navy, the army, and the revenue officers has not increased since that time.

The peace establishment was then as follows:—(See Sir John Sinclair's History of the Revenue.)

Navy, — — — —	£300,000
Army, — — — —	212,000
Ordnance, — — —	40,000
Civil List, — — —	462,115
	£1,014,115

The parliament, however, settled the whole annual peace establishment at £1,200,000.[19] If we go back to the time of Elizabeth, the amount of all the taxes was but half a million, yet the nation sees nothing during that period, that reproaches it with want of consequence.

All circumstances then taken together, arising from the French revolution, from the approaching harmony and reciprocal interest of the two nations, the abolition of court intrigue on both sides, and the progress of knowledge in the science of government, the annual expenditure might be put back to one million and an half, viz.

Navy, — — — —	£500,000
Army, — — — —	500,000
Expenses of government, —	500,000
	£1,500,000

Even this sum is six times greater than the expenses of government are in America, yet the civil internal government in England, (I mean that administered by means of quarter sessions, juries, and assize, and which, in fact, is nearly the whole, and performed by the nation,) is less expense upon the revenue, than the same species and portion of government is in America.

It is time that nations should be rational, and not be governed like animals, for the pleasure of their riders. To read the history of kings, a man would be almost inclined to suppose that government consisted in stag-hunting, and that every nation paid a million a year to a huntsman. Man ought to have pride, or shame enough to blush at being thus imposed upon, and when he feel his proper character, he will. Upon all subjects of this nature, there is often passing in the mind, a train of ideas he has not yet accustomed himself to encourage and communicate. Restrained by something that puts on the character of prudence, he acts the hypocrite upon himself as well as to others. It is, however, curious to observe how soon this spell can be dissolved. A single expression, boldly conceived and uttered, will sometimes put a whole company into their proper feelings; and whole nations are acted upon in the same manner.

As to the offices of which any civil government may be composed, it matters but little by what names they are described. In the routine of business, as before observed, whether a man be styled a president, a king, an emperor, a senator, or anything else, it is impossible that any service he can perform, can merit from a nation more than ten thousand pounds a year; and as no man should be paid beyond his services, so every man of a proper heart will not accept more. Public money ought to be touched with the most scrupulous consciousness of honour. It is not the produce of riches only, but of the hard earnings of labour and poverty. It is drawn even from the bitterness of want and misery. Not a beggar passes, or perishes in the streets, whose mite is not in that mass.

Were it possible that the Congress of America, could be so lost to their duty, and to the interest of their constituents, as to offer George Washington, as president of America, a million a year, he would not, and he could not, accept it. His sense of honour is of another kind. It has cost England almost seventy millions sterling, to maintain a family imported from abroad, of very inferior capacity to thousands in the nation; and scarcely a year has passed that has not produced some new mercenary application. Even the physicians' bills have been sent to the public to be paid. No wonder that jails are crowded, and taxes and poor-rates increased. Under such systems, nothing is to be looked for but what has already happened; and as to reformation, whenever it come, it must be from the nation, and not from the government.

To show that the sum of five hundred thousand pounds is more than sufficient to defray all the expenses of government, exclusive of navies and armies, the following estimate is added for any country, of the same extent as England.

In the first place, three hundred representatives, fairly elected, are sufficient for all the purposes to which legislation can apply, and preferable to a larger number. They may be divided into two or three houses, or meet in one, as in France, or in any manner a constitution shall direct.

As representation is always considered, in free countries, as the most honourable of all stations, the allowance made to it is merely to defray the expense which the representatives incur by that service, and not to it as an office.

If an allowance, at the rate of five hundred pounds *per ann.* be made to every representative, deducting for non-attendance, the expense, if the whole number attended for six months, each year, would be		£75,000
The official departments cannot reasonably exceed the following number, with the salaries annexed:		
Three offices, at ten thousand pounds each,		30,000
Ten ditto,	at £5,000 each	50,000
Twenty ditto,	at £2,000 each	40,000
Forty ditto,	at £1,000 each	40,000
Two hundred ditto,	at £ 500 each	100,000
Three hundred ditto,	at £ 200 each	60,000
Five hundred ditto,	at £ 100 each	50,000
Seven hundred ditto,	at £ 75 each	52,500
		£497,500

If a nation choose, it can deduct four *per cent.* from all offices, and make one of twenty thousand *per ann.*

All revenue officers are paid out of the moneys they collect, and therefore, are not in this estimation.

The foregoing is not offered as an exact detail of offices, but to show the number and rate of salaries which five hundred thousand pounds will support; and it will, on experience, be found impracticable to find business sufficient to justify even this expense. As to the manner in which office business is now performed, the Chiefs, in several offices, such as the post office, and certain offices in the exchequer, &c. do little more than sign their names three or four times a year; and the whole duty is performed by under clerks.

Taking, therefore, one million and an half as a sufficient peace establishment for all the honest purposes of government, which is three hundred thousand pounds more than the peace establishment in the profligate and prodigal times of Charles the Second, (notwithstanding, as has been already observed, the pay and salaries of the army, navy, and revenue officers, continue the same as at that period), there will remain a surplus of upwards of six millions out of the present current expenses. The question then will be, how to dispose of this surplus.

Whoever has observed the manner in which trade and taxes twist themselves together, must be sensible of the impossibility of separating them suddenly.

First. Because the articles now on hand are already charged with the duty, and the reduction cannot take place on the present stock.

Secondly. Because, on all those articles on which the duty is charged in the gross, such as *per* barrel, hogshead, hundredweight, or ton, the abolition of the duty does not admit of being divided down so as fully to relieve the consumer, who purchases by the pint, or the pound. The last duty laid on strong beer and ale, was three shillings *per* barrel, which, if taken off, would lessen the purchase only half a farthing *per* pint, and consequently, would not reach to practical relief.

This being the condition of a great part of the taxes, it will be necessary to look for such others as are free from this embarrassment, and where the relief will be direct and visible, and capable of immediate operation.

In the first place, then, the poor-rates are a direct tax which every housekeeper feels, and who knows also, to a farthing, the sum which he pays. The national amount of the whole of the poor-rates is not positively known, but can be procured. Sir John Sinclair, in his History of the Revenue, has stated it at £2,100,587. A considerable part of which is expended in litigations, in which the poor, instead of being relieved, are tormented. The expense, however, is the same to the parish from whatever cause it arises.

In Birmingham, the amount of the poor-rates is fourteen thousand pounds a year. This, though a large sum, is moderate, compared with the population. Birmingham is said to contain seventy thousand souls, and on a proportion of seventy thousand to fourteen thousand pounds poor-rates, the national amount of poor-rates, taking the population of England at seven millions, would be but one million four hundred thousand pounds. It is, therefore, most probable, that the population of Birmingham is over-rated. Fourteen thousand pounds is the proportion upon fifty thousand souls, taking two millions of poor-rates as the national amount.

Be it, however, what it may, it is no other than the consequence of the excessive burden of taxes, for, at the time when the taxes were very low, the poor were able to maintain themselves; and there were no poor-rates.[20] In the present state of things, a labouring man, with a wife and two or three children, does not pay less than between seven and eight pounds a year in taxes. He is not sensible of this, because it is disguised to him in the articles which he buys, and he thinks only of their dearness; but as the taxes take from him, at least, a fourth part of his yearly earnings, he is consequently disabled from providing for a family, especially, if himself, or any of them, are afflicted with sickness.

The first step, therefore, of practical relief, would be to abolish the poor-rates entirely, and in lieu thereof, to make a remission of taxes to the poor of double the amount of the present poor-rates, viz. four millions annually out of the surplus taxes. By this measure, the poor will be benefited two millions, and the housekeepers two millions. This alone would be equal to a reduction of one hundred and twenty millions of the national debt, and consequently equal to the whole expense of the American war.

It will then remain to be considered, which is the most effectual mode of distributing this remission of four millions.

It is easily seen, that the poor are generally composed of large families of children, and old people past their labour. If these two classes are provided for, the remedy will so far reach to the full extent of the case, that what remains will be incidental and, in a great measure, fall within the compass of benefit clubs, which, though of humble invention, merit to be ranked among the best of modern institutions.

Admitting England to contain seven million of souls; if one-fifth thereof arc of that class of poor which need support, the number will be one million four hundred thousand. Of this number, one hundred and forty thousand will be aged poor, as will be hereafter shown, and for which a distinct provision will be proposed.

There will then remain one million two hundred and sixty thousand, which, at five souls to each family, amount to two hundred and fifty-two thousand families, rendered poor from the expense of children and the weight of taxes.

The number of children under fourteen years of age, in each of those families, will be found to be about five to every two families; some having two, and others three; some one, and others four; some none, and others five; but it rarely happens that more than five are under fourteen years of age, and after this age they are capable of service or of being apprenticed.

Allowing five children (under fourteen years) to every two families,

The number of children will be — — — — —	630,000
The number of parents were they all living, would be	504,000

It is certain, that if the children are provided for, the parents are relieved of consequence, because it is from the expense of bringing up children that their poverty arises.

Having thus ascertained the greatest number that can be supposed to need support on account of young families, I proceed to the mode of relief or distribution, which is,

To pay as a remission of taxes to every poor family, out of the surplus taxes, and in room of poor-rates, four pounds a year for every child under fourteen years of age; enjoining the parents of such children to send them to school, to learn reading, writing, and common arithmetic; the ministers of every parish, of every denomination, to certify jointly to an office, for that purpose, that this duty is performed.

The amount of this expense will be,

For six hundred and thirty thousand children, at four pounds *per ann.* each, — — — — —	£2,520,000

By adopting this method, not only the poverty of the parents will be relieved, but ignorance will be banished from the rising generation, and the number of poor will hereafter become less, because their abilities, by the aid of education, will be greater. Many a youth, with good natural genius, who is apprenticed to a mechanical trade, such as a carpenter, joiner, millwright, shipwright, blacksmith, &c. is prevented getting forward the whole of his life, from the want of a little common education when a boy.

I now proceed to the case of the aged.

I divide age into two classes. First, the approach of age beginning at fifty. Secondly, old age commencing at sixty.

At fifty, though the mental faculties of man are in full vigour, and his judgement better than at any preceding date, the bodily powers for laborious life are on the decline. He cannot bear the same quantity of fatigue as at an earlier period. He begins to earn less, and is less capable of enduring wind and weather; and in those more retired employments where much sight is required, he fails apace, and sees himself, like an old horse, beginning to be turned adrift.

At sixty his labour ought to be over, at least from direct necessity. It is painful to see old age working itself to death, in what are called civilized countries, for daily bread.

To form some judgement of the number of those above fifty years of age, I have several times counted the persons I met in the streets of London, men, women, and children, and have generally found that the average is about one in sixteen or seventeen. If it be said that aged persons do not come much in the streets, so neither do infants; and a great proportion of grown children are in school, and in work-shops as apprentices. Taking then sixteen for a divisor, the whole number of persons in England, of fifty years and upwards of both sexes, rich and poor, will be four hundred and twenty thousand.

The persons to be provided for out of this gross number will be, husbandmen, common labourers, journeymen of every trade and their wives, sailors, and disbanded soldiers, worn out servants of both sexes, and poor widows.

There will be also a considerable number of middling tradesmen, who having lived decently in the former part of life, begin, as age approaches, to lose their business, and at last fall to decay.

Besides these, there will be constantly thrown off from the revolutions of that wheel, which no man can stop, nor regulate, a number from every class of life connected with commerce and adventure.

To provide for all those accidents, and whatever else may befall, I take the number of persons, who at one time or other of their lives, after fifty years of age, may feel it necessary or comfortable to be better supported, than they can support themselves, and that not as a matter of grace and favour, but of right, at one third of the whole number, which is one hundred and forty thousand, as stated above, and for whom a distinct provision was proposed to be made. If there be more, society, notwithstanding the show and pomposity of government, is in a deplorable condition in England.

Of this one hundred and forty thousand, I take one half, seventy thousand, to be of the age of fifty and under sixty, and the other half to be sixty years and upwards.—Having thus ascertained the probable proportion of the number of aged persons, I proceed to the mode of rendering their condition comfortable, which is,

To pay to every such person of the age of fifty years, and until he shall arrive at the age of sixty, the sum of six pounds *per ann.* out of the surplus taxes; and ten pounds *per ann.* during life after the age of sixty. The expense of which will be,

Seventy thousand persons at £6 *per ann.*	£420,000
Seventy thousand ditto at £10 *per ann.*	700,000
	£1,120,000

This support, as already remarked, is not of the nature of a charity, but of a right. Every person in England, male and female, pays on an average in taxes, two pounds eight shillings and sixpence *per ann.* from the day of his (or her) birth; and, if the expense of collection be added, he pays two pounds eleven shillings and sixpence; consequently, at the end of fifty years he has paid one hundred and twenty-eight pounds fifteen shillings; and at sixty, one hundred and fifty-four pounds ten shillings. Converting, therefore, his (or her) individual tax into a tontine, the money he shall receive after fifty years, is but little more than the legal interest of the net money he has paid; the rest is made up from those whose circumstances do not require them to draw such support, and the capital in both cases defrays the expenses of government. It is on this ground that I have extended the probable claims to one third of the number of aged persons in the nation.—Is it then better that the lives of one hundred and forty thousand aged persons be rendered comfortable, or that a million a year of public money be expended on any one individual, and him often of the most worthless or insignificant character? Let reason and justice, let honour and humanity, let even hypocrisy, sycophancy and Mr Burke, let George, let Louis, Leopold, Frederic, Catherine, Cornwallis, or Tippoo Saib, answer the question.[21]

The sum thus remitted to the poor will be,

To two hundred and fifty-two thousand poor families, containing six hundred and thirty-thousand children,	— £2,520,000
To one hundred and forty thousand aged persons	— 1,120,000
	£3,640,000

There will then remain three hundred and sixty thousand pounds out of the four millions, part of which may be applied as follows:

After all the above cases are provided for, there will still be a number of families who, though not properly of the class of poor, yet find it difficult to give education to their children; and such children, under such a case, would be in a worse condition than if their parents were actually poor. A nation under a well-regulated government, should permit none to remain uninstructed. It is monarchical and aristocratical government only that requires ignorance for its support.

Suppose then four hundred thousand children to be in this condition, which is a greater number than ought to be supposed, after the provisions already made, the method will be,

To allow for each of those children ten shillings a year for the expense of schooling, for six years each, which will give them six months schooling each year and half a crown a year for paper and spelling books.

The expense of this will be annually[22] — — — — £250,000

There will then remain one hundred and ten thousand pounds.

Notwithstanding the great modes of relief which the best instituted and best principled government may devise, there will be a number of smaller cases, which it is good policy as well as beneficence in a nation to consider.

Were twenty shillings to be given immediately on the birth of a child, to every woman who should make the demand, and none will make it whose circumstances do not require it, it might relieve a great deal of instant distress.

There are about two hundred thousand births yearly in England, and if claimed, by one fourth,

The amount would be — — — — — — — £50,000

And twenty shillings to every new-married couple who should claim in like manner. This would not exceed the sum of £20,000.

Also twenty thousand pounds to be appropriated to defray the funeral expenses of persons, who, travelling for work, may die at a distance from their friends. By relieving parishes from this charge, the sick stranger will be better treated.

I shall finish this part of the subject with a plan adapted to the particular condition of a metropolis, such as London.

Cases are continually occurring in a metropolis, different to those which occur in the country, and for which a different, or rather an additional mode of relief is necessary. In the country, even in large towns, people have a knowledge of each other, and distress never rises to that extreme height it sometimes does in a metropolis. There is no such thing in the country as persons, in the literal sense of the word, starved to death, or dying with cold from the want of a lodging. Yet such cases, and others equally as miserable, happen in London.

Many a youth comes up to London full of expectations, and with little or no money, and unless he gets immediate employment he is already half undone; and boys bred up in London, without any means of a livelihood, and as it often happens of dissolute parents, are in a still worse condition; and servants long out of place are not much better off. In short, a world of little cases are continually arising, which busy or affluent life knows not of, to open the first door to distress. Hunger is not among the postponable wants, and a day, even a few hours, in such a condition, is often the crisis of a life of ruin.

These circumstances, which are the general cause of the little thefts and pilferings that lead to greater, may be prevented. There yet remain twenty thousand pounds out of the four millions of surplus taxes, which, with another fund hereafter to be mentioned, amounting to about twenty thousand pounds more, cannot be better applied than to this purpose. The plan then will be,

First, To erect two or more buildings, or take some already erected, capable of containing at least six thousand persons, and to have in each of these places as many kinds of employment as can be contrived, so that every person who shall come may find something which he or she can do.

Secondly, To receive all who shall come, without enquiring who or what they are. The only condition to be, that for so much, or so many hours work, each person shall receive so many meals of wholesome food, and a warm lodging, at least as good as a barrack. That a certain portion of what each person's work shall be worth shall be reserved, and given to him, or her, on their going away; and that each person shall stay as long, or as short time, or come as often as he choose, on these conditions.

If each person stayed three months, it would assist by rotation twenty-four thousand persons annually, though the real number, at all times, would be but six thousand. By establishing an asylum of this kind, persons to whom temporary distresses occur, would have an opportunity to recruit themselves, and be enabled to look out for better employment.

Allowing that their labour paid but one half the expense of supporting them, after reserving a portion of their earnings for themselves, the sum of forty thousand pounds additional would defray all other charges for even a greater number than six thousand.

The fund very properly convertible to this purpose, in addition to the twenty thousand pounds, remaining of the former fund, will be the produce of the tax upon coals, so iniquitously and wantonly applied to the support of the Duke of Richmond. It is horrid that any man, more especially at the price coals now are, should live on the distresses of a community; and any government permitting such an abuse, deserves to be dismissed. This fund is said to be about twenty thousand pounds *per annum.*

I shall now conclude this plan with enumerating the several particulars, and then proceed to other matters.

The enumeration is as follows:

First, Abolition of two million poor-rates.

Secondly, Provision for two hundred and fifty-two thousand poor families.

Thirdly, Education for one million and thirty thousand children.

Fourthly, Comfortable provision for one hundred and forty thousand aged persons.

Fifthly, Donation of twenty shillings each for fifty thousand births.

Sixthly, Donation of twenty shillings each for twenty thousand marriages.

Seventhly, Allowance of twenty thousand pounds for the funeral expenses of persons travelling for work, and dying at a distance from their friends.

Eighthly, Employment, at all times, for the casual poor in the cities of London and Westminster.

By the operation of this plan, the poor laws, those instruments of civil torture, will be superseded, and the wasteful expense of litigation prevented. The hearts of the humane will not be shocked by ragged and hungry children, and persons of seventy and eighty years of age begging for bread. The dying poor will not be dragged from place to place to breathe their last, as a reprisal of parish upon parish. Widows will have a maintenance for their children, and not be carted away, on the death of their husbands, like culprits and criminals; and children will no longer be considered as increasing the distresses of their parents. The haunts of the wretched will be known, because it will be to their advantage; and the number of petty crimes, the offspring of distress and poverty, will be lessened. The poor, as well as the rich, will then be interested in the support of government, and the cause and apprehension of riots and tumults will cease.—Ye who sit in ease, and solace yourselves in plenty, and such there are in Turkey and Russia, as well as in England, and who say to yourselves, 'Are we not well off,' have ye thought of these things? When ye do, ye will cease to speak and feel for yourselves alone.

The plan is easy in practice. It does not embarrass trade by a sudden interruption in the order of taxes, but effects the relief by changing the application of them; and the money necessary for the purpose can be drawn from the excise collections, which are made eight times a year in every market town in England.

Having now arranged and concluded this subject, I proceed to the next.

Taking the present current expenses at seven millions and a half, which is the least amount they are now at, there will remain (after the sum of one million and an half be taken for the new current expenses, and four millions for the before-mentioned service) the sum of two millions; part of which to be applied as follows:

Though fleets and armies, by an alliance with France, will, in great measure, become useless, yet the persons who have devoted themselves to those services, and have thereby unfitted themselves for other lines of life, are not to be sufferers by the means that make others happy. They are a different description of men to those who form or hang about a court.

A part of the army will remain at least for some years, and also of the navy, for which a provision is already made in the former part of this plan of one million, which is almost half a million more than the peace establishment of the army and navy in the prodigal times of Charles the Second.

Suppose then fifteen thousand soldiers to be disbanded, and that an allowance be made to each of three shillings a week during life, clear of all deductions, to be paid in the same manner as the Chelsea College pensioners are paid, and for them to return to their trades and their friends; and also that an addition of fifteen thousand sixpences per week be made to the pay of the soldiers who shall remain; the annual expense will be,

To the pay of fifteen thousand disbanded soldiers, at three shillings per week, — —	£117,000
Additional pay to the remaining soldiers, —	19,500
	£136,500

Suppose that the pay to the officers of the disbanded corps be of the same amount as the sum allowed to the men, — — —	117,000	
		253,500
To prevent bulky estimations, admit the same sum to the disbanded navy as to the army, and the same increase of pay, — — —		253,500
Total		£507,000

Every year some part of this sum of half a million (I omit the odd seven thousand pounds for the purpose of keeping the account unembarrassed) will fall in, and the whole of it in time, as it is on the ground of life annuities, except the increased pay of twenty-nine thousand pounds. As it falls in, a part of the taxes may be taken off; for instance, when thirty thousand pounds fall in, the duty on hops may be wholly taken off; and as other parts fall in, the duties on candles and soap may be lessened, till at last they will totally cease.

There now remains at least one million and an half of surplus taxes.

The tax on houses and windows is one of those direct taxes, which, like the poor-rates, is not confounded with trade; and, when taken off, the relief will be instantly felt. This tax falls heavy on the middling class of people.

The amount of this tax by the returns of 1788, was,

	l.	*s.*	*d.*
Houses and windows by the act of 1766,	385,459	11	7
Ditto ditto by the act of 1779,	130,739	14	$5\frac{1}{2}$
Total	516,199	6	$0\frac{1}{2}$

If this tax be struck off, there will then remain about one million of surplus taxes, and as it is always proper to keep a sum in reserve, for incidental matters, it may be best not to extend reductions further, in the first instance, but to consider what may be accomplished by other modes of reform.

Among the taxes most heavily felt is the commutation-tax. I shall, therefore, offer a plan for its abolition, by substituting another in its place, which will effect three objects at once:

First, That of removing the burden to where it can best be borne.

Secondly, Restoring justice among families by a distribution of property.

Thirdly, Extirpating the overgrown influence arising from the unnatural law of primogeniture, and which is one of the principal sources of corruption at elections.

The amount of the commutation tax by the returns
of 1788, was, — — — — — — £771,657 0 0

When taxes are proposed, the country is amused by the plausible language of taxing luxuries. One thing is called a luxury at one time, and something else at another; but the real luxury does not consist in the article, but in the means of procuring it, and this is always kept out of sight.

I know not why any plant or herb of the field should be a greater luxury in one country than another, but an overgrown estate in either is a luxury at all times, and as such is the proper object of taxation. It is, therefore, right to take those kind tax-making gentlemen up on their own word, and argue on the principle themselves have laid down, that of *taxing luxuries*. If they, or their champion Mr Burke, who, I fear, is growing out of date like the man in armour, can prove that an estate of twenty, thirty, or forty thousand pounds a year is not a luxury, I will give up the argument.

Admitting that any annual sum, say for instance, one thousand pounds, is necessary or sufficient for the support of a family, consequently the second thousand is of the nature of a luxury, the third still more so, and by proceeding on, we shall at last arrive at a sum that may not improperly be called a prohibitable luxury. It would be impolitic to set bounds to property acquired by industry, and therefore it is right to place the prohibition beyond the probable acquisition to which industry can extend; but there ought to be a limit to property, or the accumulation of it, by bequest. It should pass in some other line. The richest in every nation have poor relations, and those often very near in consanguinity.

The following table of progressive taxation is constructed on the above principles, and as a substitute for the commutation-tax. It will reach the point of prohibition by a regular operation, and thereby supersede the aristocratical law of primogeniture.

TABLE I

A tax on all estates of the clear yearly value of
fifty pounds, after deducting the land-tax, and up

					s.	*d.*
To £500	—	—	—	0	3 per pound
From 500 to 1000	—	—	—	0	6 per pound
On the second thousand		—	—	0	9 per pound
On the third ditto	—	—	—	1	0 per pound
On the fourth ditto	—	—	—	1	6 per pound
On the fifth ditto	—	—	—	2	0 per pound
On the sixth ditto	—	—	—	3	0 per pound
On the seventh ditto	—	—	—	4	0 per pound
On the eighth ditto	—	—	—	5	0 per pound
On the ninth ditto	—	—	—	6	0 per pound
On the tenth ditto	—	—	—	7	0 per pound
On the eleventh ditto		—	—	8	0 per pound
On the twelfth ditto	—	—	—	9	0 per pound
On the thirteenth ditto		—	—	10	0 per pound
On the fourteenth ditto		—	—	11	0 per pound
On the fifteenth ditto		—	—	12	0 per pound
On the sixteenth ditto		—	—	13	0 per pound
On the seventeenth ditto		—	—	14	0 per pound
On the eighteenth ditto		—	—	15	0 per pound
On the nineteenth ditto		—	—	16	0 per pound
On the twentieth ditto		—	—	17	0 per pound
On the twenty-first ditto		—	—	18	0 per pound
On the twenty-second ditto		—	—	19	0 per pound
On the twenty-third ditto		—	—	20	0 per pound

The foregoing table shows the progression per pound on every progressive thousand. The following table shows the amount of the tax on every thousand separately, and in the last column, the total amount of all the separate sums collected.

TABLE II

	d.		l.	s.	d.
An estate of £50 *per ann.* at	3	per pd. pays	0	12	6
100	3		1	5	0
200	3		2	10	0
300	3		3	15	0
400	3		5	0	0
500	3		7	5	0

After 500*l.*—the tax of sixpence per pound takes place on the second 500*l.*—consequently an estate of 1,000*l. per ann.* pays 21*l.* 15*s.* and so on.

		s.	d.		l.	s.	Total amount l.	s.
For the 1st	500 at	0	3	per pound	7	5	21	15
2nd	500 at	0	6		14	10		
2nd	1000 at	0	9		37	10	59	5
3rd	1000 at	1	0		50	0	109	5
4th	1000 at	1	6		75	0	184	5
5th	1000 at	2	0		100	0	284	5
6th	1000 at	3	0		150	0	434	5
7th	1000 at	4	0		200	0	634	5
8th	1000 at	5	0		250	0	880	5
9th	1000 at	6	0		300	0	1180	5
10th	1000 at	7	0		350	0	1530	5
11th	1000 at	8	0		400	0	1930	5
12th	1000 at	9	0		450	0	2380	5
13th	1000 at	10	0		500	0	2880	5
14th	1000 at	11	0		550	0	3430	5
15th	1000 at	12	0		600	0	4030	5
16th	1000 at	13	0		650	0	4680	5
17th	1000 at	14	0		700	0	5380	5
18th	1000 at	15	0		750	0	6130	5
19th	1000 at	16	0		800	0	6930	5
20th	1000 at	17	0		850	0	7780	5
21st	1000 at	18	0		900	0	8680	5
22d	1000 at	19	0		950	0	9630	5
23d	1000 at	20	0		1000	0	10630	5

At the twenty-third thousand the tax becomes twenty shillings in the pound, and consequently every thousand beyond that sum can produce no profit but by dividing the estate. Yet formidable as this tax appears, it will not, I believe, produce so much as the commutation tax; should it produce more, it ought to be lowered to that amount upon estates under two or three thousand a year.

On small and middling estates it is lighter (as it is intended to be) than the commutation tax. It is not till after seven or eight thousand a year that it begins to be heavy. The object is not so much the produce of the tax, as the justice of the measure. The aristocracy has screened itself too much, and this serves to restore a part of the lost equilibrium.

As an instance of its screening itself, it is only necessary to look back to the first establishment of the excise laws, at what is called the Restoration, or the coming of Charles the Second. The aristocratical interest then in power, commuted the feudal services itself was under by laying a tax on beer brewed for *sale*; that is, they compounded with Charles for an exemption from those services for themselves and their heirs, by a tax to be paid by other people. The aristocracy do not purchase beer brewed for sale, but brew their own beer free of the duty, and if any commutation at that time were necessary, it ought to have been at the expense of those for whom the exemptions from those services were intended;[23] instead of which it was thrown on an entire different class of men.

But the chief object of this progressive tax (besides the justice of rendering taxes more equal than they are) is, as already stated, to extirpate the overgrown influence arising from the unnatural law of primogeniture, and which is one of the principal sources of corruption at elections.

It would be attended with no good consequences to enquire how such vast estates as thirty, forty, or fifty thousand a year could commence, and that at a time when commerce and manufactures were not in a state to admit of such acquisitions. Let it be sufficient to remedy the evil by putting them in a condition of descending again to the community, by the quiet means of apportioning them among all the heirs and heiresses of those families. This will be the more necessary, because hitherto the aristocracy have quartered their younger children and connexions upon the public in useless posts, places, and offices, which when abolished will leave them destitute, unless the law of primogeniture be also abolished or superseded.

A progressive tax will, in a great measure, effect this object, and that as a matter of interest to the parties most immediately concerned, as will be seen by the following table; which shows the net produce upon every estate, after subtracting the tax. By this it will appear, that after an estate exceeds thirteen or fourteen thousand a year, the remainder produces but little profit to the holder, and consequently will pass either to the younger children, or to other kindred.

TABLE III

Showing the net produce of every estate from one thousand to twenty-three thousand pounds a year.

No. of thousands per ann.	Total tax subtracted	Net produce
	£	£
1000	21	979
2000	59	1941
3000	109	2891
4000	184	3816
5000	284	4716
6000	434	5566
7000	634	6366
8000	880	7120
9000	1100	7820
10,000	1530	8470
11,000	1930	9070
12,000	2380	9620
13,000	2880	10,120
14,000	3430	10,570
15,000	4030	10,970
16,000	4680	11,320
17,000	5380	11,620
18,000	6130	11,870
19,000	6930	12,170
20,000	7780	12,220
21,000	8680	12,320
22,000	9630	12,370
23,000	10,360	12,370

N.B. The odd shillings are dropped in this table.

According to this table, an estate cannot produce more than 12,370*l.* clear of the land tax and the progressive tax, and therefore the dividing such estates will follow as a matter of family interest. An estate of 23,000*l.* a year, divided into five estates of four thousand each and one of three, will be charged only 1129*l. which is but five per cent.* but if held by one possessor will be charged 10,630*l.*

Although an enquiry into the origin of those estates be unnecessary, the continuation of them in their present state is another subject. It is a matter of national concern. As hereditary estates, the law has created the evil, and it ought also to provide the remedy. Primogeniture ought to be abolished, not only because it is unnatural and unjust, but because the country suffers by its operation. By cutting off (as before observed) the younger children from their proper portion of inheritance, the public is loaded with the expense of maintaining them; and the freedom of elections violated by the overbearing influence which this unjust monopoly of family property produces. Nor is this all. It occasions a waste of national property. A considerable part of the land of the country is rendered unproductive by the great extent of parks and chases which this law serves to keep up, and this at a time when the annual production of grain is not equal to the national consumption.[24] —In short, the evils of the aristocratical system are so great and numerous, so inconsistent with everything that is just, wise, natural, and beneficent, that when they are considered, there ought not to be a doubt that many, who are now classed under that description, will wish to sec such a system abolished.

What pleasure can they derive from contemplating the exposed condition, and almost certain beggary of their younger offspring? Every aristocratical family has an appendage of family beggars hanging round it, which in a few ages, or a few generations, are shook off, and console themselves with telling their tale in alms-houses, work-houses, and prisons. This is the natural consequence of aristocracy. The peer and the beggar are often of the same family. One extreme produces the other: to make one rich many must be made poor; neither can the system be supported by other means.

There are two classes of people to whom the laws of England are particularly hostile, and those the most helpless; younger children and the poor. Of the former I have just spoken; of the latter I shall mention one instance out of the many that might be produced, and with which I shall close this subject.

Several laws are in existence for regulating and limiting workmen's wages. Why not leave them as free to make their own bargains, as the law-makers are to let their farms and houses? Personal labour is all the property they have. Why is that little, and the little freedom they enjoy to be infringed? But the injustice will appear stronger, if we consider the operation and effect of such laws. When wages are fixed by what is called a law, the legal wages remain stationary, while everything else is in progression; and as those who make that law, still continue to lay on new taxes by other laws, they increase the expense of living by one law, and take away the means by another.

But if those gentlemen law-makers and tax-makers thought it right to limit the poor pittance which personal labour can produce, and on which a whole family is to be supported, they certainly must feel themselves happily indulged in a limitation on their own part, of not less than twelve thousand a year, and that of property they never acquired, (nor probably any of their ancestors) and of which they have made so ill a use.

Having now finished this subject, I shall bring the several particulars into one view, and then proceed to other matters.

The first EIGHT ARTICLES are brought forward from page 213

1. Abolition of two million poor-rates.

2. Provision for two hundred and fifty-two thousand poor families, at the rate of four pounds per head for each child under fourteen years of age; which, with the addition of two hundred and fifty thousand pounds, provides also education for one million and thirty thousand children.

3. Annuity of six pounds (per ann.) each for all poor persons, decayed tradesmen, or others (supposed seventy thousand) of the age of fifty years, and until sixty.

4. Annuity of ten pounds each for life for all poor persons, decayed tradesmen, and others (supposed seventy thousand) of the age of sixty years.

5. Donation of twenty shillings each for fifty thousand births.

6. Donation of twenty shillings each for twenty thousand marriages.

7. Allowance of twenty thousand pounds for the funeral expenses of persons travelling for work, and dying at a distance from their friends.

8. Employment at all times for the casual poor in the cities of London and Westminster.

Second Enumeration

9. Abolition of the tax on houses and windows.

10. Allowance of three shillings per week for life to fifteen thousand disbanded soldiers, and a proportionable allowance to the officers of the disbanded corps.

11. Increase of pay to the remaining soldiers of 19,500*l.* annually.

12. The same allowance to the disbanded navy, and the same increase of pay, as to the army.

13. Abolition of the commutation tax.

14. Plan of a progressive tax, operating to extirpate the unjust and unnatural law of primogeniture, and the vicious influence of the aristocratical system.[25]

There yet remains, as already stated, one million of surplus taxes. Some parts of this will be required for circumstances that do not immediately present themselves, and such part as shall not be wanted, will admit a further reduction of taxes equal to that amount.

Among the claims that justice requires to be made, the condition of the inferior revenue officers will merit attention. It is a reproach to any government to waste such an immensity of revenue in sinecures and nominal and unnecessary places and offices, and not allow even a decent livelihood to those on whom the labour falls. The salary of the inferior officers of the revenue has stood at the petty pittance of less than fifty pounds a year for upwards of one hundred years. It ought to be seventy. About one hundred and twenty thousand pounds applied to this purpose, will put all those salaries in a decent condition.

This was proposed to be done almost twenty years ago, but the treasury-board then in being startled at it, as it might lead to similar expectations from the army and navy; and the event was, that the King, or somebody for him, applied to parliament to have his own salary raised a hundred thousand a year, which being done, everything else was laid aside.

With respect to another class of men, the inferior clergy, I forbear to enlarge on their condition; but all partialities and prejudices for, or against, different modes and forms of religion aside, common justice will determine, whether there ought to be an income of twenty or thirty pounds a year to one man, and of ten thousand to another. I speak on this subject with the more freedom, because I am known not to be a Presbyterian; and therefore the cant cry of court sycophants, about church and meeting, kept up to amuse and bewilder the nation, cannot be raised against me.

Ye simple men, on both sides the question, do ye not see through this courtly craft? If ye can be kept disputing and wrangling about church and meeting, ye just answer the purpose of every courtier, who lives the while on the spoil of the taxes, and laughs at your credulity. Every religion is good that teaches man to be good; and I know of none that instructs him to be bad.

All the before-mentioned calculations, suppose only sixteen millions and a half of taxes paid into the exchequer, after the expense of collection and drawbacks at the custom-house and excise-office are deducted; whereas the sum paid into the exchequer is very nearly, if not quite, seventeen millions. The taxes raised in Scotland and Ireland are expended in those countries, and therefore their savings will come out of their own taxes; but if any part be paid into the English exchequer, it might be remitted. This will not make one hundred thousand pounds a year difference.

There now remains only the national debt to be considered. In the year 1789, the interest, exclusive of the tontine, was 9,150,138*l.* How much the capital has been reduced since that time the minister best knows. But after paying the interest, abolishing the tax on houses and windows, the commutation tax, and the poor rates; and making all the provisions for the poor, for the education of children, the support of the aged, the disbanded part of the army and navy, and increasing the pay of the remainder, there will be a surplus of one million.

The present scheme of paying off the national debt appears to me, speaking as an indifferent person, to be an ill-concerted, if not a fallacious job. The burden of the national debt consists not in its being so many millions, or so many hundred millions, but in the quantity of taxes collected every year to pay the interest. If this quantity continue the same, the burden of the national debt is the same to all intents and purposes, be the capital more or less. The only knowledge which the public can have of the reduction of the debt, must be through the reduction of taxes for paying the interest. The debt, therefore, is not reduced one farthing to the public by all the millions that have been paid; and it would require more money now to purchase up the capital, than when the scheme began.

Digressing for a moment at this point, to which I shall return again, I look back to the appointment of Mr Pitt, as minister.

I was then in America. The war was over; and though resentment had ceased, memory was still alive.

When the news of the coalition arrived, though it was a matter of no concern to me as a citizen of America, I felt it as a man. It had something in it which shocked, by public sporting with decency, if not with principle. It was impudence in Lord North; it was want of firmness in Mr Fox.

Mr Pitt was, at that time, what may be called a maiden character in politics. So far from being hackneyed, he appeared not to be initiated into the first mysteries of court intrigue. Everything was in his favour. Resentment against the coalition served as friendship to him, and his ignorance of vice was credited for virtue. With the return of peace, commerce and prosperity would rise of itself; yet even this increase was thrown to his account.

When he came to the helm the storm was over, and he had nothing to interrupt his course. It required even ingenuity to be wrong, and he succeeded. A little time showed him the same sort of man as his predecessors had been. Instead of profiting by those errors which had accumulated a burden of taxes unparalleled in the world, he sought, I might almost say, he advertised for enemies, and provoked means to increase taxation. Aiming at something, he knew not what, he ransacked Europe and India for adventures, and abandoning the fair pretensions he began with, became the knight-errant of modern times.

It is unpleasant to see character throw itself away. It is more so to see oneself deceived. Mr Pitt had merited nothing, but he promised much. He gave symptoms of a mind superior to the meanness and corruption of courts. His apparent candour encouraged expectations; and the public confidence, stunned, wearied, and confounded by a chaos of parties, revived and attached itself to him. But mistaking, as he has done, the disgust of the nation against the coalition, for merit in himself, he has rushed into measures, which a man less supported would not have presumed to act.

All this seems to show that change of ministers amounts to nothing. One goes out, another comes in, and still the same measures, vices, and extravagance are pursued. It signifies not who is minister. The defect lies in the system. The foundation and the superstructure of the government is bad. Prop it as you please, it continually sinks into court government, and ever will.

I return, as I promised, to the subject of the national debt, that offspring of the Dutch-Anglo Revolution, and its handmaid the Hanover succession.

But it is now too late to inquire how it began. Those to whom it is due have advanced the money; and whether it was well or ill spent, or pocketed, is not their crime. It is, however, easy to see, that as the nation proceeds in contemplating the nature and principles of government, and to understand taxes, and make comparisons between those of America, France, and England, it will be next to impossible to keep it in the same torpid state it has hitherto been. Some reform must, from the necessity of the case, soon begin. It is not whether these principles press with little or much force in the present moment. They are out. They are abroad in the world, and no force can stop them. Like a secret told, they are beyond recall; and he must be blind indeed that does not see that a change is already beginning.

Nine millions of dead taxes is a serious thing; and this not only for bad, but in a great measure for foreign government. By putting the power of making war into the hands of foreigners who came for what they could get, little else was to be expected than what has happened.

Reasons are already advanced in this work showing that, whatever the reforms in the taxes may be, they ought to be made in the current expenses of government, and not in the part applied to the interest of the national debt. By remitting the taxes of the poor, *they* will be totally relieved, and all discontent on their part will be taken away; and by striking off such of the taxes as are already mentioned, the nation will more than recover the whole expense of the mad American War.

There will then remain only the national debt as a subject of discontent; and in order to remove, or rather to prevent this, it would be good policy in the stock-holders themselves to consider it as property, subject like all other property, to bear some portion of the taxes. It would give to it both popularity and security, and as a great part of its present inconvenience is balanced by the capital which it keeps alive, a measure of this kind would so far add to that balance as to silence objections.

This may be done by such gradual means as to accomplish all that is necessary with the greatest ease and convenience.

Instead of taxing the capital, the best method would be to tax the interest by some progressive ratio, and to lessen the public taxes in the same proportion as the interest diminished.

Suppose the interest was taxed one halfpenny in the pound the first year, a penny more the second, and to proceed by a certain ratio to be determined upon, always less than any other tax upon property. Such a tax would be subtracted from the interest at the time of payment, without any expense of collection.

One halfpenny in the pound would lessen the interest and consequently the taxes, twenty thousand pounds. The tax on waggons amounts to this sum, and this tax might be taken off the first year. The second year the tax on female servants, or some other of the like amount might also be taken off, and by proceeding in this manner, always applying the tax raised from the property of the debt towards its extinction, and not carry it to the current services, it would liberate itself.

The stock-holders, notwithstanding this tax, would pay less taxes than they do now. What they would save by the extinction of the poor-rates, and the tax on houses and windows, and the commutation tax, would be confidently greater than what this tax, slow, but certain in its operation, amounts to.

It appears to me to be prudence to look out for measures that may apply under any circumstance that may approach. There is, at this moment, a crisis in the affairs of Europe that requires it. Preparation now is wisdom. If taxation be once let loose, it will be difficult to reinstate it; neither would the relief be so effectual, as to proceed by some certain and gradual reduction.

The fraud, hypocrisy, and imposition of governments, are now beginning to be too well understood to promise them any long career. The farce of monarchy and aristocracy, in all countries, is following that of chivalry, and Mr Burke is dressing for the funeral. Let it then pass quietly to the tomb of all other follies, and the mourners be comforted.

The time is not very distant when England will laugh at itself for sending to Holland, Hanover, Zell, or Brunswick for men, at the expense of a million a year, who understood neither her laws, her language, nor her interest, and whose capacities would scarcely have fitted them for the office of a parish constable. If government could be trusted to such hands, it must be some easy and simple thing indeed, and materials fit for all the purposes may be found in every town and village in England.

When it shall be said in any country in the world, my poor are happy; neither ignorance nor distress is to be found among them; my jails are empty of prisoners, my streets of beggars; the aged are not in want, the taxes are not oppressive; the rational world is my friend, because I am the friend of its happiness: when these things can be said, then may that country boast its constitution and its government.

Within the space of a few years we have seen two Revolutions, those of America and France. In the former, the contest was long, and the conflict severe; in the latter, the nation acted with such a consolidated impulse, that having no foreign enemy to contend with, the revolution was complete in power the moment it appeared. From both those instances it is evident, that the greatest forces that can be brought into the field of revolutions, arc reason and common interest. Where these can have the opportunity of acting, opposition dies with fear, or crumbles away by conviction. It is a great standing which they have now universally obtained; and we may hereafter hope to see revolutions, or changes in governments, produced with the same quiet operation by which any measure, determinable by reason and discussion, is accomplished.

When a nation changes its opinion and habits of thinking, it is no longer to be governed as before; but it would not only be wrong, but bad policy, to attempt by force what ought to be accomplished by reason. Rebellion consists in forcibly opposing the general will of a nation, whether by a party or by a government. There ought, therefore, to be in every nation a method of occasionally ascertaining the state of public opinion with respect to government. On this point the old government of France was superior to the present government of England, because, on extraordinary occasions, recourse could be had to what was then called the States General. But in England there are no such occasional bodies; and as to those who are now called Representatives, a great part of them are mere machines of the court, placemen, and dependants.

I presume, that though all the people of England pay taxes, nor an hundredth part of them are electors, and the members of one of the houses of parliament represent nobody but themselves. There is, therefore, no power but the voluntary will of the people that has a right to act in any matter respecting a general reform; and by the same right that two persons can confer on such a subject, a thousand may. The object, in all such preliminary proceedings, is to find out what the general sense of a nation is, and to be governed by it. If it prefer a bad or defective government to a reform, or choose to pay ten times more taxes than there is occasion for, it has a right so to do; and so long as the majority do not impose conditions on the minority, different to what they impose on themselves, though there may be much error, there is no injustice. Neither will the error continue long. Reason and discussion will soon bring things right, however wrong they may begin. By such a process no tumult is to be apprehended. The poor, in all countries, are naturally both peaceable and grateful in all reforms in which their interest and happiness is included. It is only by neglecting and rejecting them that they become tumultuous.

The objects that now press on the public attention are, the French Revolution, and the prospect of a general revolution in governments. Of all nations in Europe, there is none so much interested in the French Revolution as England. Enemies for ages, and that at a vast expense, and without any national object, the opportunity now presents itself of amicably closing the scene, and joining their efforts to reform the rest of Europe. By doing this, they will not only prevent the further effusion of blood, and increase of taxes, but be in a condition of getting rid of a considerable part of their present burdens, as has been already stated. Long experience however has shown, that reforms of this kind are not those which old governments wish to promote; and therefore it is to nations, and not to such governments, that these matters present themselves.

In the preceding part of this work, I have spoken of an alliance between England, France, and America, for purposes that were to be afterwards mentioned. Though I have no direct authority on the part of America, I have good reason to conclude, that she is disposed to enter into a consideration of such a measure, provided, that the governments with which she might ally, acted as national governments, and not as courts enveloped in intrigue and mystery. That France as a nation, and a national government, would prefer an alliance with England, is a matter of certainty. Nations, like individuals, who have long been enemies, without knowing each other, or knowing why, become the better friends when they discover the errors and impositions under which they had acted.

Admitting, therefore, the probability of such a connexion, I will state some matters by which such an alliance, together with that of Holland, might render service, not only to the parties immediately concerned, but to all Europe.

It is, I think, certain, that if the fleets of England, France, and Holland were confederated, they could propose, with effect, a limitation to, and a general dismantling of all the navies in Europe, to a certain proportion to be agreed upon.

First, That no new ship of war shall be built by any power in Europe, themselves included.

Secondly, That all the navies now in existence shall be put back, suppose to one-tenth of their present force. This will save to France and England at least two millions sterling annually to each, and their relative force be in the same proportion as it is now. If men will permit themselves to think, as rational beings ought to think, nothing can appear more ridiculous and absurd, exclusive of all moral reflections, than to be at the expense of building navies, filling them with men, and then hauling them into the ocean, to try which can sink each other fastest. Peace, which costs nothing, is attended with infinitely more advantage, than any victory with all its expense. But this, though it best answers the purpose of nations, does not that of court governments, whose habited policy is pretence for taxation, places, and offices.

It is, I think, also certain, that the above confederated powers, together with that of the United States of America, can propose with effect, to Spain, the independence of South America, and the opening those countries of immense extent and wealth to the general commerce of the world, as North America now is.

With how much more glory, and advantage to itself, does a nation act, when it exerts its powers to rescue the world from bondage, and to create itself friends, than when it employs those powers to increase ruin, desolation, and misery. The horrid scene that is now acting by the English government in the East-Indies, is fit only to be told of Goths and Vandals, who, destitute of principles, robbed and tortured the world they were incapable of enjoying.

The opening of South America would produce an immense field of commerce, and a ready money market for manufactures, which the eastern world does not. The East is already a country full of manufactures, the importation of which is not only an injury to the manufactures of England, but a drain upon its specie. The balance against England by this trade is regularly upwards of half a million annually sent out in the East-India ships in silver; and this is the reason, together with German intrigue, and German subsidies, there is so little silver in England.

But any war is harvest to such governments, however ruinous it may be to a nation. It serves to keep up deceitful expectations which prevent a people looking into the defects and abuses of government. It is the *lo here!* and the *lo there!* that amuses and cheats the multitude.

Never did so great an opportunity offer itself to England, and to all Europe, as is produced by the two Revolutions of America and France. By the former, freedom has a national champion in the Western world; and by the latter, in Europe. When another nation shall join France, despotism and bad government will scarcely dare to appear. To use a trite expression, the iron is becoming hot all over Europe. The insulted German and the enslaved Spaniard, the Russ and the Pole, are beginning to think. The present age will hereafter merit to be called the Age of reason, and the present generation will appear to the future as the Adam of a new world.

When all the governments of Europe shall be established on the representative system, nations will become acquainted, and the animosities and prejudices fomented by the intrigue and artifice of courts, will cease. The oppressed soldier will become a freeman; and the tortured sailor, no longer dragged along the streets like a felon, will pursue his mercantile voyage in safety. It would be better that nations should continue the pay of their soldiers during their lives, and give them their discharge and restore them to freedom and their friends, and cease recruiting, than retain such multitudes at the same expense, in a condition useless to society and themselves. As soldiers have hitherto been treated in most countries, they might be said to be without a friend. Shunned by the citizen on an apprehension of being enemies to liberty, and too often insulted by those who commanded them, their condition was a double oppression. But where genuine principles of liberty pervade a people, everything is restored to order; and the soldier civilly treated, returns the civility.

In contemplating revolutions, it is easy to perceive that they may arise from two distinct causes; the one, to avoid or get rid of some great calamity; the other, to obtain some great and positive good; and the two may be distinguished by the names of active and passive revolutions. In those which proceed from the former cause, the temper becomes incensed and soured; and the redress, obtained by danger, is too often sullied by revenge. But in those which proceed from the latter, the heart, rather animated than agitated, enters serenely upon the subject. Reason and discussion, persuasion and conviction, become the weapons in the contest, and it is only when those are attempted to be suppressed that recourse is had to violence. When men unite in agreeing that a *thing is good,* could it be obtained, such as relief from a burden of taxes and the extinction of corruption, the object is more than half accomplished. What they approve as the end, they will promote in the means.

Will any man say, in the present excess of taxation, falling so heavily on the poor, that a remission of five pounds annually of taxes to one hundred and four thousand poor families is not a *good thing*? Will he say, that a remission of seven pounds annually to one hundred thousand other poor families—of eight pounds annually to another hundred thousand poor families, and often pounds annually to fifty thousand poor and widowed families, are not *good things*? And to proceed a step farther in this climax, will he say, that to provide against the misfortunes to which all human life is subject, by securing six pounds annually for all poor, distressed, and reduced persons of the age of fifty and until sixty, and of ten pounds annually after sixty is not a *good thing*?

Will he say, that an abolition of two million of poor-rates to the housekeepers, and of the whole of the house and window-light tax and of the commutation tax is not a *good thing*? Or will he say, that to abolish corruption is a *bad thing*?

If, therefore, the good to be obtained be worthy of a passive, rational, and costless revolution, it would be bad policy to prefer waiting for a calamity that should force a violent one. I have no idea, considering the reforms which are now passing and spreading throughout Europe, that England will permit herself to be the last; and where the occasion and the opportunity quietly offer, it is better than to wait for a turbulent necessity. It may be considered as an honour to the animal faculties of man to obtain redress by courage and danger, but it is far greater honour to the rational faculties to accomplish the same object by reason, accommodation, and general consent.[26]

As reforms, or revolutions, call them which you please, extend themselves among nations, those nations will form connexions and conventions, and when a few are thus confederated, the progress will be rapid, till despotism and corrupt government be totally expelled, at least out of two quarters of the world, Europe and America. The Algerine piracy may then be commanded to cease, for it is only by the malicious policy of old governments, against each other, that it exists.

Throughout this work, various and numerous as the subjects are, which I have taken up and investigated, there is only a single paragraph upon religion, viz. '*that every religion is good, that teaches man to be good.*'

I have carefully avoided to enlarge upon the subject, because I am inclined to believe, that what is called the present ministry wish to see contentions about religion kept up, to prevent the nation turning its attention to subjects of government. It is, as if they were to say, '*Look that way, or any way, but this.*'

But as religion is very improperly made a political machine, and the reality of it is thereby destroyed, I will conclude this work with stating in what light religion appears to me.

If we suppose a large family of children, who, on any particular day, or particular circumstance, made it a custom to present to their parent some token of their affection and gratitude, each of them would make a different offering, and most probably in a different manner. Some would pay their congratulations in themes of verse or prose, by some little devices, as their genius dictated, or according to what they thought would please; and, perhaps, the least of all, not able to do any of those things, would ramble into the garden, or the field, and gather what it thought the prettiest flower it could find, though, perhaps, it might be but a simple weed. The parent would be more gratified by such variety, than if the whole of them had acted on a concerted plan, and each had made exactly the same offering. This would have the cold appearance of contrivance, or the harsh one of control. But of all unwelcome things, nothing could more afflict the parent than to know, that the whole of them had afterwards gotten together by the ears, boys and girls, fighting, scratching, reviling, and abusing each other about which was the best or the worst present.

Why may we not suppose, that the great Father of all is pleased with variety of devotion; and that the greatest offence we can act, is that by which we seek to torment and render each other miserable. For my own part, I am fully satisfied that what I am now doing, with an endeavour to conciliate mankind, to render their condition happy, to unite nations that have hitherto been enemies, and to extirpate the horrid practice of war, and break the chains of slavery and oppression, is acceptable in his sight, and being the best service I can perform, I act it cheerfully.

I do not believe that any two men, on what are called doctrinal points, think alike who think at all. It is only those who have not thought that appear to agree. It is in this case as with what is called the British constitution. It has been taken for granted to be good, and encomiums have supplied the place of proof. But when the nation comes to examine into its principles and the abuses it admits, it will be found to have more defects than I have pointed out in this work and the former.

As to what are called national religions, we may, with as much propriety, talk of national Gods. It is either political craft or the remains of the Pagan system, when every nation had its separate and particular deity. Among all the writers of the English church clergy, who have treated on the general subject of religion, the present Bishop of Llandaff has not been excelled, and it is with much pleasure that I take the opportunity of expressing this token of respect.

I have now gone through the whole of the subject, at least, as far as it appears to me at present. It has been my intention for the five years I have been in Europe, to offer an address to the people of England on the subject of government, if the opportunity presented itself before I returned to America. Mr Burke has thrown it in my way, and I thank him. On a certain occasion three years ago, I pressed him to propose a national convention to be fairly elected for the purpose of taking the state of the nation into consideration; but I found, that however strongly the parliamentary current was then setting against the party he acted with, their policy was to keep everything within that field of corruption, and trust to accidents. Long experience had shown that parliaments would follow any change of ministers, and on this they rested their hopes and their expectations.

Formerly, when divisions arose respecting governments, recourse was had to the sword, and a civil war ensued. That savage custom is exploded by the new system, and reference is had to national conventions. Discussion and the general will arbitrates the question, and to this, private opinion yields with a good grace, and order is preserved uninterrupted.

Some gentlemen have affected to call the principles upon which this work and the former part of *Rights of Man* are founded, 'a new fangled doctrine.' The question is not whether those principles are new or old, but whether they are right or wrong. Suppose the former, I will show their effect by a figure easily understood.

It is now towards the middle of February. Were I to take a turn into the country, the trees would present a leafless winterly appearance. As people are apt to pluck twigs as they walk along, I perhaps might do the same, and by chance might observe, that a *single bud* on that twig had begun to swell. I should reason very unnaturally, or rather not reason at all, to suppose *this* was the *only* bud in England which had this appearance. Instead of deciding thus, I should instantly conclude, that the same appearance was beginning, or about to begin, everywhere; and though the vegetable sleep will continue longer on some trees and plants than on others, and though some of them may not *blossom* for two or three years, all will be in leaf in the summer, except those which are *rotten.* What pace the political summer may keep with the natural, no human foresight can determine. It is, however, not difficult to perceive that the spring is begun.—Thus wishing, as I sincerely do, freedom and happiness to all nations, I close the

SECOND PART

APPENDIX

As the publication of this work has been delayed beyond the time intended, I think it not improper, all circumstances considered, to state the causes that have occasioned the delay.

The reader will probably observe, that some parts in the plan contained in this work for reducing the taxes, and certain parts in Mr Pitt's speech at the opening of the present session, Tuesday, 31 January, are so much alike, as to induce a belief, that either the Author had taken the hint from Mr Pitt, or Mr Pitt from the Author.—I will first point out the parts that are similar, and then state such circumstances as I am acquainted with, leaving the reader to make his own conclusion.

Considering it almost an unprecedented case, that taxes should be proposed to be taken off, it is equally as extraordinary that such a measure should occur to two persons at the same time; and still more so (considering the vast variety and multiplicity of taxes) that they should hit on the same specific taxes. Mr Pitt has mentioned, in his speech, the tax on *Carts* and *Waggons*—that on *Female Servants*—the lowering the tax on *Candles*, and the taking off the tax of three shillings on *Houses* having under seven windows.

Every one of those specific taxes are a part of the plan contained in this work, and proposed also to be taken off. Mr Pitt's plan, it is true, goes no farther than to a reduction of three hundred and twenty thousand pounds; and the reduction proposed in this work to nearly six millions. I have made my calculations on only sixteen millions and an half of revenue, still asserting that it was 'very nearly, if not quite, seventeen millions.' Mr Pitt states it at 16,690,000. I know enough of the matter to say, that he has not *overstated* it. Having thus given the particulars, which correspond in this work and his speech, I will state a chain of circumstances that may lead to some explanation.

The first hint for lessening the taxes, and that as a consequence flowing from the French Revolution, is to be found in the ADDRESS and DECLARATION of the Gentlemen who met at the Thatched-House Tavern, 20 August 1791. Among many other particulars stated in that Address, is the following, put as an interrogation to the government opposers of the French Revolution. '*Are they sorry that the pretence for new oppressive taxes, and the occasion for continuing many old taxes will be at an end?*'

It is well known, that the persons who chiefly frequent the Thatched-House Tavern, are men of court connexions, and so much did they take this Address and Declaration respecting the French Revolution and the reduction of taxes in disgust, that the Landlord was under the necessity of informing the Gentlemen, who composed the meeting of the twentieth of August, and who proposed holding another meeting, that he could not receive them.[27]

What was only hinted at in the Address and Declaration, respecting taxes and principles of government, will be found reduced to a regular system in this work. But as Mr Pitt's speech contains some of the same things respecting taxes, I now come to give the circumstances before alluded to.

The case is: This work was intended to be published just before the meeting of Parliament, and for that purpose a considerable part of the copy was put into the printer's hands in September, and all the remaining copy, as far as page 230, which contains the parts to which Mr Pitt's speech is similar, was given to him full six weeks before the meeting of Parliament, and he was informed of the time at which it was to appear. He had composed nearly the whole about a fortnight before the time of Parliament meeting, and had printed as far as page 203, and had given me a proof of the next sheet, up to page 212. It was then in sufficient forwardness to be out at the time proposed, as two other sheets were ready for striking off. I had before told him, that if he thought he should be straitened for time, I would get part of the work done at another press, which he desired me not to do. In this manner the work stood on the Tuesday fortnight preceding the meeting of Parliament, when all at once, without any previous intimation, though I had been with him the evening before, he sent me, by one of his workmen, all the remaining copy, from page 203, declining to go on with the work *on any consideration*.

To account for this extraordinary conduct I was totally at a loss, as he stopped at the part where the arguments on systems and principles of government closed, and where the plan for the reduction of taxes, the education of children, and the support of the poor and the aged begins; and still more especially as he had, at the time of his beginning to print, and before he had seen the whole copy, offered a thousand pounds for the copyright, together with the future copyright of the former part of the *Rights of Man*. I told the person who brought me this offer that I should not accept it, and wished it not to be renewed, giving him as my reason, that though I believed the printer to be an honest man, I would never put it in the power of any printer or publisher to suppress or alter a work of mine, by making him master of the copy, or give to him the right of selling it to any minister, or to any other person, or to treat as a mere matter of traffic, that which I intended should operate as a principle.

His refusal to complete the work (which he could not purchase) obliged me to seek for another printer, and this of consequence would throw the publication back till after the meeting of Parliament, otherways it would have appeared that Mr Pitt had only taken up a part of the plan which I had more fully stated.

Whether that gentleman, or any other, had seen the work, or any part of it, is more than I have authority to say. But the manner in which the work was returned, and the particular time at which this was done, and that after the offers he had made, are suspicious circumstances. I know what the opinion of booksellers and publishers is upon such a case, but as to my own opinion, I choose to make no declaration. There are many ways by which proof sheets may be procured by other persons before a work publicly appear; to which I shall add a certain circumstance, which is,

A ministerial bookseller in Piccadilly who had been employed, as common report says, by a clerk of one of the boards closely connected with the Ministry (the Board of Trade and Plantation of which Hawksbury is president) to publish what he calls my Life (I wish that his own life and the lives of all the Cabinet were as good) used to have his books printed at the same printing-office that I employed; but when the former part of *Rights of Man* came out, he took his work away in dudgeon; and about a week or ten days before the printer returned my copy, he came to make him an offer of his work again, which was accepted. This would consequently give him admission into the printing-office where the sheets of this work were then lying; and as booksellers and printers are free with each other, he would have the opportunity of seeing what was going on.—Be the case however as it may, Mr Pitt's plan, little and diminutive as it is, would have had a very awkward appearance, had this work appeared at the time the printer had engaged to finish it.

I have now stated the particulars which occasioned the delay, from the proposal to purchase, to the refusal to print. If all the gentlemen are innocent, it is very unfortunate for them that such a variety of suspicious circumstances should, without any design, arrange themselves together.

Having now finished this part, I will conclude with stating another circumstance.

About a fortnight or three weeks before the meeting of Parliament, a small addition, amounting to about twelve shillings and six pence a year, was made to the pay of the soldiers, or rather, their pay was docked so much less. Some gentlemen who knew, in part, that this work would contain a plan of reforms respecting the oppressed condition of soldiers, wished me to add a note to the work, signifying, that the part upon that subject had been in the printer's hands some weeks before that addition of pay was proposed. I declined doing this, lest it should be interpreted into an air of vanity, or an endeavour to excite suspicion (for which, perhaps, there might be no grounds) that some of the Government gentlemen, had, by some means or other, made out what this work would contain: and had not the printing been interrupted so as to occasion a delay beyond the time fixed for publication, nothing contained in this appendix would have have appeared.

THOMAS PAINE

ENDNOTES

RIGHTS OF MAN

[1] Since writing the above, two other places occur in Mr Burke's pamphlet, in which the name of the Bastille is mentioned, but in the same manner. In the one, he introduces it in a sort of obscure question, and asks —'Will any ministers who now serve such a king, with but a decent appearance of respect, cordially obey the orders of those whom but the other day, *in his name*, they had committed to the Bastille?' In the other, the taking it is mentioned as implying criminality in the French guards who assisted in demolishing it. —'They have not' (says he) 'forgot the taking the king's castles at Paris.'—This is Mr Burke, who pretends to write on constitutional freedom.

[2] I am warranted in asserting this, as I had it personally from M. de Lafayette, with whom I have lived in habits of friendship for fourteen years.

[3] An account of the expedition to Versailles may be seen in No. 13 of the *Révolution de Paris*, containing the events from the 3rd to the 10th of October 1789.

[4] It is a practice in some parts of the country, when two travellers have but one horse, which like the national purse will not carry double, that the one mounts and rides two or three miles ahead, and then ties the horse to a gate and walks on. When the second traveller arrives, he takes the horse, rides on, and passes his companion a mile or two, and ties again; and so on—*Ride and tie.*

[5] The word he used was *renvoyé*, dismissed or sent away.

[6] When in any country we see extraordinary circumstances taking place, they naturally lead any man who has a talent for observation and investigation, to enquire into the causes. The manufactures of Manchester, Birmingham, and Sheffield, are the principal manufactures in England. From whence did this arise? A little observation will explain the case. The principal, and the generality of the inhabitants of those places, are not of what is called in England, *the church established by law*; and they, or their fathers, (for it is within but a few years), withdrew from the persecution of the chartered towns, where test-laws more particularly operate, and established a sort of asylum for themselves in those places. It was the only asylum that then offered, for the rest of Europe was worse.—But the case is now changing. France and America bid all comers welcome, and initiate them into all the rights of citizenship. Policy and interest, therefore, will, but perhaps too late, dictate in England, what reason and justice could not. Those manufactures are withdrawing, and

are arising in other places. There is now erecting at Passy, three miles from Paris, a large cotton-mill, and several are already erected in America. Soon after the rejecting the Bill for repealing the test-law, one of the richest manufacturers in England said in my hearing, 'England, Sir, is not a country for a dissenter to live in—we must go to France.' These are truths, and it is doing justice to both parties to tell them. It is chiefly the dissenters who have carried English manufactures to the height they are now at, and the same men have it in their power to carry them away; and though those manufactures will afterwards continue to be made in those places, the foreign market will be lost. There are frequently appearing in the London Gazette, extracts from certain acts to prevent machines and persons, as far as they can extend to persons, from going out of the country. It appears from these, that the ill effects of the test-laws and church-establishment begin to be much suspected; but the remedy of force can never supply the remedy of reason. In the progress of less than a century, all the unrepresented part of England, of all denominations, which is at least a hundred times the most numerous, may begin to feel the necessity of a constitution, and then all those matters will come regularly before them.

[7] When the English Minister, Mr Pitt, mentions the French finances again in the English Parliament, it would be well that he noticed this as an example.

[8] Mr Burke, (and I must take the liberty of telling him he is very unacquainted with French affairs), speaking upon this subject, says, 'The first thing that struck me in the calling the States-General, was a great departure from the ancient course;'—and he soon after says, 'From the moment I read the list, I saw distinctly, and very nearly as it has happened, all that was to follow.'—Mr Burke certainly did not see all that was to follow. I endeavoured to impress him, as well before as after the States-General met, that there would be a *revolution*; but was not able to make him see it, neither would he believe it. How then he could distinctly see all the parts, when the whole was out of sight, is beyond my comprehension. And with respect to the 'departure from the ancient course,' besides the natural weakness of the remark, it shows that he is unacquainted with circumstances. The departure was necessary, from the experience had upon it, that the ancient course was a bad one. The States-General of 1614 were called at the commencement of the civil war in the minority of Louis XIII; but by the clash of arranging them by orders, they increased the confusion they were called to compose. The Author of *L'Intrigue du Cabinet* (Intrigue of the Cabinet), who wrote before any revolution was thought of in France, speaking of the States-General of 1614, says, 'They held the public in suspense five months; and by the questions agitated therein, and the heat with which they were put, it appears that the Great' (*les grands*) 'thought more to satisfy their *particular* passions, than to procure the good of the nation; and the whole time passed away in altercations, ceremonies, and parade.' L'Intrigue du Cabinet, vol. i. p. 329.

OBSERVATIONS ON THE DECLARATION OF RIGHTS

[9] There is a single idea, which, if it strikes rightly upon the mind either in a legal or a religious sense, will prevent any man, or any body of men, or any government, from going wrong on the subject of Religion; which is, that before any human institution of government was known in the world, there existed, if I may so express it, a compact

between God and Man, from the beginning of time; and that as the relation and condition which man in his *individual person* stands in towards his Maker, cannot be changed, or anyways altered by any human laws or human authority, chat religious devotion, which is a part of this compact, cannot so much as be made a subject of human laws; and that all laws must conform themselves to this prior existing compact, and not assume to make the compact conform to the laws, which, besides being human, are subsequent thereto. The first act of man, when he looked around and saw himself a creature which he did not make, and a world furnished for his reception, must have been devotion, and devotion must ever continue sacred to every individual man, *as it appears right to him*; and governments do mischief by interfering.

[10] See page 16 of this work.—N.B. Since the taking of the Bastille, the occurrences have been published: but the matters recorded in this narrative, are prior to that period; and some of them, as may be easily seen, can be but very little known.

MISCELLANEOUS CHAPTER

[11] See Estimate of the Comparative Strength of Great Britain, by G. Chalmers.

[12] See Administration of the Finances of France, Vol. III by M. Necker.

[13] Administration of the Finances of France, Vol. III.

[14] Whether the English commerce does not bring in money, or whether the Government sends it out after it is brought in, is a matter which the parties concerned can best explain; but that the deficiency exists, is not in the power of either to disprove. While Dr Price, Mr Eden (now Auckland), Mr Chalmers, and others, were debating whether the quantity of money in England was greater or less than at the Revolution, the circumstance was not adverted to, that since the Revolution, there cannot have been less than four hundred millions sterling imported into Europe; and therefore, the quantity in England ought at least to have been four times greater than it was at the Revolution, to be on a proportion with Europe. What England is now doing by paper, is what she would have been able to have done by solid money, if gold and silver had come into the nation in the proportion it ought, or had not been sent out; and she is endeavouring to restore by paper, the balance she has lose by money. It is certain, that the gold and silver which arrive annually in the register-ships to Spain and Portugal, do not remain in those countries. Taking the value half in gold and half in silver, it is about four hundred tons annually; and from the number of ships and galloons employed in the trade of bringing those metals from South America to Portugal and Spain, the quantity sufficiently proves itself, without referring to the registers.

In the situation England now is, it is impossible she can increase in money. High taxes not only lessen the property of the individuals, but they lessen also the money-capital of a nation, by inducing smuggling, which can only be carried on by gold and silver. By the politics which the British Government have carried on with the Inland Powers of Germany and the Continent, it has made an enemy of all the Maritime Powers, and is therefore obliged to keep up a large navy; but though the navy is built in England, the naval Stores must be purchased from abroad, and that from countries where the greatest part must be paid for in gold and silver. Some fallacious rumours have been set afloat in England to induce a belief of money, and, among others, that of the French refugees bringing great quantities. The idea is ridiculous. The general part of the money in France is silver; and it would take upwards of twenty of the largest broad wheel wagons, with ten horses each, to remove one million sterling of silver. Is it then to be supposed, that a few people fleeing on horse-back, or in post-chaises, in a secret manner, and having the French Custom-House to pass, and the sea to cross, could bring even a sufficiency for their own expenses?

When millions of money are spoken of, it should be recollected, that such sums can only accumulate in a country by slow degrees, and a long procession of time. The most frugal system chat England could now adopt, would not recover, in a century, the balance she has lost in money since the commencement of the Hanover succession. She is seventy millions behind France, and she must be in some considerable proportion behind every country in Europe, because the returns of the English Mint do not show an increase of money, while the registers of Lisbon and Cadiz show an European increase of between three and four hundred millions sterling.

CHAPTER I
OF SOCIETY AND CIVILIZATION

[1] That part of America which is generally called New England, including New Hampshire, Massachusetts, Rhode Island, and Connecticut, is peopled chiefly by English descendants. In the state of New York, about half are Dutch, the rest English, Scottish, and Irish. In New Jersey, a mixture of English and Dutch, with some Scottish and Irish. In Pennsylvania, about one third are English, another Germans, and the remainder Scottish and Irish, with some Swedes. The States to the southward have a greater proportion of English than the middle States, but in all of them there is a mixture; and besides those enumerated, there are a considerable number of French, and some few of all the European nations lying on the coast. The most numerous religious denomination are the Presbyterians; but no one sect is established above another, and all men are equally citizens.

CHAPTER III
OF THE OLD AND NEW SYSTEMS OF GOVERNMENT

[2] For a character of aristocracy, the reader is referred to *Rights of Man*, Part I, page 53.

CHAPTER IV
OF CONSTITUTION

[3] The whole amount of the assessed taxes of France, for the present year, is three hundred millions of livres, which is twelve millions and a half sterling; and the incidental taxes are estimated at three millions, making in the whole fifteen millions and a half; which, among twenty-four millions of people, is not quite thirteen shillings per head. France has lessened her taxes since the revolution, nearly nine millions sterling annually. Before the revolution, the city of Paris paid a duty of upwards of thirty percent on all articles brought into the city. This tax was collected at the city gates. It was taken off on the first of last May, and the gates taken down.

[4] What was called the *livre rouge*, or the red book, in France, was not exactly similar to the court calendar in England; but it sufficiently showed how a great part of the taxes was lavished.

[5] In England the improvements in agriculture, useful arts, manufactures, and commerce, have been made in opposition to the genius of its government, which is that of following precedents. It is from the enterprise and industry of the individuals, and their numerous associations, in which, tritely speaking, government is neither pillow nor bolster, that these improvements have proceeded. No man thought about the government, or who was *in*, or who was *out*, when he was planning or executing those things; and all he had to hope, with respect to government, was, *that it would let him alone*. Three or four very silly ministerial newspapers are continually offending against the spirit of national improvement, by ascribing it to a minister. They may with as much truth ascribe this book to a minister.

[6] With respect to the two houses, of which the English Parliament is composed, they appear to be effectually influenced into one, and, as a legislature, to have no temper of its own. The minister, whoever he at any time may be, touches it as with an opium wand, and it sleeps obedience.

But if we look at the distinct abilities of the two houses, the difference will appear so great, as to show the inconsistency of placing power where there can be no certainty of the judgement to use it. Wretched as the state of representation is in England, it is manhood compared with what is called the house of Lords; and so little is this nick-named house regarded, that the people scarcely inquire at any time what it is doing. It appears also to be most under influence, and the furthest removed from the general interest of the nation. In the debate on engaging in the Russian and Turkish war, the majority in the house of peers in favour of it was upwards of ninety, when in the other house, which is more than double its numbers, the majority was sixty-three.

The proceedings on Mr Fox's bill, respecting the rights of juries, merits also to be noticed. The persons called the peers were not the objects of that bill. They are already in possession of more privileges than that bill gave to others. They are their own jury, and if any of that house were prosecuted for a libel, he would not suffer, even upon conviction, for the first offence. Such inequality in laws ought not to exist, in any country. The French constitution says, That *the law is the same to every individual, whether to protect or to punish. All are equal in its sight.*

[7] As to the state of representation in England, it is too absurd to be reasoned upon. Almost all the represented parts are decreasing in population, and the unrepresented parts are increasing. A general convention of the nation is necessary to take the whole state of its government into consideration.

[8] It is related that in the canton of Berne, in Switzerland, it had been customary, from time immemorial, to keep a bear at the public expense, and the people had been taught to believe, that if they had not a bear they should all be undone. It happened some years ago, (hat the bear, then in being, was taken sick, and died too suddenly to have his place immediately supplied with another. During this interregnum the people discovered, that the corn grew, and the vintage flourished, and the sun and moon continued to rise and set, and everything went on the same as before, and, taking courage from these circumstances, they resolved not to keep any more bears; for, said they, 'a bear is a very voracious, expensive animal, and we were obliged to a pull out his claws, lest he should hurt the citizens'.

The story of the bear of Berne was related in some of the French newspapers, at the time of the flight of Louis XVI, and the application of it to monarchy could not be mistaken in France; but it seems, that the aristocracy of Berne applied it to themselves, and have since prohibited the reading of French newspapers.

[9] It is scarcely possible to touch on any subject, that will not suggest an allusion to some corruption in governments. The simile of '*fortifications*', unfortunately involves with it a circumstance, which is directly in point with the matter above alluded to.

Among the numerous instances of abuse which have been acted or protected by governments, ancient or modern, there is not a greater than that of quartering a man and his heirs upon the public, to be maintained at its expense.

Humanity dictates a provision for the poor; but by what right, moral or political, does any government assume to say, that the person called the Duke of Richmond, shall be maintained by the public? Yet, if common report is true, not a beggar in London can purchase his wretched pittance of coal, without paying towards the civil list of the Duke of Richmond. Were the whole produce of this imposition but a shilling a year, the iniquitous principle would be still the same; but when it amounts, as it is said to do, to not less than twenty thousand pounds *per ann.* the enormity is too serious to be permitted to remain.—This is one of the effects of monarchy and aristocracy.

In stating this case, I am led by no personal dislike. Though I chink it mean in any man to live upon the public, the vice originates in the government; and so general is it become, that whether the parties are in the ministry or in the opposition, it makes no difference: they are sure of the guarantee of each other.

CHAPTER V
WAYS AND MEANS

[10] In America, the increase of commerce is greater in proportion than in England. It is, at this time, at least one half more than at any period prior to the revolution. The greatest number of vessels cleared out of the port of Philadelphia, before the commencement of the war, was between eight and nine hundred. In the year 1788, the number was upwards of twelve hundred. As the state of Pennsylvania is estimated as an eighth part of the United States in population, the whole number of vessels must now be nearly ten thousand.

[11] When I saw Mr Pitt's mode of estimating the balance of trade, in one of his parliamentary speeches, he appeared to me to know nothing of the nature and interest of commerce; and no man has more wantonly tortured it than himself. During a period of peace, it has been havocked with the calamities of war. Three times has it been thrown into stagnation, and the vessels unmanned by impressing, within less than four years of peace.

[12] Rev. William Knowles, master of the grammar school of Thetford, in Norfolk.

[13] Politics and self-interest have been so uniformly connected, that the world, from being so often deceived, has a right to be suspicious of public characters: but with regard to myself, I am perfectly easy on this head. I did not, at my first setting out in public life, nearly seventeen years ago, turn my thoughts to subjects of government from motives of interest; and my conduct from that moment to this, proves the fact. I saw an opportunity, in which I thought I could do some good, and I followed exactly what my heart dictated. I neither read books, nor studied other people's opinions. I thought for myself. The case was this:

During the suspension of the old governments in America, both prior to, and at the breaking out of hostilities, I was struck with the order and decorum with which everything was conducted: and impressed with the idea, that a little more than what society naturally performed, was all the government that was necessary: and that monarchy and aristocracy were frauds and impositions upon mankind. On these principles I published the pamphlet *Common Sense.* The success it met with was beyond anything since the invention of printing. I gave the copyright up to every state in the union, and the demand ran to not less than one hundred thousand copies. I continued the subject in the same manner, under the title of *Crisis,* till the complete establishment of the revolution.

After the declaration of independence, Congress unanimously, and unknown to me, appointed me secretary in the foreign department. This was agreeable to me, because it gave me the opportunity of seeing into the abilities of foreign courts, and their manner of doing business. But a misunderstanding arising between congress and me, respecting one of their commissioners then in Europe, Mr Silas Deane, I resigned (he office, and declined, at the same time, the pecuniary offers made me by the ministers of France and Spain, M. Gérard and Don Juan Mirralles.

I had by this time so completely gained the ear and confidence of America, and my own independence was become so visible as to give me a range in political writing, beyond, perhaps, what any man ever possessed in any country; and what is more extraordinary, I held it undiminished to the end of the war, and enjoy it in the same manner to the present moment. As my object was not myself, I set out with the determination, and happily with the disposition, of not being moved by praise or censure, friendship or calumny, nor of being drawn from my purpose by any personal altercation; and the man who cannot do this, is not fit for a public character.

When the war ended, I went from Philadelphia to Borden-Town, on the east bank of the Delaware, where I have a small place. Congress was at this time at Prince-Town, fifteen miles distant; and General Washington had taken his headquarters at Rocky-Hill, within the neighbourhood of Congress, for the purpose of resigning up his commission, (the object for which he accepted it being accomplished,) and of retiring to private life. While he was on this business, he wrote me the letter which I here subjoin.

Rocky-Hill, Sept. 10, 1783

I have learned since I have been at this place, that you are at Borden-Town. Whether for the sake of retirement or economy, I know not. Be it for either, for both, or whatever it may, if you will come to this place, and partake with me, I shall be exceedingly happy to see you at it.

Your presence may remind Congress of your past services to this country; and if it is in my power to impress them, command my best exertions with freedom, as they will be rendered cheerfully by one, who entertains a lively sense of the importance of your works, and who, with much pleasure, subscribes himself,

Your sincere friend,

G. WASHINGTON

During the war, in the latter end of the year 1780, I formed to myself a design of coming over to England; and communicated it to General Greene, who was then in Philadelphia, on his route to the southward, General Washington being then at too great a distance to communicate with immediately. I was strongly impressed with the idea, that if I could get over to England, without being known, and only remain in safety till I could get out a publication, that I could open the eyes of the country with respect to the madness and stupidity of its government. I saw that the parties in parliament had pitted themselves as far as they could go, and could make no new impressions on each other. General Greene entered fully into my views; but the affair of Arnold and André happening just after, he changed his mind, and, under strong apprehensions for my safety, wrote very pressingly to me from Annapolis, in Maryland, to give up the design, which, with some reluctance, I did. Soon after this I accompanied Col. Lawrens, son of Mr Lawrens, who was then in the Tower, to France, on business from Congress. We landed at L'Orient; and while I remained there, he being gone forward, a circumstance occurred, that renewed my former design. An English packet from Falmouth to New-York, with the government dispatches on board, was brought into L'Orient. That a packet should be taken, is no extraordinary thing; but that the dispatches should be taken with it, will scarcely be credited, as they are always slung at the cabin window, in a bag loaded with cannon ball, and ready to be sunk at a moment. The fact, however, is as I have stated it, for the dispatches came into my hands, and I read them. The capture, as I was informed, succeeded by the following stratagem:—The captain of the Madame privateer, who spoke English, on coming up with the packet, passed himself for the captain of an English frigate, and invited the captain of the packet on board, which, when done, he sent some of his own hands back, and secured the mail. But be the circumstance of the capture what it may, I speak with certainty as to the government dispatches. They were sent up to Paris, to Count Vergennes, and when Col. Lawrens and myself returned to America, we took the originals to Congress.

By these dispatches I saw into the stupidity of the English cabinet, far more than I otherwise could have done, and I renewed my former design. But Col. Lawrens was so unwilling to return alone; more especially, as among other matters, we had a charge of upwards of two hundred thousand pounds Sterling in money, that I gave in to his wishes, and finally gave up my plan. But I am now certain, that if I could have executed it, that it would not have been altogether unsuccessful.

14 It is difficult to account for the origin of charter and corporation towns, unless we suppose them to have arisen out of, or been connected with, some species of garrison service. The times in which they began justify this idea. The generality of those towns have been garrisons; and the corporations were charged with the care of the gates of the towns, when no military garrison was present. Their refusing or granting admission to strangers, which has produced the custom of giving, selling, and buying freedom, has more of the nature of garrison authority than civil government. Soldiers are free of all corporations throughout the nation, by the same propriety that every soldier is free of every garrison, and no other persons are. He can follow any employment, with the permission of his officers, in any corporation town throughout the nation.

15 See Sir John Sinclair's History of the Revenue. The land-tax in 1646 was £2,473,499.

16 Several of the court newspapers have of late made frequent mention of Wat Tyler. That his memory should be traduced by court sycophants, and all those who live on the spoil of a public, is not to be wondered at. He was, however, the means of checking the rage and injustice of taxation in his time, and the nation owed much to his valour. The history

is concisely this: — In the time of Richard the Second, a poll-tax was levied, of one shilling per head, upon every person in the nation, of whatever estate or condition, on poor as well as rich, above the age of fifteen years. If any favour was shown in the law, it was to the rich rather than to the poor; as no person could be charged more than twenty shillings for himself, family, and servants, though ever so numerous; while all other families, under the number of twenty, were charged per head. Poll-taxes had always been odious; but this being also oppressive and unjust, it excited, as it naturally must, universal detestation among the poor and middle classes. The person known by the name of Wat Tyler, whose proper name was Walter, and a tiler by trade, lived at Deptford. The gatherer of the poll-tax, on coming to his house, demanded tax for one of his daughters, whom Tyler declared was under the age of fifteen. The tax-gatherer insisted on satisfying himself, and began an indecent examination of the girl, which enraging the father, he struck him with a hammer, that brought him to the ground, and was the cause of his death.

This circumstance served to bring the discontents to an issue. The inhabitants of the neighbourhood espoused the cause of Tyler, who in a few days was joined, according to some histories, by upwards of fifty thousand men, and chosen their chief. With this force he marched to London, to demand an abolition of the tax, and a redress of other grievances. The court, finding itself in a forlorn condition, and unable to make resistance, agreed, with Richard at its head, to hold a conference with Tyler in Smithfield, making many fair professions, courtier like, of its dispositions to redress the oppressions. While Richard and Tyler were in conversation on these matters, each being on horseback, Walworth then mayor of London, and one of the creatures of the court, watched an opportunity, and like a cowardly assassin, stabbed Tyler with a dagger; and two or three others falling upon him, he was instantly sacrificed.

Tyler appears to have been an intrepid disinterested man, with respect to himself. All his proposals made to Richard, were on a more just and public ground, than those which had been made to John by the Barons; and notwithstanding the sycophancy of historians, and men like Mr Burke, who seek to gloss over a base action of the court by traducing Tyler, his fame will outlive their falsehood. If the Barons merited a monument to be erected in Runnymede, Tyler merits one in Smithfield.

[17] Foreign intrigue, foreign wars, and foreign dominions, will in a great measure account for the deficiency.

[18] I happened to be in England at the celebration of the centenary of the revolution of 1688. The characters of William and Mary have always appeared to me detestable; the one seeking to destroy his uncle, and the other her father, to get possession of power themselves; yet, as the nation was disposed to think something of that event, I felt hurt at seeing it ascribe the whole reputation of it to a man who had undertaken it as a job, and who, besides what he otherwise got, charged six hundred thousand pounds for the expense of the little fleet that brought him from Holland, George the First acted the same close-fisted part as William had done, and bought the Duchy of Bremen with the money he got from England, two hundred and fifty thousand pounds over and above his pay as king; and having thus purchased it at the expense of England, added it to his Hanoverian dominions for his own private profit. In fact, every nation that does not govern itself, is governed as a job. England has been the prey of jobs ever since the Revolution.

[19] Charles, like his predecessors and successors, finding that war was the harvest of governments, engaged in a war with the Dutch, the expense of which increased the annual expenditure to £1,800,000, as stated under the date of 1666; but the peace establishment was but £1,200,000.

[20] Poor-rates began about the time of Henry the Eighth, when the taxes began to increase, and they have increased as the taxes increased ever since.

[21] Reckoning the taxes by families, five to a family, each family pays on an average, 12*l.* 17*s.* 6*d.* *per ann.* To this sum are to be added the poor-rates. Though all pay taxes in the articles they consume, all do not pay poor-rates. About two millions are exempted, some as not being housekeepers, others as not being able, and the poor themselves who receive the relief. The average, therefore, of poor-rates on the remaining number, is forty shillings for every family of five persons, which makes the whole average amount of taxes and rates, 14*l.* 17*s.* 6*d.* For six persons, 17*l.* 17*s.* For seven persons, 20*l.* 16*s.* 6*d.*

The average of taxes in America, under the new or representative system of government, including the interest of the debt contracted in the war, and taking the population at four million of souls, which it now amounts to, and it is daily increasing, is five shillings per head, men, women, and children. The difference, therefore, between the two governments, is as under,

	England			America		
	l.	*s.*	*d.*	*l.*	*s.*	*d.*
For a family of five persons	14	17	6	1	5	0
For a family of six persons	17	17	0	1	10	0
For a family of seven persons	20	16	6	1	15	0

[22] Public schools do not answer the general purpose of the poor. They are chiefly in corporation towns, from which the country towns and villages are excluded; or, if admitted, the distance occasions a great loss of time. Education, to be useful to the poor, should be on the spot; and the best method, I believe, to accomplish this, is to enable the parents to pay the expense themselves. There are always persons of both sexes to be found in every village, especially when growing into years, capable of such an undertaking. Twenty children, at ten shillings each, (and that not more than six months each year) would be as much as some livings amount to in the remote parts of England; and there are often distressed clergymen's widows to whom such an income would be acceptable. Whatever is given on this account to children answers two purposes, to them it is education, to those who educate them it is a livelihood.

[23] The tax on beer brewed for sale, from which the aristocracy are exempt, is almost one million more than the present commutation tax, being by the returns of 1788, 1,666,152*l.* and consequently they ought to take on themselves the amount of the commutation tax, as they are already exempted from one which is almost one million greater.

[24] See the reports on the corn trade.

[25] When inquiries are made into the condition of the poor, various degrees of distress will most probably be found, to render a different arrangement preferable to that which is already proposed. Widows with families will be in greater want than where there are husbands living. There is also a difference in the expense of living in different countries; and more so in fuel.

Suppose then fifty thousand extraordinary cases, at the rate		£
of 10*l.* per family per ann.	— — — — —	500,000
100,000 Families, at 8*l.* per family per ann.	— — —	800,000
100,000 Families, at 7*l.* per family per ann.	— — —	700,000
104,000 Families, at 5*l.* per family per ann.	— — —	520,000
And instead of ten shillings per head for the education of other children, to allow fifty shillings per family for that purpose to Fifty thousand families		250,000
		2,770,000
140,000 Aged persons as before,	— — — —	1,120,000
		3,890,000

This arrangement amounts to the same sum as stated in page 266, including the 250,000*l.* for education; but it provides (including the aged people) for four hundred and four thousand families, which is almost one third of all the families in England.

[26] I know it is the opinion of many of the most enlightened characters in France (there always will be those who see farther into events than others) not only among the general mass of citizens, but of many of the principal members of the former National Assembly, that the monarchical plan will not continue many years in that country. They have found out that as wisdom cannot be made hereditary, power ought not; and that, for a man to merit a million sterling a year from a nation, he ought to have a mind capable of comprehending from an atom to a universe; which, if he had, he would be above receiving the pay. But they wished not to appear to lead the nation faster than its own reason and interest dictated. In all the conversations where I have been present upon this subject, the idea always was, that when such a time, from the general opinion of the nation, shall arrive, that the honourable and liberal method would be, to make a handsome present in fee simple to the person whoever he may be, that shall then be in the monarchical office, and for him to retire to the enjoyment of private life, possessing his share of general rights and privileges, and to be no more accountable to the public for his time and his conduct than any other citizen.

APPENDIX

[27] The gentleman who signed the address and declaration as chairman of the meeting, Mr Horne Tooke, being generally supposed to be the person who drew it up, and having spoken much in commendation of it, has been jocularly accused of praising his own work. To free him from this embarrassment, and to save him the repeated trouble of mentioning the author, as he has not failed to do, I make no hesitation in saying, that as the opportunity of benefiting by the French Revolution easily occurred to me, I drew up the publication in question, and showed it to him and some other gentlemen; who, fully approving it, held a meeting for the purpose of making it public, and subscribed to the amount of fifty guineas to defray the expense of advertising. I believe there are at this time, in England, a greater number of men

acting on disinterested principles, and determined to look into the nature and practices of government themselves, and not blindly trust, as has hitherto been the case, either to government generally, or to parliaments, or to parliamentary opposition, than at any former period. Had this been done a century ago, corruption and taxation had not arrived to the height they are now at.